Introduction to
CRIMINAL
INVESTIGATION

Edited by

Michael L. Birzer and Cliff Roberson

CRC Press
Taylor & Francis Group
Boca Raton London New York

CRC Press is an imprint of the
Taylor & Francis Group, an **informa** business

CRC Press
Taylor & Francis Group
6000 Broken Sound Parkway NW, Suite 300
Boca Raton, FL 33487-2742

© 2012 by Taylor & Francis Group, LLC
CRC Press is an imprint of Taylor & Francis Group, an Informa business

No claim to original U.S. Government works

Printed in the United States of America on acid-free paper
Version Date: 20110804

International Standard Book Number: 978-1-4398-3934-8 (Paperback)

Visit the Taylor & Francis Web site at
http://www.taylorandfrancis.com

and the CRC Press Web site at
http://www.crcpress.com

CONTENTS

Section 6 PUTTING IT ALL TOGETHER

PREFACE

The diligent investigation of crime is both necessary and critical. Many years ago, police reformers O.W. Wilson and R.C. McLaren wrote in their classic textbook on police administration, "The purpose of the detective or criminal investigation function is to investigate certain serious crimes in order to arrest and convict the perpetrators and to recover stolen property" (Wilson and McLaren, 1977, p. 364). It is undeniable that the basic purpose of the criminal investigation function in the 21st century has for the most part remained unchanged. The investigation of crime is an important mandate of the police. All police agencies, large and small, rural and urban, perform criminal investigations; consequently, the manner in which investigators are trained is neither uniform nor consistent. Some neophyte investigators receive sophisticated training in order to learn the craft, while others simply learn on the job while assigned to a senior criminal investigator. Often, the first exposure that an investigator may have to crime scene investigation techniques goes back to their college days, as a student, taking an introduction course to criminal investigation. We reminded ourselves often of this as we crafted this introductory textbook on criminal investigation.

AUDIENCE AND STYLE

This book is suitable for use in college-level introduction to criminal investigation courses. Law enforcement personnel who want to learn how to become better investigators may also benefit from the book. Likewise, the book would be ideal as a reference guide for recruits attending police academies. Finally, the book is appropriate for the reader who simply desires to know why the police do what they do during a criminal investigation. We present this textbook with a high order of practicability, while at the same time maintaining rigorous academic standards of the content presented herein. It is rare to find an edited book that introduces criminal investigation. We present to the reader one such book. This textbook represents a collection of essays written by authorities on criminal investigation. The 20 chapters in this text give the reader a comprehensive overview of the criminal investigation process. We have woven together some of the most important and evolving areas of criminal investigation. Some of the contributors to this textbook are practicing or retired law enforcement personnel, while others are former investigators who have embarked on academic careers. Still others are attorneys who bring years of legal experience working as criminal prosecutors to obtain convictions of perpetrators responsible for crimes. It is our belief that combining the expertise of law enforcement authorities with academicians who study crime and law enforcement practices is the gold standard of an effective textbook on criminal investigation.

ORGANIZATION OF THE BOOK

This text is organized into six parts. Part 1 presents two chapters. You may recall the old cliché regarding how do you know where you are going if you don't know where you've been. Having some knowledge of the history of criminal investigation will assist the reader in placing the topic in proper context. We feel this is essential for students. As such, in Chapter 1, John Eterno provides an excellent abbreviated history of criminal investigation in Western society. This chapter is written in a manner so as not to bog the reader down with a voluminous amount of historical details, but it does provide what you need to know to place criminal investigations into proper historical context. In Chapter 2, Bryan Courtney presents some basic introductory remarks on the field of criminal investigation. Aspiring police officers and investigators will greatly benefit from this chapter. The chapter discusses the qualifications of becoming an investigator, the selection process, and ideal training requirements. The first two chapters of this text are designed to present the basic foundation necessary to study criminal investigation in a more detailed fashion.

Part 2 is made up of five chapters that focus on preliminary considerations of the criminal investigation process. In Chapter 3, Michael Birzer details crime scene search techniques. The chapter also includes a discussion of planning the search, the actual search, and the post-search debriefing. In any criminal investigation, law enforcement authorities rely heavily on field notes and written reports to recall at a later date intricate details about the crime. Many actors in the criminal justice system, including attorneys, judges, presentence investigators, and possibly jurors, will read the investigator's report; therefore, it is important to ensure that the investigative report is completed correctly and, more importantly, is readable. In Chapter 4, Gene Scaramella takes up a discussion of field notes and report writing. The chapter details how effective field notes and report writing are critical. In Chapter 5, Scott Mire and Robert Hanser provide an excellent overview of interview and interrogation. The chapter is a gold mine of information and offers many practical tips that will assist the investigator in preparing for the interview or interrogation. Moreover, the chapter offers specific techniques that have been time tested to be effective. In Chapter 6, Cory Rodivich provides an overview of the kinds of evidence that crime scene investigators may encounter. The chapter begins with a thorough discussion of the nature and type of evidence that may be found at the crime scene. The chapter concludes with a hands-on discussion of how to collect, package, and preserve different types of evidence. The role of forensic science in the investigation of crime has evolved significantly in recent years; in Chapter 7, Cory Rodivich provides a constructive overview of the contributions of forensic science to criminal investigations. The chapter discusses the forensic analysis of evidence and concludes with a tour of the crime lab, where the reader will be introduced to the instruments and equipment that are commonly found in most crime labs.

The five chapters in Part 3 focus on property crimes, auto theft, arson, and financial crimes. In Chapter 8, Matthew O'Deane examines vandalism. The chapter provides a thorough discussion of the most common types of vandalism in the United States: tagging and gang graffiti. The chapter offers prevention tips and basic investigative protocols that should be followed in order to effectively prosecute the perpetrators. Chapter 9 focuses on larceny and burglary. In this chapter, Walt Wywadis does an excellent job of discussing larceny and burglary from the preliminary investigation through the follow-up investigation. The chapter discusses offender characteristics and presents prevention techniques. In Chapter 10, Don Munday examines the investigation of auto theft in a step-by-step manner and discusses common methods and tools that perpetrators use to steal autos. Moreover, the chapter clearly outlines the steps to be followed in both the preliminary and follow-up investigation. In Chapter 11, Cliff Roberson provides an overview of arson investigations. Arson investigations can be both challenging and complex and should be approached with diligence. The chapter begins with a detailed description of the duties of the first responder and then proceeds to describe the steps that should be taken to preserve an arson scene. The chapter concludes with a comprehensive discussion of specific investigative steps that should be taken. Michael Palmiotto tackles financial crimes in Chapter 12. The chapter presents an overview of financial crimes while at the same time providing practical techniques that should be followed during the investigation.

Part 4 consists of three chapters. In Chapter 13, Gregg Etter and Roger Pennel discuss homicide and assault investigations. The chapter provides a thorough discussion of mode, method, and opportunity; the role of the medical examiner; manners of death; and types of evidence that may be encountered by investigators. Chapter 14 is written by John Padget and centers on the investigation of sex crimes. The chapter describes the nature of sex crime investigations and the critical role of the first responder. The chapter culminates with an overview of specific steps that should be followed during the investigation of a sex crime. In Chapter 15, Harrison Watts examines robbery investigation by discussing the categories of robbery, parties to the crime, and specific investigative steps. The chapter concludes with a discussion what is required for the successful prosecution of robbery.

The three chapters in Part 5 center on specialized investigations. The use of illegal drugs is considered to be a serious crime problem in the United States; in Chapter 16, Don Vespa provides a thoughtful overview of the investigation of illicit drug trafficking, including initiating the investigation, establishing and managing confidential informants, steps in the investigation, and a variety of surveillance techniques used in undercover operations. With the barrage of technological advancements, millions of children find themselves regularly in front of the computer on the Internet, and it is not uncommon to hear news reports of a child being solicited online by a sexual predator. Cybercrimes represent a significant growing threat in our society. In Chapter 17, Mark McCoy discusses the various types of cybercrimes and offers a timely protocol on how these cases should be investigated. In Chapter 18, Gregg Etter provides a complete overview of the investigation of gang-related crimes. He discusses the cultural characteristics of gangs and provides information centering on the primary and secondary crimes committed by gangs. Motivations for gang-related crimes are also covered in the chapter. The chapter offers a comprehensive discussion of effective gang investigative techniques and concludes with an overview of anti-gang programs that have been shown to be effective.

Part 6 concludes the book with two chapters. In Chapter 19, Frank DiMarino discusses the legal issues centering on criminal investigation. Among the topics discussed are criminal law, felonies, misdemeanors, and factors that should be taken into account during the crime scene investigation and upon the initial arrest of the suspect. Rounding out the text is Chapter 20, in which Cliff Roberson and Gwynne Birzer provide an overview of how to prepare a case for court. Topics in the chapter include testimony in court, accuracy of police reports, chain of custody of evidence, personal credibility, and insightful tips for testifying in court.

LET THE VENTURE BEGIN

Whether you are a student taking a first course in criminal investigation or perhaps a neophyte investigator looking to hone your skills, we sincerely hope the textbook adequately fulfills your needs. We now invite you to turn the pages ahead and embark upon a fascinating journey through the world of criminal investigation.

REFERENCE

Wilson, O.W. and McLaren, R.C. (1977). *Police Administration*, 4th ed. New York: McGraw-Hill.

EDITORS

Michael L. Birzer, EdD, is professor of criminal justice and director of the School of Community Affairs at Wichita State University. His research interests include police behavior, advancing the adult learning theory of andragogy into criminal justice education and training, the intersection of race and police contacts, and qualitative research methods (phenomenology, ethnomethodology, and ethnography). His non-academic experience includes over 18 years of service with the Sedgwick County Sheriff's Department in Wichita, KS, where he obtained the rank of lieutenant. Books he has co-authored with Cliff Roberson include *Introduction to Private Security: Theory Meets Practice* (Prentice Hall, 2010); *Police Field Operations: Theory Meets Practice* (Allyn & Bacon, 2008); and *Policing Today and Tomorrow* (Prentice Hall, 2007).

Cliff Roberson, LLM, PhD, is a professor emeritus at Washburn University and academic chair, Graduate School of Criminal Justice, Kaplan University. He is also managing editor of *Police Practices and Research: An International Journal* and *Professional Issues in Criminal Justice Journal*. He has written numerous texts and articles on criminal justice and has over 30 years' experience in academia as a professor, dean, and associate vice president. His non-academic experience includes service as Director of Programs, National College of District Attorneys; chief defense counsel for offenders, Texas Board of Criminal Justice; head, Military Law Branch, U.S. Marine Corps Headquarters; and Marine judge advocate.

CONTRIBUTORS

Gwynne Birzer, JD, a practicing attorney in the state of Kansas, earned her undergraduate degree in criminal justice from Washburn University, Topeka, KS, in 1989. She earned her law degree from Washburn University School of Law in 1992. In 1993, she became an assistant district attorney and prosecuted sexual offenses and child abuse cases for 5 years. She also served as a special assistant attorney general, prosecuting sexually violent offenders across the state of Kansas. In 1998, she entered private practice and taught trial techniques as an adjunct instructor at Washburn University. She is currently an associate attorney at the law firm of Hite, Fanning & Honeyman, LLP, where she focuses her practice on civil defense and litigation with emphasis on medical malpractice. She also serves as an adjunct professor teaching about the American courts and judicial system at Wichita State University.

Bryan Courtney is executive director of the Missouri–Regional Community Policing Institute at Missouri Western State University, St. Joseph. MO–RCPI is a member of U.S. Department of Justice, COPS Office, national RCPI training network. Courtney is currently coordinating a Bureau of Justice Assistance (BJA) project, RCPI National Network Delivery of BJA Training, which provides a wide range of BJA training throughout the nation to federal, state, and local law enforcement. Courtney has been with the MO–RCPI since 1997. He received his undergraduate degree in criminal justice at Missouri Western State University and his master's degree in criminal justice at Washburn University in Topeka, KS. He was a police officer in Maryville, MO, for 6 years.

Frank DiMarino, JD, LLM, is dean of the School of Criminal Justice, Kaplan University, and executive editor of the journal *Professional Issues in Criminal Justice*. From 1991 to 2007, he served as a Financial Institution Fraud Coordinator and Environmental Crimes Coordinator while prosecuting white collar criminals as an assistant U.S. Attorney in Savannah, GA. Frank's other legal experience includes serving as chief of the Criminal Law Division, Fort Stewart, GA, and as assistant U.S. Attorney, Miami, FL. In Washington, D.C., he worked as a senior trial attorney with the General Crimes Section, Multi-District Fraud Unit, Division of Enforcement, Commodity Futures Trading Commission. He also served as appellate counsel and branch chief of the U.S. Army Legal Services Agency, Falls Church, VA, and as prosecutor and officer-in-charge of the military post legal office in Nuremberg, Germany.

Gregg W. Etter, Sr., EdD, is an assistant professor of criminal justice at the University of Central Missouri, Warrensburg. He served 29 years with the Sedgwick County Sheriff's Office in Wichita, KS, retiring as a lieutenant. Dr. Etter earned his bachelor's and master's degrees from Wichita State University and his doctorate from Oklahoma State University. He is a member of the American Society of Criminology, Academy of Criminal Justice Sciences, and the National Sheriff's Association. He is rated as a gang expert by the National Gang Crime Research Center.

John A. Eterno, PhD, is associate dean of graduate studies in criminal justice at Molloy College, Rockville Centre, NY, and is a retired captain from the New York Police Department. He is managing editor of *Police Practice and Research*. His books include *Policing within the Law: A Case Study of the New York City Police Department* (Praeger, 2003); *Police Practices in Global Perspective* (Rowman & Littlefield, 2009; with Dilip Das), and *Unveiling Compstat: The Global Policing Revolution's Naked Truths* (Taylor & Francis, forthcoming; with Eli Silverman). He has testified as a policing expert, appeared in various media outlets (e.g., ABC, CBS), and consulted widely. His most recent peer-reviewed articles have appeared in *Professional Issues in Criminal Justice*, *International Journal of Police Science & Management*, *Women and Criminal Justice*, and *Criminal Law Bulletin*.

Robert D. Hanser, PhD, is the head of the department of criminal justice at the University of Louisiana at Monroe. In addition to teaching undergraduate and graduate courses in criminal justice, Dr. Hanser conducts pre-service and in-service training for police and correctional officers at the North Delta Regional Training Academy. He is a licensed professional counselor in the states of Louisiana and Texas, a licensed addictions counselor in Louisiana, a certified anger resolution therapist, and a certified gang specialist in gang counseling. His research and teaching interests focus on human behavior and mental health issues within the field of criminal justice.

Mark R. McCoy, EdD, is an associate professor at the University of Central Oklahoma Forensic Science Institute, where he is administrator of the Digital Evidence and Cyber Security Program. He retired after 20 years of service with the Oklahoma State Bureau of Investigation (OSBI), where he was the first supervisor of the OSBI Computer Crime Unit. He is a member of the International Association of Computer Investigative Specialists and is a certified forensic computer examiner. Dr. McCoy has a master's degree in forensic science and a doctorate in occupational and adult education.

Scott M. Mire, PhD, is currently an assistant professor of criminal justice at the University of Louisiana at Lafayette. He is a former police officer and U.S. border patrol agent. Following his service as a border patrol agent, Dr. Mire was employed by the Texas Police Corps as a training coordinator while he pursued his doctorate in criminal justice at Sam Houston State University, Huntsville, TX. As a training coordinator, Dr. Mire was responsible for all curriculum development in addition to providing training in all aspects of law enforcement. More recently, Dr. Mire has authored or co-authored several journal articles and book chapters. In addition, he has co-authored three textbooks in the areas of correctional counseling, ethics in criminal justice, and understanding the correlates of violence.

Donald Munday, EdD, has over 22 years of experience as a commissioned law enforcement officer. Dr. Munday served with the Wichita Police Department, where his responsibilities included patrol, crime prevention, community policing, critical stress debriefing, Crime Stoppers, vice and organized crime, bunco, exploited and missing children, and planning and research. He then became the chief of police for the city of Bel Aire, KS. Dr. Munday has been teaching criminal justice courses in university settings for many years. He has also authored two criminal justice undergraduate programs of study. He holds a bachelor's degree in human resources management; a master's in management from Friends University, Wichita, KS; and a doctorate in occupational and adult education from Oklahoma State University. Dr. Munday is an elected faculty member of the Alpha Phi Sigma National Criminal Justice Honor Society and has been a presenter at the Academy of Criminal Justice Sciences and other state and national conferences. Currently, he is a director at Pratt Community College–Wichita.

Matthew O'Deane, PhD, has been a police officer in California since 1992. He is currently an investigator for the San Diego County District Attorney's Office and is a former police officer, detective, and sergeant of the National City, CA, Police Department. He holds a doctorate in public policy from Walden University and is an adjunct professor for Kaplan University. Dr. O'Deane has also written two books on the subject of gangs, the *Gang Investigator's Handbook: A Law-Enforcement Guide to Identifying and Combating Violent Street Gangs* (Paladin Press, 2008) and *Gangs: Theory, Practice, and Research* (LawTech Custom Publishing, 2010).

John Padgett, PhD, is a native of Augusta, GA, and is curårently serving as a core faculty member in Capella University's Public Safety program. He obtained his associate's degree in criminal justice from Georgia Military College, Milledgeville; his bachelor's degree in business administration from Brenau University, Gainesville, GA; his master's degree in education from Troy University, Troy, AL; and his doctorate in professional psychology, specializing in terrorism and violence, at Walden University. He is 26-year law enforcement veteran, an administrative law hearing officer, director of law enforcement training, professor, and core faculty member. His most notable law enforcement convictions include the investigation and apprehension of two serial child molesters, two serial rapists, and the first serial murderer in Augusta, GA.

Michael J. Palmiotto, PhD, is a professor of criminal justice at Wichita State University. He is a former police officer in New York State and has experience in establishing and operating a police training facility. He has a master's degree from John Jay College (CUNY) and a doctorate from the University of Pittsburgh. Dr. Palmiotto is the author of ten books, as well as numerous book chapters and articles on policing and criminal justice.

Roger L. Pennel, PhD, is a professor of criminal justice at the University of Central Missouri. He served nearly 7 years with the Joplin, MO, Police Department, achieving the rank of sergeant. He also served 26 years in the U.S. Army Reserve and retired as a Criminal Investigations Division (CID) investigator. Dr. Pennel earned his associate's degree from Jasper County Community College, his bachelor's degree from Missouri Southern University, and his master's and doctorate degrees from Sam Houston State University, Huntsville, TX.

Cory Rodivich is a crime scene supervisor with the Wichita, KS, Police Department. He is responsible for the daily operation and supervision of the crime scene investigation section, including the direction and supervision of investigative work at major crime scenes. Supervisor Rodivich holds a master's degree in criminal justice from Wichita State University, where he currently serves as an adjunct professor in the criminal justice and forensic science programs. He holds the honor of being the first law enforcement professional from Kansas to attend the renowned National Forensic Academy, where he was elected class president by his colleagues. Supervisor Rodivich has instructed police officers and scene investigators throughout the Midwest as a consultant for the Regional Community Policing Institute at Wichita State University. His professional affiliations include the International Association for Identification, the International Association of Bloodstain Pattern Analysts, and the Association for Crime Scene Reconstruction. He is certified as a Crime Scene Investigator through the International Association for Identification.

Gene L. Scaramella, EdD, currently serves as the Dean of Graduate Studies for Ellis University. He received his doctorate in leadership and educational policy studies from Northern Illinois University, DeKalb, and his master's degree in law enforcement administration and bachelor's degree in law enforcement administration from Western Illinois University, Macomb. Dr. Scaramella served as a police officer for 16 years with both the Arlington Heights, IL, Police Department and the Chicago Police Department.

Donald F. Vespa, resident agent in charge (retired) for the Drug Enforcement Administration, St. Louis Division, has extensive operational experience in investigative surveillance techniques, informant utilization, undercover operations, and narcotic case development, and he has over 22 years experience in drug law enforcement. Vespa has served as a DEA High Intensity Drug Trafficking Areas (HIDTA) task force commander, DEA state and local task force group supervisor, and DEA resident agent in charge.

J. Harrison Watts, PhD, is an assistant professor in the criminal justice and legal studies department at Washburn University. Dr. Watts is a former police practitioner with 15 years of progressive law enforcement experience in Texas. He has 10 years of administrative-level management experience with assignments including sergeant in the criminal investigations division, deputy chief constable, inspector general, and city commissioner. His research interests are focused on police policy and management.

Walter J. Wywadis is Deputy Chief of Police, Topeka, KS, Police Department. He attended Kansas State University on a football scholarship and later became a Topeka police officer. He has served in the field of investigations as an investigator, supervisor, and division commander. Wywadis holds a bachelor's degree in criminal justice and a master's degree in management from Friends University, Wichita, KS. He is a graduate of the FBI National Academy and the Police Executive Research Forum sponsored Senior Management Institute for Police (SMIP) at Boston University.

1

Foundations

CHAPTER 1

A Brief History of Criminal Investigation

John A. Eterno
Malloy College

CHAPTER OBJECTIVES

After reading this chapter, you should be able to do the following:

1. Explain the purpose of criminal investigation.
2. Discuss ancient civilizations' attempts at investigation.
3. Describe "thief takers" and their importance to the history of criminal investigation.
4. Describe the "Bow Street Runners."
5. Identify and describe the history of Scotland Yard.
6. Describe the importance of the U.S. Postal Service to the history of criminal investigation in the United States.
7. Explain the development of criminal investigation in the United States.
8. List some of the key figures involved in the history of criminal investigation.
9. Describe the Federal Bureau of Investigation (FBI).
10. Discuss the mission of the FBI.
11. Identify paths of employment in the wide-ranging field of criminal investigations.

Chapter Outline

- Overview of Criminal Investigation
- Origins of Western Society's Criminal Investigation
- English Influence
- Development of Criminal Investigation in the United States
- Contemporary Employment in Criminal Investigation

OVERVIEW OF CRIMINAL INVESTIGATION

Crime exists in every human society. Social scientists call this phenomenon a *cultural universal*. Crime, then, is an inescapable truth of human existence as we know it. Before crime can occur, however, there must be laws, formal government-created rules that can be obeyed or disobeyed. Legal scholar Alan Dershowitz (2002) observed that laws develop and change based on human experience. The many varieties of cultures and human experiences have paved the way for many different laws and enforcement institutions, including those familiar to most Americans. Civilizations throughout history have addressed the need for lawmaking; the Code of Hammurabi, Ten Commandments, *Magna Carta*, and U.S. Constitution are examples of milestones of law.

With law comes order, some predictability about behavior. This helps society's institutions to function in a workable way (e.g., people feel safe enough to conduct business, citizens can travel safely, people do not worry too much about personal belongings). At the same time, however, laws create a class of people we call *criminals*—those who transgress the boundaries created by the laws. Law enforcement authorities must then be deployed to investigate, arrest, and prosecute these people. To Americans, and most in the Western world, the rule of law legislated through the people's representatives is commonplace and generally taken for granted. Of course, law in a democratic society is not the only method of political rule. Throughout the world and its history, police have been and continue to be involved in other types of crimes, such as political crimes against a regime. Indeed, law enforcement can become the defining aspect of a state—for example, a police state (e.g., Nazi Germany). Investigations, therefore, inherently depend on the type of legal system in place and the personalities of those in power, among many other factors. Many countries, for example, operate under Islamic law or socialist law. Importantly, then, the focus of this chapter is on democratic law and the investigation of crimes therein.

The many different types of crimes can range from minor ones such as petit theft to violent crimes such as serial murder. The following short list of crimes is neither exhaustive nor exclusive but is meant to give the reader an idea of the vastness of criminal activity: white collar crimes, victimless crimes, street crimes, property crimes, violent crimes, gang-related crimes, hate crimes, domestic violence, occupational crimes, corporate crimes, computer crimes, sex crimes, terrorism, etc. Investigations of criminal behavior can be very complicated, specialized, and technical. These occupations often call for highly educated and extremely motivated individuals (e.g., medical examiners have advanced degrees in medicine).

Although police officers in our society do investigate and take reports for most criminal acts, detectives or investigators with special skills are called in for more serious crimes such as homicide, sex crimes, and kidnappings, among other major crimes. These detectives have special skills that come from education, training, and experience. Some criminals are exceedingly cunning or gruesome and require a team of investigators to capture them. Serial killer Albert Fish is a particularly interesting example in American history. He murdered at least 15 children in the metropolitan New York area in the 1920s and 1930s.

He was trusted by people due to his kind demeanor and his grandfatherly appearance. His behavior seems to have steadily gotten worse when his wife left him when he was 49. He was a vicious man and a cannibal (Anon., 2007, paragraph 4):

> In 1928, Fish indulged his taste for human flesh on a 12-year-old girl named Grace Budd. She was the daughter of parents who knew and trusted Fish. When Fish offered to take her to a party for children, they let him do so without any misgivings. Instead of a party, Fish took Grace to his cottage in Westchester County, New York. Stripping himself naked, Fish strangled the child, and then beheaded and dismembered her with a meat cleaver. He then cooked her body parts into a stew seasoned with onions and carrots. Albert Fish then consumed this grisly repast down to the last awful morsel, and then he vanished.

This is only one example of the absolutely horrifying nature of this killer. After another incident in July 1924, where a police officer's son went missing in Staten Island, a borough on the south side of New York City, investigators were feverishly called in: "In a short period of time, Manhattan fingerprint experts and police photographers were enlisted in the case as well as some two hundred and fifty plainclothesmen" (Bardsley, 2010). Fish was not caught until a break in the case occurred in July 1934. At that point, most thought the case would never be solved, and only one investigator was still involved in the case, Detective William King. Fish sent a letter to Delia Budd, Grace's mother, in which he provided the gruesome details of her murder. Following a lead from the envelope, the investigators were able to find Fish (Bardsley, 2010):

> But, Detective King realized that the details of his meeting with the Budds and Grace were accurate. Also, the handwriting on this horrible letter was identical to the letter the elderly kidnapper had written ... six years earlier. The envelope had an important clue: a small hexagonal emblem had the letters N.Y.P.C.B.A. which stood for the New York Private Chauffeur's Benevolent Association. ... A young janitor [at the N.Y.P.C.B.A.] came forward, admitting that he had taken a couple of sheets of paper and a few envelopes. He had left the stationery in his old rooming house at 200 East 52nd Street. The landlady was shocked when she was given "Frank Howard's" description. He sounded just like the old man who had lived there for two months, the old man who had checked out of her rooming house just a couple of days earlier. The former tenant had called himself Albert H. Fish. ... Finally, the post office told Detective King that it had intercepted a letter for Albert Fish. ... On December 13, 1934, the landlady called Detective King. Albert Fish was at the rooming house looking for his letter. The old man was sitting with a teacup when King opened the door. Fish stood up and nodded when King asked him if he was Albert Fish. Suddenly, Fish reached into his pocket and produced a razor blade which he held in front of him. Infuriated, King grabbed the old man's hand and twisted it sharply, "I've got you now," he said triumphantly.

Criminal investigators seek to uproot and bring to justice such horrid lawbreakers. Influenced by what they have seen and heard in the media, students may think that detective skills are innate to everyone, but they are not.

ORIGINS OF WESTERN SOCIETY'S CRIMINAL INVESTIGATION

Although the science of criminal investigation would not be developed until modern times, some interesting developments date back to ancient civilizations. The medical field is clearly the most important of the professions in determining the cause of death. Even in ancient Egypt, physicians conducted autopsies, and autopsies can be documented back to at least the time of the ruler Imhotep in 2980 B.C. (Ramsland, 2007). One interesting case, which occurred in 44 B.C., was the killing of Julius Caesar, on whom a physician, Antistius, performed an autopsy. It was announced in the Roman Forum that one of his stab wounds was through the heart, killing him. Interestingly, the Latin word for "forum" is *forensis*, meaning a marketplace or a place of debate. In Roman times, if one person accused another of a crime, it would be taken to the Forum for debate. The best debater won the case. The Latin word *forensis*, then, is the basis for the word "forensics" today (Ramsland, 2007).

An interesting development in England occurred circa 1000 A.D. Under the rule of King Richard, an official called a *crowner* would perform various duties for the king. This office would eventually evolve and be called *coroner*. In addition to the duties involved in protecting the king's interests, these officials not only collected taxes but also "summoned inquest juries for people who were seriously wounded or who had died from 'misadventure'" (Ramsland, 2007, p. 5). Determining how a person died was important because it affected how much money the king got. By the 13th century, this official became the person who investigated all dead bodies. Although physicians may have been called in to help, little accurate scientific methodology was applied at the time; therefore, coroners relied on many different criteria to determine the cause of death, which, of course, led to interesting if not outright outlandish conclusions. Also during the 13th century, the specialty of legal medicine began to be offered at the University of Bologna in what is now modern-day Italy (Ramsland, 2007). It should be noted that, from 486 through 1500 A.D., punishment was arbitrary, and trials by ordeal or executions of the innocent were not uncommon (McKenzie, 1996). One could hardly call the investigatory practices of whatever law enforcement there was fundamentally fair and just.

ENGLISH INFLUENCE

THIEF TAKERS

Ancient civilizations and early European practices developed the roots of modern-day investigations, but it was the lure of money and the advancement of science that served as the catalysts for advances in detective work. In 18th-century England, changes in approaches to crime fighting were instrumental in the development of modern-day investigations. Constables and watchmen were the common law enforcement practice of the time. Mostly, these men assisted victims in taking an offender to a magistrate, but it was also hoped that their presence would deter would-be criminals, as private citizens were expected to bear the brunt of enforcing the law and doing any investigatory work. As cities became more populated, urban problems such as poverty and crime began to escalate. The difficulties of relying on private citizens for law enforcement became obvious, but the solution to this problem was not so clear. As early as the 1600s, men known as "thief takers" could be found (Beattie, 2006). For a reward or fee, these men used their knowledge of criminals and criminal behaviors to negotiate between perpetrators and victims for the return of some or all of the stolen property, or they helped bring the perpetrator to justice. Thief takers became far more numerous in the mid-1700s because the monetary rewards for capturing criminals grew larger. These rewards came from both the government and newspapers (Emsley et al., 2011).

Beattie (2006, p. 16) wrote that, "Over the quarter century between 1720 and 1745, and again briefly between 1750 and 1752, the reward for the conviction of a robber in London was 140 pounds, a sum that approached three or four years' income for even a skilled workman." Notwithstanding the inevitable corruption that such a system led to, many believed that these methods were to some extent successful, at least compared to the constable and watchmen, who felt little or no responsibility to investigate incidents.

BOW STREET RUNNERS

Thief takers might take a perpetrator to a local magistrate, and one place to find a magistrate was at the Bow Street office, which was set up in 1739; however, it was not until Henry Fielding took control in 1748 that a remarkable shift in the activities occurred. Because the area had an extraordinarily high rate of crime, Fielding initiated the practice of having a group of law enforcers be proactive in finding and bringing to justice perpetrators. Beattie (2006, p. 16) wrote,

> For in the winter of 1749–50, with reports increasing of violence, … Fielding had taken what was to turn out to be an important initiative by persuading a group of men, including constables and ex-constables, to devote themselves to seeking out and apprehending serious offenders and bringing them to Bow Street for examination and commitment to trial.

This, in itself, was a critical innovation, but Fielding took it a step further. Without a source of funding, the experiment devised by Fielding could easily have failed, and, in fact, it was on the brink of failing (Beattie, 2006). Although rewards were still coming in, they were expensive for the government to maintain, led to corruption, and were inefficient. Further, they were hardly adequate for this unique operation. Fielding provided the government with a clear alternative to rewards: Give him money to pay for his group and advertise the reporting of crimes and descriptions. Bow Street then began to pay its men directly for their services. Clearly, Fielding took a major step forward in the development of modern-day policing and detective work. Indeed, he has been credited with establishing the first detective unit (Germann et al., 1978, as cited in Roberg et al., 2009, p. 34).

By 1765, after Fielding had died and his half-brother John had taken over, Bow Street had clerical staff and regular people to help. This arrangement eventually caught on: "More rotation offices were set up in Middlesex and Westminster. In 1792, the Middlesex Justices Act created seven police offices in the metropolis, each with three stipendiary magistrates and six constables charged with detecting and arresting criminals" (Emsley et al., 2011).

SCOTLAND YARD

By the early 1800s, it was clear that changes were needed in the way laws were enforced, and the British Parliament set up committees to study the issues of crime and policing in 1812, 1818, and 1822 (MPS, 2011a). It was not until 1829, though, that the British Home Secretary, Sir Robert Peel, created the first modern police force in London through the Metropolitan Police Act (i.e., the Act for Improving the Police in and near the Metropolis). Although the police had developed a military structure, the intent of Peel was that the force not be military but civilian, and he deliberately chose uniforms for his officers that had no resemblance to those of the military (McKenzie, 1996). Today, both styles of policing, military and civilian, have become commonplace, depending on the country and the particular police force. Peel chose Scotland Yard for his first headquarters, and the name has become synonymous with the Metropolitan Police.

Prevention was the key to Peel's reforms; however, there was no immediate acceptance of the police. Gaining public trust was critical: "Peel's reforms, particularly in regards to discipline, were not only intended to promote and preserve the public peace, but to promote and preserve the public trust. Prior to these reforms, the public's faith in the existing police watch systems was faint" (Anderson, 2001, p. 78). Initially, the police primarily had an influence on the everyday quality of life, as they enforced laws against public drunkenness, fights, and similar minor violations.

DETECTIVES

It was not until 1842 that the Detective Branch was established, but "it soon became apparent that a detective force was needed to work in conjunction with the uniformed, beat patrol officers. Authority was given for the creation of a distinct detective force within the Metropolitan Police in 1842" (Emsley et al., 2011). Today, detectives are fewer in number compared to the uniformed patrol officers, and they tend to think of themselves, in general, as vastly more skilled than the typical officer. As Emsley and Shpayer-Makov (2006, p. 12) stated, "In their memoirs and in the way that they use the media, detectives commonly have liked to stress their knowledge of offenders, their shrewdness, their cunning, and, in more recent times, their ability to deploy science and technology." Unfortunately, such skills and information can lead to corrupt activities. Indeed, scandal among plainclothes officers is not uncommon: "Metropolitan Police detectives in the late twentieth century have demonstrated the problems in setting police officers on relatively modest incomes to investigate high-earning entrepreneurs dealing in, for example, drugs and pornography. Detective officers in such situations are exposed to dangerous levels of temptation and the potential for serious corruption … especially when the detectives regard themselves as elite" (Emsley and Shpayer-Makov, 2006, p. 13). Nevertheless, it is clear that the special skills of detectives are clearly necessary for proper investigations.

The difficulties of being a detective, including corruption and politics, among many other possible troubles, should not be underestimated. A very early case can be found in the then newly formed Detective Branch of the London Metropolitan Police (MPS, 2011b):

> Jonathan Whicher was one of the original members of the Detective Branch. … In 1860, he was called in to assist the investigation into the horrific murder of 4-year-old (Francis) Savile Kent. … When the nursemaid, Elizabeth Gough, reported the child missing at 7:15 am to Mrs. Kent, a search commenced for the child, who was found dead in an outside privy with his throat cut and a stab wound to the chest. … The local magistrates soon became impatient for results …. They asked the Home Office for assistance from Scotland Yard without the agreement of the local Chief Constable, and it was after a second request from them that Detective Inspector Jonathan Whicher, then the most senior and well known of the detectives at Scotland Yard, was sent. Whicher concentrated on a missing night dress, possibly blood stained, belonging to Constance, and there was also circumstantial evidence against her. The magistrates directed Constance's arrest and gave Whicher seven days to prepare a case. Mr. Kent provided a barrister for his daughter who dominated proceedings. Constance was released on bail and the case was later dropped. The reaction in the newspapers was sympathetic to Constance, Whicher was heavily criticised, notwithstanding the difficulties he had faced, and his reputation never recovered. … Five years later, in April 1865, after a period abroad and in a religious institution in Brighton, Constance attended Bow Street magistrates court and confessed to the murder. Her motive had apparently been to exact revenge against the second Mrs. Kent for her treatment of Constance's mother. … The confession from Constance came too late to save the career of Jonathan Whicher who had been pensioned before Constance's appearance at Bow Street confirmed his original suspicion. It is a classic illustration of how early investigations were directed heavily by magistrates, of the influence which well-to-do people could exert over local police officers, and of the importance of immediately searching and questioning the whole household at the scene of a crime, regardless of social status.

DEVELOPMENT OF CRIMINAL INVESTIGATION IN THE UNITED STATES

While Sir Robert Peel was working on creating a police force in England, the American experience with policing was also beginning, and parallels can be drawn between the two experiences. They both had in common the rise of cities and their inherent problems of crime and poverty. Also, the United States began to, at least to some extent, follow the model developed by Peel: "The police departments established from the 1830s to 1850s—Boston in 1837, New York in 1844, Philadelphia in 1854—were loosely based on the Peelian model of the London police" (Roberg et al., 2009, p. 37). One of the greatest differences between the two, uniquely American, was the large number of local departments with only tangential centralized federal government control. Further, the nature of the American system was such that local law enforcement developed more quickly compared to federal enforcement. Indeed, law enforcement at the federal level was put together in piecemeal fashion. As Johnson (1981, pp. 74–75) stated:

> Each department which exercised some control over domestic affairs (Treasury, Post Office, etc.) had particular law enforcement problems … they evolved as each department evolved. Federal law enforcement, therefore, developed haphazardly, with no central supervision in response to specific needs. … Federal officers had neither a separate identity nor a general assignment to uphold the law. Rather, they worked within a particular government bureaucracy where they investigated specific crimes.

Recall that Peel established his force due to an act of Parliament; not so for the American police, as each locale set up its own department, and federal agencies concentrated on their own areas of responsibilities. This was at least partially the result of the American federalism style of government. Johnson (1981) compared the American and British experiences with police from 1829 to 1860: "London's police therefore had a highly centralized command. … By contrast, an American chief of police had many masters. So did his patrolmen. Mayors and aldermen interfered often and without thought about the consequences … there was no single standard of behavior" (p. 32). Also, it was not until the American Civil War in the 1860s that it was ultimately decided that the federal government was supreme. Prior to that, the neophyte democracy still had many lingering questions regarding the power of the states.

Today, investigations in the United States are accomplished by an array of local, state, and federal agencies, reflecting the power structure of our complex government. According to the U.S. Department of Justice (BJS, 2007), 17,876 state and local law enforcement agencies employed 1,076,897 employees in 2004. Many of these are small agencies that do not have detectives. For these smaller agencies, when an incident requiring further investigation occurs, detectives from state, county, or other local departments are called in. Adding to the state and local numbers, at the federal level 30 agencies have 100 or more law enforcement officers who are full time and authorized to carry firearms and make arrests (BJS, 2007).

THE EARLY AMERICAN EXPERIENCE: THE POSTAL SERVICE

Understanding the development of investigations in the United States is no simple matter. It appears that necessity was definitely the mother of invention. One of the earliest attempts at investigations in the United States involved the Postal Service. In the 1800s, the U.S. Postal Service was one of the most important agencies, and laws against tampering with the mail date back as far as the beginning of the nation in 1789. Such laws required enforcement, though. As the nation grew, Americans used the mail system to transport cash or other valuables, making the Postal Service ripe for criminal activity. In the early 19th century, it became obvious that some substantial enforcement was needed. Special agents were hired who not only investigated crime but also performed a variety of inspection duties (Johnson, 1981); these special agents did investigations but were not full-time detectives. Furthermore, before 1830, very few of these special agents existed: "Postmasters general probably employed no more than a dozen special agents at any one time" (Johnson, 1981, p. 78)

In 1836, Congress passed a law that allowed the hiring of full-time special agents with arrest powers; these special agents became the first formal police force within the executive branch of the federal government. These new special agents were finally full-time investigators (Johnson, 1981, pp. 79–80):

> [Post Office detectives] developed the habit of making thorough investigations as systematically and as unobtrusively as possible. J. Holbrook, a special agent in the 1850s, used methods which convey some of the meticulous care these men adopted. In a case involving the theft of several letters containing money, Holbrook disguised himself as a traveler. This permitted him to survey the mail route, observe the routines of the postmasters, and learn the habits of local postal employees in casual conversations with local inhabitants. When he noticed that a venerable postmaster happened to own a coat somewhat too grand for his income, Holbrook arranged a trap to test his suspicions. He sent a packet containing marked bills along this mail route, confirmed that it had disappeared upon its arrival at the suspected post office, and caught the old postmaster with his wallet full of the marked money. Such detective methods seem to have been fairly typical throughout the century.

The Postal Service is one of the earliest examples in American history of the use of detectives who were exclusively government agents; however, a fairly common practice, even for the government, was to hire private detectives.

ALLAN PINKERTON

One of the most well known private detectives was Allan Pinkerton. In the 19th century, he created one of the most famous detective agencies known throughout the world and which still exists today—the Pinkerton National Detective Agency. The Pinkerton Agency is credited with saving President-Elect Abraham Lincoln's life in 1861 in Baltimore, among their many other accomplishments (Anon., 2011). Pinkerton was born in Scotland in 1819. His father was a police sergeant who died when Pinkerton was young, and his family was very poor. As a young man, he got involved in a movement that called for political and social reform. When the government issued a warrant for his arrest, Pinkerton fled to the United States in 1842. His career as a law enforcement officer began after he caught counterfeiters while cutting wood near Chicago. His reputation growing, he was given an appointment as a deputy sheriff. Although the actual dates are in doubt, sometime around

1849 he was appointed as the city police's first and, for a while, only detective. He soon quit that job. Pinkerton himself said that he left that job because of "political interference" (Mackay, 1996, p. 68).

Interestingly, and a fact not often cited in biographies of Pinkerton, at this point in his life he was "eagerly snapped up by the United States Post Office which appointed him Special United States Mail Agent" (Mackay, 1996, p. 69). As we know from our earlier discussion, the Postal Service was one of the most professional investigative bodies of its time. Pinkerton went undercover and brilliantly solved a case, determining that "one of the sorters, Theodore Dennison, had a brother named Perry who had once been arrested for pilfering mail in another town. Allan, in his guise as a recently arrived Scottish immigrant, befriended the Dennisons and learned that they were, in fact, nephews of the Chicago postmaster" (Mackay, 1996, p. 69). Shortly after this excellent piece of undercover work, Pinkerton left the post office and created the North-Western Detective Agency (later Pinkerton and Co.); however, it should be noted that Pinkerton did not invent the private detective nor the private detective agency. Although he was certainly very good at it, a French detective, Eugene Francois Vidocq, is generally considered to be the first modern detective. Vidocq created an agency in 1832 or 1833, well before Pinkerton (Brown, 2006; Emsley et al., 2006; Mackay, 1996). Pinkerton's name, however, has become synonymous with investigations. He certainly popularized such work and enjoyed many successes. He was even hired by the Union during the Civil War to obtain military information about the Confederate states (Anon., 2011).

Pinkerton also helped popularize a romanticized notion of criminals. Unlike the numerous theories of crime that exist today, all essentially sociologically or psychologically based, the image of a criminal as an equal adversary for detectives began to emerge. Walker (1977, p. 22) observed that, "Between 1874 and 1885 Pinkerton published more than eighteen books on crime and criminals. ... Pinkerton wrote that 'romance and tradition have for a long period of time accredited the cracksman with being the most expert in their profession.' The police officer was expected to match wits with these expert criminals."

THE FBI

The Postal Service and the Treasury Department (Secret Service) were early federal government investigative bodies. Today, the preeminent federal agency for law enforcement inquiries is the Federal Bureau of Investigation (FBI). Although many other federal agencies conduct investigations, those agencies tend to concentrate on very specific crimes; for example, the Drug Enforcement Agency (DEA), Bureau of Alcohol, Tobacco, Firearms, and Explosives (ATF), and Internal Revenue Service (IRS) all do investigations, but their work is specifically tailored to the mission of the particular agency. The FBI, however, is unique in that its mission is far more general in nature. Indeed, its mission statement reads (FBI, 2011a):

> To protect and defend the United States against terrorist and foreign intelligence threats, to uphold and enforce the criminal laws of the United States, and to provide leadership and criminal justice services to federal, state, municipal, and international agencies and partners.

Investigations by the FBI can overlap with those of other federal agencies, and the FBI may even take over. The well-known raid that took place in February 1993 on the Branch Davidians in Waco, Texas, was initially an ATF operation. The FBI was called in to assist after a raid by the ATF was unsuccessful, leaving four of its agents dead. A 51-day standoff followed after the FBI took charge; it ended badly, and many of the Davidians died after the FBI stormed the compound. The raid is still controversial today.

After 9/11, the FBI took on added significance in the war on terror. President George W. Bush created the Department of Homeland Security (DHS) to ensure that all of the federal agencies involved in law enforcement were properly sharing information and working together. The FBI, however, clearly has absorbed the lion's share of federal investigations, in addition to acquiring an enormous amount of expertise.

The FBI was created relatively recently compared to some of its counterparts (e.g., U.S. Postal Service, Secret Service). Indeed, the oversight body of the FBI, the Department of Justice (DOJ), was not created until 1870. The DOJ often utilized the Secret Service and private detectives for their investigations (FBI, 2011b). What was to become the FBI was not created until 1908. In that year, Attorney General Charles Bonaparte under President Theodore Roosevelt assigned ten former Secret Service employees and some others to be special agents; however, the specific reason for formation of the agency was political. There was a fight between the President and Congress over corruption, and the Secret Service agents on loan to the DOJ were subject to severe criticism for an investigation they did on a U.S. Senator. Jeffreys-Jones (2007, p. 39) summarized the situation:

> In 1904, Secret Service detectives on loan to Justice had obtained evidence that led to the conviction of a number of land fraudsters, including U.S. Senator John H. Mitchell (R-Ore.). ... Unhappy about the investigation to which he had been subjected, Congress directed a barrage of criticism at the Secret Service. This culminated, in the spring of 1908, in a legislative ban on the Treasury Department's loan of Secret Service detectives to any other department. Faced with this ban, the executive created the Justice Department's own detective force.

When the terms of the Attorney General and President were completed in 1909, they recommended that the 34 agents then assigned become a permanent force. The next Attorney General, George Wickersham, named this group of agents the Department of Investigation (FBI, 2011b), and the Bureau was given its current name in 1935. In 1924, J. Edgar Hoover became the director of the FBI. He made many changes and oversaw a rapid expansion of the Bureau. In 1932, the FBI began releasing its Most Wanted lists. During World War II, the FBI collected intelligence and tracked down deserters. Today, terrorism, cybercrime, white collar crime, and organized crime are among the many federal crimes investigated by the Bureau. The FBI is the main domestic investigative agency for the U.S. government, and it reports to the Attorney General. The FBI, however, does not have the disciplinary powers of state and local police forces. Those police forces, who do the vast majority of police work in the United States, run their own departments under local authority.

CONTEMPORARY EMPLOYMENT IN CRIMINAL INVESTIGATION

In today's world, there is no shortage of criminal behavior. In fact, the United States has the dubious distinction of having the highest prison population rate in the world and is the largest consumer of the world's illegal drugs (Eterno and Das, 2010). On a global level, transnational crime and terrorism are ever increasing as modern technology and transportation systems expand to more and more countries. Opportunities for careers in investigation should be widely available for the foreseeable future; however, this field offers so many potential career paths that it is beyond the scope of this chapter to explain them all. Instead, readers interested in careers as investigators are given a broad outline on how to proceed.

Preparing for a career as an investigator requires one to be aware of the possible tracks one can take. In very general terms, one can work in a laboratory setting or in a field setting. For those thinking of working in a laboratory (say, examining DNA), the requisite educational path would be one in the hard sciences, with a major in biology, chemistry, forensic science, or other related subject. This would allow entrance to graduate-level programs to prepare for work in a laboratory setting. In addition to DNA analysis, forensic investigations can involve, for example, fingerprints, firearms, poisons, polygraph testing, human remains, autopsies, accounting, computers, applied psychology, and much more.

Working in the field as an investigator requires a different set of skills. Although knowledge of forensics is helpful, generally a detective working in the field would not be required to develop a sophisticated, higher education in the sciences. Those interested in field investigations would more likely major in criminal justice or a related discipline. These careers generally involve becoming a sworn officer. The skills required are very different and include an understanding of criminal and procedural laws, methods of interrogation, understanding a crime scene, developing a case for prosecution, understanding *modus operandi*, spotting patterns in criminal behavior, understanding the causes of criminality, and much more.

Choosing which track to take will depend on one's interests and abilities; for example, those interested in accounting might seek to become experts in white collar crime. This very wide range of potential careers makes it important for future investigators to think about what they would like to do in the future as soon as possible so their education can be tailored to achieving that goal. Those interested in becoming an FBI special agent, for example, should know that the FBI has five entry-level programs: accounting, computer science/information technology, language, law, and diversified (combination of full-time experience and education).

As you read through this book, certain topics may be more appealing to you, and you may even consider embarking on a career in one; however, you need to do your homework to find out what it takes to become that particular type of investigator and to determine job opportunities in that field. Some careers are more likely to have openings than others. Importantly, students should talk to an advisor and a practitioner as early in their college career as possible.

QUESTIONS FOR DISCUSSION

1. Discuss some of the skills required to expose the serial killer Albert Fish.
2. Based on the discussions regarding ancient civilizations and early investigations, is it necessary to have a fair and just system to properly investigate crime?
3. Why did modern-day detectives develop?
4. Are detectives more prone to corruption? If so, why? If not, why not?
5. The United States has a unique system of law enforcement. Can it be made more efficient? If so, how? If not, why not?
6. If you wish to become an investigator, what are some steps you can take to reach your goal?

BIBLIOGRAPHY

Anderson, J. (2001). Iron Discipline, Then and Now. *Law & Order*, 49(8):77–78.

Anon. (2007). *Albert Fish, the Grandfatherly Ghoul*, http://twistedminds.creativescapism.com/most-notorious/albert-fish/af-murders/.

Anon. (2011). Allan Pinkerton. In *Encyclopaedia Britannica Online*, http://www.britannica.com/EBchecked/topic/461110/Allan-Pinkerton.

Bardsley, M. (2010). *Albert Fish: The Manhunt*, http://www.trutv.com/library/crime/serial_killers/notorious/fish/8.html; *Albert Fish: A Clue,* http://www.trutv.com/library/crime/serial_killers/notorious/fish/10.html.

Beattie, J.M. (2006). Early Detection: The Bow Street Runners in Late Eighteenth Century London. In Emsley, C. and Shpayer-Makov, H., Eds., *Police Detectives in History, 1750–1950* (pp. 15–32). Burlington, VT: Ashgate Publishing.

BJS. (2007). *Census of State and Local Law Enforcement Agencies, 2004.* Washington, D.C.: U.S. Department of Justice, Bureau of Justice Statistics (bjs.ojp.usdoj.gov/content/pub/pdf/csllea04.pdf).

Brown, H.G. (2006). Tips, Traps and Tropes: Catching Thieves in Post-Revolutionary Paris. In Emsley, C. and Shpayer-Makov, H., Eds., *Police Detectives in History, 1750–1950* (pp. 33–60). Burlington, VT: Ashgate Publishing.

Dershowitz, A. (2002). *Shouting Fire: Civil Liberties in a Turbulent Age.* Boston: Little, Brown and Company.

Emsley, C. and Shpayer-Makov, H., Eds. (2006). *Police Detectives in History, 1750–1950.* Burlington, VT: Ashgate Publishing.

Emsley, C., Hitchcock, T., and Shoemaker, R. (2011). Crime and Justice—Policing in London, *Old Bailey Proceedings Online* (http://www.oldbaileyonline.org/static/Policing.jsp).

Eterno, J.A. and Das, D.K., Eds. (2010). *Police Practices in Global Perspective.* Lanham, MD: Rowman & Littlefield.

FBI. (2011a). *Quick Facts.* Washington, D.C.: Federal Bureau of Investigation (http://www.fbi.gov/quickfacts.htm).

FBI. (2011b). *Origins (1908–1910).* Washington, D.C.: Federal Bureau of Investigation (http://www.fbi.gov/about-us/history/brief-history).

Germann, A.C., Day, F.D., and Gallati, R.R. (1978). *Introduction to Law Enforcement and Criminal Justice.* Springfield, IL: Charles C Thomas; cited by Roberg, R., Novak, K., and Cordner, G. (2009). *Police and Society.* New York: Oxford University Press.

Jeffreys-Jones, R. (2007). *The FBI: A History.* New Haven, CT: Yale University Press.

Johnson, D.R. (1981). *American Law Enforcement: A History.* St. Louis, MO: Forum Press.

Mackay, J. (1996). *Allan Pinkerton: The First Private Eye*. New York: John Wiley & Sons.

McKenzie, I. (1996). *The History of Criminal Investigation*. Austin, TX: Raintree Steck-Vaughn.

MPS. (2011a). *History of the Metropolitan Police: Time Line 1829–1849*. London: Metropolitan Police Service (http://www.met.police.uk/history/timeline1829-1849.htm).

MPS. (2011b). *History of the Metropolitan Police: Constance Kent and the Road Hill House Murder*. London: Metropolitan Police Service (http://www.met.police.uk/history/constance.htm).

Ramsland, K. (2007). *Beating the Devil's Game: A History of Forensic Science and Criminal Investigation*. New York: Berkley Books.

Roberg, R., Novak, K., and Cordner, G. (2009). *Police and Society*. New York: Oxford University Press.

Walker, S. (1977). *A Critical History of Police Reform*. Lexington, MA: D.C. Heath and Company.

CHAPTER 2

Introducing Criminal Investigation

Bryan Courtney
Missouri Western College

CHAPTER OBJECTIVES

After reading this chapter, you should be able to do the following:

1. List and describe the qualifications necessary to become a criminal investigator.
2. List and describe specific training for criminal investigators.
3. Explain the role of the initial responding officer at a crime scene.
4. List and describe the goals of criminal investigations.
5. Describe the functions of a criminal investigator in documenting a crime scene.
6. Describe the role of criminal investigations in the overall police mission and comprehend the challenges facing the criminal investigations unit in a community policing environment.

Chapter Outline

- Introducing Criminal Investigation
- Qualifications for Becoming a Criminal Investigator
- Selection Process
- Specialized Training for Criminal Investigators
- Role of the Patrol Officer in the Preliminary Investigation
- Role and Function of the Criminal Investigator

INTRODUCING CRIMINAL INVESTIGATION

Criminal investigations and the criminal investigator carry with them near mythical status and high regard from those within law enforcement and from society at large. The entertainment industry has had a long affection for criminal investigations and the criminal investigator. Countless novels, movies, and television programs have presented exciting tales about the criminal detective. Visit any bookstore and you will find a "Crime" section whose shelves are lined with stories about notorious crimes and criminals. Pop culture portrays criminal investigations as an exciting career filled with car chases, gun battles, and a continual game of chess played between criminal investigators and the perpetrators.

If you were to ask criminal justice students or recruits in a police academy what their career goals are, often their answers would focus on the general area of criminal investigations. This chapter is designed to provide an overview of what it takes to be a criminal investigator, ranging from the basic skill sets necessary to become a criminal investigator to the common qualifications law enforcement agencies require for the position of detective. This chapter also reviews the selection process within law enforcement agencies for detectives and provides a summary of the training recommended or required for criminal investigators. Additionally, this chapter provides an examination of the role that patrol officers fill in the preliminary investigation. Specific job functions of the detective, such as crime scene management, documenting the crime scene through photography, and crime scene sketching, are explored, as well as the role that criminal investigators serve within the context of the overall mission of the police in our society.

QUALIFICATIONS FOR BECOMING
A CRIMINAL INVESTIGATOR

Qualifications for becoming a criminal investigator in most agencies generally include the requirement of prior experience in the patrol division (DMPD, 2011). The minimum time required in patrol before becoming eligible to bid for a detective position within the organization is agency specific but generally ranges from 6 months to 6 years (BLS, 2011). A review of numerous departmental detective job postings revealed that most commonly a minimum of 3 years of patrol experience was necessary before applying for any specialized position, including detective (KCPD, 2011).

The minimum qualifications for entering an organization's selection process for a position in the criminal investigations unit will vary by agency, depending on its size, specialization, and responsibilities. As an example, with regard to the Alexandra Police Department: "The Criminal Investigation Section's primary responsibility is to conduct the follow-up investigations of crimes that occur within the City. Examples of these investigations are homicides, death cases, rapes and other felony sex offenses, commercial robberies, offenses wherein juveniles are victims or suspects, financial crimes, computer crimes, domestic violence, stalking, child welfare (ex: CHINS, child abuse, cases involving Child Protective Services), missing persons, and other serious investigations requiring intensive specialized or confidential investigation" (APD, 2011). One can speculate that this or any agency would favor those candidates from patrol who enter the criminal investigator selection process having developed skills and acumen in any of these specialized areas.

General qualifications may also include demonstrated interpersonal skills illustrating that the detective candidate is able to successfully build relationships outside of the organization across gender, ethnic, generational, and political groups (Bennett and Hess, 2007). Also key is that law enforcement agencies will evaluate the candidate's demonstrated ability to develop solvability factors during preliminary investigations while in patrol. Additionally, the organization will evaluate if the detective candidate has been able to successfully build professional relationships and has effectively communicated with the criminal investigations unit from his or her patrol position. Criminal investigation is a process of discovering, preparing, identifying, and presenting evidence. Organizations will look for candidates who have demonstrated these skills, as well as the ability to perform deductive reasoning, a logical process in which a conclusion follows from specific facts (Bennett and Hess, 2007). It has long been said that the greatest predictor of future performance is past performance; law enforcement agencies will look to promote candidates for detective positions that have a demonstrated history of assisting the criminal investigations unit in successful clearance of criminal investigations.

SELECTION PROCESS

Generally, the process begins with a job posting, which informs department personnel of an opening in the criminal investigations unit. Interested officers submit their interest in the position following department policy, which typically requires sending a résumé to the patrol officer's supervisor. The supervisor will evaluate if the interested party has met the minimum qualifications for the position; if so, the supervisor will enter the interested officer into the candidate pool. Applicants will be screened for eligibility for the promotional process through reviews of the candidate's experiences and expertise as they relate to the qualifications of the posted position. Upon being entered into the promotional process for detective the candidate will generally have to successfully navigate a selection process consisting of an assessment center, written test, panel interview, role play, group exercise, and in-basket (KCPD, 2011).

Larger agencies may require candidates who meet the minimum requirements for the rank of detective or investigator to successfully complete the agency's promotional academy. The Madison Police Department requires all of the detective and investigator candidates who have successfully passed the department's screening process for admission to the promotional academy to complete a week of technical competency skills specific to the rank and training in general quality improvement methods and leadership skills. Those candidates who score 70% or higher are allowed to continue on to the assessment center (MPD, 2011). The assessment center is essentially a job simulation consisting of various exercises designed to assess the qualifications and developmental potential of each candidate. The exercises are based on job-related situations and are designed as interpersonal and administrative exercises. A typical assessment center will be comprised of five sections for all ranks: written exam, interview, in-basket assignment, role-play situation, and a group exercise. Nearly all agencies will require a written test in the promotion process that generally covers organizational policy, procedure, state law, and in some cases materials from a reading list assigned to the candidates during the selection process (MPD, 2011).

Interviews are generally included in the selection process for positions in the criminal investigations unit. Interviews are conducted by a promotion panel and serve to evaluate the candidate's skills, knowledge, and abilities to perform the functions required of the position. Interview topics can include familiarity with department policies and procedures and applicable statutes, as well as the candidate's motivation to become a detective, initiative, problem-solving and organizational skills, history of teamwork, report writing ability, crime scene expertise, tactical response, and view of the role of detective within the department and in an interagency capacity (MPD, 2011).

Role plays included in the selection process generally focus on crime scene processing for investigators and interviewing for detectives. Group exercises for detectives and investigators can include debate, major incident simulation, and demonstration of communication skills. The in-basket exercise for detectives generally includes a simulated case assignment for the candidate to work. Evaluation criteria for the assessment center can include scoring the candidate's communication skills, both internal and external to the organization, in addition to problem solving and case feedback (MPD, 2011).

Candidates are scored based on their performance throughout the selection process by the promotion panel. Generally, departments post a list in rank order of those who completed the promotion process. Open positions will be filled by the highest ranking candidates on the promotional list, which is typically posted for 12 months (DPD, 2011). Candidates who are promoted to the criminal investigations unit generally enter the unit on a probationary basis and are subject to review at the end of the probationary period. New detectives who successfully pass the evaluation at the end of their probationary period will remain in that capacity; those who do not may be removed or retrained. Candidates not promoted during the life of the promotional list will need to repeat the selection process to be eligible for future detective or investigator position openings within the criminal investigations unit (KCPD, 2011).

SPECIALIZED TRAINING FOR CRIMINAL INVESTIGATORS

The old-school image of the criminal investigator suggests that the successful clearance of criminal investigations is the result of the detective beating the streets in search of clues, and the only technology required of the position is shoe leather. The criminal investigator of today, though, needs to have a wide range of technical acumen. The modern criminal investigator has many resources available to aid in the investigative process, and most require specialized training. Specific training for detectives will generally focus on the necessary skill sets directly related to the role and function of criminal investigators, including crime scene processing methodology skills such as crime scene assessment, observing the crime scene, documenting the crime scene, conducting effective and efficient crime scene searches, and processing and analyzing the crime scene.

Specific skills that are very useful to criminal investigations and that often require specialized training include (Swanson et al., 2006):

- Applying light technology
- Recovering fingerprints
- Casting impression evidence
- Bloodstain pattern analysis
- Bullet trajectory analysis
- Applying light technology

ROLE OF THE PATROL OFFICER IN THE PRELIMINARY INVESTIGATION

The role of the patrol officer in criminal investigations has evolved over the years from the traditional model focusing on random preventive patrol and responding to calls for service (Kelling, 1974). The traditional view of the patrol officer's role in criminal investigations was based on the premise that a criminal investigation did not actually begin until the detectives arrived on the scene. The role of the patrol officer was simply to get to the crime scene as quickly as possible, arrest any suspect still onsite, care for the injured, identify witnesses, and secure the scene until the detectives arrived to take over the criminal investigation. Research has shown that the actions of the initial responding officer to a crime scene is critical to the successful conclusion of a criminal investigation when that officer takes on an expanded role in the preliminary investigation (Greenberg and Wasserman, 1979).

To examine the ideal role of the patrol officer in preliminary investigations it is necessary to define "preliminary investigation." Every individual law enforcement agency will have its own policies and protocols in effectively directing what steps the patrol officers within a specific agency will take in reference to preliminary investigations. Generally, the role of patrol officers in preliminary investigations can be defined using the acronym PRELIMINARY (Greenberg and Wasserman, 1979):

Proceed to the scene promptly and safely.
Render assistance to the injured.
Effect the arrest of the criminal.
Locate and identify witnesses.
Interview the complainant and the witnesses.
Maintain the crime scene and protect the evidence.
Interrogate the suspect.
Note conditions, events, and remarks.
Arrange for collection of evidence.
Report the incident fully and accurately.
Yield the responsibility to the follow-up investigator.

INITIAL RESPONSE FUNCTIONS OF PATROL OFFICERS AT A CRIME SCENE

The initial responding officer will proceed to the scene of the crime after learning of the crime scene from a citizen contact, because of self-initiated activity, or most frequently because of a radio communication from the department call center. The initial responding patrol officer is not directly responsible for the processing of the crime scene; however, the officer does serve a vital role in the successful clearance of criminal investigations (Gardner, 2000). Specific objectives of the initial patrol officer response to a crime scene should include mentally documenting information. Dispatch will provide information provided by the calling party which can be anywhere between 100% accurate and timely to incomplete, inaccurate, and minus a logical time sequence of events. A very necessary and important skill for patrol officers is to take in information, mentally document it, and remain open to new information as it develops. Information may be communicated via radio transmissions or may be gained through personal observations, witness input, or suspect input. Any of this new information may contradict or even conflict with initial information. Suppose, for example, a call center dispatches a patrol officer to a crime scene where a citizen caller has described a suspect driving from the area of the crime scene in a green van that is on fire. Upon arriving in the area of the crime scene, the officer observes a blue van that is on fire leaving the area of the crime scene. Obviously, the patrol officer would process the new information gained from personal observation—a blue van is on fire, is leaving the crime scene, and is very likely the suspect vehicle. The officer in this example would process all available information and take appropriate actions based on this new information.

Later, in the reporting process, it will be very important for the patrol officer to be able to translate this mental documentation into report form. In-car cameras, recorded phone lines, and recorded radio transmissions are excellent resources for documenting the initial response to a crime scene. These audio and visual recordings provide a record that can later be utilized if necessary in the report-writing process to corroborate or dispute the mental notes taken by the patrol officer upon arriving at the crime scene.

OFFICER SAFETY CONCERNS FOR PATROL OFFICERS IN THE INITIAL RESPONSE TO A CRIME SCENE

Officer safety is always a priority, and a heightened concern for officer safety should occur as officers are approaching a known crime scene. The natural response by patrol officers when directed to a crime scene is to get there quickly. It is very important to temper the need to get to the scene quickly with the safety of the responding officer and with citizen safety. In 2009, 48 officers were feloniously killed in the line of duty, 47 officers were accidentally killed while on duty, and 34 of those deaths resulted from automobile accidents (FBI, 2010). It is very important for patrol officers responding to a crime scene to remember that they cannot be of service if they fail to arrive at the scene.

The responding patrol officer must be open to any and all sources of information and open to new information when approaching a crime scene. The responding officer may have received some information from dispatch or other sources in reference to any weapons, natural hazards, manmade hazards, or any other potential threats at the crime scene and should take all of this information into consideration when arriving at the scene (Gardner, 2000). Many times, the information about what exactly the potential threats are at a crime scene is incomplete at best and many times completely unknown. Officers should work to develop a strong tactical acumen and use their training and experience to protect themselves and others in the initial approach to crime scenes. In the initial approach to a crime scene it is very important to determine if there is a crime in progress and if the suspect is still at the scene. If a suspect is at the scene, the patrol officer must determine if there are multiple suspects and whether or not the officer has the tactical acumen to arrest the suspects. If the suspect has left the scene prior to arrival of the patrol officer, is an injured victim present? If so, does the victim present any threat to the officer's safety? When the responding officer has determined that no threats to the officer's safety are present and declares the scene secure, the officer can begin rendering assistance to any injured victims.

PATROL OFFICER RESPONSIBILITY FOR CARING FOR THE INJURED AT THE CRIME SCENE

The role of the patrol officer has multiple demands, including providing medical assistance to victims in need of emergency medical care. Many crimes committed against persons result in injuries and death. Initial responding patrol officers arriving at a crime scene who encounter physical injuries requiring medical assistance should activate emergency medical services (EMS) to assist the victims. It may be necessary to perform lifesaving functions such as cardiopulmonary resuscitation (CPR), stop bleeding wounds, or provide an airway, among a wide range of other life-saving activities, while waiting for EMS to arrive at the scene. Having an ongoing medical emergency taking place in the middle of a crime scene presents some challenges to preserving crime scene integrity and evidence (Gardner, 2000). With EMS on the scene and caring for the crime victim, the initial responding officers can turn their attention solely to managing the crime scene, particularly minimizing EMS damage to the crime scene, maintaining crime scene security, and controlling anyone at the crime scene (Gardner, 2000).

SECURING THE CRIME SCENE

Controlling who is in the crime scene involves identifying victims, witnesses, suspects, other officers, EMS, etc. who are within the crime scene area. It is important to identify those parties who are critical to the investigation and are performing investigative functions and to ensure that they are the only persons actually inside the crime scene (Gardner, 2000). It is very common for other officers to migrate to an active crime scene to see what happened. Victim's family members, friends, witnesses, and onlookers may also migrate to the crime scene for their own personal reasons or curiosity. The initial responding officer should quickly put up a crime scene tape barrier to keep those not directly involved in the investigation out of the scene. Some officers, victims, witnesses, and onlookers may resist when asked to step back from the crime scene. It is important that the officer use a firm but respectful tone and approach to ensure that all comply and that the integrity of the crime scene is preserved (Colwell and Huth, 2010).

TURNING THE CRIME SCENE OVER TO THE CRIMINAL INVESTIGATIONS UNIT

The role of the initial responding officer to a crime scene is so critical that research findings indicate that the majority of criminal investigations that are successfully concluded relied heavily on the observations of the initial responding officer (Greenberg and Wasserman, 1979). The research concluded that the initial responding officer was critical in the preliminary investigation in gathering specific information described as solvability factors that would increase the likelihood of successfully concluding investigations. A key role for patrol officers in the preliminary criminal investigation is to collect as much solvability factor information at the crime scene as possible, including (Greenberg and Wasserman, 1979):

- Immediate availability of witnesses
- Naming of a suspect
- Information about a suspect's location
- Information about a suspect's description
- Information about a suspect's identification
- Information about the suspect's vehicular movement
- Information about traceable property
- Information about significant *modus operandi*
- Information about significant physical evidence

After the initial responding officer has arrived at the crime scene, cared for the injured, arrested the suspect, identified victims and witnesses, secured the scene, and set up the crime scene barrier, eventually the criminal investigations unit detectives will arrive on the scene and the officer will turn the crime scene over to the investigators. Historically, the dynamics of the relationship between patrol officers and detectives has been a source of potential friction. Police scholar and former Wichita Police Chief O.W. Wilson stated that, "The communication of information between patrol officers and investigators is a vital factor in the success of criminal investigations. Investigators should make every effort to foster the cooperation and enthusiasm of patrol officers through frequent personal contacts, by making certain that beat officers receive acknowledgment in reports and press releases, and by fostering preliminary investigations by patrolmen. One of the fastest ways to stop the cooperation between patrol officers and investigators is to have the latter reword the preliminary investigation as if the patrol officer were not to be trusted" (Greenberg and Wasserman, 1979).

Ideally, law enforcement as a whole has embraced the patrol officer as a critical component of criminal investigations overall and specifically in preliminary investigation. Every agency should work toward meaningful communication and partnerships between patrol personnel and investigations personnel to increase the likelihood of successful closure of criminal investigations. Turning over a crime scene from patrol to the criminal investigations unit in a professional manner is an excellent avenue for easing potential friction and can serve as a catalyst for fostering a closer relationship between patrol officers and detectives, potentially improving the successful closure rate of criminal investigations. The first step in turning over the crime scene to the criminal investigations unit requires the initial responding officer to provide a proper debrief of the crime scene to the responding detective. The debrief should include a detailed summary of the officer's initial observations approaching the scene; initial observations upon arriving at the scene; any and all of the solvability factors information the officer was able to collect, including pointing out any witnesses to the detective, any fragile evidence or evidence that may rapidly deteriorate, and any secondary crime scenes; and explaining the crime scene barrier (Gardner, 2000). When the initial responding officer has clearly communicated all observations, actions, and solvability factors to the detective and the detective clearly communicates to the officer that the information has been received and that investigations now has the scene, the officer can assume a supporting role, begin the report writing process, or take whatever action the situation or department policy dictates once the scene is released to the criminal investigations unit.

DOCUMENTING THE CRIME SCENE

The criminal investigator's primary goal in processing a crime scene is the identification, collection, preservation, and reporting of evidence found at the crime scene. Properly documenting the crime scene is critical to successful completion of criminal investigations. Crime scene documentation consists of four key steps (Bennett and Hess, 2007):

1. Notes
2. Photography
3. Sketches
4. Report

All four components of crime scene documentation are interdependent in properly recalling the crime scene later in court (Bennett and Hess, 2007).

Crime Scene Photography

The study of crime scene photography can be an exhaustive and complex exploration into camera technology, technique, focus and depth of field, digital vs. film, and so on (Redsicker, 2000). This chapter focuses only on general guidelines for photographing almost any crime scene, keeping in mind the goal that crime scene photographs must accurately record the condition, orientation, spatial relationships, and physical evidence within the crime scene (Gardner, 2000).

General Crime Scene Photography Guidelines

General guidelines for effective crime scene photography include the following (Swanson et al., 2006):

- Photograph the crime scene as soon as possible.
- Photograph the crime scene with a partner who will keep an accurate photo log detailing the time, photo number, and location within the crime scene where the photo was taken.
- Capture overall photographs depicting the general condition and layout of the crime scene.
- Capture evidence-establishing, mid-range photographs that serve to identify small items of physical evidence within the overall crime scene.
- Capture close-up photographs of evidence.
- Photograph the crime scene from eye level to maintain a normal orientation view of the scene.
- Photograph fragile areas of the crime scene first.
- Photograph all stages of the crime scene investigation, including discoveries of evidence.
- Photograph evidence before it is collected and placed into custody.
- Photograph evidence to scale; when a scale is used, take a photograph without a scale before inserting a scale next to the evidence.
- Use a fish-eye lens for overall interior photographs.
- Include a 360-degree view of exterior crime scenes.
- Photograph points of entry and exit from inside and out.
- Capture multiple images of important evidence from overall scene, mid-range, and close-up perspectives.
- Prior to entering the scene, speak with the officer involved in the preliminary investigation to gain an overall view of the crime scene and to determine what sketches or photographs may have been taken prior to the criminal investigators' arrival.

It is critical that criminal investigators be aware that, to be admissible in court, crime scene photographs must be material, relevant, accurate, free of distortion, and non-inflammatory. The court will evaluate crime scene photographs to determine if they will be allowed into evidence in a trial proceeding based on specific criteria: Crime scene photographs must be *material*; a material photograph is directly related to the specific case and subject. Crime scene photographs must be *relevant*; a relevant photograph assists in supporting and illustrating witness testimony. Crime scene photographs must be *competent*; a competent photograph is an accurate representation of what was photographed. Its chain of custody has been accurately documented and maintained, and the photograph was secured until presentation as evidence in court.

Crime Scene Sketches

Crime scene sketches are excellent tools in crime scene documentation; when completed in a professional manner, they accurately portray the physical facts within a crime scene, create a permanent record of the location of physical evidence and their spatial relationships within a crime scene, illustrate the sequence of events at the crime scene, and assist in creating a picture of the crime scene for those not present at the crime scene (Bennett and Hess, 2007). Additionally, crime scene sketches can be utilized by the prosecution, as crime scene sketches are admissible in court.

The most common type of crime scene sketch is the rough sketch. The rough sketch is as simple as it sounds—an outline of the crime scene drawn freehand, generally with a pencil, depicting the overall scene and placement of objects and evidence within the outline (Bennett and Hess, 2007). Sketching should begin after the preliminary investigation and after the crime scene photographs have been taken. The steps in sketching a crime scene include observing and planning, measuring distances, outlining the area, locating objects and evidence within the outline, recording details, making notes, creating a sketch legend and scale, and reassessing the sketch (Swanson et al., 2006).

Observing and planning the sketch require looking at the crime scene and creating a mental image of the scene to document in the form of a rough sketch of an outline of the crime scene. Locating objects and evidence within the crime scene involves measuring distances and creating a record of the spatial relationships of objects both outside and inside the crime scene. All measurements should be taken with a steel tape measure and from fixed objects that cannot be moved or removed. Common fixed objects are walls, trees, corners of structures, and curbs. Two common techniques for plotting objects and evidence within crime scenes are the rectangular-coordinate method, where two adjacent walls serve as fixed points from which distances are measured at right angles, and the baseline method, a process of creating a straight-line axis and measuring at right angles from the straight line to the object or evidence and recording the distance between the two (Swanson et al., 2006).

After completing the crime scene rough sketch, the investigator should accurately document in crime scene notes any observations of the crime scene that could not be sketched. Crime scene notes provide further explanation and supporting information such as the weather conditions at the time of the crime scene investigation, lighting conditions, and what people were present (Gardner, 2000). Anyone who has ever looked at a map is familiar with a map legend. The map legend gives users detailed information, such as scale, points of interest, highway rest stops, and so on. A crime scene sketch should also have an accompanying legend. The crime scene legend should contain the case number, type of crime, victim name, complainant name, location, date, time, criminal investigator's name, who assisted in the sketch, scale, direction of north relative to the sketch, and who created the sketch (Bennett and Hess, 2007). The final step in sketching the crime scene is to reassess the sketch to make sure that all relevant information has been included and that the sketch is an accurate representation of the crime scene.

ROLE AND FUNCTION OF THE CRIMINAL INVESTIGATOR

The functions of a criminal investigator are generally consistent, regardless of unit specialization or the size of the law enforcement agency. The functions of the criminal investigator include (Bennett and Hess, 2007):

- Determining if a crime has occurred
- Collecting evidence in order to identify suspects
- Arresting suspects
- Recovering property
- Documenting findings in a clear and concise manner for presentation to the prosecutor and for use in the criminal judicial system

Properly defining the role of the criminal investigator must begin with an examination of the overall mission of policing to illustrate the roles that criminal investigations and detectives fill in meeting that mission. Policing in the United States has experienced a shift in the manner in which police services are delivered largely as a result of the evolving philosophy of community policing. Driven by research, citizen dissatisfaction with police services, public policy, and federal dollars, many police agencies are adopting community policing as a strategy. Community policing advocates a department-wide shift in the delivery of police services that puts an emphasis on problem solving, community partnerships, and organizational change (PERF, 1996).

The greatest boost to the community-oriented era of policing occurred with the passing of the Violent Crime Control and Law Enforcement Act of 1994. The act authorized expenditures of over $8 billion over 6 years to add 100,000 police officers to communities across the country and to promote the implementation of community policing. Furthermore, the Act also prompted Attorney General Janet Reno to create the Office of Community Oriented Policing Services (COPS) in the U.S. Department of Justice. The COPS Office has been tasked with the responsibility for putting the additional officers on the streets and providing training and technical assistance to the nation's communities and police departments in developing strategies for implementing community policing. The COPS Office defines community policing "as a policing philosophy that promotes and supports organizational strategies to address the causes and reduce the fear of crime and social disorder through problem-solving tactics and community-police partnerships" (Cohen, 2001).

In her Report to Congress on the COPS Office, Attorney General Reno (2000, pp. 2–3) made an eloquent argument of support for community policing:

> When President Clinton signed into law the Violent Crime and Control and Law Enforcement Act of 1994, he fulfilled a promise he made when he first took office—that his administration would provide local communities the resources to add 100,000 community policing officers to the nation's streets. Six years later, this historic legislation has made a difference. As of this summer, over 105,000 community policing officers have been funded. More than 30,000 grants have been awarded

to over 12,000 law enforcement agencies, covering 87% of the country. Crime has dropped to its lowest level since 1968, as police officers work hand-in-hand with the community forging new partnerships and working together to solve problems.

By walking the beat and sharing in the life of neighborhoods, thousands of community oriented policing officers funded by the COPS program are redefining the relationship between law enforcement and community. As community members get to know the person behind the badge, and police officers learn the hopes and fears of the residents they serve, perceptions change. Trust grows. New and creative ways of dealing with longstanding problems are developed. Unique partnerships are developed among groups and organizations where previously there was skepticism or even hostility. Crime decreases, the fear of crime decreases, and neighborhoods thrive.

Another of the many benefits of the COPS program, and a critical part of its legacy, has been its focus on training. COPS' regional network of training institutes across the country has trained officers in areas including building partnerships within the community, supporting victims of domestic violence, and problem solving. COPS also has made a substantial contribution to numerous integrity initiatives and is continuing to develop additional resources to strengthen this critical area. I know that the COPS program has contributed significantly to a safer America. We must not rest on our success, nor become complacent. We must continue our progress. My hope is that the important work of the COPS program will go on, as we continue to change the face of law enforcement for the 21st century.

Trojanowicz and Bucqueroux (1990) defined community policing as "requiring the police to provide full-service policing, proactive and reactive, by involving the community directly as partners in the process of nominating, prioritizing, and solving problems including crime, fear of crime, illicit drugs, social and physical disorder, and neighborhood decay." The San Diego Police Department states that, "Our Mission is to maintain Peace and Order by providing the highest quality police services in response to community needs by: Preventing Crime, Apprehending Criminals, Developing Partnerships, Respecting Individuals" (SDPD, 2011).

Community policing requires a proactive approach in which police, citizens, and community stakeholders work in collaboration to address crime and disorder within the community. The role of the criminal investigator within the overall mission of policing is usually limited to a largely reactive one. The criminal investigator's functions with regard to collecting evidence, arresting suspects, recovering property, and documenting findings for presentation to the prosecutor and for use in the criminal judicial system are critical to meeting the organizational missions of reducing crime and protecting property. The focus of community policing has been on the patrol function, with little focus on the role of criminal investigations in providing services within a community policing framework. The challenge for law enforcement agencies is to explore how the criminal investigations unit can function within a community policing framework.

What cannot be lost in this discussion is the importance of the role of the criminal investigator in conducting the follow-up investigation. The criminal investigator's ability to successfully close criminal investigations will ensure that offenders are arrested and entered into the criminal justice system, victims will see justice, and personal property will be returned.

QUESTIONS FOR DISCUSSION

1. Discuss the minimum qualifications for being promoted from patrol into the criminal investigations unit.
2. List the common steps in the promotional process for detective.
3. Discuss what the first responding officer should do when arriving at the scene of a crime.
4. What is a preliminary investigation?
5. List and discuss the importance of solvability factors.
6. What are the criminal investigator's primary goals in documenting a crime scene?
7. Discuss the following as they relate to crime scene photographs: material, relevant, free of distortion, and non-inflammatory.
8. What are two common methods of plotting objects and evidence within a crime scene?
9. Discuss the basic functions of a criminal investigator.
10. Discuss how the basic functions of a criminal investigator serve to meet the overall mission of policing and how they fit into a community policing environment.

BIBLIOGRAPHY

APD. (2011). *How to Become a Police Officer: Selection Process*. Alexandria, VA: City of Alexandria (www.alexandriava.gov/police/info/default.aspx?id=9066).

Bennett, W. and Hess, K. (2007). *Criminal Investigation*, 8th ed. Belmont, CA: Thomson Wadsworth.

BLS. (2011). *Occupational Outlook Handbook, 2010–11 Edition*. Washington, D.C.: U.S. Department of Labor, Bureau of Labor Statistics (www.bls.gov/oco/ocos160.htm).

Cohen, D. (2001). *Problem-Solving Partnerships: Including the Community for a Change*. Washington, D.C.: U.S. Department of Justice, Office of Community Policing Services (http://www.cops.usdoj.gov/ric/ResourceDetail.aspx?RID=163).

Colwell, J. and Huth, C. (2010). *Unleashing the Power of Unconditional Respect: Transforming Law Enforcement and Police Training*. Boca Raton, FL: CRC Press.

DMPD. (2011). *Minimum Qualifications for Police Officer*. Des Moines, IA: Iowa Department of Public Safety (http://www.dps.state.ia.us/commis/prtb/qualifications.shtml).

DOJ. (2011). *Community Oriented Policing Services: Community Policing Defined*. Washington, D.C.: U.S. Department of Justice (http://www.cops.usdoj.gov/Default.asp?Item=36).

DPD. (2011). *Operations Manual for the Police Department of the City and County, Denver, Colorado*. Denver, CO: Denver Police Department (www.denvergov.org/Portals/326/documents/intro.pdf).

FBI. (2010). *Law Enforcement Officers Killed & Assaulted, 2009*. Washington, D.C.: Federal Bureau of Investigation (http://www2.fbi.gov/ucr/killed/2009/aboutleoka.html).

Gardner, R. (2000). *Practical Crime Scene Processing and Investigation*. Boca Raton, FL: CRC Press.

Greenberg, I. and Wasserman, R. (1979). *Managing Criminal Investigations*. Washington, D.C.: U.S. Department of Justice, National Institute of Law Enforcement and Criminal Justice.

KCPD. (2011). *Personnel Policy*. Kansas City, MO: Kansas City Police Department (www.kcpd.org/masterindex/files/ppbm/500/504-6.pdf).

Kelling, G. (1974). *Kansas City Preventive Patrol Experiment: A Summary Report*. Washington, D.C.: Police Foundation.

MPD. (2011). *Madison Police Department Promotional Process for Investigators, Detectives, and Sergeants*. Madison, WI: Madison Professional Police Officers Association (www.mppoainfo.com/news/promotional_process.html).

PERF. (1996). *Themes and Variations in Community Policing*. Washington, D.C.: Police Executive Research Forum.

Redsicker, D. (2000). *The Practical Methodology of Forensic Photography*, 2nd ed. Boca Raton, FL: CRC Press.

Reno, J. (2000). *Attorney General's Report to Congress*. Washington, D.C.: U.S. Department of Justice, Office of Community Oriented Policing Services.

SDPD. (2011). *Mission Statement*. San Diego, CA: San Diego Police Department (http://www.sandiego.gov/police/about/chief/index.shtml).

Swanson, C., Chamelin, N., Territo, L., and Taylor, R. (2006). *Criminal Investigation*, 9th ed. New York: McGraw-Hill.

Trojanowicz, R. and Bucqueroux, B. (1990). *Community Policing: How to Get Started*. Cincinnati, OH: Anderson Publishing.

2

Preliminary Considerations

CHAPTER 3

Crime Scene Search

Michael L. Birzer

Wichita State University

CHAPTER OBJECTIVES

After reading this chapter, you should be able to do the following:

1. Describe the purpose and scope of crime scene search.
2. Describe the legal requirements of the crime scene search.
3. Identify and discuss preliminary crime scene search considerations.
4. Identify and discuss crime scene search methods.
5. Describe the protocol if evidence is discovered in the search.

Chapter Outline

- Introduction
- Purpose of Search
- Planning the Search
- Legal Considerations
- Search Methods
- Post-Search Survey

INTRODUCTION

The actions taken during a crime scene investigation can play a critical role in the successful resolution of a case. Proper treatment and preservation of the crime scene are vital to the identification and ultimate prosecution of the perpetrators. A crime scene that is handled in a haphazard manner can be detrimental to successful resolution of the case, not to mention a police department's reputation. The diligent investigation of the crime scene is both necessary and critical (Birzer and Roberson, 2008). An important part of any investigation is the crime scene search. This chapter introduces the crime scene search, and the purpose and scope of the crime scene search are discussed along with legal considerations that must be acknowledged. Finally, the chapter provides a detailed discussion of planning the search as well as specific search techniques. The student will find the information presented in this chapter an effective building block to learning about the critical nature of the crime scene search. Police officers reading this chapter will find the information to be a fresh review of the fundamentals of the crime search. Although the information presented in this chapter is generic enough to be applied in most jurisdictions, police officers are always advised to check with their agency's standard operating procedures for crime scene search techniques.

PURPOSE OF SEARCH

O'Hara and O'Hara (2003, p. 6) informed us that, "An investigation can be considered a success if all the available information relevant and material to the issues or allegations of the case is uncovered." Oftentimes the crime search is the underpinning for discerning available information that is relevant and material to the issues and allegations of the case. Throughout this book we emphasize that the primary purpose of crime scene investigation is to help establish what happened and to identify the responsible person. This is done by carefully documenting the conditions at a crime scene and identifying all relevant physical evidence. The ability to identify and properly collect physical evidence is often critical to prosecuting violent crimes. The crime scene search plays an important role in the crime scene investigation. Actions taken at the outset of an investigation, such as the initial crime scene search, can play an important role in the resolution of a case. Careful, thorough investigation is important to ensure that potential physical evidence is not tainted or destroyed or potential witnesses overlooked.

The purpose of the crime scene search is to discover evidence that will be useful in determining what happened, with the ultimate goal of identifying the person or persons responsible for committing the crime, and thus resolving the case. Evidence discovered at the crime scene will play a crucial role later at the criminal trial in establishing the truth and convicting the guilty parties. The general scope of the crime scene can cover structures of any kind, including but not limited to vehicles, open fields, mass transit systems, water vessels, waterways, aircraft, and the like. In some cases, there may be multiple crime scenes for one crime. Suppose, for example, that a shooting happens in a residence and the suspect subsequently places the body in the trunk of his car and drives the body to an open field located in a rural area where he buries the body in a shallow grave. In this situation, there are three separate crime scenes: the residence where the shooting took place, the vehicle that was used to transport the body, and the open field where the body was buried. Investigators would be responsible for diligent searches for evidence at each of these areas.

PLANNING THE SEARCH

Several preliminary tasks should be completed prior to the actual search of the crime scene. Many are discussed in other chapters in this book, but it is necessary to at least mention them here to lay the foundation for what should be done before the crime scene is searched.

CRIME SCENE BOUNDARIES

The boundaries of the crime scene should be determined as soon as possible. These boundaries define the areas that potentially could contain evidence and will have to be searched. Defining and controlling the crime scene boundaries provide a means for protecting and securing the crime scene. The number of crime scenes and their boundaries are determined by the type of crime and its location. It is recommended that boundaries be established beyond the initial scope of the crime scene. Boundaries can always be reduced in size if necessary, but they cannot easily be expanded when the investigation has begun. Boundaries of the crime scene should begin at a specific focal point and extend outward to include where the crime occurred, potential points and paths of entry and exit, and places where the victim or evidence may have been moved. Be aware of trace and impression evidence while assessing the scene. Persons present within the crime scene boundaries should not smoke, chew tobacco, use the bathroom, eat or drink, move any items including weapons (unless necessary for the safety and well-being of persons at the scene), adjust the thermostat, or open windows or doors. The scene should be maintained as it was found. Items at the crime scene should not be touched unnecessarily. Any item that is touched or moved or disturbed in any manner at the crime scene should be documented.

CRIME SCENE SECURITY

First and foremost, the scene commander or search leader should ensure that the scene has been secured, and he or she should be debriefed as to who had access to the scene (e.g., fire personnel, responding patrol officers, paramedics, news media, curious citizens). It is of the utmost importance to secure the crime scene to avoid contaminating the scene. Furthermore, a record should be kept of any person who accessed the crime scene. Investigators should consider all case information or statements from witnesses or suspects carefully in their objective assessment of the scene. It is not uncommon for investigations to change course a number of times during such an inquiry, and physical clues, initially thought irrelevant, may become crucial to a successful resolution of the case (Osterburg and Ward, 2004).

The search leader should evaluate the scene before entering or allowing other personnel to enter the area. It should be determined where other personnel have walked, and those areas should be marked; personnel should attempt to adhere to that path of travel, if practical, to avoid additional destruction or contamination of evidence. An initial attempt should be made to visually locate the essential items of evidence and to make mental or written notes about what will have to be measured, photographed, and collected.

A pivotal responsibility of the crime scene team is to ensure that there is no immediate threat to others. The investigator or first responder should scan the area for sights, sounds, and smells that may represent a danger to personnel (e.g., hazardous materials such as gasoline or natural gas). If the situation involves a clandestine drug laboratory, biological weapons, or radiological or chemical threats, the appropriate personnel or agency should be contacted prior to entering the scene. The scene should be approached in a manner designed to reduce the risk of harm to officers and maximize the safety of victims, witnesses, and others in the area. The investigator should survey the scene for dangerous persons and control the situation. If necessary, additional assistance should be summoned to the scene for the purpose of control and ensuring the safety of all personnel.

For the overall protection the crime scene, it is important to control, identify, and remove persons at the crime scene as well as limit the number of persons who enter the crime scene. The initial responding officers should identify persons at the crime scene and control their movement. They should immediately control all individuals at the scene and prevent individuals from altering or destroying physical evidence by restricting their movement, location, and activity while maintaining safety at the scene. It is not uncommon for passersby to stop at the crime scene to take a look or for news reporters to quickly congregate on the scene after hearing the call come in over the police scanner. In a matter of minutes, the crime scene can become a spectacle. This is why it is important to ask all unauthorized and nonessential personnel to leave the crime scene promptly. In essence, all individuals at the crime scene should be identified, including suspects, witnesses, bystanders, and medical and other assisting personnel. Controlling the movement of persons at the crime scene and limiting the number of persons who enter the crime scene are essential to maintaining scene integrity, safeguarding evidence, and minimizing contamination.

INITIAL WALKTHROUGH

According to the Department of Justice (DOJ, 2000), the crime scene walkthrough provides an overview of the entire scene, identifies any threats to scene integrity, and ensures protection of physical evidence. Written and photographic documentation provides a permanent record. The investigator in charge should conduct a walkthrough of the scene with individuals responsible for processing the scene. During this walkthrough, the investigator in charge should avoid contaminating the scene by using the established path of entry. It is important to prepare preliminary documentation of the scene as observed. Fragile or perishable evidence should be identified and protected (e.g., consider climatic conditions, crowds, hostile environment). Ensure that all evidence that could be compromised is immediately documented, photographed, and collected. Conducting a scene walkthrough prior to the search gives the investigator in charge an overview of the entire scene. It provides the first opportunity to identify valuable or fragile evidence and to determine initial investigative procedures, providing for a systematic examination and documentation of the scene. Written and photographic documentation records the condition of the scene as first observed and provides a permanent record. During the initial walkthrough it is important to determine which areas should be searched, paying special attention to potential problem areas. Transient physical evidence should be identified and protected. A determination should be made about personnel and equipment needs. Furthermore, specific assignments should be made of police personnel. The importance of taking extensive notes to document the scene, physical and environmental conditions, and personnel movements cannot be overemphasized (Birzer and Roberson, 2008).

EVALUATE POTENTIAL EVIDENCE

Based on the preliminary walkthrough of the crime scene, crime scene investigators should make an effort to establish the types of evidence most likely to be encountered. The investigator should literally try to reenact the crime in his or her mind. Consider, for example, where the perpetrator might have entered the crime scene, where he was standing, where he might have exited, where the victim was located when the suspect entered, or where a struggle most likely occurred. Prior to the search it is important to ensure that the proper collection and packaging equipment is sufficient for the crime scene. Sound investigative practice dictates that it is best to concentrate on the most transient evidence and work to the least transient forms of evidence. Focus first on the easily accessible areas in open view and progress eventually to possible out-of-view locations, looking for purposely hidden items. It is also important for the investigator to consider whether the evidence appears to have been moved inadvertently. Evaluate whether or not the scene and evidence appear intentionally contrived.

PHOTOGRAPHING AND VIDEOTAPING

Prior to the crime scene search, the entire scene should be carefully photographed and videotaped if possible. The aim of photographing the crime scene is to capture the most useful amount of detail possible. When evidence or any part of the crime scene is being photographed, three types of crime scene photographs are generally obtained: overall or long-range photographs, mid-range photographs, and close-up photographs. This protocol provides a clear concept of how each object related to the area. The perpetrator's point of entry and point of exit should be photographed in the same manner (e.g., overall, mid-range, close-up). Likewise, the points of entry and exit should be shown in such a manner that any marks of force will be shown clearly. A scale may also be used and depicted in the photographs. Overall photographs of a residence should depict the house numbers. This same procedure should be followed for both property and person crimes; for example, when photographs of an assault victim are taken, overall photographs should be taken, mid-range photographs of the injury or trauma, and close-up photographs of the same. In some cases, aerial photographs of a crime scene may be helpful, especially when the scene is located in a rural area. In crimes such as a rape–homicide, infrared ultraviolet photography of the body may detect latent bite marks due to hemorrhaging in tissue under the skin. The location of foreign hairs and fibers, biological fluids, and stains can also be photographed. For a more thorough discussion on photographing the crime scene, the reader is directed to Chapter 2.

CRIME SCENE SKETCH

A sketch or diagram of the crime scene establishes a permanent record of items, conditions, and distance/size relationships (Birzer and Roberson, 2008). The sketch may illustrate, for example, the location of a weapon or drops of blood relative to the victim. Sketches and diagrams are an ideal supplement to photographs. A rough sketch drawn at the scene is normally not drawn to scale and is used as a model for the finished sketch. In general, the following should be included on the rough sketch:

- Specific location
- Date
- Time
- Case identifier
- Preparer
- Weather conditions
- Lighting conditions
- Scale or scale disclaimer
- Compass orientation
- Evidence
- Measurements
- Key or legend

In some cases, number designations on the sketch can be coordinated with the same number designations on the evidence log. The crime scene sketch should illustrate the basic perimeter, the location of fixed objects such as furniture, and the location of any evidence, in addition to providing the appropriate measurements, a key or legend, and compass orientation.

EVIDENCE CUSTODIAN

One evidence custodian should be assigned to log evidence as it is discovered during the search. The evidence custodian should ensure that any item of evidence is photographed in the position where it was found prior to collection and should log where the evidence was found, the date and time when it was found, and who found it, in addition to maintaining a chain of custody and control of the evidence. The evidence custodian should also coordinate the packaging of all evidence collected at the crime scene and should thoroughly document the circumstances behind the collection of a piece of evidence, including who discovered the evidence, the time and date of discovery, and any special circumstances. Assigning an evidence custodian limits the number of crime scene personnel who may handle evidence, which could become an issue when a suspect is identified and the case subsequently goes to trial.

SPECIAL CONSIDERATIONS

In some special cases prior to the search, crime scene authorities may find it necessary to bring in specialists. Such specialists may come from a variety of disciplines, as dictated by the specific crime scene, to assist in the collection of evidence found during the search. Specialists may include medical examiners, anthropologists, odontologists, entomologists, computer investigative specialists, bomb technicians, geologists, and blood pattern analysts.

PRE-SEARCH MEETING

Prior to initiating the search, the search team leader should meet with all personnel who will be involved in the search. The search team leader should fully debrief the search team as to what is known up to that point in the investigation and about the general scope and purpose of the search. Search patterns that will be used should be identified and assignment of search personnel made. The evidence custodian should also be named at the pre-search meeting. The search leader should maintain control during the entire search process, including ensuring the safety of personnel at all times. All search personnel should be made aware of the location of the command post. Birzer and Roberson (2008, p. 177) provided the following pre-search search planning checklist:

1. The crime scene has been properly secured and contained.
2. An on-duty prosecutor has been called and briefed (for a major crime scene).
3. A search warrant (if applicable) has been obtained for the premises.
4. Search personnel have been briefed about the crime scene and the nature of evidence that is likely to be discovered. Search personnel should also be briefed as to the type of search technique that will be used. In cases where bodily fluids or other biological evidence may be collected, search personnel should wear the proper protective clothing.
5. The initial walkthrough, video recording, and sketches have been made of the entire crime scene.
6. Sufficient evidence packaging material is on hand.
7. Specific personnel have been designated evidence collectors; for example, a search member who finds some evidence will summon the designated evidence collector, at which time the evidence will be photographed, documented, and collected. Having a specific person designated as evidence collector reduces the chain of custody of the evidence. The chain of custody tracks the movement of evidence through its collection, safeguarding, and analysis lifecycle by documenting each person who handled the evidence, the date and time it was collected or transferred, and the purpose for the transfer.

LEGAL CONSIDERATIONS

An important first step in the crime scene investigation is to evaluate search and seizure issues to determine the necessity of obtaining consent to search or a search warrant. Consent to search is given by a person who has legal care, custody, and control of the property or location. If consent to search is obtained, it should be in writing (Birzer and Roberson, 2008). Most police agencies have a form for consent to search among their written forms. Consent searches are a legitimate means of obtaining evidence, but it is always best to obtain a search warrant. The gold standard, when in doubt, is to obtain a search warrant. The controlling principles governing search warrants are generally provided by the U.S. Constitution's Fourth Amendment, which is part of the Bill of Rights and guards against unreasonable searches and seizures (Birzer and Roberson, 2007). The procedure for obtaining a search warrant involves the presentation of an affidavit to a judge or magistrate by a law enforcement officer requesting that the magistrate issue the search warrant based on the probability of criminal activity (Birzer and Roberson, 2008). For a detailed discussion on the laws pertaining to search procedures, the reader is directed to Chapter 20.

SEARCH METHODS

Recall that the purpose of the crime scene search is to discover any and all evidence that will be useful in determining what actually happened, with the ultimate goal of developing suspects. Physical evidence is any object that can establish that a crime has been committed or any object that can link a suspect to a crime or can provide a link between the victim and a crime. Physical evidence introduced in a trial is in the form of a physical object, which is intended to prove a fact. Physical evidence can conceivably include all or part of any object. Suppose, for example, that the victim is stabbed with a hunting knife, which is later recovered; the hunting knife is physical evidence. Physical evidence can also include imprints or compressions; this type of evidence may include footwear patterns, tire tracks, tool marks and scratches, and bite marks. Physical evidence may also be in the form of trace materials, which may include paints and other deposits, hair and other fibers, pollens, glass, and polymers. Several types of crime scene search patterns may be used and will vary depending on the nature of the crime scene and the type of terrain; for example, the method used to search a crime scene where the victim was murdered inside of a house will differ significantly from a case where the victim was taken to a rural area and murdered in a field. It is always best to define the limits of the search in very broad terms. The crime scene search must be thorough and systematic. If an investigator fails to recognize an item as a piece of evidence or improperly collects the item, that item will not serve any purpose in the investigation.

STRIP METHOD

The strip method is ideal to use when investigators are covering a large search area looking for a sizeable object (see Figure 3.1A). The strip method requires that the area be blocked out in the form of a rectangle. Search team members then proceed at the same pace along paths parallel to one side of the rectangle. As with all search methods discussed in this chapter, when evidence is discovered, that person announces the discovery and the search is halted until the evidence is collected. Prior to collecting the evidence a photograph may be taken of the discovery, and an investigator who has been assigned to collect the evidence may be called to collect the evidence. After the evidence is collected, the search is continued. When the searchers reach the end of the rectangle, they turn around and begin to walk back along new lanes or paths.

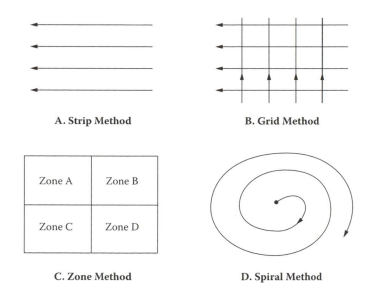

FIGURE 3.1 Search methods.

GRID METHOD

The grid method is a modification of the strip method (see Figure 3.1B). A grid search is simply two parallel searches, offset by 90°, performed one after the other. The grid search method requires that the area be searched along horizontal and vertical lines of a grid. The grid search is very thorough as the search is done in opposite directions.

ZONE METHOD

The zone method entails the crime scene being divided into zones or quadrants for individual searching (see Figure 3.1C). Depending on the size of the area, zone quadrants may be cut into another set of zone quadrants. The zone search method is ideal to use in an indoor crime scene because these scenes typically represent readily definable zones.

ELEVATION ZONE SEARCH

An elevation zone search is used for indoor crime scenes where, for example, evidence such as blood splatters and bullet holes may be present at different levels of a room. This search is conducted one elevation zone at a time (e.g., floor to waist, waist to chin, chin to ceiling).

SPIRAL METHOD

For the spiral search method, the collection of evidence is carried out in a circular pattern working toward a fixed point at the center (see Figure 3.1D). One of two methods may be used when conducting a spiral search: an outward search or an inward search. In the outward spiral search, investigators follow each other in the path of a spiral, beginning at the outside and spiraling in toward the center. In an inward spiral search, investigators begin in the center of the search area and proceed to circle around in an outward motion. The spiral method is generally used for special conditions of the search. There is always the possibility that, when using the inward spiral method, evidence could be destroyed as investigators walk toward the center to begin the search.

WHEEL METHOD

The wheel method is similar to the spiral method. In the wheel method, the search area is considered to be essentially circular. The search team gathers at the center of the circle and proceeds outward along the radii. This search method may have to be repeated several times depending on the size of the circle. The wheel search method does have a few limitations. One limitation is the increase in relative area to be observed as the investigator departs from the center (O'Hara and O'Hara, 2003). The wheel method is also difficult when searching larger areas and is usually reserved for smaller crime scenes.

POST-SEARCH SURVEY

At the conclusion of the search, the search leader or scene commander should conduct a final survey of the search site. The final search survey should include a critical review of the search. All aspects of the search should be discussed jointly with the search team in an effort to identify any part of the scene or evidence that might have been overlooked. All documentation made during the search should be double checked to ensure its accuracy and completeness. Moreover, it is also important to verify that all evidence has been accounted for prior to leaving the scene. All equipment utilized in the search should be retrieved. A final glance at the crime scene should be taken to make sure that hiding places or difficult-to-access areas have not been overlooked. Finally, search team members should be reminded not to release any particulars about evidence that was collected to news outlets or other non-authorized persons unless authorized by the crime scene commander.

QUESTIONS FOR DISCUSSION

1. Discuss the general purpose of the crime scene search.
2. Discuss preliminary considerations regarding the crime scene search.
3. Compare and contrast the various search methods discussed in this chapter.
4. Identify and discuss which search method would be most effective for an indoor room with a significant amount of blood splatter evidence on the walls and ceiling.
5. Discuss why the post-search survey is important.

BIBLIOGRAPHY

Birzer, M.L. and Roberson, C. (2007). *Policing Today and Tomorrow*. Upper Saddle River, NJ: Prentice Hall.

Birzer, M.L. and Roberson, C. (2008). *Police Field Operations: Theory Meets Practice*. Boston, MA: Pearson Allyn & Bacon.

DOJ. (2000). *Crime Scene Investigation: A Guide for Law Enforcement*. Washington, D.C.: U.S. Department of Justice, Office of Justice Programs (http://www.ncjrs.gov/pdffiles1/nij/178280.pdf).

O'Hara, C.E. and O'Hara, G.L. (2003). *Fundamentals of Criminal Investigation*, 7th ed. Springfield, IL: Charles C Thomas.

Osterburg, J. and Ward, R. (2004). *Criminal Investigation*, 4th ed. Cincinnati, OH: Anderson Publishing.

CHAPTER 4

Report Writing

Gene L. Scaramella

Ellis University

CHAPTER OBJECTIVES

After reading this chapter, you should be able to do the following:

1. Describe, in a general sense, why effective writing skills are of critical importance.
2. Identify and elaborate on the many purposes of police reports.
3. Compare and contrast the differences between the general offense case report, the supplemental or follow-up report, and specialized reports such as inventory reports, field contact reports, and other miscellaneous reports.
4. Identify the issues or rifts between prosecutors and police regarding police reports.
5. Describe the actions that can be taken by police officers to mitigate potential civil litigation.
6. Explain the importance of having an up-to-date understanding of both statutory and case law when completing formal reports.
7. Identify various reasons why the careful documentation of field interviews is important for investigative purposes.
8. Explain why police officers should be concerned about their department's policies regarding the use of field notes.

Chapter Outline

- Introduction
- Police Reports
- Supplemental or Investigative Reports
- Field Notes
- Concluding Remarks

INTRODUCTION

Before proceeding to a discussion inclusive only of police report writing, a few words regarding the importance of effective writing in a general sense seem to be in order. Regardless of the job one seeks to attain, hiring managers who represent organizations looking for specific skill sets in job applicants (ranging from positions in general office work to executive level management in a variety of workplaces) all identify, as one of the top criteria for successful employment, effective communication skills, both written and oral. As this chapter focuses on writing, it is the importance of written communication skills that will be emphasized throughout. Nevertheless, it should be noted that effective oral and other nonverbal forms of communication such as body language are very important, as well. One who cannot articulate their thoughts orally or use appropriate body language during presentations or courtroom testimony will be at a distinct disadvantage.

A relatively recent survey conducted by Stevens (2005) focused on the satisfaction levels of more than 100 employers in Silicon Valley (the technology center of our country, located in California) with their newly hired college graduates. Communication skills, particularly those pertaining to writing, emerged as one of the most significant sources of employer dissatisfaction. In response to a particular survey question asking employers to rate their level of satisfaction with new employee writing skills, the mean score on a five-point Likert scale fell below the minimum 4.0 level of satisfaction (p. 4). Employer responses to a similar, open-ended question on the survey bore remarkably similar results. Responses included such concerns as "lack of attention to detail"; "noting typographical errors on résumés and cover letters"; "seemed reluctant to write"; "they must understand they need to write the essay rather than bullet-list ideas"; and "our recent hires can't organize their thoughts on paper and can't proofread" (p. 4). Unfortunately, many of those surveyed indicated having to terminate employees who lacked this fundamental but critical skill we call writing.

Similarly, in a study conducted by the U.S. Department of Labor's Office of Disability Employment Policy (ODEP, 2008), more than 400 employers were asked to identify competencies needed by young people attempting to enter the 21st-century workforce. Of the six core competencies identified, effective writing skills made the list. As stated in their report, "Sometimes your supervisors may specifically ask you for your opinion or ask you to express your opinion in writing" (p. 3). Again, this fundamental but critical skill called writing emerged as a requisite for attaining gainful employment.

POLICE REPORTS

> Veteran officer to rookie partner: "What are you doing, writing a novel? Listen kid, if you can't fit it on the back of a matchbook it's too much information."

Let us hope that the direction given to the new officer by the field training officer highlighted above is no longer a significant issue in the field of policing. Once upon a time, however, being as brief as possible and taking shortcuts on reports were serious problems in the field. Changes in education requirements for entry and promotion, as well as increased focus on professionalizing the field, have improved this situation through the years, but it remains somewhat problematic even today. Moreover, this issue varies from department to department and is affected by a number of different variables, such as technology; supervisory likes and dislikes; formal education; effective training, both basic and in-service; and the ability of the field training officer to instill in young officers the importance of the written report at the very beginning of their careers. In likewise fashion, supervisory personnel must advocate for and sustain officers' commitment to effective report writing on a continuous basis and at all levels of the agency. The remaining portion of this chapter addresses the various types of reports utilized by law enforcement agencies, such as general incident reports, supplemental investigative reports, field notes, and the like. Although there may be subtle differences in the format or style of these reports, it is important to note that there are many more common denominators than there are differences.

THE MANY PURPOSES OF REPORT WRITING

Jetmore (2008, p. 2) identified many critical purposes of a police report, which include, but are not limited to, the following:

1. The written report serves or functions as a permanent record for incidents reported to and actions taken by representatives of an agency, either in response to those reported incidences or actions initiated on their own.
2. The written report supplies, or should supply, the context and details of an incident via the age-old golden rule of writing (i.e., who, what, when where, why, and how).
3. The written report serves as a resource for incidents that require additional agency action, such as a follow-up investigation of a crime reported to patrol officers.
4. The written report serves as an instrument that is relied upon by the various legal authorities functioning within the criminal justice system, such as judges, prosecutors, defense counsel, and those involved with civil litigation when a matter reported to or taken by a department's representative is at issue. Traffic accident reports are a good example of this sort of civil litigation.
5. The written report provides information for an agency's strategic operations and planning, ranging from crime analysis and manpower allocations to budgeting and tactics for emergency response preparedness.
6. The written report serves as a mechanism for local, state, and national database systems that provide vital information to law enforcement agencies throughout the country ranging in purpose from information on fugitives to data used for crime mapping.

Additional attributes of written reports include comprehensiveness, legibility, chronology of events, absence of misspelled words, use of proper grammar, and lack of repetition unless absolutely necessary.

BLAST FROM THE PAST 1

While writing this chapter many memories from my past career with the Chicago Police Department came to mind. Allow me to share a few of those memories regarding the writing of reports in the two boxes found in this chapter. One thing that always struck me as being very odd was that, when it came time to write the narrative portion of case reports, the use of proper grammar seemed to somehow escape the abilities of many officers. For example, most reports would start out "R/O reported to above location. Complainant said unknown male subjects removed money from his pants and fled E/B from scene." Narratives that were more detailed would carry on in similar fashion and more often than not would lack critical details, contain misspelled words, use poor grammar, and, to my amazement, have no paragraph breaks. Most case reports do have fields for the recording of a variety of pertinent information, such as an incident or report number; the offense name; address of incident; offense and location codes (UCRs); complainant, victim, and witness identities; offender description or identity; vehicle information, if applicable; and other routine information. These fields, however, do not and should not obviate the need for using proper grammar while writing the narrative section of the report. Going back to the quote above, here is an improved way of writing the same thing:

> In summary, the Reporting Officer (R/O) was dispatched to the stated location regarding a radio call of a theft. Upon arriving at the scene, the R/O was met by the victim, who stated that at approximately 2030 hours on this date, while he was exiting his detached garage at the rear of his lot, he was confronted by the male offender described above. The offender told the victim, "Hand over your watch and wallet if you know what's good for you." The victim complied and the offender then fled on foot E/B through the alley.

Although such a report would certainly contain many more details, including any actions the officer took, such as sending a flash message of the offender, the point is to notice the differences in grammar and clarity between the two quotations. It is with the type of formality and clarity found in the latter writing that all reports should be written. As my field training officer told me more than 30 years ago, if you get in the habit of writing good reports from the get go, you'll have no problems later on (e.g., in court, with supervisors, during depositions). In retrospect, that was the best and most practical advice he ever gave me.

Jetmore's (2008) emphasis on the reliance of well-written reports by a variety of legal authorities within the criminal justice system is worthy of more attention. Police officers face a double-edged sword in this regard. Not only must their reports be thorough and written using proper grammar and spelling, but they must also be written in such a way so as to lay out chronologically the course of events that may have led to an eventual arrest. Important legal doctrines pertaining to such issues as reasonable suspicion, probable cause, search and seizure requirements, use of force, and high-speed vehicle pursuits, among others, are all governed by statutory law, constitutional provisions, and man-made law, also referred to as case law, which stems from judicial interpretation. Case law is very fluid in nature, always changing. Any officer who does not keep up to date regarding the ever-evolving court decisions and laws that affect police practice operate at a severe disadvantage. The consequences of preparing improper or flawed reports are numerous and significant—for example, it could mean the acquittal of a defendant charged with a very serious criminal offense.

Suppose Officer X was on routine patrol in his marked squad car when he noticed the driver of the car traveling next to him giving him a "suspicious look." Officer X then got behind the vehicle in question, activated his emergency lights, and pulled the car over. The officer then approached the car and asked the driver for his license, registration, and proof of insurance. The driver complied, and Officer X returned to his squad car to check the driver and vehicle for any wants or warrants. The computer check indicated no wants or warrants. Still believing the driver to be "suspicious," Officer X then had the driver step out

---

BLAST FROM THE PAST 2

Case Management and Report Writing

Organizationally, the Chicago Police Department is divided into five geographic areas and 25 different police districts. Each of the five area headquarters has somewhere between four and six police districts located therein. All crime reports made by district personnel are forwarded to their respective area detective headquarters for follow-up or other forms of disposition. Detectives from the case management units of those detective areas then review each report and assign them to the appropriate detective unit for follow-up or take other administrative action. As one can imagine, with a police force of more than 13,000 members, hundreds of reports are generated on a daily basis, and each one is read by detective personnel from those case management units.

My partner's father worked in the case management unit of one of those area headquarters and, from time to time, if we had business in that facility we would stop by and shoot the breeze with him. He and the detectives he worked with in the case management unit often commented to us about the incredibly poor quality of case reports that crossed their desks. Their complaints ranged from illegibility, poor grammar, misspellings, and insufficient details to improper classification of offenses, lack of any preliminary follow-up investigative efforts, and, perhaps the most egregious of all, that supervisors had signed off on those reports. In a joking fashion, the case management detectives would place copies of many of the worst reports on a bulletin board in their office to let visiting officers and command staff personnel see just how poor many of the reports really were. On a more serious note, a few of the many negative effects associated with poor quality reports include significant and unnecessary delays of investigative efforts, needless duplication of effort, placing successful prosecutions at risk, and an overall drain on budgetary resources.

of his vehicle and he conducted a search of the driver's person. The driver had no contraband items on his person. Still trusting his instincts, the officer then began a thorough search of the inside of the driver's auto, checking under the front and rear seats, the glove compartment, and under the dashboard. The result was the same—no contraband items were found. Still going with his instincts, Officer X then opened the trunk of the driver's vehicle. To his delight, there in plain view were several handguns and assault rifles and three large plastic bags containing a white, powdery substance, which he suspected to be cocaine. Officer X then placed the driver under arrest, seized the contraband, requested a tow for the auto to be impounded, and transported the arrestee to the station for processing.

Once at the station, and after bragging a bit to some of his fellow officers about his "sixth sense," he began the daunting task of preparing the mountain of paperwork necessary for completing the arrest process. After checking off all of the boxes in the reports he then found himself having to write the narrative sections. Being the honest and dutiful officer that he was he wrote that he had initially stopped the arrestee's vehicle because of the "suspicious look" the arrestee had given him. He then continued describing the ensuing course of events. When Officer X finally went off duty, he left the station feeling as proud as a peacock for the fine job he had done. When Officer X reported for duty the next day, however, his mood was to change drastically. There was a message waiting for him requesting that he call the prosecutor's office. Officer X then placed the call and was connected to the prosecutor handling his case. Expecting to be congratulated on a job well done, the officer was shocked as the prosecutor began chastising him for his "shoddy police work." The prosecutor also informed him that, because the initial stop of the vehicle was not based on any lawful justification, the charges were being dropped and the arrestee was being released. The officer was also informed that his actions would more than likely expose his agency to civil litigation.

Officer X was furious and immediately began telling anyone at the station who would listen to him how bad the prosecutor's office was and that it was no wonder there is so much crime when prosecutors don't want to do their jobs. At the same time, the prosecutor who had spoken to Officer X was telling other prosecutors in his office what a terrible job Officer X had done, exclaiming that if only officers would do their jobs correctly they would be able to put more offenders in jail. This scenario is carried out over and over again in jurisdictions all across the country. (See "Criminal Incident Report" in the Appendix for a good example of a well-written general offense or incident report.)

With regard to this type of rift between the police and prosecutors, Jacoby et al. (1999) discussed several points of contention from both sides of the fence; more importantly, they offered many sound recommendations for mitigating these issues to ultimately improve the overall quality of police reports. Following are typical comments made by police officers and prosecutors that Jacoby et al. (1999, p. 17) identified:

1. Said by the police about prosecutors:
   - "Sure there is some delay but blame the desk sergeant, not me."
   - "What they want depends on which assistant is on the warrant desk."
   - "We give them as much information as we have at the time but they want it all wrapped up in a neat package."

2. Said by the prosecutors about the police:
   - "I know they aren't Shakespeare, but can't these guys even write?"
   - "I'm a trial lawyer. I don't have time to train everyone in report writing."
   - "A major weakness in our prosecutions is because of the lousy police reports."

Regardless of how frequently these police–prosecutor issues arise, the bottom line is the whole focus of this chapter—the absolute necessity of writing good police reports. Jacoby et al. (1999) offered some sound recommendations for improving this situation, the most notable of which include the following:

- Impress upon supervisors the importance of carefully reviewing reports before approving them. If the reports examined are lacking sufficient detail or otherwise written poorly, have the officers who wrote them redo them.
- Proper and continuous in-service training on report writing should be provided and mandated by police agencies.
- Support should be provided by prosecutors if extenuating circumstances are involved.

In conclusion of this section, it should be noted that many jurisdictions already have policies and procedures in place that directly involve input from the prosecutor's office before charges can proceed. For example, the Cook County, Illinois, State's Attorney's Office has a felony review unit. Officers wishing to charge arrestees with crimes classified as felonies are required to call the felony review unit and describe the details of the case to a prosecutor. Based on the facts of the case as described by the officer, the felony review unit will either approve or deny the charge. Additionally, most prosecutors' offices provide the law enforcement agencies in their respective jurisdictions with examples or templates of how the various criminal complaints used during the arrest process should be worded.

Although these safeguards and the technical assistance provided by prosecutors help mitigate certain legal issues, they do not ensure that police reports are written well. That responsibility must be shouldered by many, including police academy training personnel via inclusion of appropriate curricular activities, in-service training required of officers by their respective agencies, a commitment from the supervisory ranks of these agencies to carefully review reports before giving approval, and a desire on the part of individual officers to write effective reports. Absent these efforts, the problems cited above will likely continue.

WRITING GOOD REPORTS AND CAREER ENHANCEMENT

It is certainly worth noting that if newer patrol officers establish a reputation for writing quality reports the likelihood of having an opportunity to move into an investigative unit within their department increases dramatically. In addition to writing quality reports, it is the officers that go that extra mile by conducting preliminary investigations whose reputations will be bolstered. Conversely, the reputations of officers who are not thorough and write poor to average reports will more than likely prevent them from assignment to an investigative unit.

With respect to the vast majority of police departments in this country, when a vacancy in the detective division, for example, occurs, departmental notices are sent asking officers who are qualified (e.g., have minimum number of years on the job, meet educational requirements) to submit their requests for consideration. It is important to keep in mind that crime reports turned in by patrol officers are routed to the detective division for follow-up investigation. Normally, the unit commanders or designated supervisory personnel read these reports and assign them to individual detectives for follow-up. By and large, this is how new officers become known or establish their reputations in this regard.

As an example, when called to a burglary at a residence and after recording the necessary information for the report, the officer should inform the victim and other occupants of the residence to avoid disturbing the areas surrounding the forced entry or any other areas or items in the house that may have been touched by the offender. The officer should then summon the crime scene investigation unit to the scene for processing. A dutiful officer will then conduct a neighborhood canvas, which involves attempting to contact residents of other homes or employees of businesses that are in close proximity to the residence to ascertain if they saw or heard anything unusual during the time in question. That also means documenting the names, addresses, and contact information of individuals at those locations. If nobody was at home during the time of inquiry, that should be noted as well. This demonstrates to detective division personnel that the officer did a thorough job and provided sufficient detail in the report to assist with and enhance the follow-up investigation. If officers conduct their business in this way on a consistent basis, this will have a very serious and positive impact on decisions to assign or not assign them to vacancies.

POLICE REPORTS AND CIVIL LIABILITY

Unfortunately, we live in a litigious society, and police officers, as well the agencies that employ them, are extremely vulnerable to civil litigation. The nature of police work lends itself to these potentialities. Litigation arising from claims of, for example, false arrest, unlawful searches and seizures, excessive use of force, negligent operation of a motor vehicle resulting in injury or death (i.e., high-speed vehicle pursuit), negligent training, and negligent supervision and retention of personnel is commonplace in the field of policing. Police agencies can reduce the frequency of these kinds of lawsuits by having lawful and up-to-date policies and procedures, providing ongoing training to their personnel regarding legal updates and other issues that affect police practice, and providing effective supervision. Individual officers can likewise mitigate the frequency of lawsuits by adhering to the policies and procedures of their respective agencies, by following the law (statutory and case law), and, most of all, by writing the narrative sections of their reports properly and effectively. As Scarry (2008) so aptly stated, "Officers sometimes neglect their report writing, but it has very serious consequences if left unattended. What officers write in their reports stays with them forever. The words on the paper cannot be changed, and an omission of critical details cannot later be added to a report without calling the report's veracity into doubt." Defense attorneys in criminal cases and plaintiffs' attorneys in civil cases will always try to attack the weakest link in opposing counsels' cases. In both of these legal venues, sadly, the weakest links are oftentimes poorly written police reports. Police officers always talk about covering their behinds, commonly referred to as "CYA." The best way to accomplish this goal is by writing effective and detailed reports. Stressing the importance of this in the context of potential civil liability, Scarry (2008) offered many sound recommendations, such as:

- Document any and all injuries during an arrest or similar encounter incurred by either the officer or arrestee, regardless of how minor the injury may have been. As mentioned earlier, if any pertinent details are omitted from the report and raised later, the veracity of the officer will be called into question.
- Document all statements made by offenders, victims, and witnesses. For the same reason cited above, if it's not documented in the report but brought up later, doubts may very well be formed by the trier of facts, either the judge or members of a jury.
- Officers must document in detailed fashion why they took the actions they did, particularly surrounding incidents involving the use of force. Officers must lay out the events that led to a physical altercation and describe the circumstances regarding their reasons for using force.

Although these recommendations are very straightforward and should be considered as simply using common sense, there are a variety of reasons why reports are not written according to Hoyle, so to speak. Some officers are just plain lazy and want to get through the report as quickly as possible. Others do not want to work overtime, so they rush through their reports. Still others might not choose their words wisely. As Scarry (2008) noted, this kind of haste can have severe consequences with regard to the civil liability of both the department and the individual officer.

SUPPLEMENTAL OR INVESTIGATIVE REPORTS

The most common investigative report is the supplemental report. As the name indicates, it is a report that begins from the point of the end of the initial report and documents further police action taken relevant to a particular case. The most common supplemental report is prepared by investigative personnel. As you may recall from earlier in the chapter, crime reports completed by patrol division personnel are routed to the agency's primary investigative unit for further investigation or other form of disposition.

Let's say, for example, that Detective Richard "Dick" Tracey has received a case for follow-up that involved the armed robbery of a convenience store the evening before. After thoroughly reviewing the original report, as well as any other supplemental reports that may have been completed, such as one completed by evidence technicians called to the scene, Detective Tracey's investigation may take any number of twists and turns. He will more than likely begin by contacting the victim or any other witnesses who may have been present during the robbery. Arrangements would then be made to interview these persons to see if the information they provide him is consistent with the details contained in the original report and to see if they can provide any further details that may aid in identifying the offender. If the victim or a witness got a good look at the offender and Detective Tracy eventually ends up developing a solid lead on the offender, a photo or in-person line-up may be in order.

Let's now assume that the victim and a witness have made a positive identification after viewing a photo line-up. Detective Tracey then goes out and locates said suspect, takes him into custody, and brings him to the station for interrogation. He then informs the suspect of his rights under Miranda. The suspect waives said rights and agrees to be questioned without an attorney present. Tracey begins questioning the suspect and eventually confronts him with the fact that he has been identified in a photo line-up as being the offender. After hearing this information, the suspect then confesses to the crime and agrees to provide a written statement.

Although the circumstances described above may seem straightforward and not overly complicated, let's examine all of the information that must be contained in Tracey's supplemental report:

1. Tracey must note the dates and times he made contact with the victim and witness and what information they relayed to him regarding the robbery.
2. Tracey must also note the dates and times the victim and witness came to the police station to view the photo line-up. The photos used in the line-up must be incorporated into the file and must be consistent with relevant case law and department directives regarding how many photos are to be used and how they are presented to the victim or witness. Also, the photos of the subjects must be similar in nature (e.g., same race, age range, height, weight).
3. Detective Tracey must then document the time, date, and location where the suspect was placed under arrest and whether or not the suspect resisted arrest or attempted to flee or was taken into custody without incident. Any corresponding action taken by Tracey must then be documented as well.
4. Upon arriving at the station with the suspect but before the questioning begins, Tracey must document the fact that the suspect was advised of his rights under Miranda and that the suspect understood those rights. It is highly recommended that the suspect's acknowledgment of receiving his rights be done in writing and with a witness present. Most agencies have standardized forms for this procedure.
5. Because the suspect in this case waived his rights to have an attorney present and agreed to be questioned, Tracey must also document that waiver, again in writing and in the presence of a witness. The ensuing questioning should or could be documented in a number of ways (Wallace and Roberson, 2009). The questions and answers could be documented by Tracey or another detective taking handwritten notes of the responses and later included in their report. Other, more recent methods of documenting information obtained through questioning include audiotaping or videotaping the interrogation, particularly when the crime is of a serious and violent nature, such as an armed robbery, sexual assault, or murder. More and more law enforcement agencies are beginning to adopt

policies requiring videotaped interrogations so that any future claims of impropriety made by offenders about the conduct of the police can be refuted. Finally, the length of time taken during the interrogation should be noted. Lengthy interrogations should be avoided whenever possible, and the suspect should be given periodic breaks to use the restroom, eat, and drink. These breaks should be documented as well so as to refute any potential allegations of duress by the suspect at a later time.

6. Because the offender in this case confessed to the crime, a statement written by the offender in his own writing should be obtained. That statement should be signed and dated along with the time. The suspect's confession should also be witnessed and signed and dated by that person, as well. In circumstances like this, a videotape of the confession is highly recommended. If the agency involved prohibits the videotaping of interrogations and confessions, then careful documentation as described above will suffice.

As you can see, what initially seemed like a relatively easy case to prepare actually required a significant amount of careful planning and documentation. Not only must Tracey's report be written well in terms of clarity and the proper use of grammar and correct spelling, but it must also contain sufficient detail and documentation regarding the steps taken by Tracey to conform to a variety of legal requirements, as well as pertinent departmental policies and regulations. Absent this type of detail and careful preparation, the report will more than likely open up several possible lines of attack by defense counsel. (See the Appendix for an example of a supplemental report.) Hess et al. (2010, p. 90) aptly stated that, "The effective report writer attends to both content and form because they are equally important. A well-written report helps the criminal justice system operate more effectively and efficiently, saves the department time and expense, reduces liability for the department and the officer, and reflects positively on the investigator who wrote it."

Examples of other types of supplemental reports include evidence inventory reports, evidence technician reports, and forensic laboratory request and results reports, among many others. They may vary in form and the information contained therein, but all require the same level of detail and adherence to the basic mechanics of writing as any other report. Reports such as these become part of a permanent case file and are subject to discovery for trial purposes; thus, the factual information contained in them must be consistent. Such information includes dates; times; locations; identities of victims, witnesses, and offenders; and any actions taken by various other personnel involved with the case. In addition, any action taken by police personnel must always be laid out to demonstrate conformity with the law and department policies. Let's examine a few examples of these reports.

CRIME SCENE TECHNICIAN REPORTS

Of the reports mentioned, the crime scene or evidence technician reports possibly require the most detail and precision. When technicians are called to a crime scene for processing, an abundance of detailed information must be carefully recorded and eventually incorporated into their reports. Although the list of things that evidence technicians must do is a mighty long one, some of the most important points of information to be gathered are as follows:

- They must record the date and time of arrival, who summoned them, who was on the scene at the time of their arrival, any witnesses to the crime, and whether or not the scene was possibly contaminated by first responders (police and/or paramedics), the victim's friends, or co-habitants. They must determine if the scene was protected before their arrival and, if so, record the name of the officer who protected the scene and the names of anyone entering the scene prior to their arrival. In other words, they must record all pertinent information relative to the crime scene prior to their arrival and the scene being turned over to their exclusive control.
- As they begin processing the scene, they must carefully note their actions and note, for example, the areas and objects they may have examined for fingerprints or the presence of blood, the procedures used for collecting any potential evidence, the proper identification of each piece of evidence collected, at what time the evidence was transported to the crime laboratory or evidence storage facility and by whom, and the nature of any requested laboratory tests.
- Technicians must also make detailed sketches of the crime scene that are drawn to scale, using appropriate measurements and devices. Detailed photographs of the scene and the evidence collected must be taken and logged. Some agencies go a step further and require a videotaping of the scene in addition to the still photographs to provide viewers with a more broad and thorough perspective.
- Anytime any piece of evidence originally collected from the scene is subsequently moved for any reason, the chain-of-custody log becomes a crucial, legal document. The chain-of-custody log documents any and all movement of evidence, along with the purpose of said movement and to whom the evidence was turned over. This log must be carefully maintained from the time the evidence was collected up to the point at which it is brought to court at the request of either prosecutors or defense counsel. It should be noted that claims of an improper custody chain are often made by defense counsel when all due diligence is not taken by the preparers of those reports.

Thus, as was the case with the more general supplemental report, what initially may seem like a straightforward task instead involves a tremendous amount of detail, careful planning, and coordination. (See "Crime Scene/Evidence Technician Report" in the Appendix for an example of a crime scene technician's supplemental report.)

TRAFFIC ACCIDENT REPORTS

Another good example of this genre of reports is the traffic accident report, particularly when the crash involves serious personal injury or death. Normally, the first responder or patrol officer will complete the initial report. These reports contain many fields of information regarding the number of vehicles or pedestrians involved; the identities of the drivers and passengers; the positions in the vehicles of any passengers; identification of the vehicles involved (e.g., license plate numbers; year, make, and model of the vehicles; vehicle identification numbers); the directions of travel of each vehicle prior to impact; the areas of damage to the vehicles; possible intoxication or other vehicle code violations on the part of the drivers and action taken, if any; a basic sketch that indicates the names of the streets and direction of travel of each vehicle prior to collision, the point of collision, and the point at which the vehicles came to rest; and a narrative section describing the information contained in the sketch.

The completion of these reports can be fairly routine, but if serious injuries or deaths result from the accident then chances are more than good that either a criminal prosecution or civil litigation will follow. Thus, most departments have certified, specially trained traffic accident investigators, commonly referred to as traffic accident reconstructionists, who will conduct a more thorough and scientific investigation regarding the details of the accident. Their reports are not unlike the ones completed by crime scene technicians with respect to the detail and planning involved. These reports, along with the courtroom testimony of the officers who prepared them, will be the center of attention regarding any subsequent criminal or civil actions taken. Moreover, the attention to detail in these reports and knowledge of the law surrounding their specialty play pivotal roles in the outcome of any litigation. (See the Appendix for reference to a detailed traffic accident report template.)

FIELD CONTACT REPORTS

Most, if not all, police departments have reports for officers to complete when they encounter suspicious persons. Circumstances that lead to the completion of such a report most often occur when street officers, on routine patrol, observe persons acting suspiciously. Officers Friendly and Crusty, for example, observed a male subject walking down a street in a residential area in the early morning hours; he was constantly looking from side to side and behind him, as if to see if anyone was watching him. The officers confronted the subject, performed a protective search under the provisions of the *Terry v. Ohio* case, requested identification, and inquired as to what the subject was doing in the area, where he came from, and other pertinent questions. Seasoned officers such as Friendly and Crusty will record all of the information and circumstances surrounding such encounters in great detail. The person's identity, address, date of birth, physical characteristics, clothing worn, and questions asked of the person by the officers and responses given should be carefully documented in the field contact report.

A new officer or someone not acquainted with policing might ponder why Officers Friendly and Crusty went through so much trouble. The officers could have just checked the man's name through the computer for any warrants and, if the subject was not wanted, just let him go and be done with it. The value of field contact reports is that they place an individual at a certain place at a certain time and date. These reports also contain, or should contain, detailed physical descriptions of the subjects, along with clothing worn and other pertinent details.

These reports are not just thrown in a file cabinet and forgotten about. With today's technology, most departments enter these reports into databases which makes retrieval of any such reports on a certain date, time, or a proximate location an easy process. The person encountered by Officers Friendly and Crusty may have committed a serious crime minutes before being spotted by the officers. Detectives place great importance on these reports, and many offenders have been identified and arrested for crimes ranging from sexual assault, robbery, and burglary all the way to murder as a result of the information contained in those reports. These reports also serve as potentially valuable leads for investigators working on "cold cases." (See "Field Contact/Interview Report" in the Appendix for an example of a field contact card or report.)

CURFEW AND SCHOOL ABSENTEE REPORTS

The importance of these reports is much like that of the field contact report. In addition to young persons staying out too late or skipping school, many of these minors may have been involved in or may be about to be involved in criminal activities shortly before police officers initially come in contact with them. From an investigative perspective, such reports place individuals at a certain place at a certain date and time. From a crime prevention point of view, these encounters may very well have prevented a crime from taking place. Either way, it's a win–win situation for the police and the public they serve.

FIELD NOTES

Before proceeding to the concluding remarks section of this chapter, a few words regarding the use of field notes are in order. Simply defined, field notes are nothing more than notes written in small notebooks carried by officers to record information that is later incorporated into a formal report. Most police officers carry such notebooks in their pockets so they can jot down an array of information, such as names and contact information for victims, witnesses, and offenders; locations and times; vehicle identification information; comments made by victims, witnesses, and offenders; and numerous other details necessary for completion of an official report.

The issue involved in using these is whether or not to include field notes as a permanent part of a case file. This matter is determined by department policy; some agencies do so, some do not. If the policy is not to maintain field notes, this is not an issue; however, in those agencies that do require this officers are well advised to use their notebooks for official purposes only. It would prove very embarrassing for an officer to be asked by defense counsel in open court why he has notations for grocery items to pick up on his way home from work. Moreover, as insignificant as this may appear, good defense attorneys can raise much doubt in the minds of the judge and jury members regarding the officer's level of professionalism and lack of adherence to department policy. The moral of the story is that if a law enforcement agency requires, by department policy, that officers' field notes are to become part of the permanent file, then officers must get used to using field notes only for official business and not personal matters.

CONCLUDING REMARKS

It is hoped that the information contained in this chapter has demonstrated the critical role that report writing plays in the law enforcement profession and the broader criminal justice system. Reports serve several functions, perhaps the most important of which is to aid our legal system in the prosecution of persons charged with criminal offenses. As stressed throughout the chapter, a poorly prepared police report may very well result in defendants literally getting away with murder or other serious crimes. In addition, several of the more common types of reports were discussed in detail. Although all reports may differ slightly in style and purpose, these and numerous other kinds of reports not identified here all share many more commonalities than differences. Finally, several vital and fundamental recommendations for writing effective reports were directed at both individual police officers and their respective agencies. Let's conclude by revisiting those recommendations.

RECOMMENDATIONS FOR INDIVIDUAL OFFICERS

1. The basic mechanics of writing, such as the use of proper grammar, punctuation, and correct spelling, must guide each and every report written.
2. Start getting used to writing all reports in an effective manner at the beginning of one's career. This will make doing so a routine matter throughout one's career.
3. Be sure to address all of the who, what, when, where, why, and how issues, if possible.
4. Tell the story in a logical and carefully planned manner.
5. Include all of the pertinent details of an incident in the narrative.
6. Keep up to date regarding statutory and case law relevant to the field of policing.
7. To the extent possible, develop and maintain positive working relationships with prosecutors.
8. Time permitting, preliminary investigators (normally patrol officers) should take the initial report as far as it can go. Neighborhood canvasses and other extra efforts demonstrate professionalism and go a long way toward gaining a good reputation in one's own agency which very likely will assist officers in getting reassigned or promoted to an investigations division.
9. Do not rely too much on the spelling and grammar check functions of word processing programs. Those functions do not identify all mistakes. Not only are the basic mechanics of writing important but also careful planning regarding the conveyance of the story is crucial.

RECOMMENDATIONS FOR POLICE ADMINISTRATORS

1. The necessary curricula and time designated to report writing must be available at the recruit training level. Police academy recruits who do not demonstrate proficiency in this regard should be required to participate in remedial writing instruction.

2. It is critical for report writing to be at the top of the list when field training officers are assessing the performance of rookie officers. Field training officers should be encouraged to consistently reinforce to their rookies just how important effective report writing is, for all of the reasons highlighted throughout this chapter.

3. Department administrators must provide for periodic in-service training opportunities for all agency members in reference to effective report writing.

In the final analysis, the police officer's pen is indeed mightier than the proverbial sword!

QUESTIONS FOR DISCUSSION

1. In general terms, explain why good writing abilities are so important in our professional and private lives. Offer some examples in support of your position.

2. What are some of the factors or variables that positively contribute to the development of what we call effective police report writing? Identify and elaborate at least three such factors.

3. Why is up-to-date knowledge of statutory and case law such a critical factor when completing official reports? Provide examples.

4. What benefits are accrued by officers who are known to be good report writers by members of their respective agencies? Do these benefits apply in any other context within the criminal justice system? Why or why not?

5. Why is it important for police officers to document in detail incidents involving suspicious persons and circumstances? Provide examples.

6. What is the determining factor for an officer's decision to either include or exclude field notes from their permanent case files?

BIBLIOGRAPHY

Anon. (2010). 9 Tips for Rookie Success. *Police Link*, 258, July 1 (http://policelink.monster.com/benefits/articles/142427-9-tips-for-rookie-success?page=10).

Baker, B. (2006). *Becoming a Police Officer: An Insider's Guide to a Career in Law Enforcement.* Bloomington, IN: iUniverse (http://www.careerpoliceofficer.com/).

Hess, K., Bennett, W., and Orthmann, C. (2010). *Criminal Investigation*, 9th ed. Florence, KY: Cengage Learning.

Iowa DOT. (2011). *Iowa Accident Report Form*. Ames: Iowa Department of Transportation (http://www.iowadot.gov/mvd/ods/accidents.htm).

Jacoby, J., Gilchrist III, P., and Ratledge, E. (1999). *Prosecutor's Guide to Police–Prosecutor Relations.* Washington, D.C.: Jefferson Institute for Justice Studies (http://www.jijs.org/publications/pros-pubs/Police-Pros.pdf).

Jetmore, L. (2008). Investigations: Investigative Report Writing. *Law Officer*, January 31 (http://www.lawofficer.com/article/magazine-feature/investigative-report-writing).

Miranda v. Arizona, 384 U.S. 436 (1966).

ODEP. (2008). *Essential Skills to Getting a Job: What Young People with Disabilities Need to Know—Work Ethic, Communication, and Problem Solving*. Washington, D.C.: Office of Disability Employment Policy, U.S. Department of Labor (http://www.dol.gov/odep/documents/essential_job_skills.pdf).

Scarry, L. (2008). Report Writing: What You Fail to Report Could Have Negative Consequences in Civil Litigation. *Law Officer*, January 30 (http://www.lawofficer.com/article/magazine-feature/report-writing).

Stevens, B. (2005). What Communication Skills Do Employers Want? Silicon Valley Recruiters Respond. *Journal of Employment Counseling*, March 1 (http://www.allbusiness.com/sector-56-administrative-support/administrative/1189004-1.html).

Terry v. Ohio, 392 U.S. 1 (1968).

Wallace, H. and Roberson, C. (2009). *Written and Interpersonal Communication Methods for Law Enforcement*, 4th ed. Upper Saddle River, NJ: Pearson Education.

APPENDIX

SUPPLEMENTAL REPORT

Crime/Incident	Date/Time of Original Report		Case Number
Burglary (residential)	10 Aug 2007, 1400 hrs		20074H-47065

Complaint's/Victim's Name (Last, First, Middle)		Res. Phone
Jones, John, James		788-555-6785

Complaint's/Victim's Residence Address		Bus. Phone
787 Roundview Cir, Baltimore, MD 21000		788-555-1200

Date/Time of Original Crime/Incident	Date/Time of This Report
7 Aug 2007 to 10 Aug 2007, 1700 to 1400 hrs	12 Aug 07, 1800 hrs

Source: Baker, B.M., *Follow-up Report*, CareerPoliceOfficer.com, 2011 (http://www.careerpoliceofficer.com/PoliceandVictims/police_report_writing/follow-up_report.html).

Narrative

After a thorough inventory of his home, Mr. Jones discovered that the following additional items were taken in the burglary:

One (1) television; Sony; 12 inch; serial number unknown; value: $50.00

Two (2) pillow cases; pink in color (taken from second floor rear guest bedroom); value: $20.00

Total additional value: $70.00

Mr. Jones further reports that one of his neighbors had observed two men loitering in the block during the time frame of this incident. I responded to the neighbor's residence where I spoke with the following witness:

Mr. Reuben Castle

M-W-55; DOB: 12 Feb 1952

782 Roundview Cir
Baltimore, MD 21000
Res. Phone: 785-555-3824
Bus. Phone: Same (Self-Employed)

Mr. Castle reports he observed two white males placing items into a dark colored, late-model SUV which was parked in front of the victim's residence. Mr. Castle states he earlier noticed the men when they were sitting inside the vehicle for an extended period of time. Later, he noticed the men standing beside the vehicle looking around as if they were waiting or looking for someone. His last observation occurred when he saw the men placing two (2) bags inside the vehicle.

I asked Mr. Castle if he remembered the color of the bags? Mr. Castle paused for a moment and then stated, "You know, they looked like they were pink." Asked if he could describe the size and shape of the bags and the type, Mr. Castle responded, "Just bags … some kind of cloth bags." Mr. Castle's description of the bags he observed is consistent with the two pink pillow cases reported taken in this report.

Mr. Castle's observations occurred between 1200 and 1300 hrs on 8 Aug 2007.

Mr. Caste provided the following suspect descriptions:

Suspect #1: M-W-20 to 25; 5-10 to 6-00; thin build; 130 to 150 lbs; medium length red hair; freckles on face and arms; white tee shirt; blue jeans with holes in both knees; white tennis shoes; NFD

Suspect #2: M-W-20 to 25; 5-08 to 5-10; stocky build; 180 to 190 lbs; short dark hair; dark sun tan; large tattoo on right forearm; green t-shirt; blue jeans; dark color shoes; NFD

Vehicle: Dark colored late model SUV with Maryland registration possibly containing the letters: B and F; NFD

TRAFFIC ACCIDENT REPORT TEMPLATE

Access http://www.iowadot.gov/mvd/ods/accidents.htm and open the PDF document entitled "Iowa Accident Report Form" for a good example of a traffic accident report template.

CRIMINAL INCIDENT REPORT

Access http://searchwarp.com/swa220385.htm and examine the narrative provided concerning the report of a domestic violence incident. This is a good example of a well-written narrative summary of the incident, and it answers the who, what, when, where, why, and how questions that are so critical for effective report writing.

CRIME SCENE/EVIDENCE TECHNICIAN REPORT

Access http://www.crimescene.com/noir/1958_crime_report.html and examine the initial crime scene report. Be sure to also access the links at the bottom of the page, particularly the one named "Evidence." These various reports are excellent examples of thorough and detailed reports and correctly demonstrate the amount of detail required.

FIELD CONTACT/INTERVIEW REPORT

Access the following two websites and examine the templates used by the New York and New Orleans City Police Departments. Notice that the template used by the New York City Police Department requires significantly more detail, which may potentially provide valuable data and documentation for a future criminal investigation and which is more consistent with pertinent statutory and case law than the report template used by the New Orleans Police Department. The report used by the latter agency has received much recent scrutiny regarding legal issues surrounding its use.

http://media.nola.com/crime_impact/photo/terry-form-new-torkjpg-20110028f7fbd2bc.jpg

http://media.nola.com/crime_impact/photo/terry-form-new-orleamsjpg-51a1a24bc0999695.jpg

CHAPTER 5

Interview and Interrogation

Scott M. Mire
University of Louisiana at Lafayette

Robert D. Hanser
University of Louisiana at Monroe

CHAPTER OBJECTIVES

After reading this chapter, you should be able to do the following:

1. Understand the process of interviewing a person.
2. Understand the process of interrogating a suspect.
3. Understand the key principles of interview and interrogation practices.
4. Understand the importance of allowing fact to guide the process of interview and interrogation.

Chapter Outline

- Introduction
- Interviewing Individuals
- Interrogating Suspects
- Key Principles of Interview and Interrogation
- Conclusion

INTRODUCTION

The process of interviewing persons and interrogating suspects has received an enormous amount of attention from scholars and practitioners over the past several decades. Both the interview and the interrogation consist of a sometimes deeply personal interactions between law enforcement personnel and members of the community. And, as is generally the case with social science topics involving human behavior, we have yet to see that substantial breakthrough where all questions are answered and the mysteries of effective interview and interrogation are laid to rest. In fact, in spite of technology and other modern advances,

American law enforcement elicits a confession from a suspect only 45 to 60% of the time. In other words, for all practical purposes, we are still not much better than chance in being able to solicit a confession from a suspect as a result of interview and interrogation tactics.

This chapter is aimed at exploring some of the most important aspects of successfully conducting interviews and interrogations. The primary objective is to explore some of the most basic factors widely believed to have a direct impact on whether a suspect will confess. Before going any further, however, it is important to clearly illuminate the population we are most interested in. Some suspects who are selected for interrogation will never confess. Consider the example of a suspect involved in narcotics trafficking who had been previously arrested on several occasions: "I wasn't going to tell them anything. It wouldn't have mattered what they said. I had been through that before and found out the hard way that I was better off keeping my mouth shut. I was prepared to sit in jail for as long as I had to and just do my time. And what was funny was that when they realized that I wasn't going to give them any information they got angry and began threatening me. One said he would be sure that I spent the rest of my life in jail. It was kind of funny coming from the same detective that had just lectured me on the importance of telling the truth and being honest."

On the opposite end of this spectrum are those who are going to confess regardless of the tactics employed by investigators. For these individuals, the reasons for confessing are usually very personal and tied to extreme shame that produces profound psychological and emotional suffering. For those individuals in this group, the confession serves as a cleansing of emotion, substantially reducing their suffering and ultimately resulting in their life being much more tolerable. The confession is much more about them reducing their own levels of stress than it is about individual investigators or their method of interrogation.

Between these two extremes is a group of individuals who may confess depending on the circumstances. And, unlike the other two groups, the tactics employed by investigators are crucial when dealing with this group of suspects. These individuals, and especially those who have had limited contact with the police in the past, are often overwhelmed with trepidation. Often, and especially for those individuals who are guilty, their biggest concern is what is going to happen to them. The interview and interrogation process is aimed precisely at these individuals, and it is critical that the process be carried out in a manner that is most likely to solicit a confession, as opposed to shutting them off, a state whereby no useful information is provided.

INTERVIEWING INDIVIDUALS

It is important to understand that, although the terms are often used interchangeably, an interview is different from an interrogation. Generally, interviews should precede the interrogation phase; they involve gathering baseline data from a person potentially associated with a criminal event. During the interview, investigators have two primary objectives:

1. Come to know and understand the individual.
2. Determine whether the individual is a suspect and whether or not to proceed to interrogation.

The importance of getting to know the individual during the interview cannot be over-emphasized. A practical example unique to each reader may help to illuminate this point. Think back to some point in your past or even recently when you determined that a person (usually a good friend) was a terrible liar. Every time this person tried to fudge the truth, you could always tell. In fact, you would know immediately that this person was beginning to stretch the truth, and you were so accurate in your observations that after a while the person no longer even resisted your objections. This is when people who have been effectively challenged on their quest to stretch the truth are often heard to say, "Okay, it was really 2, not 5." Or, "Well, yeah, you're right. It wasn't quite that big, but you know what I mean." Some clue, either verbal or behavioral, has alerted the listener to the likelihood that a false statement or a stretching of the truth is about to follow. The point here is that this clue is identifiable on a consistent basis, sometimes with 100% accuracy. The reason for this is because a listener who has become so accustomed to a speaker's mannerisms is immediately able to detect deviations from normal and becomes suspicious. In essence, the listener knows the speaker very well. Over time, more and more variations on telling a lie become apparent. This same phenomenon is also often the case for children and their parents. Parents are often so in tune with their children that they are usually able to detect immediately when their child is telling a lie.

How do these examples tie into our discussion? Ultimately, they represent one extreme of the interview process. In other words, detectives rarely know the people they interview so well that they are able to detect deception so readily and with such accuracy. In fact, it is more often the case that detectives either do not know the interviewee at all or the extent of the relationship is very limited; therefore, the interview is best thought of as the process through which investigators get to know the interviewee as well as possible. Based on this logic, the chances of investigators accurately predicting the truthfulness of interviewees are directly related to the amount of interaction they have with the interviewees (see Figure 5.1). Using an analogy related to scientific research, the amount of interaction would be synonymous with the size of the sample. Generally, the larger the sample, the

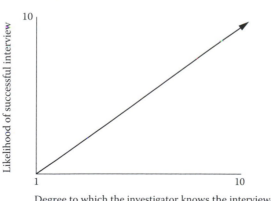

Degree to which the investigator knows the interviewee

FIGURE 5.1   Likelihood of successful interview.

greater the chances of reaching valid and reliable results. The ultimate goal of the interview is for investigators to get to know the interviewee as well as possible so they can establish a baseline of truthfulness based on the mannerisms and characteristics of the interviewee while responding to direct questions.

One example of an interview process that has been well documented is the Behavioral Analysis Interview (BAI) (Blair, 1999). The BAI provides a strategic and methodological approach to assessing the likelihood of whether the interviewee may be involved in the incident being investigated. As noted by Horvath et al. (2008), the BAI is not intended to detect specific acts of deception but rather to be used as a tool to provide directions and guidance for evaluating the totality of the interview and whether it is likely that someone is being deceptive.

Generally, the BAI consists of three parts. Initially, background information is collected that serves as the initial process of getting to know the interviewee. As pointed out earlier, this is a critical part of the interview. We suggest that as much time as possible be allocated for gathering background information. In this phase of the interview, investigators may ask questions relating to where the interviewee lives, the interviewee's relatives, etc. Investigators may ask questions about favorite sports teams and players as well as the interviewee's favorite movies and genres of music. In essence, the investigator is attempting to create a connection with the interviewee or, in other words, a good rapport that will serve as the foundation for later questions that may be more uncomfortable and intrusive.

The second part of the BAI usually consists of investigative questions. These types of questions generally attempt to ascertain whether an interviewee could have committed the crime in question. In other words, they try to determine the actions of the interviewee during the estimated time frame of the alleged commissioning of some criminal act. Although it is not very common, it is possible to completely eliminate an interviewee from further suspicion during the phase of investigative questions. An example could include an interviewee establishing an air-tight alibi for where they were during the commission of the crime in question. In most circumstances, however, interviewees are further questioned about their opportunity, access, motivation, and propensity to commit a crime (Horvath et al., 2008).

The third phase of the BAI includes questions related to behavior that are meant to draw out differences in verbal and nonverbal behavior from both innocent and guilty interviewees. As an example, interviewees may be asked what they understand the purpose of the interview to be and how they feel about being interviewed about some specific incident (Horvath et al., 1994, 2008; Inbau et al., 1986, 2001).

What is critical to understand and remember with regard to the interview is that any result should be a reflection of the totality of the interview and not one single phase of the interview or a single response to a particular question within a phase. Horvath et al. (2008) provided five specific guidelines that should always be considered when attempting to interpret the messages and behaviors observed during the BAI:

1. Evaluate any deviations from the suspect's normal behavior. There are no unique behavioral indicators that are consistently associated with innocence or guilt. It is the suspect's deviation from his or her normal behavior that is significant. Such normal behavior is especially reflected in responses to questions regarding personal history, which are generally less emotionally provocative for both guilty and innocent persons. For the innocent person, items in the investigative and behavior-provoking categories are less provocative than they are for a guilty person. Therefore, it is the consistency within and between categories that is important.

2. Evaluate the nonverbal behaviors as they occur in response to a particular question and be attentive to repetition of these behaviors—that is, their consistency across questions.

3. Evaluate verbal and nonverbal behaviors in conjunction with each other. Look for discrepancies between the two channels.

4. Consider underlying factors that could affect the validity of behavior analysis. Examples of these include the seriousness of the offense, what the suspect was told about the offense, the suspect's emotional stability, and the suspect's cultural and social environment.

5. Consider the suspect's behavior in conjunction with factual analysis. When there is a discrepancy between known facts and a suspect's behavioral indicators, the interviewer must be cautious in rendering a definite opinion of the suspect's involvement.

INTERROGATING SUSPECTS

Before reading about the general features of an interrogation, remember that the interview is meant to identify possible suspects who may have engaged in some criminal activity. The interview is generally a nonconfrontational process where investigators obtain important information and also identify baseline reactions demonstrated by interviewees. When an interviewee has been determined to be a possible suspect, the next phase of questioning is carried out in the form of an interrogation. In addition, we would like to caution readers that the literature is far from being in agreement on the best methods for soliciting a confession from a suspect. In Europe, for example, a growing body of literature suggests that suspects are more likely to confess when engaged with a style characterized by less confrontation and more sensitivity (Hakkanen et al., 2008). In the United States, this view is much less prevalent, as the general assumption is that suspects are motivated to lie and should be interrogated as such. As a result, two significant distinctions can be made between the interview and interrogation:

1. Purpose
2. Tactics

The purpose of an interrogation is to obtain a confession. The purpose of an interview is to determine whether someone should be considered a suspect in the commission of a criminal act; therefore, if a person reaches the interrogation phase, then at least theoretically the question is not whether this person is involved but how. Did the suspect directly carry out some criminal act or was the suspect involved in the commission of a criminal act? Based on the different assumptions associated with interviews and interrogations, the approaches are different. The primary distinction is the use of confrontation when conducting an interrogation. Investigators are much more direct when conducting an interrogation and often use accusatory statements to obtain information. Some examples could include the following:

Interview: John, do you have any idea of what happened to Mr. Citizen?
Interrogation: John, we know you were involved in the death of Mr. Citizen.
Interview: John, do you know why someone might have wanted to injure Mr. Citizen?
Interrogation: John, either you killed Mr. Citizen yourself or you helped someone kill Mr. Citizen because you wanted his money.

Numerous publications and training manuals can be found on how to interrogate suspects in ways that are most likely to elicit a confession (Aubry and Caputo, 1980; Gordon and Fleisher, 2002; Holmes, 2003; Walkley, 1987; Walters, 1996). The one manual, however, that is still most widely used was developed by Inbau et al. (2001). Originally developed in the 1960s, the manual is now in its fourth edition and describes the Reid technique for conducting interrogations. The Reid technique is based on numerous observations of the administering of the polygraph exam and the responses and reactions of those individuals found to be deceptive.

To begin, the Reid technique calls for a particular setting in which the interrogation should take place; for example, the room should be relatively small and should be located in the police station. Further, the setting should be soundproof to limit distractions and minimally furnished. The psychology behind such a setting is to attempt to raise anxiety levels within a suspect by creating unfamiliar surroundings and enhancing the idea of isolation. In some cases, the greater the feelings of anxiety and isolation, the greater the likelihood of a confession (Inbau et al., 2001). Once the correct setting has been been achieved, the Reid technique consists of nine steps aimed at driving a suspect toward confession:

1. *Confrontation*—In this phase of the interrogation, investigators make it very clear that they believe the suspect is responsible for or involved in the commission of a crime. The speech is direct and automatic: "John, the reason we are here is because you committed this crime. I am not asking you. I am telling you that you committed this crime. The evidence is clear, and everyone I have spoken to says the same thing. You did it." The primary objective of the confrontational phase is to quickly raise the suspect's stress level and begin the process of logically laying out evidence showing the suspect's involvement.

2. *Theme development*—When investigators have confronted a suspect with strong assertions of his guilt, the next phase is to begin to explore themes that may serve to justify the suspect's criminal actions. This is a very important phase of the Reid technique. Often, suspects feel an abundance of shame related to their criminality, and they need some type of justification to be able to reduce the shame and subsequently disclose their actions. Consider a suspect accused of sexually molesting a child. In some cases, investigators may be well served in developing a theme whereby they express how they also see some children as being extremely sexy. The purpose of this theme is to create some justification for the suspect, thus reducing his shame. Some suspects may respond with, "Yes! I can't believe you feel the same way. I thought I was the only one who had those kinds of feelings and thoughts."

3. *Stopping denials*—When the investigation has begun to develop themes based on the evidence, it is important to stop a suspect's denials before the investigator and the interrogation get taken off track. The point is to stay on theme and within the domain of evidence with as few distractions as possible.

4. *Overcoming objections*—At this point in the interrogation, many suspects will object to the theme presented by investigators. This is different that a denial of committing the crime. Here is an example of a suspect objecting to a theme: "I could not kill another person. I saw my dad murder my mom when I was 12 years old." In order to overcome such an objection, one reply available to investigators could be, "John, I understand. You are correct, you could never PLAN to kill another person like your dad had planned to murder your mom. In fact, he had probably planned to kill her for years."

5. *Getting the suspect's attention*—In this phase of the interrogation, many suspects are very unsure of themselves. Especially when successful themes have been presented suspects will often find themselves more isolated than ever. The goal is now to offer support to the suspect. "John, I know you were under stress. You had been trying for a long time. Anyone would have been stressed under those circumstances. Hell, you lasted a lot longer than I could have."

6. *Suspect loses resolve*—Suspects who are provided support by an investigator will often feel as though they have an ally and that they are being understood. Unfortunately, for some suspects, this may be the first time they ever felt heard. As a result, they will begin to let their guard down and lose some of the resolve necessary to maintain their lies and deception.

7. *Offering alternatives*—In some cases, when suspects begin to lose their resolve, the path to confession is quick and uninterrupted. Others, however, may need alternatives or contrasts for the most shameful aspects of the crime: "John, either you planned to kill your wife or you were so upset when you found out she was having an affair, you blew up. You were out of control." These two contrasts will often result in a suspect who has begun to lose resolve indicating which scenario is most accurate. At this point, the indicators will often be subtle, such as a gentle nod of the head or putting their head in the palms of their hands.

8. *Bringing the suspect into the conversation*—In this phase of the interrogation, the suspect has usually given some indication as to which alternative is most accurate. For all practical purposes, the confession has begun and the goal is to allow the suspect to provide as much information as possible. In some cases, additional investigators may be brought in, and suspects once again rely on the most socially acceptable rationale for the commission of their crime. The result is that the suspect confesses to now another person.

9. *Confession*—The final stage of the interrogation is simply ensuring that the confession will be admitted in a trial. The voluntariness of the confession will be captured, and usually suspects will be asked to provide their confession in writing.

A PRACTICAL EXAMPLE

On September 1, 2003, Detective Victor Lauria of the Novi Police Department in Detroit, Michigan, used his training in the Reid technique to interrogate Nikole Michelle Frederick (Layton, 2010). Frederick's 2-year-old stepdaughter, Ann Marie, was brought to the emergency room near death, with obvious signs of extensive child abuse. Frederick was her primary caretaker and was watching Ann Marie in the time before the trip to the hospital. The interrogation took place over 2 days, with Frederick being charged with the crime immediately following the first sit-down. Lauria began with a simple interview, just talking in a non-threatening way to establish Frederick's baseline reactions:

Lauria: How would you rate yourself as a mother?

Frederick: Um, I think I'm, I'm pretty good. I mean I, I am a little bad with being stern and stricter, you know, letting them get away with things.

Lauria: How would you describe Ann Marie?

Frederick: She was a very hard baby. She would, uh, cry all the time. Always wanted to be held. … I mean Annie just, I mean she always looks like she's beaten. She's always climbing or you know. I always can see a little bit of bruising and scrapes or whatever on her back. Her shins are always bruised.

Because Frederick appeared to be making excuses for Ann Marie's injuries and setting up a justification—"She was a very hard baby"—and because she was taking care of Ann Marie when the injuries occurred, Lauria predicted guilt and began interrogating her. He proceeded to subtle confrontation, letting Frederick know how she would be caught:

Lauria: There's a whole line of study in police work that can determine how injuries occur and how old the injuries are.

Frederick: … I don't even think we'll find out exactly what happened because the only one that really knows is her and it's gonna be awfully hard trying to get her to say if anything happened, you know. I'm not trying to be rude or anything, I was just wondering how long this is going to take.

Lauria: Well, like I said, one of the things we're able to do with those [bruises] is we can date bruises based upon, you know, whether they're new bruises just coming in, or whether they're bruises that are already starting to heal because, you know, doctors and forensic scientists and pathologists study those type of things.

Frederick: Okay.

Lauria: Can you think of any reason why they would determine that those bruises were caused in the last 24 hours and that somebody would suspect that you did this?

Frederick: Um, other than that I was there, no.

…

Lauria: Do you suspect anybody of doing this?

Frederick: No, I don't. And that's what I'm saying, and I, I'm having a hard time believing that it was inflicted on her because, like I said, we would have heard something, too, you know.

Lauria: Out of all the people in the house that were there or came in last night, list all the people that you would vouch for that you would say absolutely would not do something to hurt Ann Marie.

Frederick: I know John wouldn't do it. I honestly don't think Brian would do it.

Lauria: Who'd vouch for you?

Frederick: Um, probably John. But, see, like, I don't, I don't necessarily, uh, believe what the doctor's saying and how they were inflicted, whatever.

Detective Lauria began developing a theme about an out-of-control situation—Frederick had not premeditated the abuse; she just hadn't been thinking clearly. But Frederick didn't like that theme. She asked the detective why he wasn't believing her story. Lauria then switched to an out-of-control "split second" in which Frederick had hurt Ann Marie. He explained that Ann Marie's injuries were definitely not from a fall. Someone else had inflicted them, possibly in a split second of irrationality. Frederick was listening now, apparently clinging to the "split second" qualification. Lauria further developed the theme by bringing up Ann Marie's difficult nature and how hard she was to care for—blaming the victim, which Frederick had already shown a tendency toward. Frederick began nodding her head, and Lauria set up an alternative. He told Frederick that "without an explanation of what happened people would assume the worst." The implied contrast had already been set up: a cold-blooded, vicious attack on a toddler vs. a momentary loss of self-control when dealing with a difficult child. The approach worked. According to Lauria's account:

> Over two days of questioning Frederick never asked how Ann Marie was doing. Near the end of the interview I pointed this out to her. She tried to convince me that she had asked several times about Ann Marie's injuries. She then asked me for an update in her condition. I told her that Ann Marie was brain dead and that she was probably not going to survive. Frederick stated, "Oh, my God. I'm gonna go for murder." I then spent another 45 minutes with various themes in an attempt to get

further information. After several attempts at denying any further knowledge or involvement in causing the injuries to Ann Marie she admitted to shaking her. After admitting to shaking her, Frederick broke down and cried. She then said, "I killed that little girl. I killed that little girl."

Ann Marie died of her injuries, and Nikole Michelle Frederick stood trial for first degree felony murder. She was found guilty and sentenced to life in prison without the possibility of parole.

KEY PRINCIPLES OF INTERVIEW AND INTERROGATION

Before transitioning into the final parts of this chapter a couple of points are worthy of mention. First, we have relied on two techniques, the BAI and the Reid interrogation system, to illustrate the differences between interviews and interrogations. This is not meant to imply, however, that we feel these techniques are superior to others. As noted above, there are other styles and techniques of conducting interviews and interrogations, and the specific methods chosen will largely be governed by the policies and procedures of individual agencies and the manner in which their leadership has been trained. Some aspects of interview and interrogation, however, are universal and do not rely on the individual techniques used to gather information and obtain confessions.

The first aspect of interviewing persons and interrogating suspects that has been shown to be effective is careful planning. This point cannot be overemphasized. It is vital that investigators gather as much background information as possible on individuals to be interviewed and especially suspects that will be interrogated. For those who will be interrogated, investigators should make every attempt to learn about their associates, past criminal involvement, employment history, and any other information that may be available. This background information will not only help investigators identify possible patterns of deception but also provide the foundation for effectively planning how to carry out the interview and interrogation (Napier and Adams, 2002; Vessel, 1998).

Another aspect of interview and interrogation that is important to understand and carry out is for investigators to follow the facts related to the incident in question. This aspect of successful interviewing and interrogation is also directly tied to a thorough background investigation prior to questioning. When investigators let facts guide their questioning they are better able to stay on point and ensure that the process remains within areas of questioning that are productive and relevant. When they allow facts to guide questions, investigators are also better positioned to challenge suspects who may be deceptive and not addressing the specific components of the questions being asked. When investigators are able to point to substantive facts driving their questions, they are also more likely to be viewed as credible by the suspect, and, especially within the criminal element, the perception of credibility is very important. If an investigator loses credibility during the interview or interrogation, the chance of success is greatly diminished. In fact, in such circumstances it may be best to stop and allow another investigator to take over the questioning or at least be present for the duration of the conversation.

A third aspect of successfully interviewing and interrogating suspects is to ask clear questions that can be understood by the suspect. Questions should be construed in a simple manner and not be overly complex. Just as important, however, is that when a clear question has been presented investigators should be patient and allow the individual to respond without interruption. For many investigators, allowing individuals to fully respond without interruption is deceptively difficult. Especially in the beginning phases of an interview or interrogation, open-ended questions, clearly framed, are usually best. Open-ended questions tend to force individuals away from one- or two-word responses. As noted by Napier and Adams (2002), open-ended questions generally make it more difficult for suspects to successfully lie, especially over time.

One caution is worth noting in relation to the framing of questions. In many circumstances, investigators will attempt to frame questions so perfectly that they actually end up doing as much or in some cases more talking than the suspect. The psychology behind this phenomenon is probably rooted in wanting to obtain the confession so badly that the basics of communication are cast aside in the pursuit of a perfect question that will somehow force the suspect to confess. This is rarely the case, however, and a confession is usually the result of various factors and probably most associated with the strength of the evidence. At any rate, many investigators make a serious error by not allowing a suspect to fully answer a question without being interrupted. Of course, we do not mean to imply that it is productive to allow someone to significantly depart from the main theme of questioning, either intentionally or unintentionally; however, every effort should be made to provide their answers.

Finally, and arguably most importantly, all interviews and interrogations should be conducted with the utmost of professionalism. This can sometimes be difficult, especially when interrogating individuals suspected of committing a heinous crime. It can be a daunting task to look into the eyes of someone who has killed another and calmly ask that person to talk you through the crime scene and the reasoning behind their gruesome act. To not remain professional, however, not only jeopardizes the confession but also may raise questions of legality regarding the entire investigative process and whether the case will be accepted for prosecution.

CONCLUSION

The process of conducting successful interviews and interrogations is often difficult. A lot of the variability is directly associated with the individual being questioned. Some will give information willingly, and some will offer no information; for others, the methods used in soliciting the information are critical and ultimately decide whether they will disclose sensitive details. It is important to understand the difference between an interview and interrogation. When conducting interviews, the questions are usually aimed at obtaining general information in order to ascertain whether the person should be considered a suspect in some criminal event. When a person is deemed a suspect, the questioning shifts to the form of an interrogation. The most significant difference between an interview and interrogation is that an interrogation usually consists of intentional and deliberate confrontation. The suspect is told that he is believed to be responsible for the commission of a criminal act. The ultimate goal in the interview and interrogation process is obtaining a confession from an individual admitting that he or she did in fact commit the criminal act or was involved in the commission of a criminal act. In the U.S. court system, a confession is powerful evidence. In fact, without a confession many prosecutors will not file charges unless there is an abundance of physical or circumstantial evidence. As a result, a great deal of importance is attached to the process of obtaining a confession. Investigators often have a great deal of pressure on them to figure out how to effectively obtain a confession from a criminal who has a lot to lose by confessing. It is a difficult process that must be carefully managed.

Prior to conducting interviews and especially interrogations, investigators should take the necessary time to obtain as much background information as possible regarding the individual to be questioned. A thorough background investigation helps investigators plan for the interview and interrogation. It also allows investigators to develop themes that identify the precise questions that need to be answered. Investigators should follow the facts when questioning suspects and allow them the time to answer questions without interruption. Finally, investigators must remain professional throughout the duration of the interview and interrogation. Professionalism is among the most salient tools an investigator has, not only to get a confession but also to ensure that the confession is admissible in court.

QUESTIONS FOR DISCUSSION

1. What is the difference between an interview and interrogation?
2. Discuss the process of developing themes within an interrogation. What is the purpose of developing a theme?
3. Identify and discuss several key principles to conducting successful interviews and interrogations. Which of the principles do you think is most important? Why?
4. In your opinion, does the court system rely too heavily on the confession for a criminal prosecution? Why?

BIBLIOGRAPHY

Aubry, A.S. and Caputo, R.R. (1980). *Criminal Interrogation*, 3rd ed. Springfield, IL: Charles C Thomas.

Baldwin, J. (1992). *Video Taping Police Interviews with Suspects: An Evaluation*, Police Research Series Paper 1. London: Home Office.

Blair, J.P. (1999). Detecting Deception: The Effects of the Reid Behavioral Analysis Interview Training, unpublished master's thesis. Macomb: Western Illinois University.

Bull, R. (1999). Police Investigative Interviewing. In Memon, A. and Bull, R., Eds., *Handbook of the Psychology of Interviewing* (pp. 279–292). Chichester: Wiley.

Cherryman, J. and Bull, R. (2000). Reflections on Investigative Interviewing. In Leishman, F., Loveday, B., and Savage, S., Eds., *Core Issues in Policing*, 2nd ed. (pp. 147–159). London: Longman.

Gordon, N. and Fleisher, W. (2002). *Effective Interview and Interrogation Techniques*. San Diego, CA: Academic Press.

Hakkanen, H., Ask, K., Kebbell, M., Alison, L., and Granhag, P.A. (2008). Police Officers' Views of Effective Interview Tactics with Suspects: The Effects of Weight of Case Evidence and Discomfort with Ambiguity. *Applied Cognitive Psychology*, 23:468–481.

Holmberg, U. (2004). Police Interview with Victims and Suspects of Violent and Sexual Crimes, Interviewees' Experiences and Interview Outcomes, unpublished Ph.D. thesis. Stockholm University.

Holmes, W. (2003). *Criminal Interrogation: A Modern Format for Interrogating Criminal Suspects Based on the Intellectual Approach*. Springfield, IL: Charles C Thomas.

Horvath, F., Blair, J.P., and Buckley, J.P. (2008). The Behavioral Analysis Interview: Clarifying the Practice, Theory, and Understanding of Its Use and Effectiveness. *International Journal of Police Science and Management*, 10(1):101–118.

Horvath, F., Jayne, B.P., and Buckley, J.P. (1994). Differentiation of Truthful and Deceptive Criminal Suspects in Behavioral Analysis Interviews. *Journal of Forensic Sciences*, 39:793–807.

Inbau, F.E., Reid, J.E., and Buckley, J.P. (1986). *Criminal Interrogation and Confessions*, 3rd ed. Baltimore, MD: Williams & Wilkins.

Inbau, F.E., Reid, J.E., and Buckley, J.P. (2001). *Criminal Interrogation and Confessions*, 4th ed. Gaithersburg, MD: Aspen.

Jones, T., Maclean, B., and Young, J. (1986). *The Islington Crime Survey, Crime Victimization, and Policing in Inner City London*. London: Gower.

Layton, J. (2010). *How Police Interrogation Works*, http://people.howstuffworks.com/police-interrogation2.html.

Milne, B. and Bull, R. (1999). *Investigative Interviewing: Psychology and Practice*. Chichester: Wiley.

Moston, S. (1996). From Denial to Admission in Police Questioning of Suspects. In Davies, G., Lloyd-Bostock, S., McMurran, M., and Wilson, C., Eds., *Psychology, Law and Criminal Justice: International Developments in Research and Practice* (pp. 91–99). Berlin: de Gruyter.

Napier, M.R. and Adams, S.H. (2002). Criminal Confessions: Overcoming the Challenges. *FBI Law Enforcement Bulletin*, 71(11):9–15.

Smith, D.J. (1983). *Police and People in London: A Survey of Londoners*. London: Policy Studies Institute.

Vessel, J.D. (1998). Conducting Successful Interrogations. *FBI Law Enforcement Bulletin*, 67(10):70–78.

Vrij, A. (2003). "We Will Protect Your Wife and Child but Only If You Confess": Police Interrogations in England and the Netherlands. In Van Koppen, P.J. and Penrod, S.D., Eds., *Adversarial Versus Inquisitorial Justice: Psychological Perspectives on Criminal Justice Systems* (pp. 55–79). New York: Plenum Press.

Walkley, J. (1987). *Police Interrogation: Handbook for Investigators*. London: Police Review Publication.

Walters, S.B. (1996). *Principles of Kinesic Interview and Interrogation*. Boca Raton, FL: CRC Press.

Williamson, T.M. (1993). From Interrogation to Investigative Interviewing: Strategic Trends in Police Questioning. *Journal of Community and Social Psychology*, 3:89–99.

CHAPTER 6

Evidence

Cory Rodivich

Wichita, Kansas, Police Department

CHAPTER OBJECTIVES

After reading this chapter, you should be able to do the following:

1. Define the term *evidence*.
2. List and describe the general categories of evidence.
3. Discuss the linkage theory and Locard's theory of exchange.
4. List and describe the major types of physical evidence.
5. Discuss the generalist concept and its application to forensic field investigation.
6. Describe the methods of identification, collection, and preservation prescribed for the major types of physical evidence.

Chapter Outline

- Nature of Evidence
- Founding Theories of Forensic Investigation
- Importance of Information Gathering
- Major Types of Physical Evidence
- Generalist Concept
- Identification, Collection, and Preservation of Physical Evidence

---

NATURE OF EVIDENCE

Evidence can be defined as anything legally submitted to a tribunal or trier of fact (judge or jury) that tends to prove or disprove a fact in question. In a very practical sense, the two fundamental questions to be answered in any criminal investigation are what happened and who did it? Many specifics must absolutely be deduced to ultimately answer these questions with a reasonable degree of certainty, but anything that assists the investigator and, in turn, the trier of fact in answering these questions can be considered evidence. The term *anything* is, of course, very broad, but as we will discuss, the word *evidence* encompasses a broad range of objects, information, and observations. Evidence can be classified into three general categories: testimonial, documentary, and physical.

TESTIMONIAL EVIDENCE

Testimonial evidence includes the statements of victims, witnesses, and suspects that are gathered during the interview or interrogation process. Testimonial evidence, while often beneficial in establishing and understanding certain factors such as motive, has one major flaw—subjectivity. Humans are subjective beings, each bringing his or her own agenda and perceptions to the interview table and witness stand. At times, an agenda can include outright perjury. More often than not, the nature of this subjectivity is less deceitful and more a matter of perspective, centering on the individual's ability to perceive and remember events. A knife may appear to be quite large to a victim at the time of the incident and in light of all of the emotions that accompany being victimized, when in actuality the weapon recovered from the suspect was a small pocketknife. A witness who overhears another witness describing some detail regarding a suspect's appearance or behavior, which he himself did not observe, may absorb that information and later change his statements after convincing himself that he, too, observed this detail. Human beings, whether victim, witness, or suspect, are capable of distorting facts, sometimes purposefully for their benefit or the benefit of others and other times unconsciously. Although testimonial evidence is not to be ignored, the importance of documentary and physical evidence in evaluating the statements of individuals must always be recognized (Gardner, 2005).

DOCUMENTARY EVIDENCE

The three primary methods used to document the people, places, and things involved in criminal investigations are photography, sketching or diagramming, and notetaking. Photographs are visual representations that provide investigators with permanent records that can be examined and analyzed subsequent to crime scene investigations and all evidence-gathering activities. Photographs, in the most basic sense, effectively demonstrate what something looks like. Information regarding the appearance of a person, place, or thing is more easily and often more effectively communicated to the trier of fact with photographs rather than with verbal recollections and descriptions. Photographs are routinely entered as evidence in criminal court proceedings, with officers or investigators testifying that each photograph is a true, clear, and accurate representation of what they observed. Photographs are increasingly valuable when they are utilized to capture transient or temporary conditions, such as the appearance of a crime scene before it is processed or searched and the presence of items contained within before they are moved, altered, or collected. Photographs are often the only way a piece of evidence can be preserved for viewing, as in the case of physical injuries on living persons. Injuries and resulting wound patterns cannot be physically removed from individuals and will change over time, if not heal completely.

Sketches are drawn and measurements are obtained to record information that cannot be captured in photographs, such as the size and dimensions of a crime scene and specific locations of objects and items contained within it, as well as their spatial relationships. Sketches and measurements made in the field can then be utilized to construct polished, scale drawings from a two-dimensional or three-dimensional perspective; these, again, can be presented to the trier of fact as true, clear, and accurate visual representations of what was observed or examined by investigators. Similar to photographs, diagrams can greatly assist the trier of fact in gaining an understanding of the people, places, and things involved and the events that occurred during both the commission and investigation of a crime.

Notes are written to document information that cannot be captured in either photographs or diagrams, such as sounds, smells, temperatures, nonvisual postmortem changes in a deceased victim, or the actual ambient lighting conditions present at a crime scene. To photograph a pitch-dark room or space, with the intention of demonstrating the appearance of the interior, light must be artificially injected into the room. The exposed photograph will show what the interior of the room looked like, but the image itself, the room being illuminated, does not accurately reflect how the room appeared to the investigator at the time the photograph was taken. Notes provide a supplement to photographs and diagrams, painting a complete and clear picture of the observations made by investigators for the trier of fact.

PHYSICAL EVIDENCE

Physical evidence takes the form of specific, tangible items collected during criminal investigations for subsequent examination, analysis, and presentation. The term *physical* does not necessarily imply that the item is visible to the eye; often, the most compelling physical evidence requires some form of development or instrumentation to visualize. The underlying importance of physical evidence is that it is real and tangible and cannot be denied; physical evidence never lies. Failure to understand the true nature and significance of physical evidence lies strictly in the human elements of its identification, collection, and examination. Properly considered, physical evidence establishes a framework of facts and objective knowledge that will guide both the investigator's understanding of the crime being investigated and the trier of fact's subsequent decision as to the guilt or innocence of the defendant (Gardner, 2005). The remainder of this chapter focuses on physical evidence.

FOUNDING THEORIES OF FORENSIC INVESTIGATION

As is discussed in the following chapter, forensic science involves the application of professional and scientific disciplines to the examination and analysis of physical evidence. The process of bringing an article of physical evidence up to the point of examination is just as intensive, involving the three main activities of identification, collection, and preservation. The most difficult aspect of this process is identification, which requires above all that the investigator be critically observant and highly inquisitive. The initial stage of the identification process involves application of the two founding theories of forensic investigation.

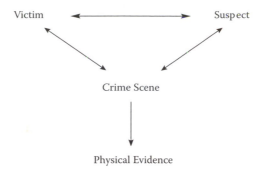

FIGURE 6.1 Linkage theory.

LINKAGE THEORY

The linkage theory is illustrated in Figure 6.1. The three main factors in the overall equation of most criminal investigations are the victim, the suspect, and the crime scene. Each of these factors can be and many times is plural in number. It is important to note that, although this chapter is not solely devoted to crime scene investigation, a definition of the term *crime scene* would be beneficial. A crime scene is traditionally thought of as a location, a home, a business, a parking lot, a vehicle, etc. This is true in every case, as the crime has to be committed somewhere, but from an evidentiary point of view this definition is very restrictive. A crime scene can, in fact, be any person, place, or thing from which physical evidence can be recovered. When considering such relevant concepts as custody, integrity, and contamination, one can see the similarities between a living room, a firearm, a victim's corpse, and a suspect's clothing.

A quintessential goal of investigations involving crimes against property and persons is to establish a linkage between these factors through physical evidence. In a very practical sense, the linkage theory targets the investigator's search by directing evidence-gathering activities toward the factor missing from the equation. Suppose that the scene of a sexual assault was reported as being the victim's home; in this case, the investigator's search would concentrate on identifying and collecting physical evidence that would place the suspect inside the scene, as that person did not reside within the victim's home. If the crime scene is a neutral location, such as a parking lot or outdoor venue, where the presence of neither the victim nor the suspect can be strictly established, then physical evidence originating from both individuals would be valuable. If the crime scene is a common location, as in cases involving domestic violence or locations with unlimited public access and traffic (such as a 24-hour convenience store), where the presence of both the victim and suspect is not extraordinary, then the face value of physical evidence can possibly be diminished. The linkage theory, therefore, also assists the investigator in assessing the probative or evidentiary value of articles of potential physical evidence—that is, whether an item tends to prove a fact in question or aids in the investigation.

Factors that can potentially strengthen the linkages among victims, suspects, and crime scenes, and thus the probative value of physical evidence, are the basic nature of the evidence itself and the context in which it is located. In some cases, especially when suspects state that they have never visited a particular scene or location, the mere presence of physical evidence, such as a fingerprint, is valuable as it refutes the suspect's statement. Some forms of biological or DNA evidence are inherently valuable just because of what they are and the implications that accompany them. If the victim and suspect both state that the suspect was invited into the victim's home and drank a glass of water prior to the sexual assault, then the suspect's fingerprint on the drinking glass is explainable and not very probative. The suspect's seminal fluid atop the couch where the assault was reported to occur not only places the suspect inside the home but also places him there in a very specific and probative context, that of sexual intercourse. Blood is inherently valuable because it establishes not only the individual's presence inside of a crime scene but also his or her active participation in a disturbance or violent crime. In the case of a non-residential burglary where a fingerprint recovered from the remaining glass within the broken window used to gain entry is identified as belonging to an employee of the business, the mere presence of the fingerprint is not entirely probative because of the employee's consistent access to the window. If the glass within the window is double-paned and the fingerprint was recovered from the exterior side of the interior glass panel, the probative value of the fingerprint has now significantly increased because of the context in which it was located; the fingerprint could not have been deposited without the exterior glass panel being shattered first.

LOCARD'S THEORY OF EXCHANGE

Edmond Locard is credited with starting the first crime laboratory in Lyons, France, in 1910. Locard's theory of exchange can be simply stated as every contact leaves a trace, meaning that when a person comes into contact with an object or another person an exchange of material (i.e., physical evidence) will occur; the person will leave something behind and take something with him. Numerous factors exist that affect the forensic value of this exchanged material, but Locard's theory of exchange faithfully serves investigators by directing them to the types of physical evidence potentially left within or taken from crime scenes and the locations of such evidence.

Locard's theory of exchange is often successfully applied by investigators trying to place themselves in the shoes of perpetrators. What would the suspect have to contact in order for him to accomplish what he did inside the scene? For a burglary incident, where the suspect's point of entry was a window unit, the ground below the window unit may bear partial footwear impressions; an air-conditioning unit located adjacent to the window may have been utilized by the suspect as a boost and may also bear footwear impressions, as well as fingerprints; and jagged glass remaining within the window frame through which the suspect crawled suggests the possibility of the suspect being injured and bleeding within the scene. As Locard's theory implies, it is important for the investigator to also realize what the suspect may have taken from the scene. Soil or vegetation from the ground below the window may be trapped in the suspect's shoes. If entry was made by prying open a door, paint from the door may be embedded on the marking edge of the tool used and retained by the suspect. Investigators should strive to identify and collect not only unknown, evidentiary samples but also known standards for subsequent comparison.

It is also important to note the interrelationship between the linkage theory and Locard's theory of exchange, with the linkage theory representing the goal and Locard's theory the means by which to achieve the goal. In the case of the scene of a sexual assault reported to be the suspect's residence, an investigator who applies the linkage theory would realize that physical evidence left by the victim would be most probative. The application of Locard's theory then alerts the investigator to the specific types of physical evidence potentially resulting from sexual intercourse. This seems very simplistic, but when presented with the absence of obvious pieces of physical evidence, such as a used condom, the investigator's search for bodily fluids will be affected by this information, as the fluids deposited by males and the fluids deposited by females during intercourse are entirely different pieces of material.

The underlying concept addressed in Locard's theory of exchange is that of transfer, the transfer of materials when people and objects come into contact. The materials that are transferred, both left behind and removed, become physical evidence that assists in establishing linkages among the victim, suspect, and crime scene. The concept of transfer can serve to direct the flow of an entire investigation; just as suspects can be tracked through cellular phone pings and stolen credit card purchases, suspects can be tracked through the continual transfer of physical evidence. Blood is transferred from the victim to the suspect's clothing in a stabbing incident, resulting in primary transfer. The victim's blood is then possibly transferred to the driver's seat of the suspect's car as he flees the scene, resulting in secondary transfer. The following day, traces of the victim's blood are then possibly transferred to the clothing of the suspect's roommate, who is also permitted to drive the vehicle, resulting in tertiary transfer. The suspect's vehicle and the roommate's clothing now constitute additional articles of physical evidence that can and should be pursued by investigators.

The possibility of transfer can be either limited or expansive based on the nature of the material involved. In the previous example, the victim's fingerprint was not able to be transferred to the suspect's clothing for a variety of reasons. The victim's blood, on the other hand, was dynamic, capable of movement and flight, offering evidentiary value of personal identification not dependent on factors such as surface characteristics and pattern formation. As will be discussed, biological/DNA evidence and those articles categorized as trace evidence are most often associated with this concept of continual transfer. Presented with these materials, a skilled, observant, and inquisitive investigator can take the concept of transfer and run with it, striving to think "outside of the box." Upon arriving at the scene of a residential robbery, for example, an investigator notices that the home interior is covered in hair shed from the victim's dog. Just as in humans, unique DNA signatures are also located in the cells of animals. Presented with statements from the victim that he and the unknown suspect fought on the living room floor during the incident, the investigator recognizes the potential transfer of pet hair to the suspect's clothing. The dog shed on the floor, resulting in primary transfer; the suspect then contacted the floor and removed pet hair, resulting in secondary transfer. The examination and comparison of exemplars collected by the investigator from the dog and samples subsequently recovered from the suspect's clothing can objectively link the suspect to the crime scene through the victim's pet.

IMPORTANCE OF INFORMATION GATHERING

Every case and every crime scene is unique, presenting a singular set of facts and circumstances. To ensure the most effective and thorough collection of physical evidence, the investigator must be knowledgeable of the facts and events surrounding the commission of the crime. This information is generally gathered in two ways: (1) from the statements of individuals involved, including the victim, suspect, witnesses, and first responders (e.g., police, fire, and EMS personnel); and (2) from observations made by the investigator during his preliminary survey of the crime scene. A skilled investigator can make determinations from his observations of the crime scene and also formulate questions for those individuals involved by applying the linkage theory and Locard's theory of exchange; doing so also targets evidence collection efforts and ultimately strengthens the case.

In the case of a sexual assault, details regarding the sexual nature of the incident can be useful information. If penetration was made in a specific manner, the investigator can expand his search to include items such as lubrication devices and the presence of blood and fecal material. Valuable evidence can also certainly be located outside of the immediate perimeter where the assault occurred. Inquiring of the victim whether the suspect utilized a condom and, if so, where the condom itself and the wrapper were disposed of can be valuable information. Also very useful is attempting to account for the suspect's actions before, during, and after the incident. If the victim reports that the suspect had never been inside of her home prior to the incident, then the mere presence of physical evidence deposited by the suspect becomes important. Insightful questions for the victim would address anything that the suspect may have touched, eaten, drunk from, or smoked, so his presence can be objectively established within the scene. If multiple cigarette butts are located within the residence, follow-up information should be sought from the victim regarding the brand of cigarettes she smokes, in an attempt to isolate a stray brand possibly originating from the suspect. If the victim reports that the suspect entered the residence's bathroom immediately following the incident, the suspect could have urinated in the toilet (also possibly leaving behind traces of seminal material) or cleaned himself with any towel, rag, or tissue present. If, upon viewing the interior of the bathroom, towels are scattered about the floor, further clarifying questions to the victim may assist in isolating a particular one. Often, items that are very common and ordinary inside of a particular location can be very important pieces of physical evidence. Recognition of the importance of such items is dependent upon the investigator's insight and ability in gathering relevant information.

Key to investigating violent crimes is the examination of the victim and any physical injuries. Examination of a shooting victim could indicate that the firearm was in close range to the victim at the time it was discharged. When the firearm is recovered, it can be processed for physical evidence linking both the victim and suspect to it; for example, material deposited by the suspect might be found on the grips and any articles required to operate the firearm, and biological evidence from the victim might be located around the muzzle and tip of the gun barrel. In a very practical sense, an examination of a shooting victim and information gathered from medical personnel and treatment can alert the investigator to the number of bullets still present inside the victim. When the number of shots fired during the incident has been established, the bullets within the victim do not have to be searched or accounted for at the scene.

The absence of such relevant case information is a regular occurrence. Scene investigators must often operate within the realm of possibility, which, as it sounds, increases their workload. What is paramount is that investigators always err on the side of caution. Physical evidence that is not properly documented or collected is always worthless.

MAJOR TYPES OF PHYSICAL EVIDENCE

Although not all inclusive, the following sections cover the major and most common types of physical evidence encountered by investigators. More detailed descriptions regarding the nature of each is included in the following chapter, along with the potential results obtained from the forensic analysis of physical evidence and the investigative information generated from these results.

FINGERPRINTS

The fingers and palms of the hands, as well as the soles of the feet, of human beings have friction ridge skin, composed of complex patterns of hills and valleys designed for gripping purposes. Within a fingerprint pattern are a number of features known as ridge characteristics or minutiae, which, based upon their identity, number, and relative location, serve as a means of personal identification.

BIOLOGICAL/DNA EVIDENCE

The chemical blueprint of life itself, DNA is found in structures contained in cells, including nuclei and mitochondria. Because bodily fluids, tissues, and organs are comprised of cells, these body materials can be used for DNA typing as a means of personal identification.

TRACE EVIDENCE

Trace evidence simply refers to physical evidence that is small in size and includes materials and substances such as hair, fibers, paint, glass, and soil.

FIREARMS EVIDENCE

Firearms evidence includes the firearms themselves and the ammunition components contained within or expelled from the gun during the firing process.

TOOLMARK EVIDENCE

Toolmarks are patterns resulting from a harder marking device, or tool, being forced against a softer object, usually in an attempt to force entry into, for example, a dwelling, business, or storage unit.

IMPRESSION EVIDENCE

Impressions most often take the form of footwear and tire-tread marks deposited on a variety of yielding or unyielding surfaces within a crime scene.

OTHER PHYSICAL EVIDENCE

Articles of physical evidence also commonly encountered by police or investigative personnel include drugs and drug paraphernalia, documents of a questionable nature, various tools and blunt- and sharp-force weapons, clothing, bedding, and beverage cans and bottles. In accordance with the linkage theory and Locard's theory of exchange, physical forms of physical evidence, such as those listed above, can be examined for additional forensic evidence, such as fingerprints, DNA, and trace evidence, to identify people and substances and thus establish linkages to aid in the investigation.

GENERALIST CONCEPT

Given the subjective nature of testimonial evidence and current trends in popular culture regarding the availability and popularity of forensic science and investigation among potential jury members, a strong emphasis has been placed on physical evidence and its analysis in the investigation and prosecution of crime. The investigation of crime scenes and the identification, collection, and preservation of physical evidence can therefore be considered as the foundations of criminal investigation. As previously discussed and is further discussed in the following chapter, numerous classifications of physical evidence exist to assist investigators in proving their cases. To ensure an efficient and effective investigation of the crime scene and all associated physical evidence, an investigator must possess not only a detailed and thorough knowledge of the identification, collection, and preservation methods prescribed to each particular classification but also the probative value of what the evidence may reveal.

Two positions within the field of forensic investigation are the *specialist*, an individual who possesses educational and professional expertise in a particular discipline such as fingerprint examination and DNA analysis, and the *generalist*, an individual who, although less formally educated, possesses a well-rounded and experienced knowledge base and skill set in a variety of forensic disciplines. Crime scene investigators may specialize in disciplines more applicable to field investigation, such as photography, death investigation, and bloodstain pattern analysis, but ideally they are generalists who can perform a variety of tasks with regard to physical evidence identification and collection and can draw conclusions about what an article of evidence may reveal upon examination. The ability of the investigator to make frontline judgments as to the probative and evidentiary value of an article of potential physical evidence can serve to direct, focus, and target the subsequent investigation of the case.

IDENTIFICATION, COLLECTION, AND PRESERVATION OF PHYSICAL EVIDENCE

The recovery of physical evidence consists of three main phases—identification, collection, and preservation—each of which presents unique challenges and responsibilities to the investigator.

IDENTIFICATION

The identification of physical evidence commences with the gathering of relevant and specific case information through observation and inquiry. Before investigators can search for evidence, they must be aware of what they are searching for. When the investigator has gained an understanding of the available facts of the case and the events occurring during commission of the crime, the next step in the process is application of Locard's theory of exchange. Directed to the types of physical evidence potentially left within the scene and their locations, the investigator can now begin the practical process of searching. Although different methodologies exist to adapt and increase the effectiveness of crime scene searches to specific surroundings, it is paramount that the search be organized and systematic to ensure that nothing is overlooked, missed, or lost, regardless if the area being searched is as contained as the interior of a residence, as expansive as an open field, or as specific as an article of furniture or the blade of a knife.

Directed to a specific surface or location, the investigator then employs a series of presumptive tests, proceeding from the least destructive means to the most destructive means. The first presumptive test is the investigator's eyes. Physical evidence can be very visible to the eye, as in the case of firearms and the ammunition components expelled from such; it can also be very invisible to the eye, as in the case of some bodily fluids and other DNA evidence. The second presumptive test is essentially another set of eyes, directing light and light sources to increase visibility. Side or oblique lighting—positioning a light source (usually a high-powered flashlight) parallel to a surface—is particularly useful in locating physical objects such as spent bullets or cartridge cases, as distinct shadows will be cast along the surrounding areas and surfaces, as well as in finding impressions such as fingerprints, toolmarks, or footwear on flat surfaces. At this stage in the process, specific types of physical evidence can require specific light sources to make them visible. The use of a forensic alternate light source (ALS) is particularly useful in dealing with various types of DNA, trace, and fingerprint evidence that respond to individual wavelengths or bandwidths of light in contrast with the surfaces upon which they are located. These visual mediums of identification constitute the least destructive presumptive tests, as they do not require the forensic evidence potentially located on items being examined to be significantly handled, moved, or altered in any way.

Proceeding to more destructive means, the methodologies for identifying physical evidence that may require further clarification or development are dependent on the specific types of evidence being sought. Various chemical and physical methods can be employed to locate fingerprints and footwear impressions not readily visible under existing or directed light. Chemical presumptive tests can be performed on suspect stains visualized with a forensic alternate light source to distinguish bodily fluids from non-evidentiary foreign material. In either case, the evidentiary material is now being significantly handled, altered, and potentially contaminated.

COLLECTION

Methods of collection likewise vary with the specific type of evidence being recovered, but, generally speaking, physical evidence is collected by collecting the whole article, sampling or removing evidence from the article, and/or photographing the article in a manner proceeding from most transient to least transient. Similar to the process of identification, the sequence in which specific articles of physical evidence are collected is extremely important. This sequence is determined by the investigator after careful observation of the nature and condition of the crime scene. Physical evidence that is transient or conditional is collected first. Transient evidence is physical evidence that is easily moved or lost due to factors outside the control of the investigator, including weather or environmental conditions. Imagine a hair strand embedded in the broken windshield of a vehicle involved in a vehicular homicide case on a windy day or a footwear impression in the snow being filled in by continued snowfall. Conditional evidence is physical evidence that is easily altered, lost, or compromised in some way, due to subsequent actions taken by the investigator. Areas and items that need to be contacted in order for the investigator to operate within the scene should be considered and examined before action is taken. If the tiled kitchen floor is in the investigator's path toward the body of a murder victim, the floor should first be examined for possible footwear impressions prior to walking on it. Trace evidence possibly located on the bedroom floor surrounding the bed where a sexual assault was reported to occur should be collected prior to the investigator approaching the bed to conduct his examination.

The idea of conditional evidence works in tandem with the generalist concept and the investigator's knowledge of forensic analysis. The possibility of recovering multiple types of forensic evidence from single objects such as firearms, soda cans, and strands of duct tape used to bind a victim is often high. Physical and chemical methods of identification and collection prescribed for a certain type of forensic evidence may adversely affect the evidentiary value of another type of evidence. DNA evidence, for example, can possibly be contaminated by any number of materials contained within chemicals used in fingerprint processing.

An introduction to the common methods for collecting major types of physical evidence is provided below. Some pieces of physical evidence, mainly impression evidence such as fingerprints, footwear, and tire treads, are capable of being examined and compared from photographs. Although photographs of these items or the surfaces that contain them are routinely taken for documentary purposes, examination-quality photographs must be taken very specifically. The camera must first be positioned in a manner 90° to the subject matter. Exposure settings on the camera must then be adjusted to maximize the area of acceptably sharp focus within the image, known as depth of field. This is especially critical for three-dimensional impressions, such as those deposited in mud or other yielding materials. To meet these two standards, the use of a tripod or copy stand is essential. The subject matter must then be composed within the frame of view so the frame is filled, with minimal dead space. A rule or scale must then be inserted into the image to establish the exact size and dimensions of the subject matter. The camera is positioned 90° to the subject matter to reduce distortion and ensure the accuracy of these measurements. In the current age of digital photography, an additional step in the process is to adjust the resolution settings on the camera to reduce file compression and ensure that the highest and sharpest level of detail is presented to the examiner. The initial consideration in this process, however, is the appropriate light source and lighting technique. As previously discussed, visualization of certain types of evidence requires the use of a forensic alternate light source, whereas others only require that light be directed from a certain position.

PRESERVATION

Preservation of physical evidence involves packaging and storing evidence following its collection. The goal of evidence preservation is twofold: (1) preservation of the evidence itself, ensuring that the item or material does not degrade or decompose, and (2) preservation of the evidentiary value of the item or material by inhibiting cross-contamination. The preservation of evidence is accomplished by ensuring that the items are dry prior to packaging, are packaged in the proper storage medium, and are stored in the proper environment following packaging. With the exception of accelerants and flammable liquids that will evaporate if not packaged in airtight containers, the preferred storage medium for the majority of physical evidence is paper. Paper is breathable, which allows residual moisture to dry and inhibits the growth of molds and bacteria, which can have a detrimental effect, particularly on biological evidence. The proper storage environment exhibits two consistent characteristics, regardless of the type of evidence: the absence of direct sunlight and consistent temperature and humidity levels. Most physical evidence can be stored appropriately under room-temperature conditions. Biological evidence and items bearing such can be refrigerated; however, with the exception of whole fluid samples, this is not necessary as long as the above standards are maintained.

The evidentiary value of physical evidence must be maintained by inhibiting cross-contamination. Cross-contamination is directly associated with Locard's theory of exchange and is caused by the inappropriate handling and packaging of physical evidence, particularly trace and biological evidence. By exposing one item to another, evidence from the first is transferred to the second and *vice versa*. Biological evidence is especially susceptible to this, as samples originating from different individuals can be present on the same object. Items such as clothing and bedding articles, where different parts can be folded onto one another and easily make contact, must be packaged accordingly to ensure the integrity of each evidentiary sample. Remember that one of the primary goals in gathering and analyzing physical evidence is to establish linkages among the victim, suspect, and crime scene. Evidence originating from each of these factors must be packaged separately to maintain the probative value of results generated from the comparisons of unknown samples and known standards.

It should also be noted that cross-contamination can occur much earlier, in the collection process. Whether in the field or in a laboratory setting, evidence handled with common tools and implements and on common surfaces can certainly result in the transfer of material between items. During the course of an investigation, it is possible that the scene investigator could respond to multiple scenes, including the residences of both the victim and the suspect, and encounter multiple persons, including the victim and suspect, in a relatively short period of time. The investigator must take precautions to safeguard against the transfer of material from one location, one item, one tool, or one person to another. This is best accomplished by the use of disposable or single-use collection implements when appropriate and the use of personal protective equipment, including gloves, masks, eye protectors, shoe covers, head covers, and disposable coveralls.

FINGERPRINTS

Three types of fingerprints are encountered by investigators. Patent prints are caused by deposits of contaminants, including blood, grease, or ink, that are visible to the naked eye. Plastic prints are deposited in soft, pliable materials, such as clay, putty, and wax. Latent prints, the type most commonly encountered by investigators, are created by the deposit of bodily secretions, including water, oils, salts, and amino acids; they are not readily visible to the eye and require some form of development.

Patent prints, depending on the contaminant material used in depositing the impression, can potentially be further developed and enhanced. Patent prints deposited with blood are the most common form of visible fingerprints encountered during scene investigations and are especially valuable because, based on the linkage theory, what better piece of evidence could be recovered than the suspect's fingerprint made with the victim's blood? Chemical reagents used in processing patent prints deposited with blood are designed to react with products present in blood (proteins and amino acids). The resulting reaction forms colors along the friction ridges that allow for better visualization. Patent prints should be photographed at examination quality before and after chemical treatment, with the substrate itself also being collected, if possible.

Plastic prints are three-dimensional impressions deposited in soft receiving surfaces. Plastic prints should be photographed at examination quality; light directed from a certain position, as will be discussed with footwear and tire-tread impressions, can possibly enhance the level of detail displayed. In these instances, photographs will most often represent the best evidence, with the substrate itself, again, being collected, if possible.

Latent prints are developed by a variety of physical and chemical means. The appropriate processing method for developing latent prints is dependent on two major factors: surface and time. Use of powder and brush remains the primary physical method for developing fingerprints on smooth, nonporous surfaces and on items found at crime scenes, such as glass, plastics, and vehicle frames. Fingerprint powders exist in a variety of forms, all designed to provide contrast with the background surface and increase visibility. The developed impressions are collected using a variety of lifting mediums, including tape, gelatin lifters, and silicon-based casting materials. Numerous chemical methods exist to process both nonporous and more textured, porous items, such as paper, tape, cardboard, and untreated wood, for latent fingerprints when both time and surface characteristics present adverse conditions.

Chemicals that react with residual body materials are particularly useful when water, the primary component within the bodily secretions forming the print, has either evaporated over time on a smooth, nonporous surface or been absorbed into a more textured, porous surface such as paper. Some chemical processes are useful when the suspected surface displays a great deal of noise, such as overlapping colors, brand names, and logos, which could easily obscure prints even after their development. Certain chemical solutions, when viewed with filtration under a forensic alternate light source, will fluoresce, thereby highlighting the impression itself and greatly reducing the background noise. Due to several practicalities, including the need for specialized pieces of equipment, shelf life of chemical mixtures, and safety of those persons involved, chemical processes are almost exclusively conducted in a laboratory setting. Fingerprints developed via strictly chemical means are incapable of being lifted and are collected and preserved through examination-quality photography.

BIOLOGICAL/DNA EVIDENCE

For the crime scene investigator, anything of biological origin (originating from an individual) is a potential source of DNA evidence. According to Locard's theory of exchange, anything that has come into contact with an individual is a potential source of DNA evidence. Clothing and jewelry, for example, are easily identifiable and simple to collect as evidence. The identification and collection of body materials, both visible and invisible (e.g., fluids and skin cells), are much more intensive and technical.

Bodily fluids are the most common form of DNA evidence encountered by scene investigators and analyzed by examiners. Some bodily fluids, depending on their individual nature and the contrast of the background surface upon which the stain lies, can be readily visible to the eye, such as blood; others, such as seminal fluid, vaginal secretions, urine, saliva, and sweat, often require the use of forensic alternate light sources to make them apparent. Generally speaking, forensic alternate light sources direct individual wavelengths or bandwidths of light toward a surface that are then either reflected or absorbed by that surface. Seminal fluid stains located on a couch cushion are an entirely different type of matter than the fibers composing the cushion; therefore, the fluid stains will reflect the wavelengths or bandwidths of light differently than the cushion's background, thereby distinguishing the stain from the cushion. Because the human eye can only visualize every wavelength within the visible spectrum of light, barrier filters placed over the eyes of the investigator and the lens of the camera greatly assist in visualizing the resulting fluorescence.

While not every substance detected on various surfaces is a bodily fluid, chemical presumptive tests designed to react with specific enzymes, such as acid phosphatase in seminal fluid and amylase in saliva, can then be employed to further indicate the presence of bodily fluids and distinguish them from other foreign materials. Blood does not fluoresce under a forensic alternate light source, but blood on dark-colored surfaces can be detected at certain wavelengths due to its absorption rate contrasting with that of the background. Most often, blood is visible at crime scenes and upon the items contained within. Various chemical solutions are available to detect latent bloodstains, possibly resulting from a suspected clean-up attempt, and to test presumptively for blood to safeguard against false positive reactions or to distinguish blood from similar-looking substances.

There are four primary methods for collecting DNA evidence from crime scenes and objects contained within. Easily portable articles, including clothing, jewelry, cigarette butts, and discarded pieces of chewing gum, can simply be collected. Some DNA samples, such as seminal fluid stains on carpet and whole urine in a toilet, can also be physically removed or cut from the substrate. DNA samples of bodily fluids and epithelial skin cells sloughed from hands in contact with rough or abrasive surfaces can also be sampled or absorbed using sterile cotton or polyester swabs. Bodily fluids in dry form can also be scraped into packaging mediums such as glassine envelopes or druggist folds using sterile, sharp implements.

As is discussed in the following chapter, the end result of a DNA analysis is a statistic that defines the probability of the chance duplication of a particular DNA profile within ethnic groups—in other words, the chance of the generated DNA profile belonging to a person other than the one represented in the submitted exemplar. The discriminatory nature and, hence, the evidentiary value of this statistic is determined by two major factors: size and purity. With regard to collection, the investigator should strive to recover and concentrate as much of the sample as possible, with as little dilution or contamination of the sample as possible. This is particularly important when articles of physical evidence can be processed for both fingerprints and DNA, such as firearms, soda cans, latex gloves, and patent prints deposited with blood, or when known DNA sources are being processed for unknown or evidentiary DNA sources, including cases involving bitemarks and fingernail scrapings, where improper or imprecise collection techniques can make the known person being processed the major contributor in a mixture of DNA profiles.

TRACE EVIDENCE

Trace evidence includes materials and substances, such as hairs, fibers, paint, glass, and soil, which are small in size and easily transferred from one person or object to another. The stray head or pubic hair shed by an unknown suspect can be a valuable piece of evidence, as hair is also a potential source of DNA. Oblique lighting and the use of a forensic alternate light source are useful techniques for observing and locating hairs at the crime scene or upon suspects' or victims' bodies and clothing. When hair strands have been located, they can be collected using tweezers, forceps, or even sticky notes and placed into primary containers, such as druggist folds or glassine envelopes. The use of tape lifts when systematically processing distinctive areas at the crime scene, including carpeting, furniture, and vehicle interiors, is also effective in isolating freshly deposited hair evidence. The identification and collection of fiber evidence are accomplished in similar ways, with the assistance of a forensic alternate light source and the use of the picking or tape-lifting methods.

Paint evidence is commonly associated with vehicle crashes or collisions and pry tools utilized in forcing entry into structures and storage mediums. Intact paint chips are ideally suited for examination, as they reveal layering characteristics; they can be collected with the use of tweezers, forceps, or tape lifts and then packaged in storage mediums such as druggist folds and glassine envelopes. Paint smears or scrapings are often the result of objects forcibly contacting each other. If feasible, the article bearing the paint smear should be collected as evidence. If necessary, the sample can be scraped into the packaging medium with a sharp instrument, taking care to recover the entire sample or as much of it as possible.

Glass fragments resulting from broken windows in burglary incidents or broken windshields and headlamps in vehicular assaults are often transferred to the victim or suspect and their clothing. The previously described collection methods of picking, scraping, and tape lifting are also effective with glass evidence. Due to the sharp and brittle nature of glass, such packaging mediums as evidence tins should be selected to ensure both safety and preservation. Large fragments of glass should be preserved intact to facilitate additional forensic examinations, such as fracture comparisons and direction of force determinations.

Soil evidence is often recovered from shoes, tires, and vehicle wheel wells and undercarriages and is associated with like forms of impression evidence. Soil samples can be taken at certain distance intervals from the impressions or areas of contact to ensure that representative samples from the areas involved are obtained. The previously described collection methods of picking, scraping, and tape lifting are also effective for soil evidence. In cases involving the compaction of soil on surfaces such as vehicle wheel wells and undercarriages, efforts should be made to recover intact samples to preserve the layering and stratification of the soil content which may be representative of particular locations.

FIREARMS EVIDENCE

Firearms and the ammunition components present within and expelled from them are visible objects; however, fired projectiles and cartridge cases ejected from specific firearms can be difficult to locate, considering the myriad factors involved in a shooting incident that can affect their behavior. Establishing the trajectories of fired projectiles using tools such as trajectory rods and lasers can assist investigators in locating both projectile fragments and spent cartridge cases by isolating the paths taken by the fired projectiles and the physical locations of shooters within scenes. Once directed to specific locations, investigators can then utilize techniques such as oblique lighting or tools such as metal detectors to assist in the search. The condition and functioning properties of a firearm, such as the status of the safety mechanism and the presence of any chambered rounds, should be noted prior to its unloading and collection. Revolvers hold ammunition inside of individual chambers within a rotating cylinder, and the chamber aligned with the barrel should be noted before the cylinder is released. Firearms should never be collected by inserting a tool inside the barrel, so as to not destroy any possible DNA or trace evidence or alter the rifling of the barrel. Likewise, fired projectiles and spent cartridge cases should never be collected using sharp or metal instruments, so as to not obliterate, obscure, or alter any identifiable markings used for comparison.

TOOLMARK EVIDENCE

Toolmarks commonly encountered by the investigator are made by prying, clawing, or cutting instruments being impressed into or slid across a surface. Portable items bearing toolmarks, such as metal strike plates on doorjambs and cut padlock bolts, should be collected intact. Samples from cut wiring, such as telephone wires cut to disable security alarms and bound copper wiring cut or stolen from electrical boxes to sell, can be cut from the remaining wiring, being sure to include the end severed by the suspect's tool. Prior to packaging, the end of the wire sample cut by the investigator should be designated to alert the examiner of which end requires his attention. Toolmarks on immovable or nonportable items can be recovered using silicone-based casting materials that are extruded or smeared onto the surface bearing the markings. Once dry, the cast can then be removed and packaged accordingly. Intact samples as described above and toolmark casts should be packaged in such a manner to avoid abrasive contact with the markings. Similarly, care must be taken to protect the blades, edges, or marking surfaces of recovered tools for subsequent comparison.

IMPRESSION EVIDENCE

Footwear and tire-tread impressions can be deposited onto two-dimensional, unyielding surfaces, such as glass, tile, linoleum, or wood flooring, and onto three-dimensional, soft, yielding surfaces, such as wet soil and snow. Similar to fingerprints, footwear and tire-tread impressions can be examined and compared using photographs. Impressions must first be photographed at examination quality, with light directed from a specific position. Two-dimensional impressions are best visualized with oblique lighting directed from a position parallel to the surface. The detail and tread patterns in three-dimensional impressions are best visualized by directing light from an angle above the surface to cast shadows from the raised areas in the impression into the valleys. An addition to photographs of lengthy tire-tread impressions is a tape measure or some form of measuring device to track the progress of capturing the entire circumference of the tire(s).

Similar to fingerprints, two-dimensional impressions can be patent or latent and, depending on certain factors, can be further enhanced or developed. Patent impressions made of dirt or soil are commonly encountered by investigators in cases such as burglaries involving forcible entry via kicking. Patent impressions deposited with blood can be further developed with similar blood reagents. Latent impressions encountered by investigators commonly take the form of residual moisture on the soles of shoes or disturbances in dusty surfaces. Latent impressions made with residual moisture can be further developed with fingerprint powder. Disturbances in dust, on the other hand, will simply be eradicated with the use of powder and a brush.

Two-dimensional impressions can be collected in a variety of ways. Patent blood impressions cannot be lifted after they have been chemically treated, thus the surface upon which the impression lies should be collected. Patent impressions deposited with dirt or soil, latent impressions developed with fingerprint powder, and impressions deposited on dusty surfaces can all be collected using various lifting mediums, including fingerprint tape and gelatin lifters. Impressions deposited on or made with dust matter can also be collected with electrostatic lifting devices. Three-dimensional impressions deposited in wet soil, snow, and other pliable mediums are collected by casting. Dental stone, a powdery substance used in dental laboratories when making crowns and similar items, is often the best suited material for casting three-dimensional impressions. The recovered lifts and casts should then be packaged in such a manner as to avoid creasing, folding, and breaking.

QUESTIONS FOR DISCUSSION

1. Define the term *evidence*.
2. List and describe the three general categories of evidence.
3. Discuss the linkage theory and its application to the identification of physical evidence.
4. Define Locard's theory of exchange and discuss the importance of the concept of transfer to forensic investigation.
5. Discuss the generalist concept and its importance to the complete and thorough processing of crime scenes and physical evidence.
6. Discuss the process of identifying physical evidence and the use of presumptive tests.
7. List and describe the collection methods for three types of physical evidence.
8. Define the terms *transient evidence* and *conditional evidence*.
9. Discuss the two major factors affecting the packaging and storing of physical evidence.

BIBLIOGRAPHY

Fish, J.T., Miller, L.S., and Braswell, M.C. (2007). *Crime Scene Investigation*. Newark, NJ: LexisNexis–Anderson Publishing.

Gaensslen, R.E., Harris, H.A., and Lee, H.C. (2008). *Introduction to Forensic Science and Criminalistics*. New York: McGraw-Hill.

Gardner, R.M. (2005). *Practical Crime Scene Processing and Investigation*. Boca Raton, FL: CRC Press.

Lee, H.C., Palmbach, T., and Miller, M.T. (2001). *Henry Lee's Crime Scene Handbook*. San Diego, CA: Elsevier Academic Press.

Saferstein, R. (2009). *Forensic Science: From the Crime Scene to the Crime Lab*. Upper Saddle River, NJ: Prentice Hall.

CHAPTER 7

Role of Forensic Science

Cory Rodivich

Wichita, Kansas, Police Department

CHAPTER OBJECTIVES

After reading this chapter, you should be able to do the following:

1. Define forensic science and its use in the criminal investigative process.
2. Identify the major responsibilities of the forensic scientist.
3. Discuss the potential information generated from the forensic analysis of physical evidence.
4. Discuss the potential results generated from the forensic analysis of physical evidence.
5. Describe the divisions of a typical, full-service crime laboratory.
6. List specialized forensic services available to investigators.

Chapter Outline

- Forensic Science and Criminal Investigation
- Responsibilities of the Forensic Scientist
- Forensic Analysis of Physical Evidence
- Results Generated from Forensic Analysis of Physical Evidence
- Modern, Full-Service Crime Laboratories
- Specialized Forensic Science Services

FORENSIC SCIENCE AND CRIMINAL INVESTIGATION

In its broadest sense, forensic science, or *criminalistics*, is the application of the natural and physical sciences, such as biology, chemistry, physics, and geology, to the law. More specifically, "Forensic science is the application of science to the criminal and civil laws that are enforced by police agencies in a criminal justice system" (Saferstein, 2009, p. 5) For the purposes of this text, forensic science is explored as it relates to its contribution to the process of investigating crime. Forensic science encompasses myriad disciplines and professions, each containing a specific knowledge base and skill set utilized in the processing and analysis of physical evidence to produce investigative leads. The two fundamental questions to be answered in any criminal investigation are what happened and who did it? Many specifics must certainly be deduced to ultimately answer these questions, with forensic science providing answers such as the identification of unknown substances, the linkage of persons and items to crime scenes, and the reconstruction of the sequence of events involved in a crime. It is imperative that the investigating officer be aware of the opportunities afforded by the application of forensic analysis and techniques.

Some forensic disciplines typically associated with the modern crime laboratory, such as drug chemistry, toxicology, and DNA analysis, are traditionally scientific, with analysis being performed in a laboratory setting utilizing processes such as microscopy, chromatography, mass spectrometry, electrophoresis, and associated pieces of equipment. Other forensic disciplines, found both inside and outside of the modern, budgeted crime laboratory, such as fingerprint examination, document examination, forensic engineering, bloodstain pattern analysis, and shooting incident reconstruction, while very technical, are traditionally less scientific and performed outside of the traditional laboratory setting. They utilize alternative pieces of equipment and rely on expert interpretation and specific, experimented principles associated with the discipline, such as the reaction of certain inks to ultraviolet and infrared energy, the structural failure rates of steel, the visual interpretation of bloodstain patterns and actions that could cause their deposit, and bullet perforation characteristics of specific materials and substances.

Regardless of the scientific or technical nature of the practicalities involved in the application of a forensic discipline, scientists must always be aware of their primary responsibilities and discharge them methodically, reliably, and consistently.

RESPONSIBILITIES OF THE FORENSIC SCIENTIST

The role of the forensic scientist is to generate investigative leads by applying the principles and techniques of the physical and natural sciences in the analysis of physical evidence and to provide expert testimony regarding the results and conclusions of the analysis.

ANALYSIS OF PHYSICAL EVIDENCE

The many types of physical evidence potentially recovered during criminal investigations were discussed in the previous chapter. The common factor shared by these various types of evidence is revealed in their analyses. The analysis of physical evidence must be grounded in scientific inquiry: "Science derives its integrity from the adherence to strict guidelines that ensure the careful and systematic collection, organization and analysis of information, a process known as the scientific method" (Saferstein, 2009, p. 25).

The scientific method is initiated by the formulation of a question requiring investigation, one as general as the identity of the perpetrator of a particular crime or one as specific as the location of the shooter in a homicide investigation. Based upon careful and inquisitive observation of the crime scene, for example, forensic scientists then formulate a hypothesis or plausible explanation proposed to answer the question. Developing ways to test the hypothesis through experimentation is the heart of the scientific method. The testing process must be controlled, thorough, and generally accepted as valid by the scientific community. Finally, when the hypothesis is validated by data generated from extensive and continuous experimentation, it becomes suitable as scientific evidence for use in criminal investigations and criminal court proceedings.

The inherent principles of the scientific method, specifically applied to criminal investigation, provide a safeguard by which the conclusions generated from the analysis of physical evidence cannot be tainted by bias or human emotion or compromised by the distortion or ignorance of contradictory evidence. In the context of criminal investigations, the scientific method distinguishes evidence from coincidence, pursues generalities to the level of specific details, disallows hypotheses more extraordinary than the facts themselves, allows tests to either prove or disprove alternative explanations, qualifies possible alternative results, and quantifies their degree of certainty (James and Nordby, 2005).

EXPERT WITNESS TESTIMONY

Trial courts have broad discretion in accepting individuals with expertise in a particular subject matter as expert witnesses. The competency of these experts may be established by educational degrees, attendance and participation in specialized training courses, membership in professional organizations, the amount and substance of professional publications, and, most importantly, the number of years of occupational experience. Generally, prosecutors and lawyers engage expert witnesses when the facts of a case remain unclear, the analytical procedures in their specific field assisted in generating investigative leads or in clarifying the facts of the case, or specialized training can further educate the trier of fact, thereby helping the judge or jury make more informed decisions as to the guilt or innocence of the accused (James and Nordby, 2005). In their role as expert witnesses, forensic scientists provide testimony that establishes the validity of the science or investigative technique itself, explains the methodology employed to conduct the analysis, and reveals the results generated from the analysis and how those results impact the case presented before the court. In accordance with the scientific method, expert witnesses cannot render any opinion or conclusion with absolute certainty. At best, they may only be able to render an opinion based on a reasonable, generally accepted scientific certainty derived from training, experience and experimentation (Saferstein, 2009). In an adversarial system of justice, forensic scientists should not be advocates for either the prosecution or defense, but only advocates of the truth.

FORENSIC ANALYSIS OF PHYSICAL EVIDENCE

As discussed in the previous chapter, the objective of any crime scene investigation is to identify, collect, and preserve all physical evidence relevant to a particular case. The forensic scientist analyzes articles of physical evidence in an attempt to provide the investigator with information that may assist in solving the case. Exploring the types of information that can be generated from the analysis of physical evidence helps to clarify its value to criminal investigations.

CORPUS DELICTI

Corpus delicti is a Latin term referring to the body or elements of a crime. These elements are provisions articulated in local ordinances and state and federal statutes that the prosecutor is obligated to prove beyond a reasonable doubt to secure a conviction of the accused based on the charges filed. In a case involving illegal drug possession, for example, the green botanical substance recovered from the suspect's pockets must be established as containing *Cannabis* (marijuana). In a case involving the accused being suspected of driving a vehicle under the influence of alcohol, the prosecutor must demonstrate that the defendant's blood-alcohol content was above the legally allowed limit. In the case of an alleged sexual assault, the identification of seminal fluid on vaginal swabs obtained from the victim establishes the crucial element of penetration.

MODUS OPERANDI

Modus operandi is a Latin term for "method of operation." As criminals reoffend, they often repeat behaviors, which become known as their preferred method of operation. Some burglars, for example, will use the same tools and techniques to gain entry into structures each time. The examination of toolmark impressions recovered from entry doors pried open or footwear impressions recovered from the ground below forced window units could yield similarities that allow investigators to attribute several cases involved in a burglary trend to the same suspect.

IDENTIFICATION OF UNKNOWN SUBSTANCES OR MATERIALS

In some cases, the scientific analysis of physical evidence can identify an unknown substance or material, such as chemical accelerants used in arson or bombing incidents, bacteria (e.g., anthrax) used in terrorist or biological warfare incidents, or toxins in the bloodstream of a suspected poisoning victim.

IDENTIFICATION OF PERSONS

The reliable and accurate identification of persons involved in criminal investigations is absolutely critical to the operation of a criminal justice system. Fingerprints and biological or DNA evidence are inherently valuable because they can be used to identify people, be they suspect, victim, or witness. The ability to identify decomposed or skeletonized human remains is invaluable in cases of individual death or mass disaster incidents.

ESTABLISHMENT OF LINKAGES OR EXCLUSIONS

As described in the previous chapter, Locard's theory of exchange and the linkage theory are the founding principles of forensic investigations. Linking victims, suspects, objects, and crime scenes is the quintessential, most versatile, and most important goal of the scientific analysis of physical evidence. A bullet recovered from the body of a homicide victim and cartridge cases recovered from the crime scene can be matched to a specific firearm on which the suspect's fingerprints and DNA were found. Similarly, exclusions can prove disassociations among victims, suspects, objects, and crime scenes. Also valuable, exclusions can help guide an investigation by eliminating potential suspects or weapons and focusing investigators on the proper course of action.

PROVIDE INVESTIGATIVE LEADS

Physical evidence can provide direct information to an investigator; however, not every piece of physical evidence recovered during an investigation will be linked to a victim or suspect. As we will discuss, not every category or article of physical evidence is capable of being individualized, that is attributed to a single source; however, associations to a particular group of people (DNA evidence isolated to a particular blood type) or a particular type of object (caliber of firearm) may still be established, thereby further targeting the investigation. Recently, national databases have been developed that have made forensic science more helpful during the investigative phase, particularly in cases with no reliable witnesses or useful testimonial evidence. Databases developed for fingerprint, DNA, and firearms evidence, for example, can assist investigators in linking evidence to a known person or firearm or in connecting unsolved cases with similar physical evidence.

SUPPORT OR DISPROVE STATEMENTS OF VICTIMS, SUSPECTS, OR WITNESSES

With credibility being a constant concern regarding the testimony of those involved in criminal investigations, physical evidence and its analysis can play a vital role as an objective standard against which statements can be evaluated. The presence or absence of certain pieces of physical evidence and the conclusions drawn from such, including bloodstain patterns, gunshot residue, and bullet trajectories, can either support or rebut the statements of victims, suspects, or witnesses.

RESULTS GENERATED FROM FORENSIC ANALYSIS OF PHYSICAL EVIDENCE

The forensic analysis of physical evidence, regardless of the type or the discipline required, involves the application of a common principle: the comparison of a known standard (exemplar) against an unknown (forensic) sample collected from a crime scene, which as discussed in the previous chapter is not limited to an actual physical location. Fingerprints recovered from the interior of a stolen vehicle can be compared to the known fingerprints of a suspect obtained while the suspect was being booked for a previous crime. Seminal fluid recovered from the victim of a sexual assault during the forensic nurse's examination can be compared to the known DNA standard of the suspect. The composition of a green botanical substance discovered in the pocket of a suspect during an officer's routine pat down can be compared to the known chemical composition of marijuana.

CLASS/FAMILY CHARACTERISTICS

The first step in the analysis of physical evidence is classification. Whatever the item being examined, it must first be classified within a family or group of similar items; that is, it must be identified. Shoes, for example, are manufactured in a variety of styles, sizes, shapes, and colors. We can recognize their differing appearances while still identifying and classifying them as shoes. A group can be very broad (e.g., a white, cotton fiber), or a group can be somewhat specific (e.g., a footwear impression revealing the brand, size, and tread pattern of a shoe). An article of physical evidence that, upon examination, yields a level of detail that allows the item to be classified within a group of similar items (or people) is said to exhibit class or family characteristics.

INDIVIDUAL CHARACTERISTICS

The second step in the analysis of physical evidence is individualization, the attempt to narrow the classification until only one item remains in the class. "In forensic science, individualization can mean either of two things: (1) that in some way, by examining the various characteristics of something, it can be recognized as unique—one of a kind—among members of its class; or (2) that when a questioned or unknown object or item is compared with a known or exemplar item, they are found to have a common origin" (Gaensslen et al., 2008, p. 26). An article of physical evidence that, upon examination, yields a level of detail that allows the item (or person) to be individualized from all other members of the class or group of similar items (or people) is said to exhibit individual characteristics. It is important to realize that only certain types of physical evidence, including pattern evidence such as fingerprints, firearms/toolmarks, footwear impressions, tire-tread impressions, bite marks, and fracture comparisons, because of the level of detail potentially exhibited, are commonly able to be individualized.

Recent advances in DNA technology have ushered some biological evidence and DNA profiling into this group as well. Chemical and materials evidence, such as paint, soil, metallic residues, drugs, and fibers, cannot be strictly individualized. It is possible, however, that these types of items and other trace/transfer evidence can be associated to such a small class that in some incidents where the number and types of items, weapons, participants, and/or vehicles, for instance, can be limited in scope the classification itself can provide strong investigative leads.

INCLUSIONS

When the classification of an article of physical evidence can be narrowed, but not to the point of individualization or exclusivity, the finding is known as an *inclusion*. In other words, the questioned item could match the known. The questioned item *cannot be excluded* as having come from the known. The questioned item is consistent with the known. A sample of glass recovered from a burglary suspect's clothing or a sample of paint collected from the suspect's vehicle in a hit-and-run can be compared to known samples collected from the glass remaining within the window frame of the suspect's point of entry and paint exemplars collected from the victim's vehicle. The glass samples can be shown to share common chemical compositions and optical properties, and the paint samples can be shown to share color and layer structure. The question facing the forensic scientist is how to interpret these findings. The glass and paint have been placed into small classes, with many different glass and paint sources being excluded, but it remains unknown and impossible to evaluate how many sources exist other than the glass panel at the burglary scene and the paint covering the victim's vehicle (Gaensslen et al., 2008). Often, an inclusion is the best possible result generated from the analysis of certain types of physical evidence.

EXCLUSIONS

The opposite end of the spectrum regarding the comparison of unknown samples and known exemplars is the *exclusion*. Contrary to inclusions, exclusions are absolute. If differences exist in the class or individual characteristics between unknown samples and known exemplars, the known standard is excluded as a potential source of the questioned sample. Similar to inclusions, however, exclusions still provide investigative leads by redirecting or targeting an investigation through the elimination of potential suspects, weapons, etc. As Sir Arthur Conan Doyle stated, through his immortal character and forensic pioneer, Sherlock Holmes, in the novel *The Sign of the Four*, "When you have eliminated the impossible, whatever remains, however improbable, must be the truth."

MODERN, FULL-SERVICE CRIME LABORATORIES

Forensic laboratories can differ greatly in their capabilities, depending on funding, equipment and staffing levels. The divisions, units, or areas of emphasis within the modern, full-service crime laboratory are representative of the major types of physical evidence recovered during criminal investigations.

FINGERPRINTS SECTION

The examination of fingerprints has been an integral part of policing and forensic science for well over 100 years. The principal reason for this is that fingerprints constitute a unique and permanent means of personal identification. Fingerprint analysts have formulated three basic principles that encompass these ideas of the uniqueness and stability of fingerprint identification: "A fingerprint is an individual characteristic. No two fingers have yet been found to possess identical ridge characteristics" (Saferstein, 2009, p. 168). The fingers and palms of the hands of humans have friction ridge skin, composed of complex patterns of hills (ridges) and valleys (furrows) designed for gripping. Similar friction ridge skin can also be found on the soles of the feet. Within a fingerprint pattern are a number of features known as ridge characteristics or minutiae. Fingerprint ridges form the minutiae in three primary ways: by ending abruptly (forming a ridge ending), by splitting into two ridges (forming a bifurcation), and by being short (forming a dot). The minutiae can then combine to form additional patterns, such as two bifurcations facing each other, forming an island or enclosure (Gaensslen et al., 2008). The individuality of a fingerprint is determined by a careful examination of the identity, number, and relative location of these ridge characteristics, meaning that, if two fingerprint impressions are to match, they must reveal characteristics that are identical and have the same relative location to one another. The accuracy of fingerprint identification has been verified by the millions of individuals who have had their fingerprints classified during the last 110 years, including the nearly 50 million fingerprint records in the Federal Bureau of Investigation (FBI) database. An identical impression shared by two different people, including identical twins, who share an identical genetic makeup, has yet to be discovered.

A fingerprint does not change during an individual's lifetime (Saferstein, 2009). The skin is composed of layers of cells, with those nearest the surface making up the outer layer of skin, known as the epidermis, and those making up the inner layer of skin, known as the dermis. The shape of a boundary of cells, known as dermal papillae, separating the epidermis and dermis, determines the pattern of the ridges on the surface of the skin. Once these dermal papillae form during embryonic development, the ridge patterns and characteristics remain unchanged throughout life, except to enlarge during growth phases. Attempts to obliterate or obscure one's fingerprints will prove futile, as it is impossible to obliterate all of the ridge characteristics on the hand and the presence of permanent scars only provides new characteristics for identification.

The general ridge patterns of fingerprints allow them to be systematically classified (Saferstein, 2009). All fingerprints are divided into three classes on the basis of their general pattern, which then form the basis for all ten-finger classification systems currently in use: loops, whorls, and arches. Each pattern has its own general characteristics, which can be further subdivided into distinct groups. The original classification system, developed by Sir Edward Henry in the late 19th century, converted ridge patterns on all ten fingers into a series of letters and numbers arranged in the form of fractions. In the United States, due to the limited capacity of the original Henry system and the ever-increasing number of fingerprints on file, the FBI expanded its classification capacity by modifying the Henry system and adding additional extensions (Saferstein, 2009). This system is used by most law enforcement agencies in the United States today. A fingerprint classification system in and of itself cannot be used to identify an individual; it simply provides the examiner with an organized system of class characteristics from which a list of candidates can be generated. The identification must always be made and verified by a final, visual comparison of the questioned print's and the file print's minutiae.

Ten-print card files, however, provide little assistance in cold searches for a single fingerprint when the name of a suspect has not been generated in a specific case. The development of computerized fingerprint search systems, or Automated Fingerprint Identification Systems (AFISs), revolutionized the field by enabling timely and efficient cold searches, considering that single prints or partials of single prints are generally recovered from crime scenes or evidence. AFIS technology enables a computer to scan and digitally encode fingerprint minutiae so they can be subject to high-speed processing and searches: "The computer's search algorithm determines the degree of correlation between the location and relationship of the minutiae for both the search and file prints" (Saferstein, 2009, p. 175). During the search for a match, in databases containing both the fingerprints of known offenders and previously unmatched fingerprints recovered from crime scenes or evidence, the computer uses a scoring system that produces a list of known prints that most closely correlate to the minutiae identified on the questioned print input into the system by the examiner. All of the prints selected by the AFIS system are then visually compared against the questioned print by the examiner, who makes the final verification of the fingerprint's identity. AFIS searches can range in scope from local city, county, and state databases to, since 1999, a nationwide database, the Integrated Automated Fingerprint Identification System (IAFIS), which links state AFIS computers with the FBI database containing nearly 50 million fingerprint records.

BIOLOGY/DNA SECTION

Forensic science was again revolutionized throughout the 20th century with early advances in the analysis of blood and physiological fluid evidence and the advent of modern DNA (deoxyribonucleic acid) typing. Until the 1980s, when DNA typing was developed, forensic biologists relied on what is now referred to as *classical* or *conventional* genetic markers to try to individualize blood and bodily fluid evidence. The first major category of conventional genetic markers was blood groups. The first blood group, the ABO system, was discovered in 1901 and used extensively during the 20th century, prior to modern DNA typing. Other genetic markers, including isoenzymes, plasma proteins, and hemoglobin variants, followed suit. The analysis of biological evidence, in its conventional form, yielded typing matches between an evidence sample and a known person, representative of inclusions, indicating that the person *could be* the source of the deposited evidentiary sample. Modern DNA typing has made considerable strides toward the individualization of biological evidence.

Genetics is the study and science of inheritance, how parents pass their traits and characteristics to their offspring. By the 1940s, it was clear to scientists that DNA is the genetic material, the chemical blueprint, of life itself. DNA in humans is found in all cells that contain a nucleus, except red blood cells. As cells divide and differentiate to form the millions of cells that make up different organs and tissues, DNA is replicated; thus, each cell contains an identical copy of the person's DNA, known as the genome. Because most body cells have a copy of that person's DNA, almost any fluid, tissue, or organ can be used for DNA typing. And, because people, whether victims or suspects, are involved in the commission of crime, DNA evidence can possibly be recovered on any type of case. The bodily fluids that are most commonly encountered in forensic laboratories are blood, semen, vaginal secretions, saliva, and urine (Gaensslen et al., 2008). DNA typing technology is now sufficiently sensitive that the possibility of generating a profile from seemingly very small articles of biological evidence has greatly improved: "Bits of fingernail, dandruff flakes, the skin cell residues on cigarette butts or filter tips and shed cheek cells from the dried saliva surrounding bite marks have all been successfully DNA profiled in recent years" (Gaensslen et al., 2008, pp. 224–225).

The analysis of physical evidence bearing potential DNA material, the source of which can be specified based on the unique facts of a case, consists of several steps, including preliminary or presumptive screening to detect the possible presence of bodily fluids, confirmatory testing to prove that the material being tested for is actually present, species determination to further specify the probative value of the material (particularly useful in cases designed to enforce wildlife regulations and bloodshed incidents where the possibility of encountering animal blood is high), isolation of the actual DNA material from the known and questioned samples, analysis of specific regions or *loci* on the DNA strand so a DNA profile can be generated, and comparison of the profiles generated from both samples to determine whether the known individual is not the source of the questioned sample or can be included as a possible contributor to the questioned sample.

Each molecule of DNA consists of a long, spiral structure, the double helix, which has been likened to a twisted ladder. The "handrails" of the ladder string together the ladder "rungs." Each rung consists of two (2) of four (4) varieties of nucleic acids, which are then combined in pairs. The sequencing of these base pairs constitutes the genetic coding of DNA. The human genome consists of approximately 3 billion base pairs, about 3 million of which vary from person to person. Person-to-person differences within a particular segment of a DNA sequence are known as *alleles*. DNA typing focuses on identifying and isolating specific fragments of these alleles. Identical fragments appearing on both the known and questioned samples are considered to represent a match. To determine the likelihood of this match being mere coincidence, the particular combination of alleles is compared to the frequency with which it statistically appears in a given population (Lushbaugh and Weston, 2009).

The study of population genetics examines how often alleles at specific genetic loci occur in a population. Modern DNA technology and analysis have led forensic scientists to utilize DNA typing kits that examine multiple genetic loci, which provide a very high level of individualization. By examining multiple loci where variation occurs, a DNA profile can be produced. When comparing questioned and known DNA profiles, a difference of a single allele can exclude the known individual as the donor of the questioned sample. The more loci that exhibit the same allele pattern, the stronger and more statistically significant the evidence becomes that both samples originate from the same individual (Lushbaugh and Weston, 2009). As Gaensslen et al. (2008, p. 256) noted, "The level of individuality produced by DNA typing depends on the population genetics of the *loci* and the types that are chosen for the overall DNA profiling."

Following inclusion of the known individual in the questioned or evidence profile, statistical calculations are performed to estimate the probability of the chance duplication of the DNA profile in the population. For many complete DNA profiles, this probability is extremely low; however, although the resulting figures can be astronomical, such as 1 in 100 billion, they still remain only probabilities. They do not mean that there cannot be another person with the same profile. An additional factor to realize is that there are different estimates of the probability of chance duplication according to racial or ethnic group: "Because the frequencies of types within *loci* can and do vary in different populations, the different estimates for each of them are commonly given by the analyst so as not to mislead the courts" (Gaensslen et al., 2008, p. 258). Most DNA laboratories, based on the available data, can compute these probabilities for Caucasian, African American, and Hispanic populations. It is important to understand that in a forensic case the race or ethnic group of the depositor is not known with certainty; even in a DNA-match case with very low probabilities of chance duplication, there is still a small chance that another person shares the same profile (Gaensslen et al., 2008).

DNA analysis, as discussed thus far in the field of forensic science, commonly refers to nuclear DNA analysis. Additional structures contained in the cell, at a rate of hundreds to thousands, are mitochondria, which are responsible for making energy for the cell to function. Mitochondria contain a small quantity of their own DNA, consisting of about 16,000 base pairs, making it roughly 10,000 times smaller in size than nuclear DNA. Another feature is that mitochondrial DNA is strictly inherited maternally. The stability of the mitochondrial DNA sequence allows it to be traced through the maternal lineage for many generations. This quality has implications for the use of mitochondrial DNA typing in cases involving the identification of human remains. Mitochondrial DNA typing has also proven useful in the analysis of old, degraded, decomposed, or potentially skeletonized samples, where nuclear material is either present in only very small quantities or no longer available (Gaensslen et al., 2008).

Similar to fingerprints, DNA evidence is represented by a system of classification. DNA profiles are written as a series of numbers. Modern computer technology has allowed DNA profiles to be stored in searchable files. CODIS (Combined DNA Index System) is a computer software program developed by the FBI that maintains local, state, and national databases of DNA profiles generated from the known standards of convicted offenders and, depending on individual state legislation, arrestees (referred to as the *offender database*), unsolved crime scene evidence (referred to as the *forensic database*), and the known standards of missing persons. Similar to AFIS, CODIS allows analysts to cold search questioned samples for no-suspect cases and compare both offender and forensic samples on cases believed to be linked to the same suspect (Saferstein, 2009).

FIREARMS AND TOOLMARKS SECTION

Examinations of firearms evidence and toolmarks are explicably linked, as they require the application of common principles, skills, and equipment.

Toolmarks

A toolmark can be defined as a pattern resulting from a harder marking device, or tool, being forced against a softer object (Gaensslen et al., 2008). Toolmarks commonly encountered by forensic examiners are created by screwdrivers, pry bars, snips, wire and bolt cutters, clawing instruments, and various other tools, most often used for forced entry into, for example, a dwelling, business, storage unit, or storage medium. Toolmarks can be classified into two main types: impressions and striations. Impressions occur when a tool is forced or pushed into a surface. Striations result when a tool slides or is moved across a surface, depositing a pattern of scratches (stria) caused by tiny defects along the face, blade, or edge of the tool. Toolmarks can be recovered as a combination of the two, as in the case of a flat-head screwdriver being used to pry open a residential entry door. Striations caused by the blade of the screwdriver could be deposited on metal strike plates lining the doorjamb, while impressions caused by the round shaft of the screwdriver could be deposited in the wood door itself.

Toolmarks can exhibit either class or individual characteristics, sometimes both. Impressions most often exhibit class characteristics, as the basic size and shape of the tool is depressed into a surface. Single-bladed tools, such as pry bars and flat-head screwdrivers, can easily be distinguished from double-bladed tools, such as the claw end of a hammer or a nail-puller on the end of some pry tools. Individual characteristics are usually exhibited by large distributions of striations deposited on metal surfaces. Softer materials, such as wood, can yield or splinter, reducing contact with the blade of the tool. Cutting instruments used to cut through wire or a padlock hasp can deposit impressions that can be classified as single-edged or double-edged and also leave visible striation patterns, depending on the nature and size of the surface being cut (e.g., telephone wire vs. bound copper wiring). Impressions can potentially exhibit granular-type individual detail, depending on the condition of the tool itself and the elasticity of the surface or material being marked.

A major issue facing toolmark examination is the difficulty in accurately reproducing the toolmark recovered from the crime scene. Because the toolmark is made by imperfections on the blade, edge, or marking surface of the tool, the marks left by the tool sliding across or being impressed into a surface at a particular angle may differ from marks produced when the tool is held at a different angle. The examiner must obtain a series of exemplars, applying the suspect tool at various angles and pressures, to most accurately reproduce the evidentiary sample. The primary concern, however, for investigating officers is locating the suspect tool in a timely manner. The longer the interim between the toolmark's deposit and the toolmark examination, the greater the chance that the defects and imperfections on the tool's marking surface have been altered by continued use.

Firearms

"A firearm is a device that, using the rapid combustion of an energetic chemical, is designed to accelerate a projectile to a high velocity while directing it toward a target" (Gaensslen et al., 2008, p. 182). In order to understand the principles and practices involved in the examination of firearms evidence, an introduction to the construction and function of firearms and ammunition is warranted.

A cartridge, or live round, consists of four basic components. The cartridge case is the container of the unit, holding the other three components together; in handguns and rifles, the cartridge case is a cylindrical piece of brass or nickel-plated brass. The cartridge case is filled with a propellant (smokeless powder), which can take many shapes, including small disks, tubes, or balls. The projectile, or bullet, usually constructed of lead or copper-coated lead, is put into the cartridge case, which is then squeezed around the bullet in order to make a tight seal. The final component is the primer, which takes the shape of a soft, metal cup built into the cartridge case at the end opposite the bullet. The primer contains a small hole, known as the flash hole, in contact with the propellant. A shotshell, or live round fired through a shotgun, shares similar components, with the main difference being that shotshells usually contain multiple projectiles, or pellets, rather than a single bullet (Gaensslen et al., 2008).

When a cartridge is loaded into the firing chamber and the trigger is pulled, the firing pin strikes the primer, causing shock-sensitive material within the primer to ignite. A spark is then transferred through the flash hole to the propellant. The burning powder exudes heat and creates gases that develop high pressure inside the cartridge case. Because the bullet is sealed into the cartridge case, this pressure builds rapidly until finally the bullet is forced from the case and propelled down the firearm's barrel at high velocity. This process, regardless of the size of the ammunition and the firing action of the firearm itself, remains consistent among firearms. Differences between firearms primarily occur before and after the firing process—that is, how the cartridge enters the firing chamber and how the cartridge case is disposed of.

The majority of handguns can be classified into two distinct groups: revolvers and semiautomatic pistols. Revolvers have cylinders comprised of a number of individual chambers, each holding a single cartridge. With each successive pull of the trigger, the cylinder rotates so a new cartridge is placed into the firing chamber and aligned with the barrel. The fired cartridge cases remain in the cylinder until manually removed. In semiautomatic pistols, cartridges are contained in magazines that fit into the grip of the pistol. With each successive trigger pull, the spent cartridge case is mechanically extracted and ejected from the firing chamber; a new cartridge is then fed into the chamber from the magazine.

Long guns, or firearms with long barrels designed to be fired from the shoulder, can be classified into two major groups, rifles and shotguns. Many subclassifications exist within these two groups, based on their firing actions. The majority of rifles contain magazines, which feed new cartridges into the firing chamber. The fired cartridge cases can be mechanically extracted and ejected, as in the case of semiautomatic rifles, or manually extracted and ejected, as in the case of bolt-action and lever-action rifles, although the ejection of cartridge cases from rifles is not strictly manual. Although the shooter must manually retract and replace a bolt or lever during the entire process, mechanisms within the firearm actually make contact with the cartridge case during the ejection process. Similarly, shotguns can contain magazines, often tubular in shape and located below the barrel. The fired shotshell cases are either mechanically extracted and ejected, as in the case of semiautomatic shotguns, or manually extracted and ejected (similar to bolt-action and lever-action rifles), as in the case of pump-action shotguns. Similar to revolvers, shotshells can be manually loaded and fired, and shotshell cases can be manually removed, as in the case of single- or double-barrel break action shotguns.

As the process implies, cartridge cases and shotshell cases fired in mechanically extracting and ejecting firearms have the potential to yield more detail of forensic value because, like toolmark impressions, mechanisms within the firearm make more contact, like a pry tool on a metal strike plate, with the cartridge or shotshell case, producing additional marks of interest. The firing pin strikes the primer, producing toolmark #1. The expanding gases within the firing chamber, which produce the force that propels the bullet down the barrel, then force the cartridge or shotshell case backward in the firing chamber. The cartridge or shotshell case then strikes the breechface, the surface at the rear of the firing chamber, producing toolmark #2. Firing pins and breechfaces are machined parts, universal to firearms regardless of size or firing action. Quality firearms are manufactured by machining and metal-working blocks of hard steel (Gaensslen et al., 2008). These processes leave fine stria on the exposed surfaces of the firing pin and breechface, which can then be transferred or impressed into the primer and base of the cartridge case. In mechanically extracting and ejecting firearms, there exists the potential for two more points of comparison. Following the cartridge or shotshell case striking the breechface, the extractor mechanism latches onto the rimmed edge of the cartridge case, producing toolmark #3, and the ejector mechanism then strikes the rim of the cartridge case when discharging it from the firing chamber, producing toolmark #4.

Similar to the machined parts responsible for propelling a bullet from a cartridge case, the barrel of the firearm itself is tooled for a specific purpose. In handguns and rifles, the barrel is composed of a series of spiraling grooves known as *rifling*. Rifling is imparted to a barrel by devices containing a series of sharp raised areas (teeth) circling a central shaft. The grooves are cut by pulling or pushing this shaft through the steel barrel and turning it simultaneously. The raised areas in the barrel between the grooves are called *lands*. The desired result is the bullet emerging from the barrel in a rapid spin, following the helical path of the lands and grooves, in order to improve accuracy (Gaensslen et al., 2008). The machining process, again, leaves fine stria on the interior surface of the barrel, which can then be imparted to the bullet as it travels. Shotgun barrels, considering the plastic body of shotshells and the presence of multiple projectiles or pellets, are typically smooth and not rifled.

The examination of firearms and firearms evidence consists of three main phases. The first step in the process is testing the firearm for functionality—in other words, determining whether the firearm is capable of being fired and whether its safety features are functional. During this process, the firearm is also test fired to obtain exemplars of cartridge or shotshell cases and bullets to compare against evidence samples. The second step in the process is classification, comparing the class characteristics of the exemplars and the evidence samples. Basic class characteristics include caliber (determined by the inside diameter of the barrel), shape of the firing pin impression, number and width of the lands and grooves, and the direction of spin (right or left) imparted on the bullet. The final step in the process is individualization. If the exemplar and evidence sample share class characteristics, the examiner will then attempt to individualize the evidence sample to the exemplar (and hence the firearm) by comparing the striation patterns present on the cartridge or shotshell case and the bullet. Of considerable benefit to forensic examination, toolmarks imparted on firearms evidence by the internal mechanisms involved in a firearm's firing and function are highly reproducible. Unlike the defects and imperfections located on the blades of pry tools and cutting instruments, firearms and the surface characteristics discussed above will not typically change drastically over time with continued use.

Similar to fingerprint and DNA evidence, firearms examinations are now aided by the use of computerized databases that allow for cold searching, particularly in cases where the suspect firearm has not been recovered. The FBI maintains a central, computerized General Rifling Characteristic (GRC) file, consisting of the class description of thousands of firearms, based on the rifling characteristics imparted to fired bullets. Most of the forensic laboratories in the United States and many abroad contribute data to this file as examiners encounter firearms not already listed. Firearms examiners can enter the caliber, number of lands and grooves, width of the lands and groves, and direction of rotation noted on an evidence bullet and perform a rapid computer search for known firearms that share similar class characteristics. Maintained by the Bureau of Alcohol, Tobacco, Firearms, and Explosives, the National Integrated Ballistics Information Network (NIBIN) contains images of bullets and cartridge cases recovered from crime scenes and those test fired from recovered firearms submitted for examination. NIBIN allows these images of bullets and cartridge cases to be searched and possibly associated with the same firearm, even if the firearm has yet to be recovered, thereby establishing linkages between cases, potentially across jurisdictional lines.

Fracture Comparisons

Because similar principles, skills, and equipment are required, firearms and toolmark examiners can also be called upon to conduct fracture comparisons or physical matches. Fracture comparisons are performed in an attempt to match randomly fractured or broken pieces of a solid material or object to show that the broken pieces were originally part of the same object (Gaensslen et al., 2008). Materials commonly encountered in such comparisons include glass, plastic, and metal. Vehicular assault or hit-and-run scenes, for instance, may contain broken pieces of head lamp lenses or license plate frames. A broken fragment of a knife blade may be present inside the scene of a stabbing incident or still inside the victim's wound. If the suspect vehicle or remaining knife blade can be located prior to repair or disposal, the edges of both objects, much like a jigsaw puzzle, can be fitted together and realigned, thus linking the objects to the victim, suspect, and crime scene.

Serial Number Restoration

Another important duty assigned to the firearms examiner is serial number restoration. Firearms manufactured by legitimate sources are serialized for identification purposes. A unique serial number is mechanically imparted into the metal frame of a firearm to identify that particular firearm. Suspects who obtain a firearm illegally or use a registered firearm in the commission of a crime can attempt to obscure or eradicate the serial number through a variety of methods to preclude tracking the firearm from manufacturer to seller to owner. The pressure applied as the number is imparted into the firearm is such that it deforms the crystal structure of the metal to a depth below the actual indentations forming the number. When the crystal structure of the metal is strained or deformed, the metal is more susceptible to attack by chemicals (Gaensslen et al., 2008). The examiner first smoothes out the area where the number was originally stamped, removes any dirt or oil, and polishes the surface to a mirror-like finish. The examiner then carefully applies a strongly acidic or basic (depending on the material being processed) etching solution. The etching solution dissolves the deformed or strained metal at a faster rate than the unaltered metal, revealing the pattern of the original numbers. If the suspect doing the defacing did not go deep enough to eliminate the entire area of strain, then this process often can be repeated until the entire original serial number is restored.

IMPRESSION EVIDENCE SECTION

The examination of other forms of impression evidence, including footwear and tire-tread impressions, can also be conducted in this area, depending on the size of the laboratory and amount of these particular types of evidence being submitted, as such examinations involve similar processes of pattern recognition and matching. The skill of an experienced examiner in these areas, however, cannot be underestimated, as footwear and tire-tread examination requires a specific terminology and knowledge base.

Footwear and tire-tread impressions can be divided into two main types: two-dimensional and three-dimensional. Two-dimensional impressions are deposited on unyielding surfaces, such as tile, linoleum, concrete, or wood flooring, and can also be made on paper, plastics, carpet, or clothing. Three-dimensional impressions are those that remain after a surface has been deformed. This type of impression is predominantly deposited on exterior surfaces, such as soil, sand, or snow, but can also include impressions made in other soft, yielding materials. Although all impressions are potentially identifiable, three-dimensional impressions generally retain more specific details and characteristics (James and Nordby, 2005).

The same process of classification and individualization remains in effect. Footwear impressions, made from any shoe, sandal, or slipper, can be classified according to physical size and shape, tread pattern design, and position and degree of wear. Tire-tread impressions can be classified according to tread dimension (referring to the specific physical tire tread size), tread pattern design, wear features resulting from the erosion of rubber from frictional forces, and noise treatment (referring to the variance of the pitch, or size, of the tread design elements as they are arranged around the entire circumference of the tire). Classification of these impressions could result in determining the brand, size, make, or model of the shoe or tire depositing the impression. Individualization of these impressions results from identifying and matching such characteristics as cuts, scratches, gouges, tears, and other physical damage randomly added to or removed from the surface of the shoe sole or tire during use (James and Nordby, 2005).

TRACE EVIDENCE SECTION

Trace evidence is simply physical evidence that is small in size. From a legal perspective, including the term *trace evidence* on a search warrant expands the scope of the search to anywhere and anything. In a forensic laboratory setting, trace evidence examinations usually involve the use of microscopes or other instrumentation or chemical means to classify the origin of, for example, hair, fibers, paint, glass, soil, and ignitable liquid residues.

Hair

An examination of the morphology or structural characteristics of hair, including color, length, diameter, scale structure, and medullary index, can potentially determine whether the hair is human or animal in origin, the body area from which the hair originated, the racial origin of the depositor (especially true for Caucasian or African American head hair), and whether the hair was forcibly removed from the body of the depositor (Saferstein, 2009). Trace analysis of hair, similar to other materials, cannot, in and of itself, yield individual characteristics. Because hair is of biological origin, DNA analysis and determinations must be relied upon for any attempt at individualization.

Fibers

Fibers can be classified into two broad groups, natural and manufactured. Natural fibers are derived from animal sources, including sheep, goats, or alpacas, or plant sources, such as cotton. Manufactured fibers are fibers derived from either natural or synthetic polymers, which are substances composed of large numbers of chain-linked molecules. Fibers manufactured from raw materials, such as cotton or wood pulp, that require the extraction and chemical treatment of cellulose are classified as regenerated fibers (e.g., acetate, rayon). Most fibers currently manufactured, however, are produced solely from synthetic chemicals and are therefore classified as synthetic fibers (e.g., acrylic, nylon, polyester). Manufactured fibers are marketed under hundreds of trade names. To avoid confusion, the U.S. Federal Trade Commission has approved generic or family names for the various groups of all manufactured fibers used to produce goods such as clothing, home furnishings, and vehicle mats and seatbelts. Many of these generic classes (e.g., acrylic, nylon, polyester, spandex) are produced by numerous manufacturers and sold under a variety of trade names (Saferstein, 2009).

An examination of the morphological features of fibers, such as color, dye composition, diameter, cross-sectional shape, chemical composition, and absorption rate of infrared light, can potentially classify fibers into broad groups and then further classify manufactured fibers into generic classes. Many types of nylon, for example, are available for purchase in consumer markets. Although all types of nylon share common properties, each may differ in appearance and dye-absorption ability due to modifications in the basic chemical structure made during the manufacturing process (Saferstein, 2009). As in all areas of forensic examination, the narrower the classification, the stronger the linkage among victims, suspects, and crime scenes.

Paint

Most paints have four basic components: (1) binder, a polymeric substance used to bind paint to the surface; (2) pigments, or coloring agents; (3) fillers and additives; and (4) a carrier solvent, which allows the paint to be applied easily. The number of combinations of these basic components is substantial and makes different paints distinguishable upon analysis (Gaensslen et al., 2008). The examination of paint with regard to color, surface texture, color layer sequence, and chemical composition of binders and pigments can yield class matches between known and evidentiary samples, such as samples collected from a door utilized as the point of entry in a burglary case and samples recovered from a pry tool suspected of being used to force the door open. In traffic-related cases, an analysis of paint recovered from the crash or crime scene can often assist in identifying the color, make, and model of an unknown vehicle based on the various manufacturers' specifications.

Glass

"Glass is a hard, brittle, amorphous substance composed of sand (silicon oxides) mixed with various metal oxides. When sand is mixed with other metal oxides, melted at high temperatures and then cooled to a rigid condition without crystallization, the product is glass" (Saferstein, 2009, p. 423). Glass, based on its chemical composition and manufacturing process, can be categorized into many types, such as borosilicates, which are used in vehicle headlights; soda-lime glass, which is used in most windows and bottles; tempered glass, which is used in the side and rear windows of vehicles; and laminated glass, which is used in the front windshields of vehicles. The physical properties of density and refractive index are used for class matching glass fragments. Density, the measurement of mass per unit of volume, is a property of matter that remains the same, regardless of the size of an object. A simple procedure for determining the density of a solid is to first weigh it and then measure its volume by noting the volume of water it displaces when submerged (Saferstein, 2009). Refractive index, another physical property of matter that is not dependent on the size of an object, is defined as the ratio of the speed of light in a vacuum to the speed of light in a given medium. Refraction refers to the bending of a light wave due to a change in velocity. The refractive index of a substance varies with its temperature and the wavelength of light passing through it. This determination is best accomplished by the immersion method, in which evidentiary and known fragments of glass are immersed in a liquid medium whose refractive index is adjusted by changing temperature until it equals the refractive indices of the glass fragments. If both samples of glass exhibit minimum contrast with the immersion liquid, they can be said to have comparable refractive indices (Saferstein, 2009).

Soil

"For forensic purposes, soil may be thought of as any disintegrated surface material, natural or artificial, that lies on or near the Earth's surface" (Saferstein, 2009, p. 435). Generally, these materials are naturally occurring vegetation, rocks, minerals, and animal matter, but they can also be such manufactured trace elements as glass, paint, asphalt, and brick fragments, the presence of which gives soil particular characteristics applicable to a specific location.

Soil evidence found adhering to a victim's or suspect's clothing or shoes or to the tires and undercarriage of a vehicle can be compared to known exemplars collected from the crime scene. The forensic value of soil increases in relation to variations in its composition at the crime scene; if, for example, soil content and composition are indistinguishable for miles surrounding the crime scene, the soil evidence would have little to no value in associating soil found on the suspect with that found at the crime scene. Microscopic examination of soil is conducted for the comparative value of class characteristics, such as color, texture, presence of plant and animal material and artificial debris, and the color, geometric shape, density, and refractive index of rocks and minerals present. Considering the potential variety in soil colors, rocks, minerals, and artificial debris possibly present, trace analysts schooled in geology can be presented with many points of comparison among specimens.

Ignitable Liquid Residues

Analysis of debris and other arson- or explosion-related evidence to detect the presence of accelerants or ignitable liquid residues is a significant part of the work of most forensic laboratories. Burned debris, soggy carpeting, and a variety of other items recovered from the scene of such an incident may contain accelerant. If an ignitable liquid is present, it is usually in trace amounts and mixed with the debris and charred material. Various methods are used by analysts to process such material to concentrate or separate any ignitable liquids from the debris. Instrumental analysis of the resulting liquid isolates individual chemical compounds, which then reveal their own characteristic pattern. When a particular chemical compound has been identified, the analyst can then determine if it is flammable and whether it is known to be a component of any commonly encountered ignitable liquids, including gasoline or petroleum distillates such as kerosene, cigarette lighter fluids, charcoal starter fluids, and paint thinners (Gaensslen et al., 2008).

DRUG IDENTIFICATION SECTION

The analysis of controlled substances is another major task of most forensic laboratories. Samples of green botanical substances or white powdery or rock-like substances are first subjected to preliminary screening tests. Color tests, for example, produce characteristic colors for certain drugs and indicate the possible presence of one or more illicit substances. When positive reactions are produced, analysts then conduct more complex, confirmatory tests employing microscopic and instrumental analysis techniques to identify specific chemical structures and specific drug substances. When a drug or controlled substance has been positively identified, criminal investigation and prosecution can proceed.

TOXICOLOGY SECTION

Toxicologists detect and identify drugs and poisons (toxins) in bodily fluids, tissues, and organs. Samples may include a vial of drawn blood from a suspect in a DUI case, whole blood and urine samples from the victim of a sexual assault who reports being given a drug, or fluid and hair samples obtained from deceased victims in suspected overdose or homicidal poisoning cases. Similar to drug identification testing, analysts employ a series of screening and confirmatory tests to identify the chemical structure, or signature, of substances. As the human body is an active chemistry laboratory, few substances enter and completely leave the body in the same chemical state; therefore, a thorough understanding of how the body alters and metabolizes the chemical structure of a drug is essential to detecting its presence in appropriately collected samples (Saferstein, 2009).

QUESTIONED DOCUMENTS SECTION

A questioned document can be defined as any object with handwriting or print whose source or authenticity is in doubt. Microscopic analysis of documents, most commonly in paper form, can be utilized to compare handwriting samples based on the premise that no two individuals unconsciously write exactly alike because of variations in the physical, mechanical, and mental functions that contribute to the overall character of a person's writing. Microscopic analysis of machine-created writing, such as that produced by computer printers, photocopiers, fax machines, and typewriters, can also yield points of comparison. Continued use of printing devices results in random, irregular wear and damage to moving parts of the machine. Defect marks resulting from random debris on the glass platen, inner cover, or mechanical portions of a photocopier can produce irregularly shaped images. The transmitting terminal identifier (TTI), a header at the top of each page of a faxed document, assists in determining authenticity. Variations in the alignment of characters, along with defects in a typeface, can assist in proving the identity of a typewriter (Saferstein, 2009).

Specialized discovery techniques, mainly involving the manipulation of light and light sources, are also applied by the examiner on documents suspected of being fraudulently changed. *Alterations* (when writing on a document is somehow altered or added to) and *obliterations* (when writing is blotted out, smeared over, or obscured in some way) can be detected because inks of varying chemical composition also vary in the way in which they absorb and re-radiate infrared light. *Erasures* (when the writing is removed from a document by either chemical means or an abrasive instrument) can be detected under ultraviolet or infrared lighting to reveal discoloration from the chemical agent or under oblique, visible lighting to highlight the remaining, patterned disturbance to the upper fibers of the paper. Other specialized lighting techniques can be utilized to reveal indented writing in paper below the sheet actually being written on and writing or typing on charred documents.

Microscopic and instrumental analysis of ink and paper can also generate investigative leads from document evidence. The chemical composition and dye patterns of inks can be isolated not only to distinguish between known and questioned samples but also to reference the age of a document based on the date when a particular ink dye was produced. An analysis of the paper on which a document is written or printed can include general appearance, color, weight, presence of a watermark, fiber identification, and characterization of additives, fillers, and pigments (Saferstein, 2009).

PHOTOGRAPHY SECTION

The functions of a complete photographic laboratory are both numerous and vital, as documentation is a key aspect of any forensic investigation, whether in the field or in a laboratory setting. This section can be responsible simply for processing and storing film negatives and digital images obtained by examiners during their analyses, but technicians can also be tasked with processing photographic prints and enlargements and preparing photographic exhibits for courtroom presentations. To effectively assist examiners, forensic photographers must also be skilled in manipulating cameras and various light sources and spectra to best capture articles of physical evidence, such as impressions, whose examination can be conducted using photographs. Forensic photographers can also use their expertise and the technology made available to them to generate evidence that cannot be seen by the human eye; for example, ultraviolet and infrared photography can be used to detect document forgeries, as well as bloodstains or gunshot residue particles on dark-colored surfaces. This section can also be responsible for the analysis and enhancement of video evidence, most often involving security or surveillance videos that have captured persons, actions, or vehicles relevant to investigations.

SPECIALIZED FORENSIC SCIENCE SERVICES

Specialized forensic science services outside of the traditional crime laboratory setting are routinely available for use by law enforcement agencies and personnel.

FORENSIC MEDICINE

Forensic medicine can be divided into two distinct fields, forensic pathology and forensic nursing. Forensic pathologists are doctors of medicine with advanced forensic training who are expert in determining the cause and manner of death. The cause of death is a medical determination, a medical explanation for why a person died (e.g., gunshot injuries, sharp force trauma, blunt force trauma, asphyxiation). The manner of death (homicide, suicide, accidental, or natural) is a medicolegal determination that considers all available information, including that gathered from crime scenes, police investigations, and forensic laboratory examinations. The pathologist, or medical examiner in most jurisdictions, makes this determination after conducting an autopsy, or postmortem examination, of the decedent. Postmortem examinations generally entail, but are not limited to, the removal of the internal organs of the chest, abdomen, and head, which are then dissected to determine disease or injury, as well as the collection of fluid, tissue, and organ samples for subsequent toxicological analyses. Similar to any crime scene, the decedent is a valuable source of physical evidence, including DNA, trace evidence, and possibly impressions, which can be used to identify suspects and establish linkages. As the medical examiner holds jurisdiction over the decedent, the pathologist is also tasked with the search and collection of such evidence. In most major jurisdictions, the medical examiner's office is directly associated, both in location and administration, with the forensic laboratory.

Forensic nurses are registered nurses employed by hospitals, clinics, or other medical facilities. They have received advanced forensic training in the identification, collection, and preservation of physical evidence derived from living patients. Forensic nurses are most often involved in this process during the investigation of sexual assault incidents. Many jurisdictions, in conjunction with local police agencies and medical facilities, have assembled a Sexual Assault Nurse Examiner/Sexual Assault Response Team (SANE/SART), which is staffed with forensic nurses who conduct medical examinations of sexual assault victims. The SANE/SART examination consists of two parts: (1) physical examination of the victim to locate, document, and treat associated wounds or injuries; and (2) collection of the standardized sexual assault evidence collection kit. The sexual assault evidence collection kit serves the dual purpose of collecting known standards of biological material from the victim and collecting evidence samples of possible biological material transferred from the suspect. Components of a sexual assault evidence collection kit include vaginal and rectal swabs, pubic hair combings, and fingernail scrapings. In cases involving the suspected use of narcotics, whole blood and urine samples are also collected for toxicological analysis.

FORENSIC ANTHROPOLOGY

Forensic anthropologists are physical anthropologists specialized in examining human skeletal remains. Depending on the condition and amount of skeletal remains recovered, forensic anthropologists can provide class estimates of the age, sex, stature, and group or ethnic affiliation of the individual, in addition to analyzing any skeletal abnormalities or trauma present. Forensic anthropologists can often assist field investigators in the recovery of remains, whether scattered about the surface or buried in the ground, as they are highly skilled in the basic principles and methodology of archaeology. Forensic anthropologists can also lend their knowledge and skill to the science of forensic taphonomy, which deals with the history of a body after death. Forensic taphonomy can be an important part of a criminal death investigation, as postmortem changes in human remains can affect estimates of time since death, identification of the individual, and the ability to determine the cause and manner of death (James and Nordby, 2005). Although not directly included in the forensic anthropologist's responsibilities, an associated discipline known as forensic sculpture or forensic facial imaging involves specialists attempting to reconstruct what an individual's face may have looked like based on observable features of a recovered skull.

FORENSIC ODONTOLOGY

Forensic odontologists are forensic dentists who conduct two major types of analyses involving human teeth. The first is the identification of human remains that are so altered by decomposition, fire, or explosion that they cannot be identified by visual means. Typically, the odontologist will compare postmortem dental x-rays with dental x-rays taken when the person suspected of being the decedent was alive. Like forensic anthropologists, forensic odontologists are very useful in this manner on the scenes of mass disaster situations. The second major examination conducted by forensic odontologists is comparing known and evidentiary bite-mark impressions (Gaensslen et al., 2008).

FORENSIC ENTOMOLOGY

Entomology is the study of insect species. Forensic entomologists can analyze the life cycles of insect species (from egg to larva to pupa to adult) recovered from corpses and combine their results with environmental factors from the scene, such as temperature and length of daylight hours, to calculate an estimate of the individual's time of death when the issue is in question.

FORENSIC PSYCHOLOGY

Forensic psychologists evaluate criminal offenders to determine competence to stand trial and may also be involved in offender treatment programs. Specialists in this area may also profile criminal cases, primarily those involving serial murder or serial rape. Profilers can sometimes provide useful investigative leads about the characteristics of unidentified suspects based on their *modus operandi*, behavior patterns, and crime scene patterns.

FORENSIC ENGINEERING

Forensic engineers are professionals expertly trained in a particular engineering specialty (e.g., mechanical, electrical, civil). Forensic engineers can assist law enforcement in the investigation of transportation system disasters, materials failure cases, and building or structure collapses.

FORENSIC COMPUTER SCIENCE

Forensic computer scientists are most often tasked with three main responsibilities. The first is identifying, collecting, preserving, and examining information derived from computer hard drives, data storage media, and other electronic devices such as pagers, answering machines, and cellular telephones to generate investigative leads and assist in solving cases. The second is to find hidden or deleted information on electronic media. The third responsibility, and perhaps the most difficult and technically intensive, is tracing suspects committing computer crimes, such as circulating child pornography or gaining unauthorized access to confidential information on computer networks (Gaensslen et al., 2008).

FORENSIC RECONSTRUCTION

Reconstruction can be defined as "the use of physical evidence and its analysis to try to understand the events that produced that evidence" (Gaensslen et al., 2008, p. 27). The reconstruction of the sequence of events that occurred prior to, during, and subsequent to the commission of a crime is heavily based on observations made at crime scenes, findings from postmortem examinations of victims, and forensic analysis of recovered physical evidence. Statements of living individuals involved in the incident are also evaluated during the formulation of a reconstruction hypothesis, but, like hypotheses in general, testing conducted both in the field and in the laboratory can either support or disprove those statements. The reconstruction of a crime is very much a collaborative effort between law enforcement personnel and forensic investigators. Forensic or crime scene reconstruction can be interpretive or very scientific and mathematical. What is paramount, however, is that strict adherence to the scientific method is maintained, which, above all, includes the qualities of objectivity and falsifiability, the ability of a theory to be disproved when presented with other plausible alternatives. Reconstructionists can be well trained and highly skilled field investigators or laboratory analysts who have immediate access to the scenes of incidents, or they can be private consultants, perhaps retired after years of professional forensic experience and training, who are enlisted to provide their expertise. In either circumstance, thorough and detailed scene documentation is crucial. As previously discussed, reconstruction of the sequence of events occurring during the commission of a crime can be both interpretive and very scientific or mathematical. The three major disciplines or areas of study specifically applied to scene reconstruction are vehicle or traffic crash reconstruction, bloodstain pattern analysis, and shooting incident reconstruction, also known as *external ballistics*.

Traffic Crash Reconstruction

Crash reconstruction is grounded in the principles espoused in Newton's laws of motion and the mathematical calculations of algebra, geometry, trigonometry, and physics. Crash reconstructionists can interpret general findings based on such observations as the final resting places of vehicles or persons involved; the damage sustained by vehicles, including points of impact and paint transfer; skid marks; acceleration marks; deceleration marks; scrapes, gouges, or any other change in the roadway; and deformation of headlamp filaments indicating whether the lamps were on or off at the time of impact. After detailed and accurate measurements of the crash scene and evidence contained within are obtained, reconstructionists can then make mathematical calculations to determine the approach angle of the vehicles prior to the collision, speed at the time of impact, departure angle of the vehicles following the collision, and rates of acceleration and deceleration. Mathematical formulas can also be used to calculate the motion characteristics of vehicles airborne or in flight during traffic collisions.

Bloodstain Pattern Analysis

Identifying and interpreting bloodstains and bloodstain patterns are among the most valuable skills possessed by forensic field investigators. Grounded in fluid dynamics and physical laws, such as the effect of air resistance and gravity, viscosity, and surface tension, bloodstain pattern analysis is a very technical discipline based on science and the use of the scientific method. Bloodstain patterns deposited on victims, suspects, floors, walls, ceilings, clothing, and other relevant items can provide valuable insight into the events and sequence of events that occurred during the commission of a violent crime. The analysis of bloodstain patterns involves the consideration of such factors as number, dispersion, shape, size, volume, orientation, location, and surface textures. Information potentially generated from the interpretation and in some cases mathematical calculation of bloodstain patterns includes the basic nature of the action causing the pattern, the direction from which the blood originated, the angle at which a blood droplet struck a surface, the approximate location or position of a victim at the time a blood-drawing wound was inflicted, the approximate location of the suspect inflicting the blood-drawing wound, the minimum number of blows that struck a bleeding victim, and the movement characteristics of a bleeding individual at a crime scene (Saferstein, 2009). As blood is a fluid affected by the laws of physics, bloodstain patterns resulting from a particular action are capable of being reproduced by the analyst.

Shooting Incident Reconstruction

As previously discussed, firearms and ammunition are constructed very specifically in order for projectiles to travel aerodynamically in the direction in which they are fired, thereby increasing accuracy over distance. Similar to bloodstain patterns, the path of a fired projectile is seriously affected by the laws of physics; therefore, bullet impacts resulting from a particular firearm firing specific ammunition in a specific context and into a specific substrate can be reproduced by the analyst. The skilled reconstructionist's examination of the shooting scene, including all bullet impacts, defects imparted to the impacted substrates, and all available testimonial and physical evidence, can generate the following key information regarding a shooting incident: the number of participants involved; the number and type of firearms involved; the manner in which a firearm was fired; the distance from which a firearm was fired; the location, position, and orientation of a firearm at the moment of discharge; the direction and trajectory of projectile paths; the sequence of shooting events and bullet impacts; the presence and type of any intervening objects struck during the flight of fired projectiles; and the location, position, and orientation of participants at the moment of any firearm discharge (Chisum and Turvey, 2007).

QUESTIONS FOR DISCUSSION

1. What is forensic science and how is it utilized in the criminal investigative process?
2. Describe the major responsibilities of the forensic scientist.
3. What is the scientific method?
4. Discuss the potential information generated from the forensic analysis of physical evidence.
5. Define and differentiate between class or family characteristics and individual characteristics.
6. List the types of physical evidence that commonly exhibit individual characteristics.
7. List and describe the divisions of a typical, full-service crime laboratory.
8. Describe three forensic specialties, outside of the typical crime laboratory, that are also available to investigating law enforcement personnel.

BIBLIOGRAPHY

Chisum, W.J. and Turvey, B.E., Eds. (2007). *Crime Reconstruction*. Burlington, MA: Elsevier.

Gaensslen, R.E., Harris, H.A., and Lee, H.C. (2008). *Introduction to Forensic Science and Criminalistics*. New York: McGraw-Hill.

Girard, J.E. (2008). *Criminalistics: Forensic Science and Crime*. Sudbury, MA: Jones & Bartlett.

Houde, J. (1999). *Crime Lab: A Guide for Nonscientists*. Ventura, CA: Calico Press.

James, S.H. and Nordby, J.J., Eds. (2005). *Forensic Science: An Introduction to Scientific and Investigative Techniques*, 2nd ed. Boca Raton, FL: CRC Press.

Lushbaugh, C.A. and Weston, P.B. (2009). *Criminal Investigation: Basic Perspectives*, 11th ed. Upper Saddle River, NJ: Prentice Hall.

Saferstein, R. (2009). *Forensic Science: From the Crime Scene to the Crime Lab*. Upper Saddle River, NJ: Prentice Hall.

Saferstein, R. (2011). *Criminalistics: An Introduction to Forensic Science*, 10th ed. Upper Saddle River, NJ: Prentice Hall.

3

Property Crimes and Financial Investigations

CHAPTER 8

Vandalism

Matthew O'Deane

San Diego California District Attorney's Office

CHAPTER OBJECTIVES

After reading this chapter, you should be able to do the following:

1. Identify the impact of vandalism and what purpose it serves to those engaging in it.
2. Describe how the police respond to the vandalism problem.
3. Identify ways in which communities can prevent vandalism.
4. Discuss how vandalism cases are prosecuted and addressed in the court system.

Chapter Outline

- Introduction
- Vandalism Impact
- Taggers vs. Gangs
- Vandalism Reveals Monikers
- Graffiti Is All about Respect, or Disrespect
- Folks and People Alliances
- Police Response
- Gang Injunctions
- Graffiti Search Warrants
- Control Techniques
- Educating Parents and the Community
- Vandalism and the Media
- Vandalism Prosecution

INTRODUCTION

The most visible and most problematic form of vandalism in the United States is the unlawful application of graffiti. The existing research on graffiti does not make it easy to determine where graffiti got its start in America. If writing on cave walls counts, then the first taggers were prehistoric. More recently, during World War II, the phrase "Kilroy was here" was written on tanks and military equipment throughout Europe and was later seen in the subway systems in New York. In the 1950s, street gangs began using graffiti to mark their territory, promote their gangs, and intimidate the community. The word "graffiti" comes from the Italian word for scratch, *graffio*. Graffiti is any unauthorized inscription, word, figure, mark, or design that is written, marked, etched, scratched, drawn, or painted on real or personal property, with the intent of having it be seen by the passing public. The negative impact of graffiti on a community is significant, as it can instill feelings of fear and insecurity, it causes significant problems for local jurisdictions that have to keep the community clean, residents and businesses often flee the area, and property values plummet. The presence of graffiti vandalism is an affront to all who live, work, and visit a community. Such unauthorized inscriptions and graffiti are a major problem around the world, not just in the United States. Graffiti is often referred to as the "newspaper of the streets" in the gang and tagger subculture. If that is true, we as law enforcement officers need to make sure we get the subscription so we can tell what is going on around us. We need to understand all of the basic elements of graffiti—why it is used and what it means. Gangs use graffiti to gain recognition or express the identity of the gang, and gang members are motivated to put up graffiti to reflect their loyalty to their gang. In some cases, members may be ordered by their gang to put up graffiti to demonstrate their worthiness to join and to prove that they are committed to the gang. A gang's desire to mark their territory and let others know who they are can be exploited by investigators.

It is a critical skill to understand the graffiti in your area and to be able to read it, explain it, and document it so the graffiti can be used against the gangs and crews and their individual members. Graffiti offers many practical investigative tips; for example, it can help in identifying the size and strength of the local gang, their monikers, pending or past crimes, ongoing rivalries, and their boundaries. Gangs use graffiti to claim their turf by marking their neighborhoods with graffiti on fences, schools, sidewalks, walls, homes, and street signs. Graffiti is a very important element in the investigation of street gangs. In many ways, gang graffiti is a code, and, like most codes, it is susceptible to analysis if you take the time and effort to do so.

VANDALISM IMPACT

The dollar amount spent on graffiti cleanup is enormous. In 2000, the national cost for graffiti cleanup exceeded $4 billion dollars, which is widely seen as a very conservative estimate, as only a fraction of vandalism incidents are ever reported. The police try to work closely with other city departments, such as public works or parks and recreation, as well as private property owners, to address this problem. The average cost of removing or painting over graffiti is $552 per incident in Los Angeles County, and the county spends over $30 million per year in graffiti cleanup costs. This is not unique to Los Angeles; every major city in this country has similar issues, and graffiti vandalism has significant economic repercussions everywhere it appears. The money used to clean up the damage could be directed instead toward many more productive programs or to putting more police officers on the street or addressing a wide range of social ills. Also, business owners who have to clean up their businesses after taggers hit typically offset their costs by charging higher prices for their products. Aside from the cost, graffiti makes our cities look rundown and trashed.

One of the more costly forms of vandalism occurs when people etch or scribe their names into glass, such as commercial business or bus windows. The replacement cost of glass in windows is typically between $20 and $30 dollars per square foot, depending on the grade of the glass, thickness, cut, and whether the glass is tempered or tinted. When vandals use glass as their canvas, repairing the damage can cost up to 50 times more than for conventional graffiti painted on a concrete wall. This type of vandalism is difficult to prevent, as a number of hard objects can be used to etch glass, luan, Lucite®, or other surfaces such as anodized or polished aluminum or stainless steel. In many cases, governmental agencies are tasked with cleaning up graffiti. With budgets having to be cut everywhere, governments can ill afford the millions of dollars required to deal with graffiti. On a positive note, technology has allowed crime prevention concepts to be designed into many products to make the financial impact of vandalism less costly. These techniques are discussed later in the chapter.

The only people that I have met who enjoy looking around vandalized communities are the gang members and taggers that put the graffiti there. Graffiti is believed to have a direct link to other crimes in a neighborhood; when it is not quickly removed and is left unchallenged, it often attracts more serious criminal activity. Graffiti leads to a loss of neighborhood pride, and people begin to feel intimidated in their own neighborhoods. Graffiti lowers property values and negatively impacts local business, as people tend to avoid businesses that have been vandalized in this way. In areas where gangs are allowed to destroy property at will, the physical environment supports the gang subculture and gives the local gang more power and more control over the target area. According to the "broken window" theory proposed by Kelling and Wilson (1982), if a window in a building is broken and left unrepaired, the rest of the windows will soon be broken, as this is taken as an indicator that the community does not have any interest in how the neighborhood looks. The authors suggested that untended physical disorder, antisocial behavior, and nuisance activity all lead to the breakdown of social control and increases crime.

When residents perceive that crime is rising, they often react by avoiding public spaces such as parks, and their involvement in neighborhood events is significantly reduced. That is why gang enforcement in many neighborhoods focuses on the central community parks where gangs tend to congregate so the parks can be reclaimed for legitimate public activities. The common neighborhood response of not using public spaces for recreation and leisure because of the gang's presence disrupts social balance and community attachment to the park and subsequently decreases the community's ability to regulate criminal behavior.

As crime in a community increases, so does fear of the local gang. Those with the means to do so tend to move out of the area, leaving behind those who are either unable or unwilling to counter the presence of the local gang (Shaw and McKay, 1942). The remaining residents become even less likely to report crimes committed by the gang and less likely to provide information to the police. The community purposefully or inadvertently helps the gangs evade justice for crimes committed against the community. In areas where gangs are allowed to destroy property at will, the physical environment supports the gang subculture and gives the local gang more power and more control over the target area (BJA, 1998; Dubin, 1959; Goldstein, 1990).

In 1992, a group of police, prosecutors, and neighborhood residents in Los Angeles gathered and determined that the need for other remedies such as trash collection, graffiti cleanup, and building and code enforcement to improve the quality of life in neighborhoods should go hand in hand with each injunction (Skogan, 1988). Thus, civil gang abatement is often viewed as most effective when used as part of a coordinated effort involving law enforcement, community mobilization, and the restoration of municipal services essential to quality of life (Hanh, 1992). Graffiti may be considered a low priority compared to other crimes, but to the small business owner it is very costly, both in clean-up and in the negative perception of being in unsafe areas. One thing everyone seems to agree on is that local businesses smeared with paint and markers are suffering heavy financial and emotional costs, and it scares away potential customers, which results in businesses increasing prices to offset their losses.

TAGGERS VS. GANGS

The first thing one should do when trying to determine if graffiti is tagger or gang related is to look at the letters and the overall design or symbols used. If it has "bubble letters," for example, and contains more than one color of paint or ink or shows even a hint of skill, then it almost certainly is not gang related. If it has sharp, angular stick letters done in one color of paint it probably is gang related. Graffiti was once solely associated with gangs; however, tagger graffiti now far exceeds gang graffiti in terms of property damage. Vandalism is a significant property crime, but the crime of vandalism often escalates into a crime against a person, as violence often follows acts of vandalism. Taki 183 was probably one of the most well-known taggers; his nickname was Taki, and he lived on 183rd Street in Manhattan. Taki worked as a messenger, and wherever he made deliveries throughout Brooklyn he would also write his name. The first article about a tagger appeared in *The New York Times* in 1971, when they published an interview with Taki.

Tagger graffiti is typically more colorful and more elaborate when compared to gang graffiti. Tagger crews are loose affiliations, typically comprised of young people whose principal activity is graffiti. Some of these tagger crews will try to pass themselves off as party crews—groups of young people that evolve around social functions such as raves and house parties—to avoid the police scrutiny that their gang member friends typically receive.

Taggers come from every race and socioeconomic background; most taggers are males. Taggers can be identified in many cases by the graffiti written on their clothing, such as their shoes or inside their baseball caps; schoolbooks; notebooks; backpacks; compact disc covers; and bedroom furniture or walls. They frequently wear baggy pants and carry backpacks when headed out to vandalize, carrying with them cans of spray paint, various colors and types of magic markers, etching tools, piece books, slap tags, and cameras to photograph their creations. Many times taggers carry the tools used for etching glass or mirror surfaces such as spark plug porcelain, drill bits, screwdrivers with a sharpened tip, small rocks, or any other type of sharp instrument. They may also carry stickers that have drawings or a tagging moniker written on them. These stickers are used to "slap tag"—that is, they are slapped on a surface and are difficult to remove and generally leave a residue. Many times taggers can be identified by paint or marker residue on their fingertips, and they may carry notebooks that contain tagging drawings. They tend to visit tagging websites, subscribe to tagging magazines, or have photographs of tagging in their possession. Taggers generally tag in or near their own neighborhoods and, like traditional gang members, associate with other people who exhibit these same traits.

Tagging has long been considered a steppingstone to gang membership. The term "tag" is believed to be derived from an early group of graffiti artists who called themselves the "Tuff Artist Group." Taggers in many cases are not the same as gang members, although many taggers and their crews have turned into gangs over the years. A tagger is a person who adopts a nickname (i.e., tag) as opposed to a gang member's moniker. They write their tag in as many places as possible so it can be seen by as many people as possible. Taggers enjoy greater popularity and reknown among their peers when their tags can be seen in many locations, especially those difficult to access. Taggers have their own subculture, language, and dress that set them apart from street gangs. Their clothing tends to be very baggy to conceal their spray paint and brighter than the clothing worn by gangs. Many wear clothing designed specifically for taggers and emulate popular hip-hop culture. Some crews are all one ethnicity, but taggers as a whole care less about the race of the person and more about how often they can get the crew name up on walls, freeway signs, subway trains, buses, and other public places.

Taggers tend to be younger kids, typically 12 to 18 years old. The older kids are often referred to as "kings," the younger kids as "toys." Tagger crews can range in size from 4 to as many as 200 members. When rivalries occur between crews, they sometimes solve the dispute with a "battle," a competition where the rival crews have a designated time frame in which to mark a particular area. Their work is then judged by a predetermined third party. The winner keeps their name; the loser has to change their name.

Tagger crew names are typically three letters, although they can range from two to five letters; the letters represent the full name of the crew (e.g., RCA for Ruthless City Artists, RTS for Running the Show, SEK for South East Kings). Numbers in a crew name can derive from a phone pad number (e.g., 787 for RTS) or can be a code that represents letters (e.g., 1 = A, 2 = B). They can also be telephone area codes, penal codes, or a combination of any of these elements to add to the confusion; for example, 1972 on a wall could represent the Sycho Pathic Crew (i.e., the 19 equals S from the number/letter code, and 7 equals P and

2 equals C from the phone pad). A lot can be learned about gang members based on their monikers, and the same is true when looking at the name of a tagging crew. Many taggers consider themselves just a group of writers, not vandals; they feel that they have the talent of professional writers and as such often incorporate the term "writer" into their name. Examples include Able to Rite (ATR), Kalling All Riters (KAR), Writers Making Masterpieces (WMM), or The Write to Survive (TWTS). Some crews honor their favorite method for applying graffiti, such as Spray Kan Artists (SKA), Living on Aerosol (LOA), or Krylon Criminals (KC). Other crews honor the destructive nature of their activity, such as Trash Shit Up (TSU), City under Siege (CUS), or Leaving Serious Damage (LSD). Some names tell you what targets the gang prefers, such as All Over Buses (AOB), Rapid Transit District Killers (RTDK), or Interstate Freeway Taggers (IFT). Others tell you the ethnicity of the gang, such as Mexicans Taking Kontrol (MTK), The Mexican Kings (TMK), or Krazy Ass Mexicans (KAM). Some names give away the gender of the group, such as Bitches with Attitude (BWA), Queens Causing Trouble (QCT), or Crazy Fantasy Girls (CFG). Still other names suggest how the crews view themselves, such as Criminals Out Shooting (COS) or We're No Angels (WNA).

Taggers as we know them today have made a significant transition from the early days. Crews have become more violent, and many have been classified as "tag bangers" by police. Once a tagger crew starts to claim a turf, jump members into the group, actively attack rivals for entering their turf, and align with other gangs for protection, they are no longer a tagger crew. It is important to clarify that a tag banger *is* a gang member. From a law enforcement perspective, it is important to investigate taggers in the same manner as we do street gangs. The first thing many officers need to do is eliminate the mindset that it is "just tagging." Vandalism and property crimes take a back seat to violent crimes for many officers, but not dealing with the graffiti problem in an aggressive manner allows the gang problem to get worse. It is also important to note that many street gang members have tagger friends and may even adopt a tag so they can claim to be "just" a tagger when stopped by police.

Increasingly, they are wannabe gangsters who use the mobility and guise of a tagger crew to take their crimes beyond the boundaries of their turf. They generally work under the cover of darkness, particularly when doing extensive murals and marking freeway signs and other public places where risk of exposure is high. They will, however, deface property whenever they have the opportunity to do so. Taggers typically plan graffiti missions in advance and conduct prior surveillance of locations to check for security, cameras, and potential escape routes.

Gang graffiti serves one of the following purposes:

- Establish the presence of a gang or gangs.
- Establish turf or territory.
- Warn of impending danger or threats.
- Put down rival gangs or issue a challenge.
- Target a community at large (e.g., racist gang graffiti).

Gang members have placed a major emphasis on identifying themselves and their gang affiliation, and they use a variety of methods to communicate with each other and carry out their gang-related business, one of the most visible being graffiti. Graffiti illustrates the individual gang member's commitment to the gang and their claim to the neighborhood; it tells the world who they are and what they represent. Graffiti is also great evidence against gang members and has tremendous investigative significance for anyone who investigates gang members and gang crimes.

For Hispanic gangs from Southern California, the number 13 (often written on the streets as XIII or X3) represents the fact that these gangs are *Surenos* (Southerners). The number 13 represents the letter M, which is the 13th letter of the alphabet, and the letter M stands for "Eme," or the Mexican Mafia. Gangs from Northern California, called *Nortenos*, may use the number 14 (XIV or X4), which represents N, the 14th letter of the alphabet, and the letter N stands for Nuestra Familia. The Fresno Chankla Bulldogs, for example, use 14 to indicate that they are aligned with the north, and the Old Town National City (OTNC) gang uses 13 to indicate that they are aligned with the south. Many gang names, particularly those from Southern California, include the numbers or names of the streets on which the gang was originally founded (e.g., 18th Street and 38th Street in Los Angeles, 7th Street in San Bernardino, or 30th Street in San Diego). Many Los Angeles area gangs use telephone area codes in their graffiti. Sometimes the side of town may also be indicated by number, such as 519, which represents the East Side (i.e., 5 for E, 19 for S).

Gang graffiti helps the police investigate gangs and understand many aspects of gangs, including the different ways in which a gang can express its name. Graffiti typically helps the police identify a street gang's territory and provides other useful information, such as the monikers of individual street gang members, indications of pending gang violence, current rivalries, and overall size of the gang based on gang rosters. When detectives start from what is believed to be the center of a gang's territory and follow the graffiti out in every direction, they can define the borders of that gang. Having recent examples of graffiti around the perimeter of an area is one of the best and most accurate methods to show the gang's recent presence in the area and help prove their claim on the area to a court of law.

VANDALISM REVEALS MONIKERS

Graffiti is used to promote or enhance the names and reputations of a gang and its members. In some cases, gang members use graffiti to brag about crimes they have committed, and it is not uncommon to find graffiti at the scene of a gang crime to send the message that the gang is in control. It is common for monikers to show up on graffiti "roll calls," or *placas*; they are symbols of acceptance by the gang and are critical in gang and vandalism investigations. Just about every gang member has a nickname or moniker that they substitute for their real name. Many times a moniker is the only name by which a witness, rival gang member, or even fellow gang members will know someone, making the identification of a moniker a very critical element in many gang investigations. Monikers do not have to make sense, they do not have to be spelled correctly, and they are often helpful in identifying an

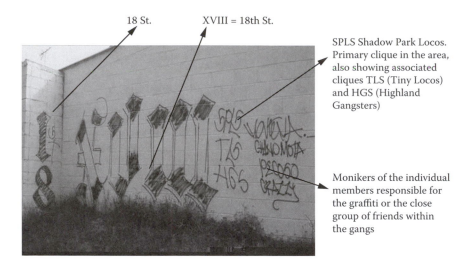

18 St.   XVIII = 18th St.

SPLS Shadow Park Locos. Primary clique in the area, also showing associated cliques TLS (Tiny Locos) and HGS (Highland Gangsters)

Monikers of the individual members responsible for the graffiti or the close group of friends within the gangs

FIGURE 8.1 Gang graffiti.

unknown offender. The moniker may reflect a distinctive aspect of a gang member's personality, physical characteristics, reputation, or other trait. These names may be quite simple and typically refer to the appearance or personality of the gang member, such as "Lonely," "Silent," "Playboy," "Droopy," "Boxer," "Popeye," "Shy Boy," "Pony," "Pirate," "Sneaky," "Speedy," "Gordo," or "Flaco." A moniker can also shed some light on the person's status or a particular talent; for example, someone known as "Trigger" or "Shooter" likely has a propensity to use or possess firearms.

Identifying the monikers of gang members is very important for documentation and conducting gang-related investigations. Gang members now use monikers so dependably that they can provide a critical source of investigative information. Self-admissions, graffiti, informant interviews, and monitoring or recording inmate visits or conversations among gang members are some ways to identify gang members' monikers during an investigation. Typically, graffiti will include the name of the gang, nicknames of the members, and slogans, messages, or symbols exclusive to the gang (see Figure 8.1). Gang names are usually abbreviated to two or three letters but the affiliation of the gang may be written out (e.g., Crips, Bloods, Surenos, Nortenos, Folks, People), as well as their slogans.

GRAFFITI IS ALL ABOUT RESPECT, OR DISRESPECT

The respect shown or not shown to every gang and every gang member is a critical concern to all gangs and all tagger crews. Respect is so important that, in some cases, if a gang member or tagger fails to disrespect a rival through hand signs, graffiti, or a simple mad-dog stare, they could be disciplined by their own gang or crew. Respect in this case really means fear. Those who join a gang or crew will constantly have to commit crimes to keep other members afraid of them. Outside the gang and tagger world, respect is something you can earn by getting an education and accomplishing your goals in life; in their world, respect is earned by being violent or by being prolific, such as in the case of a tagger. They gain the recognition they desire by applying their tag name in as many places as possible, despite the impact on the community. Because members of different gangs often live in close proximity to one another, graffiti can and usually does provoke confrontations. Gangs may misspell or alter a rival gang's name or symbol as a sign of disrespect, or they may add "Killer" to a rival gang's name; for example, a Blood member might paint "Crip Killer" or abbreviate it as "CK." A West Coast Crip gang member will use "FUCC" for the word "FUCK," because he does not want to use the letters "CK," which could be mistaken as standing for Crip Killer, which he most definitely is not. Often graffiti threatens or challenges rival gangs. A gang typically will cross out the graffiti of a rival gang or gang member or write "187" (for homicide) or some other derogatory term next to it.

FOLKS AND PEOPLE ALLIANCES

The Folks and the People alliances were established in the penitentiary system of the Illinois Department of Corrections in the mid-1970s by incarcerated gang members seeking protection through "coalition building." These groups adopted common identifiers to show other gangs the alignment of gang members. These gangs use many of the same identifiers; however, they point these identifiers to the left side or right side of their body as appropriate. The seven largest gangs in the middle portion of the United States are the Gangster Disciple Nation, comprised of the Gangster Disciples and Black Disciples (Folks); Black Gangsters or New Breeds (Folks or Independent); Latin Kings (People); Black P Stone Nation (People); Vice Lords (People); Four Corner Hustlers (People); and the Maniac Latin Disciples (Folks). These gangs account for 80% of all gang members in the metropolitan Chicago area.

POLICE RESPONSE

Many law enforcement operations targeting gangs are designed to protect the physical environment and limit social disorganization in the neighborhoods (Akiyama, 2003; Livingston, 1997; Wilson, 1988). When gang members are in possession of marker pens, spray paint cans, or other sharp objects capable of defacing private or public property, they are ready to damage property where they feel it is appropriate. As such, it is important for law enforcement to address such minor violations to limit the potential damage to public and private property and hinder gang members' ability to advertise themselves to the community. When the police apprehend gang members spray painting, marking with marker pens, scratching glass windows of shops or public transit, applying stickers, or otherwise applying graffiti on any public or private property, including but not limited to streets, alleys, residences, block walls, vehicles, or any other real or personal property, they are helping protect the environment of the neighborhood, in theory, and holding gang members responsible for even minor violations. A police agency may want to organize a trap for a tagger operation, which may include selecting an area that is heavily targeted by vandals, finding a wall to paint clean as a tempting target, and conducting surveillance. The key is to know the area well; taggers typically tend to run upon contact, so it is essential to have a sufficient number of officers to cut off potential escape routes. Video surveillance makes these cases easy to prove, and because the witnesses are police officers citizen informants are not necessary.

GANG INJUNCTIONS

Provisions of gang injunctions include restricting the possession of marker pens, spray paint cans, or other sharp objects capable of defacing private or public property, as well as spray painting, marking with marker pens, scratching, applying stickers or otherwise applying graffiti on any public or private property, including but not limited to streets, alleys, residences, block walls, vehicles, or any other real or personal property. Some injunctions contain wording that restricts damaging or vandalizing the property of another, both public and private property, including but limited to any vehicle, light fixture, door, fence, wall, gate, window, building, street sign, utility box, telephone box, trees, or power poles (Crowe, 2000). In 1982, the Los Angeles city attorney and the Los Angeles police took a new approach to addressing the problem of gang graffiti. A civil gang injunction was obtained against three gangs; Dogtown, Primera Flats, and the 62nd East Coast Crips. Seventy-two members of the three gangs were targeted with a civil gang injunction that had restrictions only aimed at reducing graffiti, including prohibiting graffiti on private property, on public property, and trespassing on private property with the intent to place graffiti. The injunction also contained an order for the gang to clean up the graffiti that displayed the name of their gangs. The graffiti attributed to these gangs covered storefronts, billboards, houses, and fences and allowed the gangs to control their territory. The injunction required the 72 named defendants to do 5 hours of community service to clean up their graffiti. The drive for this graffiti cleanup was based in part on the theories of Thrasher (1927), who suggested that gang graffiti promoted solidarity, group awareness, and attachment to a local territory.

GRAFFITI SEARCH WARRANTS

When writing search warrants in your vandalism investigations, consider seeking judicial approval to obtain the following:

1. Evidence of involvement in or creation of graffiti, tagging, or illegal "street art," including cans of spray paint, nozzles from other kinds of aerosol sprays, etching tools or other sharp or pointed objects used to etch or scratch glass and other hard surfaces, and permanent marking pens, such as Magic Markers, Sharpies, etc.
2. Evidence of membership or affiliation with any tagging crew, such as any reference to a tagger's name, and any drawings, writings, objects, or graffiti depicting taggers' names, initials, logos, monikers, slogans, or mention of tagging crew membership or affiliation, activity, or identity, whether memorialized electronically, digitally (including the central processing unit/hard drive, floppy disk, CD-ROM, or other electronic storage medium), or on paper in books, sketch pads, tablets, notebooks, and the like

3. Any paintings, drawings, photographs, photograph albums, photographic negatives, image disks, memory sticks, undeveloped film, or homemade videotapes depicting persons, vehicles, weapons, or locations that appear upon observation to be relevant to tagging crew membership or association, or depicting items believed to be evidence in the case being investigated with this warrant, or which depict evidence of any criminal activity

4. Any newspaper clippings relating details of or referring to any graffiti crime

5. Any address books, lists of, or single references to addresses or telephone numbers of persons who are determined to belong to or to be affiliated with any tagging crews

6. Deadly weapons, such as knives and accessories such as sheaths

7. Firearms, including ammunition, casings, holsters, targets, and cleaning equipment

8. Papers, documents, and effects tending to show dominion and control over said premises, including keys, fingerprints, clothing, photographs, image disks, memory sticks, photographic negatives, undeveloped film, homemade videotapes, and any other non-commercially manufactured video or audio recordings

9. Handwriting, documents, and effects bearing a form of identification such as a person's name, photograph, Social Security number, or driver's license number

10. Permission to answer incoming phone calls, either landline or cellular, during execution of the warrant; to view any videotapes seized pursuant to the warrant; and to open or download and forensically examine all computer memory, software, and programs seized pursuant to the warrant

CONTROL TECHNIQUES

Vandalism control can be accomplished in several ways: by dealing with at-risk youth who may become vandals (prevention), dealing with those that have already joined gangs or tagger crews (intervention), and holding vandals accountable for their actions (suppression).

PREVENTION

True vandalism prevention seeks to work in innovative and creative ways to enable young people to feel empowered to make safe and informed choices. One approach is to work with young people to raise their awareness of the risks of gang and tagger crew involvement, the consequences of engaging in criminal acts of vandalism, and developing exit strategies for those who are already involved in doing acts of vandalism. Vandalism prevention includes the strategies, actions, and efforts used to dissuade youth from getting involved in gangs and tagger crews, violence, and antisocial behavior. The goal is to find those youth who are most likely to join a gang in the future and offer them alternatives and support to make better choices. Examples include information campaigns, after-school and summer programs, truancy and dropout prevention, and prenatal and infancy support. Stopping youth from joining in the first place will obviously reduce gang membership and gang crime. Also proving effective is Crime Prevention Through Environmental Design (CPTED), which is defined as the proper design and effective use of the built environment to reduce crime, disorder, and the fear associated with crime.

INTERVENTION

Intervention includes the strategies, actions, and efforts used to dissuade youth from continuing their involvement in a gang and to discourage violence and antisocial behavior. Intervention targets active gang members and their close associates, and it requires aggressive outreach, ongoing recruitment, and careful planning and coordination. A multidisciplinary intervention team can provide assessment, intervention planning, and case management, relying upon the proverbial carrot and stick, where the carrot represents opportunities and the stick accountability.

The Los Angeles County Sheriff's Department and the cities of Downey, La Mirada, Norwalk, Santa Fe Springs, and Whittier launched Aware Teens against Graffiti (ATAG), an innovative delinquency prevention program that targets first-time tagging and vandalism offenders between the ages of 9 to 15 and their parents. The weekend-long program focuses on the parents receiving an intensive two-day skill-building training, and the youth offenders participating in community service projects and group discussions while being supervised by law enforcement. The goal is to get the first-time offender through the system and encourage them not to reoffend.

What motivates graffiti vandals? Some of them just want to damage property, but most get a thrill out of seeing their art or tags in places where lots of other people can see them, too. If you can deny graffiti vandals this thrill, they will go elsewhere next time or may reduce their involvement in vandalism activity altogether. Over the past several years, graffiti vandalism has exploded nationwide; particularly hard hit is San Diego, CA, where graffiti costs the city millions of dollars annually. Many individual citizens and community-based groups are working to stop the vandals and repair the damage they are causing. Also, modern advances are reducing the costs associated with repairing vandalism; for example, San Diego transit buses now have a thin layer of plastic on both sides of the glass that can be more easily replaced when vandals scratch their names in the glass, keeping transit cleaner for less money.

Law enforcement personnel report that many graffiti vandals claim to have stolen or "racked" the paint, markers, or etching tools used in their crimes. Vandals also claim that they have no problem buying spray paint from retail stores. The city's Responsible Retailer Program is a direct and practical response to this problem, where retailers voluntarily step up employee education and internal security to deprive graffiti vandals of the legitimate products they misuse to commit property crimes. The program involves in-store activities designed to reduce retail theft of potential graffiti tools and to stop the illegal sale of spray paint to customers under the age of 18. It includes training store employees, strategically placing signs at display and check-out points, and displaying potential graffiti tools in a prudent manner. Through awareness and strengthened self-policing, San Diego retailers are constricting the flow of products into the hands of those who use them in graffiti crimes. Further, by joining the program, participating retailers can curtail costly theft from their stores while demonstrating an active concern for the problems of the community in which they do business.

There are also laws that compel compliance similar to that promoted by the Responsible Retailer Program; for example, the Los Angeles Municipal Code (§47.11) states: "Every person who owns, conducts, operates, or manages a retail commercial establishment selling aerosol containers or marker pens with tips exceeding four millimeters in width, containing anything other than a solution which can be removed with water after it dries, shall store or cause such aerosol containers or marker pens to be stored in an area viewable by, but not accessible to, the public in the regular course of business without employee assistance, pending legal sale or disposition of such market pens or paint containers." The Los Angeles Municipal Code (§47.16) also states that, "Every person who owns, conducts, operates, or manages a retail commercial establishment selling glass-etching cream or any commercially available glass-etching products, whether sold separately or in a kit in an area viewable by, but not accessible to, the public in the regular course of business without employee assistance, pending legal sale or disposition of such glass etching cream or glass etching product is in violation of this section. No person who has not yet attained the age of 18 years can purchase such items. Therefore this ordinance requires anyone who displays for sale glass etching cream, or any commercially available glass etching product, whether sold separately or in a kit, to display it under lock and key and allow its sale only to persons 18 years of age or older."

The California Penal Code (§594.1) addresses the sale, purchase, or possession of aerosol paint container and mandates posting of notice by retailers: "(a) It shall be unlawful for any person, firm, or corporation, except a parent or legal guardian, to sell or give or in any way furnish to another person, who is in fact under the age of 18 years, any aerosol container of paint that is capable of defacing property without first obtaining bona fide evidence of majority and identity. (b) It shall be unlawful for any person under the age of 18 years to purchase an aerosol container of paint that is capable of defacing property. (c) Every retailer selling or offering for sale in this state aerosol containers of paint capable of defacing property shall post in a conspicuous place a sign in letters at least three-eighths of an inch high stating: Any person who maliciously defaces real or personal property with paint is guilty of vandalism which is punishable by a fine, imprisonment, or both." The California Penal Code (§594.2) also addresses the possession of specified instruments with intent to commit vandalism or graffiti: "Every person who possesses a masonry or glass drill bit, a carbide drill bit, a glass cutter, a grinding stone, an awl, a chisel, a carbide scribe, an aerosol paint container, a felt tip marker, or any other marking substance with the intent to commit vandalism or graffiti, is guilty of a misdemeanor. For the purposes of this section, 'felt tip marker' means any broad-tipped marker pen with a tip exceeding three-eighths of one inch in width, or any similar implement containing an ink that is not water soluble. Marking substance means any substance or implement, other than aerosol paint containers and felt tip markers, which could be used to draw, spray, paint, etch, or mark."

A common application of nuisance abatement laws is forcing owners to act against gang use of their buildings or face a governmental takeover; for example, landlords have been court-ordered to clean up graffiti, erect security gates, install lighting, remove abandoned cars, and evict known drug dealers. Such orders are commonly coordinated with community policing tactics to reinforce the owner's ability to act against gangs. Local building and housing codes can also be used against gang locations, compelling property owners to comply with fire, health and sanitation, and zoning requirements.

Eliminating potential targets of gang crime can be accomplished in a number of ways. Many times, physical changes to a location can make it less desirable to a gang as a target because it requires significantly more effort or increases the risk of apprehension. Sometimes, simply adding a light or a lock on a gate may be enough to make the gang member move on to an easier target. These strategies are part of a broader concept, mentioned earlier, known as Crime Prevention Through Environmental Design (CPTED). Further targets are areas where gangs tend to congregate. Many times they plan crimes at these locations, and they serve as safe havens for gang members after they have committed a crime. Having detailed information about these locations is critical to gang investigators and increases the chances of capturing suspects and solving crimes. Understanding the physical layout of these gang hangouts can aid in cutting off potential escape routes, and crime prevention techniques can be applied to make these locations less desirable.

Crime Prevention Through Environmental Design is based on the idea that situational factors such as the environment (e.g., poor lighting) can make crime more likely to occur at a particular time and place. CPTED measures can include installing additional lighting, cleaning up the area, removing graffiti, and addressing housing issues. Some locations that are well-known crime hot spots are poorly supervised, poorly managed, and inadequately lit. Changing some of those situational factors can help reduce levels of crime in these places.

Traditional local law enforcement typically operates on a reactive basis; that is, police wait for a call for service and react by arriving at the scene and, when appropriate, making an arrest. The emphasis in law enforcement circles today is to become more proactive to prevent crimes from occurring in the first place. Community policing is a proactive form of policing that still encompasses reactive law enforcement. The community policing philosophy emphasizes identification and resolution of gang problems and conditions that cause gang crime rather than focusing exclusively on individual gang incidents. The approach requires close cooperation between citizens and police officers, and many view community-oriented policing as an attractive option for addressing fears that often are prevalent among minority communities. Police agencies must sell their anti-gang program to community members so they will not consider it a form of repression against their neighborhoods and will see it for what it is: a response the community deserves to protect it and remove violent offenders from the area.

Following are some suggestions related to CPTED and reducing the threat of gangs:

- Erect fences between your business and public property to better define your boundaries and make it more difficult for graffiti vandals to get close enough to your walls.

- Remove large trees or bushes that block people's view of vandals. The best landscaping in graffiti-prone areas is short bushes planted along the walls to keep potential vandals from getting too close. Make sure to keep the bushes well trimmed.
- Use pebbles around the building to create noise when people are walking, although this will only make a difference if someone is around to hear the noise, see what is happening, and do something about it.
- Move dumpsters to the end of an alley to reduce graffiti. Call dumpster companies and ask them to keep graffiti off of dumpsters.
- If payphones or benches close to your business encourage people to hang out, see about getting them removed.
- Use motion-detector lights. Keeping the lights on all night makes it easier for people to see graffiti vandals, but it also lets the vandals see what they are doing and lets others see the graffiti when they are done. Also, if an area is usually dark, it will be more noticeable if it is suddenly lit up.
- Install video cameras, especially systems that activate by sensor and start recording when someone is on the property. These systems reduce the time needed to review recordings and more importantly can alert owners via text when the system has been activated. These systems are also beneficial when used in connection with sting operations; once a system has been triggered, officers can move into the area covertly and make an arrest.
- Conduct weekly inspections on your property and in your community to help prevent graffiti.
- Clean up graffiti right away, but only after it has been documented. Gang members and taggers take the messages they read in graffiti seriously, and the longer graffiti is left up in a neighborhood the greater the risk that the threats will be acted upon. The swift removal of the graffiti will let gangs know that people in the community will not tolerate their vandalism and that they care about their community.

One important factor to consider when instructing citizens to clean graffiti is their personal safety. Many citizens have been the victim of violent crimes because they were cleaning graffiti off of their property. In some gang neighborhoods, graffiti is cleaned by the police so the gangs see that the police are responsible for the graffiti being cleaned up, not local citizens. We do not want to turn cleaning graffiti into a death sentence for members of the community. When graffiti is not cleaned up immediately, it can often multiply as different gangs cross out their rivals' messages and add their own. The faster you remove the graffiti, the less of a thrill the vandal gets. This is an important point. Removing graffiti promptly is the best way to prevent it from occurring again. Some cleanup jobs take just a few minutes, but others can take all day.

The police encourage property owners to use graffiti-resistant surface coatings. There are products on the market, such as graffiti-proof paint, that make it easier to clean off the paint; these products can prevent spray paint, permanent marker, and ink from penetrating the surface, thus making graffiti removal simpler and allowing the use of water-based or other standard cleaning products. Applying a clear-coat finish can protect painted and unpainted surfaces. Repainting the entire wall leaves no trace of graffiti ever having been there and does not draw the attention of vandals. This approach is much more effective than painting over just the graffiti. When repainting over graffiti, it is advisable to use the same color paint as the wall or a neutral color such as gray, white, or beige. The closer the color match, the more effective it will be in preventing further vandalism. The key is to be persistent. It may be necessary to clean up the graffiti three times before the vandals realize it is not worth their effort. The vandals' objective is to have others see their tag name, so they are drawn to walls that are not routinely cleaned immediately because they know their tag will be up longer and seen by more people. Before attempting to clean up graffiti, it is important to identify the method used by the vandals to apply the graffiti and the type of surface to which it has been applied. Smooth, hard surfaces are the easiest to clean; rough, porous surfaces the most difficult. The materials used to apply the graffiti (e.g., spray paint, grease pencils, felt tip pens, water-based paint, stickers, shoe polish, crayons) affect the difficulty of cleaning up the graffiti.

Many times the most obvious removal methods work, such as soap, water, and a soft brush. Try this method first to do the least amount of damage to the surface being cleaned. If using soap and water does not work, then the use of a more powerful removal product appropriate for the application method and surface is recommended. In many cases, graffiti can be cleaned using a removal product rather than painting over it. Removing graffiti is preferred since it is easier than painting and eliminates the difficulty of matching paint.

SUPPRESSION

The involvement of law enforcement when criminal activity occurs is an appropriate response. Gang leaders and hardcore members should be targeted for aggressive suppression backed by the full force of the law. Law enforcement, parole and probation officers, and prosecutors must work together to remove dangerous and influential gang members from the community through effective use of gang intelligence (e.g., wiretaps, informants, enhancements), targeting, and vertical prosecution.

EDUCATING PARENTS AND THE COMMUNITY

Awareness is the key; for example, can people in the community recognize taggers, can they deal with them, and do they know what to do when they are the victim of graffiti vandalism? In many cases, parents are unaware of their child's involvement in tagger crews. Many parents assume a "not my child" attitude, which can be addressed by educating parents on the signs and symptoms of vandalism.

GRAFFITI REWARD PROGRAMS

Some cities offer a reward for information leading to the arrest and prosecution of suspects involved in tagging or graffiti. The Santa Clarita graffiti rewards program is available to individuals or entities that report or identify any persons responsible for acts of graffiti vandalism within the city limits of Santa Clarita. The amount of the reward is based on the information provided and the action taken. A graffiti reward program application and approval from the Los Angeles County Sheriff's Department are required before any reward funds are distributed. No rewards are awarded until each case has cleared the judicial system and sentencing has been established.

LEGAL LOCATIONS FOR GRAFFITI

Writers Block, 5010 Market Street in San Diego, is a good example of where it is legal to do graffiti; it offers an opportunity to legally practice graffiti art in a place designed for just that purpose. I have visited this location several times, and I am always surprised by the sophisticated artwork being created. Consisting of row upon row of sheets of plywood and covering a couple of acres, Writers Block allows anyone to bring their own paints and create a design. It is a place for youths to gather after school and on weekends to create street art using cans of spray paint in a controlled, supervised, and, most importantly, completely legal setting in which no private or public property is damaged.

GRAFFITI HOTLINES

Graffiti abatement hotlines allow citizens to call in and report vandalism and have it removed. San Diego's hotline, for example, receives over 4000 calls per year. In addition to reporting the graffiti, callers can learn more about prevention. A frequent complaint about these hotlines is the response time, as there is often a significant delay between a property owner calling about the graffiti and the actual removal of it. Eliminating such delays should be a consideration for any jurisdiction planning on operating a hotline. Local jurisdictions must convince the callers that their complaint of vandalism will be a priority and that it will be cleaned up right away. If the jurisdiction does not have the resources to respond to complaints in a timely manner, the value of the hotline diminishes. Crews must be able to respond to individual service calls made to the graffiti hotline as well as focus on cleanup near schools, parks, and major intersections and transit routes to have the biggest impact.

VANDALISM AND THE MEDIA

A tagger's motivation is exposure, exposure, exposure. That is why media reports avoid showing examples of vandalism on a large scale, and they do not disclose the exact locations of recently cleaned areas, as this is often a challenge to taggers to immediately vandalize it again to send the community a message. It is counterproductive to identify clean canvases for vandals.

VANDALISM PROSECUTION

Like all other gang and tagger cases, a gang expert is necessary when prosecuting vandalism cases. In 1993, I had the opportunity to be part of a 2-month undercover operation that targeted tagger crews. Officers posed as members of an Australian movie production company called Star Productions that was doing a documentary on taggers. Officers distributed posters and flyers throughout the tagger community, seeking participants for the documentary. Taggers who came into the studio thought they were going to be in the film; they were asked to fill out an information sheet, submit to an interview, and show the film crew examples of their work in the studio and in the field. Thirty-seven people were arrested during this 6-month sting operation. Letting their egos rule, these taggers unwittingly took officers who they thought were producers on a graffiti tour of the county, proudly pointing out their artwork on walls and freeways. Their admissions were captured on videotape. Hundreds of acts of vandalisms in the San Diego area were solved. The key to this operation was aggregation of the individual incidents of vandalism which caused the total dollar amount in damage to rise above the level that constitutes a felony. Expert testimony can be extremely useful in graffiti vandalism prosecutions, as it can be used to explain how graffiti vandals operate, their motivation, their terminology, and psychology. Further, this type of testimony can be used to prove damages when a damage amount is required by your offense or for the purpose of restitution.

AGGREGATION OF DAMAGES: GRAFFITI TRACKER DATABASES

The theory behind aggregation of damages is that offenders caught putting up graffiti can be charged not just with one count of vandalism but for all of the other damage for which they are responsible. This has two main benefits. One, it sends a signal to the offenders that their vandalism is being tracked. Two, a city can seek restitution from offenders for all of the damage that they have committed, not merely a single incident. The system gives law enforcement personnel real-time, street-level intelligence that allows them not only to focus on the worst graffiti offenders and their damage but also to monitor potential gang violence associated with the graffiti. Some cities have found a way to exploit graffiti by establishing a tracking program that empowers law enforcement and prosecutors to use this form of street-level intelligence in court. The law allows for aggregation of damages for felony filings with a series of graffiti vandalism against different victims when there is one intention, one general impulse, and one plan. To make this a reality, many police departments have created databases to track incidents of graffiti. Often, city workers or contractors hired to clean up graffiti or even homeowners who have to clean their fences, for example, will take photos of the graffiti before removing it. They calculate the cost to repair the damage and provide their photographs to the police for investigation. These photographs are uploaded into the tracker system, where they can be compared to similar incidents of vandalism to try to solve a series of separate vandalism offenses. Many times agencies will use GPS in their cameras to show exactly where a photograph was taken but even more important in most cases is who took the photograph, as every photograph must be authenticated. Typically, people who have taken such photographs must testify that they did, in fact, take the photographs; they must provide information about where and when they took the photographs, what graffiti they cleaned up, how many supplies they needed, and the total cost of the graffiti removal. The key to using these databases is having a standardized procedures set up in public works or graffiti abatement operations to make sure these photographs can be used.

Another advantage of graffiti tracker systems is geographic information systems (GIS) mapping software. Mapping a suspect's graffiti can demonstrate a connection between the locations of the graffiti and the location of the offender's residence. This approach has been used successfully to secure search warrants of gang members' residences. During the course of such searches, it is common to find not only instruments of the crime but also additional graffiti at the offender's residence. This graffiti can then be matched in style to the graffiti stored in tracker databases. Graffiti databases allow vandalism incidents to be fully documented against an offender for criminal prosecution and give law enforcement the ability to conduct rapid searches on offenders in a simple, effective, and comprehensive way. Known offenders, known associates, crews, and gang affiliations can be readily identified and additional arrests made. These systems can also track the costs of damages, which can help cities allocate anti-graffiti budgets and allow city attorneys and prosecutors to readily gain restitution from offenders by keeping track of the damage estimates. These systems also centralize data collection methods through one system, including information from graffiti hotlines and code enforcement officers. Digital cameras allow stakeholders to easily document vandalism for the database, and it is possible to map locations where graffiti is most prevalent. Graffiti databases can benefit a city through coordination of graffiti crime investigations across operational or political boundaries; they can help uncover graffiti patterns, track gang migrations, and develop anti-graffiti strategies; and they can build, enhance, and centralize evidence for more substantial arrests and prosecution of suspects. The automatic linking of similar incidents to develop actionable intelligence can aid in identifying suspects, witnesses, and contacts.

CALIFORNIA EVIDENCE CODE SECTION 1410.5: HANDWRITING

Unfortunately, the fact that the tagger's name is on the wall does not prove that the person who uses the name actually did anything; for example, a freeway sign may contain several names placed there by one tagger, and some taggers plagiarize or bite other taggers' monikers, especially the names of more notorious taggers. This has resulted in some police agencies employing innovative investigation techniques, among them handwriting analysis to link tags with individual taggers. This requires an expert to convince a jury that a particular act of vandalism was committed by a defendant. This effort can be aided by viewing piece books and sketches done by the defendant and comparing them with known graffiti samples. If the graffiti photographs do not definitely prove that the same person did each act of vandalism, it may be necessary to rely on admissions, other evidence, or witnesses to tie the defendant to the moniker or tag you are investigating. Sometimes the defendant can be circumstantially linked to the vandalism if the graffiti in question is close to defendant's home or the defendant passes by the vandalized locations on a regular basis.

In some cases, graffiti can be linked to specific taggers by examining their handwriting. A writing for the purpose of the evidence code includes any graffiti consisting of written words, insignia, symbols, or any other markings that convey a particular meaning (§1410.5(a)). A photograph of graffiti may be admitted into evidence for the purpose of proving that the writing was made by the defendant (§1410.5(b)). When we have a graffiti writing sample that we know has been written by our suspect, that writing is called an *exemplar*, the sample we will compare to the other unknown incidents of vandalism. Photographs of graffiti may be admitted into evidence for the purpose of proving that the writing was made by the defendant (§1410.5(b)), and they should be evaluated by an expert.

We all have different writing styles, and so do taggers and gang members when they apply their graffiti. Samples of their writing can be obtained when an officer sees a suspect actually do the writing or they can come from graffiti seized from a suspect's personal property. The police can compare known graffiti samples in several ways. The key to studying a tag or a moniker is to study each letter in the word to identify beginning and ending strokes, as well as the connecting strokes, heights of letters, and slant and spacing of letters. Look for similar curves. Do they follow the same general direction? Look at the crowns or caps on letters, the horizontal strokes or curved strokes at the top of the staff of capital letters. Look for a similar pattern in how each sample is written, the alignment of the different samples (baseline, headline, and top line in each sample), the proportion of each letter in the word, the spacing between certain letters in each sample, and how each letter, if at all, is connected in each sample. Do the slant of the letters in each sample, the spelling, trademarks such as punctuation and diacritics, and level of skill and ability of each sample match?

CALIFORNIA EVIDENCE CODE SECTION 720: EXPERT QUALIFICATIONS

A person who is qualified to testify as an expert is one who has special knowledge, skill, experience, training, or education pertaining to the subject to which his testimony relates. This knowledge may be shown by any admissible testimony, including the witness's own testimony. Qualified law enforcement experts possess great information regarding the methodology, motivation, psychology, and identification of graffiti vandals. Many officers have conducted numerous interviews with graffiti vandals and can testify as experts with regard to the inner workings of tagging crews, gangs, and their actions. This can be especially useful when prosecuting a graffiti vandal under an aggregation or conspiracy theory. Further, these experts can be used to explain the significance of evidence seized, such as graffiti photo books, sketchbooks (notebooks in which graffiti vandals practice their tagging), graffiti tools, items such as clothing containing lettering or initials of crews, or even pictures of the vandalism.

DAMAGE OR COST EXPERTS AND PROOF OF AMOUNT OF DAMAGES

Many jurisdictions hire private contractors or citizen groups to assist the city with painting over graffiti, thus putting the city in the shoes of the victim (literally and figuratively as the city is now absorbing the entire cost of the clean up). Experts can be used to verify the amount of damages incurred and the cost of repair. Certain penal code sections require that specific monetary damages be proven as part of the case in chief; hence, these experts could be vital to successful prosecution. Many public agencies have individuals who can testify to the costs of repairing or cleaning such items as signs, walls, or vehicles. Often, these costs can be greater than one might think; for example, when an overhead freeway sign is vandalized, the costs to clean it up include costs associated with closing travel lanes, bringing in the necessary trucks and equipment, and the salaries of the workers assigned to clean up the graffiti. Many cities or community groups have specific groups charged with cleaning up graffiti who can testify to the cost of the damage.

ESTABLISHING A LACK OF PERMISSION

Graffiti cases require some evidence that the defendants do not own the property vandalized; a lack of permission is helpful but not critical to such cases. These issues can sometimes be solved easily during a defendant's interview: "Do you own any of the properties in the photos I have shown you? Did you have permission from any of these property owners to tag in any of the locations in these photos? If so, which ones?" Otherwise, it is necessary to disprove ownership by calling each owner to testify as to their ownership of the property; in the case of public property, someone has to testify that it is, in fact, public property. Another alternative is to obtain certified copies of property deeds showing that the defendant was not the owner of the property at the time of the vandalism.

Vandalism trials can be time intensive; however, juries should come to have a dim view of taggers when they see how much damage they are causing in their community. One can argue that, with respect to those specific offenses relating to public property (mainly §§640.5 and 640.7), the permissive inference language of §594 should control. That language currently reads that, "with respect to real property, vehicles, signs, fixtures, or furnishings belonging to any public entity, as defined by §811.2 of the Government Code, and the Federal Government, it shall be a permissive inference that the person neither owned the property nor had the permission of the owner to deface, damage, or destroy the property." Lack of permission has been held not to be an element of the offense of vandalism, the argument being made here that it is the defendant's burden to prove that he or she had permission to vandalize property not his or her own.

It must be made clear that permission was not granted; for example, New York State Penal Law §145.60 states that "no person shall make graffiti of any type on any building, public or private, or any other property real or personal owned by any person, firm or corporation or any public agency or instrumentality, without the express permission of the owner or operator of said property." Section 30-15-1.1 of the New Mexico Code indicates that "graffiti consists of intentionally and maliciously defacing any real or personal property of another with graffiti or other inscribed material inscribed with ink, paint, spray paint, crayon, charcoal or the use of any object without the consent or reasonable ground to believe there is consent of the owner of the property."

PENALTY FOR VANDALISM

In California, if the amount of defacement, damage, or destruction is $400 or more, vandalism is punishable by imprisonment in the state prison or in a county jail not exceeding one year or by a fine of not more than $10,000; if the amount of defacement, damage, or destruction is $10,000 or more, it is punishable by a fine of not more than $50,000 or by both that fine and imprisonment. If the amount of defacement, damage, or destruction is less than $400, the vandalism is punishable by imprisonment in a county jail not exceeding one year or by a fine of not more than $1000, or by both that fine and imprisonment. If the amount of defacement, damage, or destruction is less than $400 and the defendant has been previously convicted of vandalism or affixing graffiti or other inscribed material under Sections 594, 594.3, 594.4, 640.6, or 640.7, the vandalism is punishable by imprisonment in a county jail for not more than one year or by a fine of not more than $5000, or by both that fine and imprisonment.

Upon conviction of any person for acts of vandalism consisting of defacing property with graffiti or other inscribed materials, the court may, in addition to any punishment imposed under subdivision (b), order the defendant to clean up, repair, or replace the damaged property himself or herself, or order the defendant, and his or her parents or guardians, if the defendant is a minor, to keep the damaged property or another specified property in the community free of graffiti for up to one year. Participation of a parent or guardian is not required under this subdivision if the court deems this participation to be detrimental to the defendant, or if the parent or guardian is a single parent who must care for young children.

RESTITUTION

Restitution is often an issue when a case has been successfully prosecuted. Experts can be called to testify at a restitution hearing or can be consulted with regard to the amount of restitution to request. If a minor is personally unable to pay a fine levied for acts prohibited by this section, the parent of that minor shall be liable for payment of the fine. A court may waive payment of the fine, or any part thereof, by the parent upon a finding of good cause. Section 4.24.330 of the Revised Code of Washington states that an adult or emancipated minor who commits criminal street gang tagging and graffiti under §306 of this act by causing physical damage to the property of another is liable in addition to actual damages, for a penalty to the owner in the amount of the value of the damaged property not to exceed $1000, plus an additional penalty of not less than $100 nor more than $200, plus all reasonable attorneys' fees and court costs expended by the owner.

VANDALISM TO DISSUADE WITNESSES

If vandalism is committed to dissuade a witness, violation of California Penal Code §140 may be a viable charge, in addition to the vandalism charge. Such a violation is committed by every person who willfully takes, damages, or destroys any property of any witness, victim, or any other person because the witness, victim, or informant had provided any assistance or information to a law enforcement officer, or to a public prosecutor in a criminal proceeding or juvenile court proceeding. A violation of Penal Code §140 is punishable by imprisonment in the county jail not to exceed one year or imprisonment in the state prison for two, three, or four years.

CALIFORNIA PENAL CODE SECTION 182: CONSPIRACY AND AIDING AND ABETTING

A conspiracy is committed when two or more persons conspire to commit any crime (§182(a)(1)). The prohibition to commit any crime includes municipal ordinances. Many graffiti offenses are classified as misdemeanors, so the problem of securing adequate sentences commensurate with the damages incurred by graffiti vandals is an ongoing one. If there is sufficient evidence, however, prosecuting graffiti vandals under a conspiracy theory is an option that can secure a more appropriate sentence. A conviction for conspiracy does not require completion of the underlying charge. The elements of conspiracy are (1) an agreement to commit crime, and (2) an overt act done by member of the conspiracy in furtherance of the agreement. The overt acts must be expressly alleged in the charging document. Further, at least one of the overt acts alleged must be proven beyond a reasonable doubt to obtain a conviction. When conspiracy charges are applied to graffiti vandalism cases, the punishment would be imprisonment in the state prison or in the county jail, not to exceed one year and/or a fine. One advantage to charging conspiracy in graffiti cases is that it allows prosecutors to obtain a felony conviction where otherwise we would have only a misdemeanor. Felony conspiracy should not be considered when the object of the conspiracy is the commission of a misdemeanor offense; however, such charges can and should be considered where misdemeanor charges of graffiti vandalism cannot adequately address the conduct involved.

GANG AND TAGGER PROBATION

When we have done the job of arresting and convicting a tagger or gang member engaged in vandalism, they can be placed on probation and monitored more closely than other offenders. As such, conditions of probation can be mandated to help reduce the chance the offender will commit future vandalism offenses. Following are conditions of probation set forth by California:

1. ASSOCIATIONS
   1a. You shall not associate with any persons known to you to be a member of a tagging crew. (Especially the _____ tagging crew).
   1b. You shall not associate with anyone known to you that tags or does graffiti.
   1c. You shall not associate with _____.
   1d. You shall not act in furtherance of, in association with, or for the benefit of any tagging crew.
   1e. You shall not possess any graffiti materials, including, but not limited to, spray paint cans, tips for spray cans, marker pens, liquid shoe polish, slap tags, or etching tools, etching cream, acrylic paint, paint sticks, latex/cloth or rubber gloves.
2. REGISTRATION. You shall register as a gang member. As required by Penal Code §186.30 *et seq.*, you shall report to the police/sheriff station which has jurisdiction in the area in which you reside and register within 10 days of the date of this order

or 10 days from your release from custody and every time you change residence within the next 5 years. Failure to comply with these registration requirements during the next 5 years is a crime (California Penal Code §186.33).

3. CURFEW. You shall abide by curfew limits as set by the court or the probation department. You shall not be outside your residence between the hours of _____ p.m. and _____ a.m. at any time except as set by the court or probation department to accommodate going to and from employment or emergencies or activities preapproved by the court or probation department.

4. SEARCH AND SEIZURE. You shall submit your person, property, place of residence, vehicle, and personal effects to search at anytime, with or without a warrant or reasonable cause, by any probation officer or peace officer per *United States v. Knights*, 534 U.S. 112 (2001).

5. TRUE NAME AND ADDRESS. You shall use only your true name and date of birth when questioned by any peace officer or probation officer at any time. Your current true address is: _____.

6. WEAPONS
   6a. You shall not own, carry or possess any weapons, including, but not limited to, knives, firearms, explosives, or ammunition.
   6b. You shall surrender all firearms under your control at the date of this order.
   6c. Except in the presence of a peace officer, you shall not remain in any building, vehicle, or in the presence of any person where dangerous or deadly weapons, firearms, ammunition, or explosives are known by you to exist.

7. SCHOOL. You shall not be on the grounds of any school unless enrolled in that school or with prior administrative approval.

8. VICTIMS AND WITNESSES. You shall not contact nor come within 100 yards of any victims or witnesses connected with this case. (Protective orders are attached to court files and provided to defendants.)

9. LOCATIONS. You shall not come within 100 yards of the following locations: _____.

10. CLEAN-UP CONDITIONS
    10a. You shall clean up, repair, or replace the damaged property located at _____.

    10b. You shall keep the property located at _____ free of graffiti for up to one year at your expense.

11. SUSPENSION of driver's license pursuant to Vehicle Code §13202.6.

12. WARNING. Penal Code §594.7 mandates incarceration in jail or prison for third violation of Penal Code §594, regardless of the amount of damage caused, if there was any previous incarceration for those priors.

13. OTHER. _____.

14. You shall comply with all terms, conditions of probation, and orders imposed by the court. You shall obey all laws.

I HAVE RECEIVED, READ, AND UNDERSTOOD THE ABOVE TERMS AND
CONDITIONS OF PROBATION AND AGREE TO ABIDE BY SAME.

(Signed) _____   (Dated) _____

CONDITIONS OF PROBATION FOR JUVENILE VANDALS

- Obey all laws. Obey all orders of the Probation Officer and of any court.
- Obey all instructions and orders of Parents/Guardians, Teacher(s), School Officials.
- Report to the Probation Officer as directed.
- Notify the Probation Officer before changing address, school, school schedule, or place of employment.
- Seek and maintain training or employment as directed by the Probation Officer.
- Perform hours of work under the supervision of the Probation Officer.
- Attend a school program approved by the Probation Officer. Maintain satisfactory grades, attendance, and citizenship. Promptly notify Probation Officer of every absence.
- Do not be within one block of any school ground unless enrolled, attending classes, on approved school business, or with school official, parent, or guardian.
- Do not leave your residence outside of the specified hours, except with parental consent.
- Do not stay away from your residence for more than 24 hours, nor leave Los Angeles County except at times and places specifically permitted in advance by the Probation Officer.
- Do not associate with co-minors or anyone disapproved of by your parents or the Probation Officer.
- Do not participate in any type of gang activity.
- Do not have any dangerous or deadly weapon in your possession nor remain in the presence of any unlawfully armed person.
- Do not contact, or cause any contact with, or associate with the victims or witnesses of any offense alleged against you.
- Do not associate with children except in the presence of a responsible adult.
- Do not drink any alcoholic beverages.
- Cooperate in a plan to control abuse of alcohol, controlled substances, or poisons.
- Do not use or possess narcotics, controlled substances, poisons, or related paraphernalia; stay away from places where users congregate.
- Do not own, use, or possess an electronic paging device.
- Do not associate with persons known to be users or sellers of narcotics or controlled substances, except with the prior written permission of the Probation Officer.
- Submit to urinalysis and skin checks as directed by the Probation Officer to detect the use of narcotics or controlled substances.

- Submit to testing of blood, breath, or urine to detect the use of alcohol, narcotics, controlled substances, or poisons whenever requested by any peace officer.
- Submit person, residence, or property under your control to search and seizure at any time of the day or night by any law enforcement officer with or without a warrant (WIC §790.4).
- Cooperate in a plan for psychiatric/psychological testing or treatment.
- Pay fines to the general fund of the county through the Probation Officer in such a manner as the Probation Officer shall order, in addition to any penalty assessment and surcharge (Penal Code §1464, Government Code §76000).
- Make reparation on all related losses as determined by the Probation Officer, including a service charge, as authorized by Welfare and Institutions Code §276.
- Make restitution to the restitution fund.
- Do not drive any motor vehicle.
- Surrender operator's license to the court clerk, who shall comply with §13352 of the Vehicle Code.
- If a minor, your parents are ordered, pursuant to WIC §727, to complete ten class sessions of a parent education program and to file proof of completion with the Probation Officer.
- Participate in after-school and weekend tutorial, vocational, and recreational activities as directed by the Probation Officer.
- Participate in the High School Graduate/GED/WIN program and make continuing progress toward completion of high school.
- Do not possess any lighters, matches, or other incendiary devices. Do not possess any spray cans, markers, or other marking devices.

QUESTIONS FOR DISCUSSION

1. What is the primary reason why a tagger would write on a wall?
2. What does the term "tagger" mean and where did it come from?
3. Define graffiti.
4. What laws do you have in your area designed to hold taggers responsible for their actions?
5. What is the benefit of cleaning graffiti from a community as quickly as possible?
6. What should be done before graffiti is removed?
7. Why should we remove graffiti?
8. What do you think is the primary reason why a gang member writes graffiti?

BIBLIOGRAPHY

Akiyama, C. (2003). Book Review for *Gangs, Graffiti, and Violence: A Realistic Guide to the Scope and Nature of gangs in America*, by Duane A. Leet, George E. Rush, and Anthony M. Smith. *Criminal Justice Review*, 28(1):173–175.

BJA. (1998). *Addressing Community Gang Problems: A Practical Guide*. Washington, D.C.: U.S. Department of Justice, Office of Justice Programs, Bureau of Justice Assistance.

Crowe, T. (2000). *Crime Prevention Through Environmental Design*, 2nd ed. Boston: Butterworth-Heinemann.

Davis, K. (2008). Graffiti Formats: Are They Gangs or Graffiti Crews? *Journal of Gang Research*, 15(2):1–18.

Dubin, R. (1959). Deviant Behavior and Social Structure: Continuities in Social Theory. *American Sociological Review*, 24:147–163

Ganz, N. and Manco, T. (2004). *Graffiti World: Street Art from Five Continents*. New York: Harry N. Abrams.

Goldstein, H. (1990). *Problem-Oriented Policing*. New York: McGraw-Hill.

Grody, S., Shanahan, D., and Prigoff, J. (2007). *Graffiti L.A.: Street Styles and Art*. New York: Harry N. Abrams.

Hanh, J.K. (1992). *Civil Gang Abatement: A Community-Based Policing Tool of the Office of the Los Angeles City Attorney*. Los Angeles: Los Angeles City Attorney's Office.

Kelling, G.L. and Wilson, J.Q. (1982). Broken Windows. *The Atlantic Monthly*, March.

Livingston, D. (1997). Police Discretion and the Quality of Life in Public Places: Courts, Communities, and the New Policing. *Columbia Law Review*, 97:551.

Miller, W.B. (1958). Lower Class Culture as a Generating Milieu of Gang Delinquency. *Journal of Social Issues*, 14:5–20.

Miller, W.B. (1959). Implications of Urban Lower-Class Culture for Social Work. *Social Service Review*, 33:219–236

O'Deane, M. (1993). Will They Ever Run Out of Spray Paint? *Law Enforcement Quarterly*, November.

O'Deane, M. (2008). *Gang Investigator's Handbook: A Law-Enforcement Guide to Identifying and Combating Violent Street Gangs*. Boulder, CO: Paladin Press.

O'Deane, M. (2010). *Gangs: Theory, Practice and Research*. San Clemente, CA: LawTech Custom Publishing.

Phillips, S. (1999). *Wallbangin': Graffiti and Gangs in L.A.* Chicago: University of Chicago Press.

Rahn, J. (2002). *Painting without Permission: Hip-Hop Graffiti Subculture*. Westport, CT: Greenwood Publishing Group.

Shaw, C. and McKay, H. (1942). *Juvenile Delinquency and Urban Areas*. Chicago: Chicago University Press.

Skogan, W. G. (1988). Community Organizations and Crime. In Tonry, M. and Morris, N., Eds., *Crime and Justice: A Review of Research* (pp. 39–78). Chicago, IL: The University of Chicago Press.

Thrasher, F. M. (1927/1963). *The Gang: A Study of 1,313 Gangs in Chicago*. Chicago, IL: University of Chicago Press.

Wilson, C.R. (1997). What's in a Name? Gang Monikers. *FBI Law Enforcement Bulletin*, 66(5):14–17.

Wilson, P. (1988). Preventing Vandalism and Graffiti. *Journal of Security Administration*, 11(2):28–29.

CHAPTER 9

Larceny and Burglary

Walter J. Wywadis

Topeka, Kansas, Police Department

CHAPTER OBJECTIVES

After reading this chapter, you should be able to do the following:

1. Describe the investigative processes for larceny and burglary crimes.
2. Explain crime prevention techniques used to deter property crimes.
3. Identify the importance of physical evidence in criminal investigations.
4. Describe the importance of community policing in law enforcement.
5. Define the importance of quality-of-life issues within communities.

Chapter Outline

- Introduction
- Larceny
- Burglary
- By the Numbers
- Preliminary Investigative Techniques
- Follow-Up Investigation
- Offender Characteristics
- Shoplifting
- Prevention Techniques

INTRODUCTION

The crimes of larceny and burglary are offenses considered by most large law enforcement agencies to be low-profile investigations. Depending on the size of the community and law enforcement agency, many times the cost of investigations and prosecutions outweighs what prosecutors believe to be the severity of the crime. Agencies aim considerable resources toward investigating major crimes such as robbery, assaults, rapes, and homicides. In medium and smaller agencies that do not experience numerous major crimes, these investigations are more of a priority because burglary and larceny crimes are the most likely to touch members of the community. These crimes normally do not rate front-page headlines in today's media, and some investigators consider investigating these crimes as less than glorious assignments. Larceny and burglary crimes are categorized together under the umbrella term of property crimes for statistical purposes. Law enforcement agencies organize investigative units or squads in this same fashion to investigate property crimes. This allows for improved communication among squad members through sharing of information gathered and assisting one another in case investigations. Investigating larceny and burglary can be satisfying with the proper training, knowledge, and mindset. This domain of investigations can offer a wonderful opportunity for investigators to learn the techniques and develop the skills necessary to solve major crimes.

LARCENY

The crime of larceny is the same as theft. Many jurisdictions list one or the other as offenses. Each state has different levels of classification based on specific dollar amounts to distinguish between a felony and a misdemeanor offense. By definition, the act of larceny or theft is the unlawful taking of property from another or exerting control over the property by possessing it without the authority to do so. Examples of these offenses include shoplifting and pocket picking, and acts of larceny or theft are generally associated with the act of burglary. Variations of laws enacted by different state, counties, or municipalities may specifically address the theft of gas, theft of services, and theft by deception. Motor vehicle theft has its own classification and is separate from general larceny/theft in most agencies.

BURGLARY

The crime of burglary consists of unlawfully entering or attempting to enter the property of another with the intent to commit a felony or larceny with or without force. The property can be a fixed structure, vehicle, or boat. For charging purposes, no distinction is made among these structure types, although in many jurisdictions this information is usually designated on the original offense reports filed by officers. Burglaries represent one of the most common crimes to which officers respond. Both residential and business burglaries require the same investigative techniques.

RESIDENTIAL BURGLARY

Usually residential burglary occurs while the residents are away, often during daylight hours. The perpetrator will most often look for an open or easy entrance that would involve the least amount of effort or noise. Targets are usually small items such as jewelry, cash, or anything of value that can be easily carried away. Occasionally, a burglar enters a residence when the owner is home, usually by mistake. State law normally classifies this type of burglary as aggravated burglary.

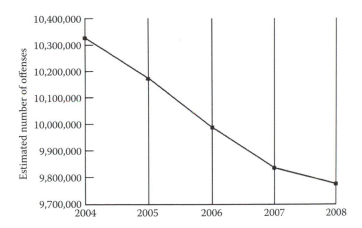

FIGURE 9.1 Property crime offenses, 5-year trend from 2004 to 2008. (From FBI, *2008 Crime in the United States: Property Crime*, Federal Bureau of Investigation, Washington, D.C., 2009.)

NON-RESIDENTIAL BURGLARY

Burglaries to businesses generally occur at night when the businesses are closed. Most often, cash registers or safes small enough to be removed are the targets, along with whatever items a business might offer that are of interest to the suspect. Entry is normally a "smash and grab," accomplished in a very short time frame, unless the suspect knows the business is not protected by alarms or cameras. The more professional or organized burglar may enter the business through the roof by cutting a hole and dropping in, by using heater or air conditioning vents, or by punching a hole through an exterior wall.

BY THE NUMBERS

According to the 2008 FBI Uniform Crime Reporting (UCR) program, property crime includes the offenses of burglary, larceny/theft, motor vehicle theft, and arson. There were an estimated 9,767,915 property crime offenses in the United States in 2008 (Figure 9.1). The estimated rate of property crimes was 3212.5 offenses per 100,000 inhabitants. An estimated $17.2 billion in losses resulted from property crimes in 2008 (FBI, 2009a). In 2008, an estimated 2,222,196 burglaries were committed, and burglary accounted for 22.7% of the estimated number of property crimes that year. Burglaries of residential properties accounted for 70.3% of all burglaries. Victims of burglary offenses suffered an estimated $4.6 billion in lost property, and overall the average dollar loss per burglary offense was $2079 (FBI, 2009b). The FBI also reported that an estimated 6.6 million acts of larceny or theft occurred nationwide in 2008; they accounted for an estimated 67.5% of all property crimes that year. The average value of property taken during an act of larceny or theft was $925 per offense. Applying the average value to the estimated number of larcenies and thefts, the loss to victims nationally was nearly $6.1 billion (FBI, 2009c).

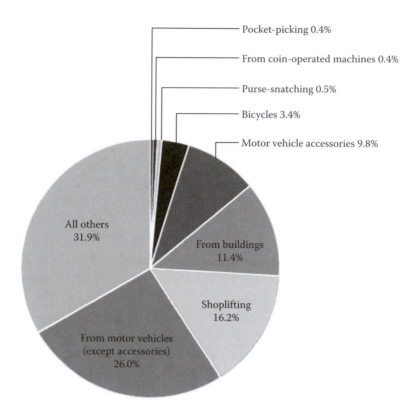

Pocket-picking 0.4%

From coin-operated machines 0.4%

Purse-snatching 0.5%

Bicycles 3.4%

Motor vehicle accessories 9.8%

All others
31.9%

From buildings
11.4%

Shoplifting
16.2%

From motor vehicles
(except accessories)
26.0%

FIGURE 9.2 Larceny–theft, percent distribution in 2008. (From FBI, *2008 Crime in the United States: Larceny–Theft*, Federal Bureau of Investigation, Washington, D.C., 2009.)

Although property crimes showed a decease from 2004 through 2008, due to aggressive prosecutions, proactive enforcement, and prevention programs, the estimated numbers reported to the FBI for larceny or theft and burglary still represent big business. The criminal element of American society will continue committing these crimes unless law enforcement, the community, and courts intervene and arrest, convict, or rehabilitate repeat offenders. These crimes and the criminals who perpetrate them lower the quality of life for all citizens within the communities they live. Citizens should not have to be afraid to go to work or school or participate in recreational activities for fear of returning home violated. Distributions of the direct costs associated with these crimes reflect themselves through higher costs of insurance, uncollected taxes, and higher prices at retail businesses. These crimes are far more startling when the data are analyzed at the national rather than at a local level (see Figure 9.2). Keep in mind that these figures represent just two types of crimes being committed nationwide.

By now, you are likely wondering what law enforcement, courts, and probation and parole officers are doing about this widespread epidemic of crime. Nationwide arrests reported by the FBI during 2008 totaled 1,687,345, or 565.2 per 100,000 inhabitants. Arrests for property crimes increased 5.6% in 2008 as compared to 2007 (FBI, 2009d). The FBI has published a report on 10-year arrest trends in which it compares 1999 to 2008 (FBI, 2009e,f):

- *2008 nationwide burglary arrest data*
  - Adult males accounted for 157,341 burglary arrests.
  - Juvenile (under 18 years old) males accounted for 43,702 arrests.
  - Adult females were arrested 29,055 times.
  - Juvenile females were arrested 6713 times.
- *2008 arrests for burglary by race*
  - 157,252 Caucasians were arrested (66.8%).
  - 73,960 Blacks were arrested (31.4%).
  - 2077 American Indian or Alaskan natives were arrested (0.9%).
  - 2118 Asian or Pacific Islanders were arrested (0.9%).
- *2008 nationwide larceny/theft arrest data*
  - Adult males accounted for 431,212 larceny/theft arrests.
  - Juvenile (under 18 years old) males accounted for 105,099 arrests.
  - Adult females were arrested 308,011 times.
  - Juvenile (under 18 years old) females were arrested 80,799 times.
- *2008 arrests for larceny/theft by race*
  - 666,360 Caucasians were arrested (68.1%).
  - 286,844 Blacks were arrested (29.3%).
  - 12,684 American Indian or Alaskan natives were arrested (1.3%).
  - 13,257 Asian or Pacific Islanders were arrested (1.4%).

As if these statistics are not alarming enough, to get a better grasp of the totality of these crimes keep in mind that not all law enforcement agencies throughout the United States report to the FBI Uniform Crime Reporting system. Many smaller jurisdictions choose not to be reporting agencies; therefore, an unknown additional number of crimes and arrests are not reported to the FBI.

PRELIMINARY INVESTIGATIVE TECHNIQUES

How a preliminary investigation proceeds in response to an incident depends on a number of factors. The size of the law enforcement agency, its budget, and community expectations govern most of the decisions, dictating how many and what kind of resources are expended. Budgetary constraints have forced agencies to examine internal policies defining how they will respond to criminal incidents. Many agencies have had to reduce positions, cut budgets, and redistrict patrol territories to maintain equal coverage of municipalities and cities. Even if an agency has implemented changes and adjusted its responses, many times political pressure or interference causes new procedures to be overridden to address pressure applied by the public. Many law enforcement agencies gauge their responses by the amount of loss reported. Whatever the size of the agency and political environment of the community, some basic techniques determine the success or failures of investigations.

Generally, the first responding officer is the most important part of any investigation. The actions taken when the officer arrives on the scene are of utmost importance, whether they are from a smaller department where officers process their own crime scenes or are from a larger department that has specialists to respond to particular types of crime scenes. An important thing to remember is that the first responding officers have overall responsibility and are in charge of making decisions regarding the crime scene and investigation until a senior officer or a ranking supervisor relieves them.

Officers should approach the scene in an organized fashion and treat every scene as if the crime has just occurred and the suspect may still be there until it is determined that it is a past crime and the scene is cleared. If the residents or owners have been within the crime scene, the officer should take an organized approach when meeting with them.

Here is a great example of the need to treat every call as if the suspect was still there. I used to be a K-9 officer working the night shift. On this particular night in the early morning hours, dispatch sent me to a call of aggravated burglary. The suspect entered the residence by way of a back entry door to a garage, and the victim confronted him. The suspect then ran from the residence. The first responding officer arrived at the scene, walked around the outside, and did not observe the suspect; he advised me to disregard the call, stating, "The suspect is gone." Because I was only a couple of blocks away, I responded to the scene anyway. Upon arrival, I walked up to the officer and asked where the suspect had been. The officer took me to the open door that the suspect kicked in to gain entry. I decided to use my K-9 partner for the heck of it. Upon giving him the command to "smell find," my K-9 left the doorway and immediately began pulling me across the back of the house and around the corner, ultimately going under a low-lying evergreen bush 20 feet from the doorway. Thinking my K-9 was tracking a cat or a rabbit, I restarted my partner at the doorway again. The K-9 trailed to the same bush. I then pulled him back and he immediately went back under the bush. This time when I pulled him back, he had a shoe in his mouth! Checking closer, I found the suspect lying under the bush right up next to the house he had just broken into. As stated previously, treat all burglary calls as if they had just occurred and the suspect is still there until determined otherwise.

Upon making contact, a good immediate approach is to advise victims not to touch or move anything, and take reasonable precautions in protecting the integrity of the scene and any evidence. Remove the victims from the scene, which removes them from the temptation to clean up. If possible, interview the victims at another location outside of the crime scene. Countless times in the author's experience, the residents or owners cannot resist moving items or picking items up that were moved, eradicating possible evidence while in the presence of the interviewing officers. This is human nature. The victims are violated, and they want normalcy to return as soon as possible in their lives. Officers should be firm but gentle in dealing with the emotions of the victims and go well beyond normal expectations in explaining the process of gathering evidence to accomplish a successful investigation. In my experience, this area is one of the biggest challenges for first responding officers.

Officers should keep in mind that victims have had their minds clouded by the media through unrealistic television shows that portray one tiny hair or drop of blood evidence being able to clear cases by the end of a hour-long show. The victim is the most important aspect of any investigation. Taking time to explain processes and providing a realistic timeline can go a very long way in helping the victim process this traumatic experience.

THE CRIME SCENE

The officer should make a determination concerning securing the crime scene area outside around the building or residence to search for possible evidence. Several things must occur if the decision is made to secure the area outside. Officers need to make sure the area secured is large enough to cover the entire area believed to be the crime scene, which can be determined by interviewing the victims and witnesses at the scene. It is far better to secure too much rather than not enough area, and later it can be difficult to get evidence found outside the crime scene area entered in court as evidence. This can be an uphill battle, and many times evidence, no matter how important it is to the case, may be excluded by the courts because it was recovered from an unprotected area. Officers should keep in mind that often a case hinges on physical evidence and its integrity during the collection processes, as often it is the only link to a suspect. This is especially important any time you are operating with a search warrant to give you legal access.

The rule of thumb that I have always gone by is to take the biggest possible area and later, when the search is completed, reduce it down; resources such as additional officers can be relieved and allowed to return to normal duties. When possible, station as many additional officers as it takes outside and around the perimeter of the crime scene and cordon off the area with crime scene tape.

The officer in charge outside at this time should start a crime scene log and note information on all persons who enter, being sure to log who enters, at what time and for what reason, and when they leave. The outside area of the business or residence is the first area processed for evidence, as it poses the greatest risk for lost evidence or possible contamination of evidence. An important rule to remember in all crime scenes is that everyone who enters or leaves a crime scene will either deposit something or take something with them. This emphasizes the importance of limiting the amount of foot traffic and the number of people who enter a crime scene.

A big problem at just about every law enforcement agency is the number of officers that will show up at a major crime scene and want to enter it. Usually, initiating a crime scene log will cut down on the number of these people entering. Rather than entering, they instead will hang around the outside to avoid having their names appear on the crime scene log and later explaining in court why they entered. In addition to having officers at the scene, natural causes, such as weather, can also contribute to a loss of critical evidence.

All points of entry and any possible points of entry may contain evidence to process. It is important to remember that many times a suspect will attempt several points of entry in an effort to find the best entry point that requires the least amount of effort. Suspects will try all doors and windows before deciding to break a window or enter a door by kicking or prying, potentially drawing attention to their activities. In most burglaries, physical evidence found at the point of entry is best. This is where the suspect will spend most of his or her time.

When the outside scene and the point of entry have been processed, the officer should take the time to walk through the crime scene with the victim to obtain knowledge of all items moved or handled. Many times, suspects bring items into a crime scene that they inadvertently leave, such as tools, gloves, hats, or even their wallets.

DEVELOPING EVIDENCE

In any crime scene, everything should be considered evidence until it is determined otherwise! Too often, items that have been disregarded at the scene as evidence have later been determined during interviews to be important evidence. When dealing with a crime scene and documenting evidence, there is one point I cannot stress enough: pictures, pictures, and more pictures! You can never take too many photographs. Photographs are inexpensive and can be discarded from the case file when it is determined that they are not needed. With today's digital media cameras, it is easy and extremely worthwhile to fill as many disks with photographs as necessary. Later, while reviewing these images with prosecutors, pictures can be eliminated as candidates for courtroom presentation. Take pictures of evidence collected, footprints, fingerprints, items moved, overall rooms, points of entry, and outside scenes around the building. The old saying that "a picture is worth a thousand words" has applied many times in court proceedings I have been involved in. Pictures often save time on the stand in testimony and give a very accurate depiction of the scene to jurors. Here are some reminders to remember when processing crime scenes:

- Fingerprints are the standard evidence being sought; they are obtained by dusting areas such as the point of entry and all items that have been moved or touched.
- Also important are photographs and cast impressions of footprints outside, around the building, on doors kicked open, and within the business or residence on floor surfaces.
- The suspect may have tracked in mud or dirt after entering. Many times these tracks inside can help determine the point of entry and potential avenues of escape.
- Blood may be found at crime scenes from suspects who have cut themselves entering or exiting. Possible comparisons through DNA and blood typing later can positively identify or exonerate a suspect.
- When a broken window is the point of entry, fibers from clothing, blood, and skin often are present and can be collected for comparisons. If no blood is found at the point of entry and within the business or residence, do not overlook the possibility that fibers are present. The suspect's clothing may have gotten snagged. Check the point of entry carefully for this type of physical evidence and collect it for future comparisons.
- Develop toolmark impressions from the point of entry if a door or window has been pried open. These impressions can later be compared to a tool or implement found at the scene, at another location, or on the suspect.
- Suspects apprehended soon after an incident may still be wearing the same clothes.

Again, think glass, dirt, blood, shoes, and fibers.

Never underestimate the value of the suspect's person for obtaining physical evidence. When I was interviewing a suspect at police headquarters I saw a glitter under the room lights in his hair. After obtaining a flashlight and looking much closer, the glitter in his hair was actual glass fragments! These glass fragments were also on his pants and in the cuffs of his pants, and they matched the type of glass from the broken window at the crime scene point of entry.

A neighborhood canvass should be performed before any crime scene investigation is complete to gain additional witness information. Many times, these canvasses reap enormous additional evidence. Maybe a vehicle was observed parked in an unusual place, or someone was observed in the area. From this new information, additional areas might possibly be pinpointed and searched for evidence, or a description of the possible suspect or their vehicle can be developed. The canvass is sometimes referred to as a door-to-door "knock and talk." Officers identify everyone contacted and document their observations. Finally, before any crime scene is released a final walk-through should be done to ensure that nothing has been missed or forgotten. This is the final chance for investigators to review the scene before releasing it to the victim.

Any officer who was involved, no matter how minor the involvement, should assemble a complete and accurate report. Many times during court proceedings, attorneys will attempt to discredit the investigation because an officer did not document one small particular aspect of the case investigation. If the first responding officer, crime scene technician, or investigator approaches the preliminary investigation in an organized fashion to obtain as much information as possible from the victim and thoroughly processes the crime scene for as much physical evidence as possible, the case is well on the way to answering the who, what, where, when, why, and how of the crime.

FOLLOW-UP INVESTIGATION

After the initial reports are completed, the case is typically sent to the Criminal Investigative Division (CID) for preliminary review. During the supervisor review process, the reports and the evidence are considered in combination with solvability factors. If the case meets these factors, an investigator is assigned the case. If the case does not meet these solvability criteria, it is logged for informational purposes; if additional information develops with regard to the case, it will be assigned. Some law enforcement agencies assign these cases as "in-house" assignments.

An investigator has the specific duty to review the case, make contact with the victim, and gather any additional information that they may have regarding the case. If no new information develops to raise the solvability factors, the case will remain logged and filed. This concept also fulfills the community expectation of follow-up on all cases. Each law enforcement agency applies its own procedures and criteria during the review process based on the size of the agency, budgetary guidelines, and community expectations.

During the follow-up investigation, it is imperative for the officer or investigator to review all reports and evidence gathered and documented, as well as the preliminary statements of the victims and witnesses. After review, the follow-up investigation usually begins by contacting the victim. This contact may clarify facts originally reported or help determine if any information not originally reported during the initial interview can move the investigation forward. Often, victims talk with neighbors, who will tell them things that they would not tell officers during the neighborhood canvass for fear of involvement or reprisal. When this happens, it gives the case investigator a reason to contact the neighbors again. In some cases, examination of the victim's background may be necessary to confirm or deny the victim as a possible suspect; for example, if victims have a history of making large insurance claims, insurance company investigators will communicate their suspicions to law enforcement agencies when such losses are reported. Insurance investigators then work in conjunction with law enforcement to help resolve the claim. In any event, the investigator should always look at the background of the victim during the follow-up phase of the investigation to rule out that he or she is a professional victim reaping the proceeds of insurance fraud.

If there are no known potential suspects, the follow-up investigation will entail developing potential suspects by examining intelligence networks within the agency and other area agencies with similar types of burglaries. Considered are the specific types of items taken, similar points of entry, the use of similar tools for prying, the presence of similar size and pattern of footprints, similar days of week or time of day, and locations of the incidents. This type of crime comparison is termed a *crime analysis*; it examines all the characteristics of the crime and compares them to those of crimes that have occurred prior to this case. Often, these similarities uncover a pattern or crime hot spot within the community that law enforcement can use in predicting future occurrences. Sharing this kind of information with other officers provides the opportunity to implement strategies such as a stake out in an attempt to catch the suspect in the act.

The Topeka Police Department is one of many law enforcement agencies utilizing CompStat (comparative statistics) meetings, which involve command staff of the agency discussing statistics and developing crime strategies to deal with reported crime. They meet once a week to examine two questions: (1) Where is crime happening? and (2) What are we doing about it? A vital part of this program is the crime analysis unit, whose responsibilities are to review all crimes reported and provide weekly updates on crime statistics, including individual crime categories, crime patterns, and developing trends. This process is referred to as *intelligence-led policing*, and it allows agencies to target high-crime areas, concentrating resources to reap the most benefit in crime reduction and apprehension. It also allows agencies to be proactive in target hardening neighborhoods and businesses by contacting them when discovered trends surface. The analysis area of law enforcement has made significant advances; analysts can predict crime patterns based on the statistics available and can estimate rates of reduction or escalation in crime rates. Gone are the days of agencies just sending police units out and randomly patrolling areas of a city and occasionally discovering or deterring crime.

Investigators can develop suspect pools because they normally have a stable of informants who can provide information about current thieves that might be active. This is sometimes risky, as many times informants will tell investigators what they want to hear just so they can get paid, or they may want to make a deal. Often the informants themselves may be the suspects, or they may give information on others to cut down on their competition. Information gained through informants must be confirmed before taking action.

Another approach to solving theft cases is to try to track the items taken. Every town has pawn shops or flea markets that buy items from the street and resell them. Countless times, I have gone into shops such as these and identified an item previously reported stolen. Reputable businesses will have information on file about the people from whom they have bought items. Once identification of an item is made, a hold can be placed on it until the victim has been notified. Usually the victim has the option of buying back the personal belonging for the price paid at the business. The author has investigated many cases where, although it was not possible to identify the suspects for prosecution, at least it was possible to make the victims happy by locating their stolen items. Also, getting information about stolen items out to these businesses and informants makes them aware of the items that were stolen, and they can report back to investigators about who is attempting to sell similar items. Case investigators then follow up on this information.

Most agencies have an affiliation with a Crime Stoppers type of program, which accepts anonymous tips on crimes, or an investigator can use the local media to get information of the crime out to the public, requesting that anyone with information contact the agency. This type of information sharing has solved cases and led to search warrants and the recovery of stolen property.

No one should know the case better than the suspect and the assigned case investigator. Investigators need to use this information to their advantage at all times. When investigators meet with and interview potential suspects, it is not unusual for comments made during these interviews to indicate that those being interviewed might know more about a case than they are letting on. At this point, investigators must decide whether the case can be solved without a confession. If the investigator has no physical evidence, it is time to regroup and work toward possible recovery of the stolen items. Countless times, when the author has asked potential suspects for written consent to search their property without a search warrant, they have given their consent in an attempt to continue to claim their innocence, even though they know the property is at their residence. They tempt fate by thinking it will not be found by investigators. Finding stolen items gives investigators more leverage to use during further interviews.

Earlier in the chapter, the importance of thoroughly processing the crime scene was explained. If the crime scene was thoroughly processed and hair, blood, fingerprints, or fibers were found and collected as evidence, the investigator can apply for a search warrant for the person of the suspect for blood, spit, hair, and fingerprints to compare to what was collected at the scene. If the investigator is lucky, the suspect already may have fingerprints on file somewhere from a previous arrest. It is always a good tactic to give suspects the opportunity to comply with a consensual waiver to confirm whether they are willing to cooperate and allow this personal physical evidence to be gathered without a search warrant. This allows investigators to keep the lines of communication open and helps gain the trust of suspects. If they refuse, use a search warrant as a last resort. I have always found it a best practice to give the suspect the opportunity to comply with a request for all of the items. The investigator is now on his or her way to positively identifying or eliminating a suspect to the crime. All of the items should be sent to a crime lab for comparisons.

If there are any possible eyewitnesses who may have seen the suspect, a photo line-up should be prepared and shown to the witnesses for possible identification. Photo line-ups are currently under scrutiny because of the number of reported incorrect identifications. Each agency will have guidelines regarding photo line-ups. If they are used, they should consist of six similar photos that include one of the possible suspect. Most recent suggestions are to have an investigator not directly involved in the case show the line-up. No suggestions should be given to the witnesses that a suspect has been placed under arrest, and witnesses should be strongly advised not to make a positive identification if they are not 100% positive. In a best-case scenario, a positive identification will be made and physical evidence recovered at the scene that positively matches to the potential suspect. Along with the stolen items recovered from the suspect's residence or vehicle, you now have a prosecutable case! This is why it is so important for the first officer responding to the scene to pay attention to proper crime scene processing, for reports to be complete and accurate, and for interviews to be conducted.

OFFENDER CHARACTERISTICS

The reasons why burglars and thieves do what they do are as varied as their methods of operation (MOs), or how they commit the crimes. Much published literature has suggested that these crimes are fueled by drug addiction, because addicts need a constant supply of funds to purchase drugs. I believe that this theory does have some validity but does not totally explain the burglary and theft problem. Generally, economic conditions of any community are a significant factor. A high rate of unemployment can have a strong bearing on the amount of crime within and around a community. Security precautions within a community can also influence the ability of criminals to locate easy targets. Sometimes people just take things because of an overwhelming desire to have them at no cost.

We have all seen the television version of professional burglars. Usually dressed in dark clothing, masked, gloved, and sneaking in the dark, they carry a bag of goodies used to pick locks; they are able to overcome the best alarm systems and likely have a dark getaway vehicle parked down the block. Some burglars do, indeed, match this description, and they go to great extremes to remain undetected. Usually these professionals do not enter homes unless they suspect great wealth lies within. They generally target businesses to try to get the biggest haul for the least amount of effort; the hauls are often in the form of cash from safes and targeted big-ticket items within the business. These organized burglary offenses are generally not detected until the victim returns home or someone reports to work at the business the next day, because the entry points are well thought out, such as rooftops that officers do not have the ability to check during patrol activities. These criminals are usually caught only when they get overconfident and sloppy. Police generally do not catch these types because they make their haul and move down the road to another city; they are transient in nature.

Serial burglars target and watch potential victims for long periods until they learn their usual routines. They often follow victims while they are going about their daily activities. These burglars may break into homes for the psychological thrill or sexual satisfaction.

They tend to take small personal items, such as underwear, jewelry, or pictures of the victim so they can relive the moment later. This type of criminal may advance to breaking into homes while the residents are home or to sexual crimes such as rape. These particular criminals are difficult to catch, and it normally takes many hours to pattern these suspects.

Most often local police spend a great deal of time chasing around unorganized burglars and thieves, who do some general targeting of homes and businesses looking for likely targets. These unorganized criminals will also target friends and family in their quest for money. Drug addicts generally fall into this category, as do juveniles. Their crimes normally consist of "smash and grabs" at businesses to take whatever items strike their fancy, along with any cash found. They also often graduate, if undetected, to prying open doors, kicking doors, and smashing windows at residences. These suspects target jewelry, cash, guns, tools, electronics, and generally anything they think that they can sell for cash. Juveniles have a tendency to target electronics and many times eat while they are in the residence.

A simple theory that explains how crime occurs proposes that, first, there must be a motivated offender; second, the offender must find a suitable target worth the effort; and, third, there must be minimal chance of apprehension. This theory certainly lends itself to burglars being viewed as "optimal foragers" (Johnson and Bowers, 2004). The optimal foraging theory suggests that, when predatory animals select hunting areas and prey, they optimize their rewards by weighing the nutritional value of the potential prey against the effort and risk involved in obtaining it. Similarly, burglars maximize their revenues by selecting neighborhoods and dwellings that require little effort to enter, contain valuable items, and give the impression that the likelihood of being apprehended is low.

SHOPLIFTING

Shoplifting costs businesses millions of dollars every year. Consumers have to absorb the added costs passed on in the form of higher prices due to shrinkage, and countless tax dollars are not collected by local and state governments. Shoplifters may be any age or gender, from any economic or ethnic background. They can be classified as either organized or unorganized. Shoplifters are the ultimate opportunists, taking advantage of heavy customer traffic times, employee shift changes, and opening and closing times. Generally, the most important aspect in successfully carrying out this crime is the ability to conceal the item on their person or within other packages or bags. They wear baggy clothing or heavy clothing in warm weather, or they carry bags or purses that are larger than average. Organized teams distract customers and employees while others are concealing items. Price tag switching or altering is a tactic used to pay an unreasonably low price for an item. Bernice Yeung (2010) wrote, "U.S. retail thefts are becoming a big moneymaker for organized crime—pulling in as much as $10 billion a year." This article was based on the arrests of a 21-member theft ring located in Georgia. They allegedly were paid $100 to $300 a day to steal cans of baby formula for eventual resale in the black market. This theft ring is part of the rising trend of organized retail crime (ORC). There are currently four bills before Congress in an effort to battle these crimes and theft rings.

PREVENTION TECHNIQUES

The best intentioned crime prevention initiatives cannot be successful without community support. This premise is primarily based on the philosophy of Sir Robert Peel, known as the father of modern-day policing. Peel observed that, "The police are the public and the public are the police." Think about it. Police acquire their authority from laws approved and determined by the public. The public decides what types of laws need to be enforced. Police agencies use public funding to provide equipment for officers and to pay wages. A law enforcement agency is useless without public trust. Thus, the public are the police, and police officers are members of the public who choose to be paid. Many of the most successful crime prevention programs are community based. Debate about the benefits of community policing has gone on for years, but, undeniably, many of today's crime prevention programs are based on facets of community policing. The basic definition of community policing varies but its methodology is unmistakable: "The police designate a community in which they will engage in problem solving, develop relationships with the population, collaborate with them to diagnose problems that have generalized impact, prescribe and implement interventions to solve the problems and continuously monitor the results" (Flynn, 1998).

SAFE STREETS

These concepts are the basis for the Safe Streets organization. Safe Streets' mission involves organizing neighborhoods and communities for action, developing leadership among youths and adults, and bringing community and strategic partners together on specific problems or opportunities relevant to building safe communities (Safe Streets, 2011). The organization operates based on the following premises:

- The best crime prevention tool is a good neighbor.
- Joint efforts are more effective than individual ones.
- There are more citizens than there are law enforcement agents.
- Citizens can be an extension of law enforcement's eyes and ears.
- Citizens provide a vast resource pool.

Safe Streets also incorporates and supports the development of neighborhood improvement associations (NIAs). Neighbors work together and organize activities as ways to improve their quality of life, developing alliances to work together in determining community issues and working with the local police to effect change. Some neighborhoods develop groups such as Citizens on Patrol that assist law enforcement in patrolling neighborhoods and contact them when suspicious activity is found. Others work on quality-of-life issues, such as cleaning up neighborhoods. Studies have shown that in neighborhoods that appear to be cared for (e.g., less trash, fewer run-down homes) crime is lower, because cared-for neighborhoods suggest neighborhood involvement. Involvement equals greater opportunities for detecting crime, thus making criminals move on to less cared for neighborhoods.

CRIME STOPPERS

Crime Stoppers is a nonprofit, community-based organization designed to assist law enforcement in reducing and solving crime. It offers cash rewards to anyone who calls in anonymously and gives useful information that leads to solving a crime. Crime Stoppers is based on the principle that "someone other than the criminal has information that can solve a crime," and it was created to combat three major problems faced by law enforcement in generating information: fear of reprisal, apathy, and reluctance to get involved (Crime Stoppers USA, 2011).

CRIME PREVENTION THROUGH ENVIRONMENTAL DESIGN

Taking into consideration the characteristics of burglars and thieves—seeking opportunistic targets, desiring to conceal themselves, and drawing the least amount of attention to themselves while plying their trade—many communities are making themselves less attractive targets by adopting Crime Prevention Through Environmental Design (CPTED). This crime prevention technique is based on the theory that the proper design of buildings can lead to reductions in crime and improve the quality of life. CPTED employs three basic principles: (1) *natural surveillance*, by creating spaces in such a way as to maximize visibility and foster positive social interaction among residents; (2) *natural access control*, by limiting access and increasing surveillance through the selection of entrances, exits, fencing, lighting, and landscaping; and (3) *natural territorial reinforcement*, by creating a sense of ownership and space. CPTED strategies incorporated in both new buildings and existing structures can improve crime prevention. Ideally, a community can implement this concept and mandate its integration in all new builds within a community.

COMMUNITY PARTNERSHIPS

Communities and law enforcement can initiate and implement community partnership strategies designed to prevent and reduce crime. Several years ago, the Topeka Police Department embarked on such a program with the local Safe Streets organization to become the Safest Capital City in America Program (with a population of 100,000 and over). The vision of this program is to compare crime statistics of cities of similar size and become the safest city with the least amount of crime reported in the national ranking. Through this program, several crime reduction initiatives have been undertaken. One such program is Lock It, Remove It, or Lose It. The city of Topeka was experiencing a large number of vehicle burglaries, and this program was developed to remind citizens to remove valuable items from their cars and make their cars less appealing to burglars. Since 2007, Topeka has experienced a 21% overall drop in crimes reported, including theft from vehicles. In 2009, Topeka had 452 fewer thefts reported than in the prior year.

Another program instituted to work in conjunction with Lock It, Remove It, or Lose It is a theft deterrence and recovery program called Record It, Report It, and Recover It. This program encourages citizens to inventory their valuables and record the identification numbers. In addition, the program introduced citizens to invisible markers that could be used to mark these items with personal identification numbers (e.g., driver's license number). The marker is not visible until it is held under blue light. The markers are made available to the public through the Topeka Police Department, neighborhood improvement associations, and local pawn shops. This program allows citizens to identify personal items that have been stolen and can assist in the recovery of them.

Citizens themselves can take actions to make their homes less appealing to burglars and thieves:

- Install outdoor lighting.
- Remove vegetation close to a residence that may be used to conceal someone, and do not plant shrubs or bushes below windows that could conceal intruders attempting to enter a home.
- Install audible alarms that draw attention when activated.
- Install good-quality deadbolt locks on all exterior doors.
- Cut up boxes that contained expensive purchased items and deposit them in trash receptacles to avoid advertising these purchases to anyone who passes by.
- On trash pickup day, bring the curbside trash receptacle in as soon as possible after pickup to avoid the appearance that no one is home.
- Pick up mail and newspapers daily; when out of town, have a neighbor retrieve them.
- Make it look as though someone is home even when you are not.
- Be suspicious of any strange vehicles or people in the neighborhood you might see when you leave or go about your daily activities.

Precautions should also be taken while at home. Never leave doors open or garage doors up when doing yard work or other chores, as open doors invite thieves. An open garage door allows thieves to walk in and take whatever they desire, undetected. Generally, people become victims when they have become very comfortable in their daily lives. By just taking a few minor precautions victimization can be avoided.

Businesses can protect themselves by taking extra precautions in day-to-day operations by implementing good business practices. No shoplifters will steal merchandise if they are obviously being watched. Make them feel watched by employees or have video cameras visible. Compare packages customers are carrying when they leave with their receipts. Minimize opportunities for customers to conceal expensive items. Keep displays away from windows in an effort to discourage "smash and grabs." To prevent switching of price tags, use tamperproof labels. Daily or weekly inventories of merchandise can detect a problem before it gets out of control. The design of business buildings can help determine if a business will be a victim of burglary or theft. Municipalities can require new buildings or residential neighborhood designs to include CPTED inspections and practices during developmental phases. The use of laminated glass can make it more difficult to smash the glass to gain entry, good commercial locks will cost a burglar more time to enter a business, and motion-sensing alarms coupled with 24/7 video surveillance can be valuable deterrents.

QUESTIONS FOR DISCUSSION

1. Explain the importance of the first responding officer at the crime scene.
2. Why are the collection and processing of physical evidence important?
3. Describe community policing.
4. What is evidence at a crime scene?
5. Describe how a community can get involved in community crime issues and how important is it with regard to crime prevention.
6. Explain practices that businesses can employ to deter crime and criminals.
7. Explain Crime Prevention Through Environmental Design (CPTED).
8. What are the characteristics of criminals who commit burglaries, and what are their tactics?
9. Explain the importance of quality-of-life issues within a community.
10. Describe how intelligence-led policing can be used to effect crime reduction.

BIBLIOGRAPHY

Crime Stoppers USA. (2011). *What Is Crime Stoppers?*, http://www.crimestopusa.com/AboutUs.asp.

FBI. (2009a). *2008 Crime in the United States: Property Crime.* Washington, D.C.: Federal Bureau of Investigation (http://www2.fbi.gov/ucr/cius2008/offenses/property_crime/index.html).

FBI. (2009b). *2008 Crime in the United States: Burglary.* Washington, D.C.: Federal Bureau of Investigation (http://www2.fbi.gov/ucr/cius2008/offenses/property_crime/burglary.html).

FBI. (2009c). *2008 Crime in the United States: Larceny-Theft.* Washington, D.C.: Federal Bureau of Investigation (http://www2.fbi.gov/ucr/cius2008/offenses/property_crime/larceny-theft.html).

FBI. (2009d). *2008 Crime in the United States: Arrests.* Washington, D.C.: Federal Bureau of Investigation (http://www2.fbi.gov/ucr/cius2008/arrests/index.html).

FBI. (2009e). *2008 Crime in the United States: Ten-Year Arrest Trends (1999–2008).* Washington, D.C.: Federal Bureau of Investigation (http://www2.fbi.gov/ucr/cius2008/data/table_32.html).

FBI. (2009f). *2008 Crime in the United States: Arrests, by Race.* Washington, D.C.: Federal Bureau of Investigation (http://www2.fbi.gov/ucr/cius2008/data/table_43.html).

Flynn, D.W. (1998). *Defining the "Community" in Community Policing.* Washington, D.C.: Police Executive Research Forum (www.policeforum.org/library/community-policing/cp.pdf).

Johnson, S. and Bowers, K. (2004). The stability of space–time clusters of burglary. *British Journal of Criminology*, 44:55–65.

Mesa, AZ, Police Department. (2011). *Crime Prevention Through Environmental Design*, www.Mesaaz.gov/POLICE/literature/pdf/CPTEDlong.pdf.

Safe Streets. (2011). *About Safe Street*, http://www.safest.org/Page.aspx?nid=7.

Yeung, B. (2010). Shoplifting, Inc., *The Crime Report*, March 4 (http://thecrimereport.org/2010/03/04/shoplifting-inc/).

CHAPTER 10

Auto Theft

Donald Munday
Pratt Community College

CHAPTER OBJECTIVES

After reading this chapter, you should be able to do the following:

1. Describe and define the crime of auto theft.
2. List the most common vehicles stolen.
3. Discuss the most common tools used by auto thieves.
4. Outline the steps of a preliminary investigation by a police officer.
5. Describe the steps of a follow-up investigation.

Chapter Outline

INTRODUCTION

Motor vehicle theft has plagued society for decades, costing insurance companies and law-abiding Americans billions of dollars every year. This crime is perceived to be a *victimless crime*, but it is not. Each person in America who pays auto insurance is subject to increased insurance premiums due to this crime.

AUTO THEFT DEFINED

According to the Federal Bureau of Investigation's Uniform Crime Reporting (UCR) Program, motor vehicle theft is defined as the "theft or attempted theft of a motor vehicle" (FBI, 2008). The UCR program considers a motor vehicle to be a self-propelled vehicle that runs on land surfaces and not on rails. Examples of motor vehicles include sport utility vehicles, automobiles, trucks, buses, motorcycles, motor scooters, all-terrain vehicles, and snowmobiles. Motor vehicle theft does not include farm equipment, bulldozers, airplanes, construction equipment, or water craft such as motorboats, sailboats, houseboats, or jet skis. The taking of a motor vehicle for temporary use by persons having lawful access is excluded from this definition. To gain a better understanding of the magnitude of motor vehicle theft, look at these numbers provided by the FBI for the year 2008:

- An estimated 956,846 thefts of motor vehicles occurred nationwide.
- There were 314.7 motor vehicle thefts per 100,000 inhabitants.
- The estimated number of motor vehicle thefts declined 12.7% compared to 2007 figures, 22.7% compared to 2004, and 16.9% compared to 1999.
- More than $6.4 billion was lost to motor vehicle thefts nationwide.
- The average dollar loss per stolen vehicle was $6751.
- About 72% of all motor vehicles reported stolen in 2008 were automobiles.

The occurrence of violent and non-violent crime in the United States is illustrated by the FBI's Crime Clock Statistics (Table 10.1); for example, according to these data, a motor vehicle theft occurs every 33 seconds. Research has shown that auto thieves can steal a vehicle in less than a minute. Many of these autos are stolen for parts, such as the airbags. Reports to law enforcement indicate that autos are stolen from shopping malls, parking lots, car dealership lots, streets, apartment complexes, and airport parking lots, among other public and private areas (Layman, 2011).

TABLE 10.1   Crime Clock Statistics

One Violent Crime	**Every 22.8 seconds**
One Murder	Every 32.3 minutes
One Forcible Rape	Every 5.9 minutes
One Robbery	Every 1.2 minutes
One Aggravated Assault	Every 37.8 seconds
One Property Crime	**Every 3.2 seconds**
One Burglary	Every 14.2 seconds
One Larceny-Theft	Every 4.8 seconds
One Motor Vehicle Theft	Every 33.0 seconds

Source: FBI, *2008 Crime in the United States: Crime Clock Statistics*, Federal Bureau of Investigation, Washington, D.C., 2009 (http://www2.fbi.gov/ucr/cius2008/about/crime_clock.html).

TABLE 10.2 Top 10 Vehicle Theft Rates in U.S. Metropolitan Statistical Areas (MSAs) in 2009

Rank	Metropolitan Statistical Area	Vehicle Thefts	Rate[a]
1	Laredo, TX	1792	742.22
2	Modesto, CA	3712	727.29
3	Bakersfield, CA	5530	684.91
4	Stockton, CA	4479	663.69
5	Fresno, CA	5875	641.89
6	Yakima, WA	1525	637.93
7	San Francisco/Oakland–Fremont, CA	26,374	610.81
8	Visalia-Porterville, CA	2440	567.88
9	Las Vegas–Paradise, NV	10,706	562.63
10	Albuquerque, NM	4815	561.25

[a] Ranked by the rate of vehicle thefts reported per 100,000 people
Source: National Insurance Crime Bureau, Des Plaines, IL, 2010.

VEHICLE THEFT TRENDS

A review of motor vehicle theft trends in 2009 reveals that Laredo, TX, owns the number one spot in the nation for vehicle thefts per 100,000 population (NICB, 2010). Table 10.2 lists the top ten cities in the nation for motor vehicle thefts in 2009, according to the National Insurance Crime Bureau (NICB, 2010). Except for Visalia–Porterville, CA, these same cities also made the 2008 top ten list; however, Visalia–Porterville, CA, was listed as number 11 in the 2008 top ten list (NICB, 2009b).

METHODS COMMONLY USED TO STEAL A VEHICLE

Over the years, law enforcement has improved their techniques of identifying stolen vehicles and the people who steal them. Also, the auto industry has made technological improvements that make it more difficult to steal a vehicle. This has forced auto thieves to change the way they do things, although some still rely on some of the older methods.

JOYRIDING

Joyriding generally refers to the theft of autos by teenagers. Offenders are usually 15 to 19 years old (Swanson et al., 2009). Teenagers look for the easiest target, such as a vehicle left running with the doors unlocked outside an apartment, house, or convenience store. The young auto thief simply opens the car door, gets in behind the steering wheel, and drives off. The motive of this crime is impressing one's peers or street gang membership initiation.

SLIDE HAMMER AND SCREW DRIVER

Auto thieves were able to use screw drivers to steal a car or truck manufactured prior to 2003. An auto thief would use a hard object to break a small back seat window to gain entry into the car. Once inside the car, the auto thief removed the lock cap of the ignition and inserted a slide hammer into the key opening to remove the lock. Once this was done, the auto thief inserted the screw driver into the ignition, started the car, and drove away. After 2003, however, the auto industry began using laser-cut ignition keys that have security computer chips in them, and the ignition was redesigned to accommodate these new keys (Helperin, 2008).

SHAVED KEY OR JIGGLER

When auto thieves discovered that a screw driver would not work, they devised the *shaved key*, also known as a *jiggler* or *master key* (Pasquale, 2006). An auto thief can grind down the face of a key but leave the ridges intact. Once this is done, the key will fit almost any auto door and ignition. The auto thief jiggles the shaved key in the door to unlock it. Once inside the auto, the thief inserts the shaved key into the ignition and again jiggles it to fool the ignition's security system. A shaved key may look a little worn and perhaps has some scratches on the face, but otherwise it is difficult to detect. These keys are valuable items to an auto thief because they can be used over and over again. Recently, the Auto Jiggler Key Set and slim jims have been advertised on the Internet, making it easier for individuals to gain access to tools that can be used to steal autos.

THE SLIM JIM

Some auto thieves still use an age-old tool called the *slim jim*, which is a thin piece of aluminum or metal with notches on both ends. The thief slides the slim jim into the crevice between the window and the door frame and uses it to manipulate the door lock to unlock the vehicle. Once inside, the auto thief can use various tools to start the car and drive away.

THEFT BY OPPORTUNITY

All over the country, on cold winter days, many car owners like to warm up their vehicles before driving them. They start their vehicles and leave them running while they go back inside. Sometimes, too, people will park in front of a convenience store and run inside, leaving their car running so it stays warm. The auto thief looking for an easy target has just found one. The thief simply opens the unlocked door, slides inside the now warm vehicle, and drives off. Some cities have enacted laws to try to prevent this type of crime from occurring.

TABLE 10.3 Top 10 Most Frequently Stolen Vehicles in the United States in 2008

Rank	Year	Make	Model
1	1994	Honda	Accord
2	1995	Honda	Civic
3	1989	Toyota	Camry
4	1997	Ford F-150	Pickup Truck
5	2004	Dodge Ram	Pickup Truck
6	2000	Dodge	Caravan
7	1996	Jeep	Cherokee/Grand Cherokee
8	1994	Acura	Integra
9	1999	Ford	Taurus
10	2002	Ford	Explorer

Source: National Insurance Crime Bureau, Des Plaines, IL, 2009.

AUTO CLONING

Over the years, auto thieves have continued to develop new ways to steal and sell stolen autos. One method is to clone the auto. The auto cloning process begins with the auto thief locating an auto that is of interest. The auto thief copies the legitimate vehicle identification number (VIN) and then steals a similar auto. The VIN of the stolen auto is replaced with the copied VIN. To complete the process, the auto thief either forges ownership documents for the cloned auto or obtains ownership documents by fraud. Once this process has been completed, the auto thief can now sell the cloned auto to an innocent party for a premium price. Typically, it is quite easy to insure and license a cloned auto if it has been purchased in another state because most licensing agencies do not check for duplicate ownership of an out-of-state auto. The National Insurance Crime Bureau has found that luxury cars are usually targeted for cloning, generating estimated illegal profits in the United States in excess of $12 million each year (NICB, 2004).

MOST FREQUENTLY STOLEN VEHICLES

Each year the types of motor vehicles stolen and the means used to steal them change due to changes in demand of the underground marketplace (see Table 10.3). These customers are looking to purchase stolen vehicles for their parts or for resale in the United States or elsewhere on the black market.

INVESTIGATION PROCESS AND TECHNIQUES

To locate stolen autos and identify suspects, law enforcement officers must continually refine their investigative and interview skills. Traditionally, the criminal is usually a few steps ahead of the investigator. To level the playing field, police officers and investigators must continually gather information and intelligence from arrested auto thieves. This information can be used to identify new auto theft techniques and possible auto theft rings. Among the many reasons, motor vehicles are stolen for:

- Their car parts
- Gang initiations
- Insurance fraud
- Joyriding by juveniles
- Chop shops
- Terrorist-related activity
- Transportation of illegal drugs
- Use in criminal acts (burglary, check forgery, identity theft, robbery)
- Vehicle cloning

The first step for a law enforcement officer is to become familiar with the vehicle identification number (VIN), which serves as the fingerprint of a specific motor vehicle. In the United States, since 1954, automobile manufacturers have utilized the VIN instead of the engine number as an identifier. Prior to 1968, although all VINs were inscribed on metal plates, they were not uniformly located on vehicles, and there was no standard method for attaching VIN plates to vehicles (Swanson et al., 2009). Later, in 1981, the U.S. National Highway Traffic Safety Administration (NHTSA) passed a regulation that required all motor vehicles to have a 17-character VIN. This action by the NHTSA standardized the identification system of vehicles sold or manufactured in this country (NHTSA, 2010).

Vehicle identification numbers after 1981 consist of combinations of 17 numbers and letters (I,O, and Q are not used). This number can be considered the fingerprint for each vehicle. The VIN can give a law enforcement officer important information, such as the owner of the vehicle, and it can help determine if the vehicle was stolen. The first three characters are the world manufacturer identifier, the next five digits describe components of the vehicle, and the last eight characters are the vehicle indicator section (Flynn, 2008). Let's decode a sample VIN: 1F2DH34B1DS234567

1	Identifies the country of origin
F	Identifies the auto manufacturer (Ford)
2	Identifies the specific make or manufacturer
D	Defines the vehicle restraint system
H34	Indicates auto body style, model, and series
B	Describes the engine type
1	Check digit character
D	Year of the vehicle
S	Assembly plant identifier
234567	Identifies the order of production

The *check digit* is very important for verifying the accuracy of a VIN. The somewhat lengthy check digit calculation is summarized briefly below:

1. A key is used to assign a numerical value to each letter in the VIN; in our example, 1 = 1, F = 6, 2 = 2, D = 4, etc.
2. A specific weight factor for each character is assigned based on its position in the VIN, except for the ninth character, which is the check digit character; in our example, the first characters has weight 8; the second, 7; the third, 6; etc.
3. The value of each character is multiplied by the weight; in our example, F would be 6 × 7 = 42). These 16 values are added together and divided by 11. The remainder represents the check digit; for example, if the remainder is the number 10, then the check digit is X, and an X is placed in the VIN.

The VIN is typically located on the left side of the dashboard. It is easily seen by looking through the windshield. It can also be found on a sticker on the driver's side door post. The sticker shows the VIN as a bar code. This bar code can be read only with special equipment (Gilbert, 2009). If the sticker is missing or the code does not match any of the hidden manufacturer-marked auto parts, this indicates that the vehicle has possibly been stolen.

To assist in deterring auto theft and to identify stolen vehicles, in 1984 Congress passed the Motor Vehicle Theft Law Enforcement Act. This new law required auto manufacturers to add permanent VIN markings to at least 14 major parts on the auto. These auto parts are in high demand by auto thieves and chop shops. The additional parts that are marked include:

- Transmission
- Both doors
- Both fender wells
- Front and rear bumpers
- Hood
- Rear quarter panels
- Engine
- Decklid
- Tailgate or hatchback

PRELIMINARY INVESTIGATION

A vehicle theft investigation can be initiated in different ways. The most common is when a vehicle owner notifies local law enforcement by calling 911 or another emergency number. The police officer or sheriff officer who receives the call from the dispatcher then responds to the location of the vehicle owner or reporting party. The first step in the preliminary investigation phase is determining if the alleged vehicle theft is factual. In some cases, the vehicle may be part of a civil dispute, recovered as a financial company repossession, or taken by a family member. It is also possible that the owner abandoned the vehicle after an accident due to intoxication or the owner simply forgot where he parked it. Typically, repossession companies notify local law enforcement agencies prior to recovering vehicles.

When the officer has determined that the vehicle has not been repossessed then other possibilities must be explored. One such possibility is that the owner may have been involved in a hit-and-run accident and left the scene and is now reporting the vehicle as stolen. Officers taking a vehicle theft report should pay attention to any noticeable injuries or any odor of alcohol, which could indicate that this is a false report. In many cases of this nature, drivers leave the scene of an accident because they fear being arrested for driving under the influence (DUI). It is recommended that the officer run a check on the owner to determine if there are any prior DUI arrests or convictions. This information can assist the officer in clarifying if an actual vehicle theft has occurred or if the report was made to cover up a hit-and-run accident involving alcohol.

When it has been decided that the vehicle has, indeed, been stolen, then the officer should begin a line of targeted and detailed inquiry with the vehicle owner or reporting party to determine:

- Owner and registration information
- Vehicle identification number and license tag information
- Make of the vehicle, year, color, body style
- Any markings or special equipment (such as rims or tires)
- When and where was the vehicle last seen
- Who drove it last
- Whether someone borrowed the vehicle and is late returning it
- Whether the key was left in the ignition
- Whether the vehicle was locked and the windows closed

The vehicle owner should provide a detailed list of items that were in the vehicle, such as a computer, credit cards (account numbers), handgun or rifle, items of identification (driver's license, military ID, Social Security card), portable DVD player, purse or wallet, vehicle military installation pass, or any other valuables, as well as their serial and/or model numbers. During the preliminary investigation, the officer should gather as much detail as possible concerning the stolen vehicle and the contents that were in it at the time of the theft, including serials numbers, to assist in the recovery of the items. In many cases, such information can assist officers and investigators in making arrests and recovering property. If the owner left a purse or wallet in the vehicle, the auto thieves may use the contents to commit identity theft. Soon after the interview with the stolen vehicle owner, the officer should make a serial numbered case and enter the VIN and other descriptors into the National Crime Information Center (NCIC) system. The NCIC entry will assist officers in identifying this vehicle throughout the country. Also, the officer should enter into the NCIC any serial numbers and descriptors of property in the vehicle at the time it was stolen.

After the officer completes the preliminary interview and the auto theft report, a visual search of the area around the owner's residence a few blocks in all directions should be conducted. There is a chance that the stolen vehicle or property may be found. In the case of joyriding by juveniles, they frequently abandon the stolen vehicle close to the site of the theft (Gilbert, 2009). Studies indicate that officers should always check the area close to the location of the offense for recovery purposes (Lu, 2003). If the officer locates the stolen vehicle, he should protect the vehicle from evidence contamination and notify the crime scene investigative unit. There may be physical evidence present that can lead to the arrest of a viable suspect.

FOLLOW-UP INVESTIGATION

The auto theft investigator must verify the information in the responding officer's preliminary report. This can be done by contacting the owner and reviewing the stolen vehicle information contained in the officer's report. When this has been done, then the investigator should become familiar with the case by reviewing all of the information available, including the vehicle owner and witness statements. From this information, the investigator may be able to connect this case to others. The investigator should also review any suspicious character reports that officers submitted around the date, time, and location of the theft. This information could give the investigator a solid person of interest to locate and interview concerning the case.

During the follow-up investigation, the investigator must keep an open mind. The vehicle theft could be a case of insurance fraud, the vehicle could have been taken to a chop shop, it could have been stolen for cloning purposes, or it might have been stolen for export to another country. There are many informational sources available to assist auto theft investigators in these types of cases. Investigators should consider these sources as investigative tools that can assist in solving a cases and locating suspects.

One such tool is the *International Association of Auto Theft Investigators* (IAATI). IAATI is a network of investigators that share knowledge and expertise. IAATI also sponsors training seminars. Another major resource to assist auto theft investigators is the National Insurance Crime Bureau (NICB). The NICB has database services available to the law enforcement community, which include the following (Swanson et al., 2009):

- *Export file*—Export declarations from the U.S. Customs Service, which can assist in the detection of illegal exports
- *Information-wanted file*—Information concerning a person who has not made payments to a financial institution but has purchased insurance on a vehicle from a NICB member company
- *Insurance theft file*—Insurance company theft records containing ownership and insurance information from over 1000 insurance companies in the United States, from the Canadian Automobile Theft Bureau (CATB), and from most European countries

- *Salvage files*—Salvage vehicle reports that are filed with insurance companies and include information on both buyers and sellers
- *VIN Assist*—No-cost service provided to the law enforcement community that validates VINs

A valuable resource that the NICB offers is their *Passenger Vehicle Identification Manual*, which is published annually. This publication contains information pertaining to vehicle theft prevention standards, VIN locations, federal safety certification labels, VIN structure, and vehicle assembly recorded information (Swanson et al., 2009).

One of the most widely utilized and valuable resources for auto theft investigators is the FBI's National Crime Information Center. Investigators and officers alike can make inquires online to NCIC concerning license plate registration information, motor vehicle information, motor vehicles wanted in conjunction with felonious criminal activity, recovered stolen license plates, and recovered stolen vehicle component parts (Swanson et al., 2009).

Investigators should take note that thefts of older vehicles have tended to remain constant. This indicates that auto thieves are targeting these vehicles for parts. It has been estimated that a stolen motor vehicle valued at $20,000 can be stripped in a chop shop and converted into $30,000 worth of parts (Layman, 2011). A recent trend has been the theft of airbags, which are resold and cost insurance companies and consumers an average of $50 million a year (Berg, 2007). Investigators should check questionable auto body shops and salvage yards for stolen parts. Intelligence information from undercover operations can assist auto theft investigators in identifying such places.

INVESTIGATIVE USE OF STOLEN VEHICLE RECOVERY SYSTEMS

There have been many advancements in stolen vehicle recovery systems that assist auto theft investigators in recovering stolen vehicles. One of the questions an investigator should ask of the vehicle owner is if the stolen vehicle has a factory-installed activated GPS system, such as General Motors' OnStar® or the aftermarket LoJack® system. OnStar combines a GPS transmitter in the vehicle with cellular technology and a monitoring center. OnStar service has assisted law enforcement in recovering stolen vehicles and locating the offenders. When the OnStar system is activated in a stolen vehicle, operators can locate the vehicle and direct officers and investigators to its exact location. If the vehicle is being driven, OnStar operators can direct officers to the path of the vehicle. When officers are behind the stolen vehicle, OnStar can actually send a signal to the engine that slows the car down (Helperin, 2008). This reduces the risk of high-speed pursuits that are a danger to citizens and pursuing officers. The LoJack recovery system utilizes FM radiofrequency technology to connect with specially equipped law enforcement vehicles. When an officer or investigator enters the VIN of a stolen vehicle into the FBI's NCIC database, the VIN is cross-checked with the LoJack database. If a match is found, then a signal is sent to a LoJack transponder hidden in the stolen vehicle. This signal activates the LoJack transponder and sends a silent signal to local law enforcement vehicles equipped with LoJack tracking units. This equipment can lead officers and investigators to the stolen vehicle (Helperin, 2009).

UNDERCOVER INVESTIGATIONS

In recent years, there has been a movement in law enforcement to conduct undercover auto theft investigations. The use of bait cars by law enforcement agencies has proven to be effective. A hidden camera is installed inside the bait car along with a GPS system and an ignition immobilizer, more commonly known as a kill switch. Investigators park the bait car in a parking lot or on the street, and surveillance teams positioned around the bait car wait for an individual to break into the car and steal it. When the offender starts the car and drives off, the ignition immobilizer is activated and the car rolls to a stop as officers approach it to arrest the offender. The auto theft is captured on video along with audio which assists in the criminal prosecution of the offender.

The emergence of corrupt auto body shops, chop shops, and salvage yards involved in the purchase and selling of stolen autos and auto parts has created a need for undercover investigations. Undercover investigators pose as auto thieves selling stolen vehicles or as someone looking for stolen auto body parts to buy or sell. These investigators may be able to purchase a stolen auto or stolen parts from the corrupt business during the initial contact, but it may take more than one meeting to establish a level of trust with the seller. Using a confidential informant (CI) to introduce an undercover investigator to the seller in many cases will assist in building this trust, but it can be risky. The CI may play both sides. During the investigation, background checks should be conducted on all individuals involved in the potential transactions. This gives the undercover investigator vital intelligence to fully understand the depth of the operation and the individuals being investigated. There may be existing outstanding warrants on these individuals or they may be on federal or state parole.

During an undercover operation, it is very important that the undercover investigator wear a well-hidden body wire so that all conversations between the parties are recorded for use in a criminal prosecution. As in any undercover operation, backup officers in the area should be monitoring the conversations in case the undercover investigator needs assistance. The undercover operation team should choose a word or phrase for the investigator to use in case of an emergency or when immediate back-up officers are needed. This procedure is a must in any "buy–bust" situation. One of the goals of the undercover investigator should be to make enough purchases of stolen property from an individual to indicate that the business is working with auto thieves as a criminal enterprise. In most jurisdictions in the United States this would culminate in the issuance of a search warrant to enable investigators to search the corrupt business for stolen autos, documents related to an illegal operation, and stolen auto parts. The execution of the search warrant may lead to recovery of stolen property, arrests of involved individuals, fruits of other crimes, and investigative leads that may solve other criminal cases.

AUTO THEFT TASK FORCE

Across the nation, many law enforcement agencies are joining together to combat and prevent auto theft by creating auto theft task forces. The crime of auto theft has no boundaries; therefore, to effectively combat and prevent this type of criminal activity there must be good communication, sharing of information, and working relationships among law enforcement agencies. Task forces allow multiple jurisdictions to work as one team covering a large geographical area.

Many well-established and effective auto theft task forces can be found throughout the country; one example is San Diego County's Regional Auto Theft Task Force (RATT). In 2010 RATT undercover investigators, along with the Naval Criminal Investigative Service (NCIS), completed "Operation Hotel California" (SDCDA, 2010). This operation was initiated in response to reports that auto thieves were targeting areas in and near military housing (Wheeler, 2010).

Undercover RATT investigators purchased drugs (e.g., cocaine, methamphetamine, ecstasy, oxycodone, heroin), stolen autos, and weapons from individuals in the San Diego area, and this undercover operation resulted in 51 grand jury indictments for auto theft, carjacking, identity theft, residential burglary, selling stolen vehicles, and the sale of controlled substances. RATT investigators recovered 46 stolen vehicles, illegal drugs, seven guns, and two ballistic vests. This operation illustrates how very effective task forces can be and how auto theft investigations can lead to identifying other types of criminal activity.

PROCESSING THE RECOVERED STOLEN VEHICLE

Stolen vehicles can be found in many different locations—parked on the street or in parking lots, parks, and malls. Occasionally, in an attempt to destroy any physical evidence, the auto thief will rig the accelerator pedal in the vehicle so it speeds into a river or creek. When a stolen vehicle is recovered by an officer on the street, a protocol must be followed in processing it for physical evidence.

PROTECTING EVIDENCE AND PROCESSING THE STOLEN VEHICLE

When an officer locates a stolen vehicle, the main focus is on securing it and protecting any and all physical evidence. The dispatcher should be notified, and a crime scene investigator should be sent to the recovery scene to properly process the stolen auto for evidence. The proper protocol for processing the stolen vehicle includes the following:

- Visually inspect the vehicle from the outside for damage, new or old. Remember to take precautions to preserve any and all trace evidence that is identified.
- Examine the exterior of the vehicle for any trace evidence such as blood, foreign substances, hair, or paint transfer. Trace samples should be carefully collected and submitted for later comparison.
- Take photographs of the vehicle's exterior, interior, and VIN located on the dashboard and door. Photographs should be taken of any property or evidence that is located inside the vehicle.
- Examine the interior of the vehicle closely for any trace evidence such as blood, fibers, hair, mud, or any other items of interest. If there are any hair brushes or combs found in the vehicle, inspect them for hair samples. Collect the hair samples

for evidence. The hair samples may identify the auto thief through DNA comparison at a later date.

- Collect all property and physical evidence. Properly package and take measures to preserve any trace evidence for future forensic lab comparisons and analysis.
- Utilize fingerprint powder on the rearview mirror and other areas of the stolen vehicle where the offender may have touched. It is not unusual for the auto thief to adjust the rearview mirror with an ungloved hand out of habit. If latent prints are located and lifted properly, then the investigator should have them run through the Automated Fingerprint Identification System (AFIS) for comparison. If the auto thief has any prior arrests or convictions, his or her fingerprints will be on file with a federal, state, or county agency.

When the stolen vehicle has been carefully and properly processed for physical evidence, then the seat position should be checked. This can assist the investigator or officer in determining the possible height of the auto thief, which, in turn, can help determine the auto thief's motive—for example, joyriding by a juvenile. Also, the information can assist in placing a person of interest in the vehicle when it was stolen.

ALTERED VINS

During an auto theft case follow-up investigation, the investigator may discover that the VIN on the vehicle may have been altered. This suspicion usually occurs when the investigator computes the check digit of the 17-digit VIN and discrepancies appear. The NICB's *VIN Assist* program aids the law enforcement community by analyzing suspicious VINs from recovered stolen vehicles (Swanson et al., 2009). Investigators can further check the validity of a suspicious VIN on a vehicle by comparing it with hidden VINs. The vehicle may still have one or more of the 14 manufacturers' marked parts that have the correct VIN number inscribed on them. If the suspicious VIN does not match a hidden VIN, then the investigator has uncovered an altered VIN.

AUTO THEFT PREVENTION AND PROGRAMS

In the United States, effective proactive approaches to addressing the crime of auto theft have been made by law enforcement agencies and various organizations. These efforts resulted in a decline in auto thefts of 12.7% in 2008 compared to data from 2007 (FBI, 2008).

THE LAYERED PROTECTION APPROACH

The National Insurance Crime Bureau recommends a layered protection approach to preventing and reducing the crime of motor vehicle theft (NICB, 2010). Each layer has a deterrent factor. The four layers of protection are (1) common sense, (2) warning devices, (3) immobilizing devices, and (4) tracking devices (see Table 10.4).

TABLE 10.4   Layered Protection

Layer 1. Common Sense
Never leave a vehicle running, and always remove the ignition key.
Lock all doors and close all windows.
Park in a well-lit area.
Layer 2. Warning Devices
Audible alarms (motion or impact sensors)
Window alarm warning stickers
Steering wheel lock (prevents the steering from turning)
Window etching (etch VIN in each window of the vehicle)
Microdot marking (identifying markings that can be traced back to the VIN)
Layer 3. Immobilizing Devices
Smart keys (contain coded computer chips that match a particular vehicle)
Fuse cut-offs (short-circuit electrical system to prevent engine from starting)
Kill switches (inhibit flow of electricity or fuel to the engine)
Starter, ignition, and fuel disablers (short-circuit electrical or fuel system)
Layer 4. Tracking Devices
GPS (e.g., OnStar)
LoJack

Source: National Insurance Crime Bureau, Des Plaines, IL, 2009.

STATEWIDE COORDINATED PROGRAMS

In 1985, the Michigan State Police and Michigan Auto Insurance Companies organized a statewide "Help Eliminate Auto Thefts" (HEAT) program to enhance auto theft awareness and prevention. HEAT coordinates citizen participation and law enforcement agencies through a 24/7, confidential, toll-free hotline and a website. The hotline and website provide a means for tipsters to report corrupt auto body shops, suspected chop shops, insurance fraud, auto theft offenders, corrupt salvage yards, and carjackings. Tipsters receive a substantial cash reward depending on the information they provide. The HEAT hotline is operated by the Michigan State Police and funded by the Michigan's Auto Insurance Companies. Over the past 25 years, the Michigan HEAT program has managed more than 8500 tips called in and recovered over 4200 stolen vehicles valued at over $51 million; over 3400 suspects have been arrested, and more than 2000 tipsters have been awarded approximately $3.5 million (PR Newswire, 2010).

The Texas Department of Public Safety administers a statewide vehicle registration program similarly titled "Help End Auto Theft" (HEAT). This program coordinates voluntary vehicle owner registration to assist law enforcement officers in identifying stolen vehicles. Vehicle owners can enroll online. The program allows law enforcement officers, between the hours of 1:00 a.m. and 5:00 a.m., to stop any vehicles that have HEAT decals affixed to a window so the officers can verify ownership of the vehicle. Border decals are also issued to alert law enforcement to verify ownership of vehicles driven across the border into Mexico (TXDPS, 2010).

VEHICLE TITLE FRAUD PREVENTION

The National Motor Vehicle Title Information System (NMVTIS) was established in response to Title II of the Anti-Car Theft Act, which was enacted to combat and prevent title fraud. The NMVTIS allows verification and validation of motor vehicle titles prior to a new title being issued. This system prevents title fraud associated with junk or salvage titles. The NMVTIS can also assist auto theft investigators by tracking VINs across the nation, such as during the investigation into the 1993 World Trade Center terrorist bombing. Another valuable NMVTIS service is prevention of the crime of auto cloning (Insurance Information Institute, 2010).

QUESTIONS FOR DISCUSSION

1. Define auto theft and discuss its impact on the United States.
2. What are some of the most common methods auto thieves use to steal a vehicle?
3. List the top 10 most frequently stolen vehicles in the United States in 2008.
4. Discuss the motives for someone to steal a vehicle.
5. Describe what a VIN is and how to decode it.
6. List the steps of a preliminary investigation that an officer should follow.
7. Discuss the resources available to auto theft investigators.
8. What are advantages of having an auto theft task force?
9. List the proper steps of processing a recovered stolen vehicle for physical evidence.
10. Explain what role an undercover investigation may play in addressing the crime of auto theft.

BIBLIOGRAPHY

Berg, B. (2007). *Criminal Investigation*, 4th ed. New York: McGraw-Hill.

FBI. (2008). *2008 Uniform Crime Report*. Washington, D.C.: Federal Bureau of Investigation.

Flynn, K. (2008). What's in a VIN? Decoding Vehicle Identification Numbers Puts the Brakes on Auto Theft, Cloning, and Chop Shop Operations. *Law Enforcement Technology*, 35(6):90–96.

Gilbert, J.N. (2009). *Criminal Investigation*, 8th ed. Upper Saddle River, NJ: Pearson Education.

Helperin, J. (2008). *Evaluating Stolen Vehicle Recovery Systems: The Pros, Cons, and Pricing*, July 9, http://www.edmunds.com/car-technology/evaluating-stolen-vehicle-recovery-systems.html.

Insurance Information Institute. (2010). *Auto Theft*. New York: Insurance Information Institute (http://www.iii.org/issues_updates/auto-theft.html).

Layman, M. (2011). *Criminal Investigations: The Art and the Science*, 6th ed. Upper Saddle River, NJ: Pearson Education.

Lu, Y. (2003). Getting Away with the Stolen Vehicle: An Investigation of Journey-after-Crime. *The Professional Geographer*, 55(4):422–433.

NHTSA. (2010). *Vehicle Identification Numbers (VIN)*. Washington, D.C.: National Highway Traffic Safety Administration (http://www.nhtsa.gov/Vehicle+Safety/Vehicle-Related+Theft/Vehicle+Identification+Numbers+%28VINs%29).

NICB. (2004). *Doing a Double-Take: Vehicle Clones Are a Street-Level Problem for Insurers*. Palos Hills, IL: National Insurance Crime Bureau (www.nicbtraining.org/Vehicle_Cloning.pdf).

NICB. (2009a). *Passenger Vehicle Identification Manual*, 80th ed. Palos Hills, IL: National Insurance Crime Bureau.

NICB. (2009b). *Thefts Cool but California Remains a Hot Spot for Hot Cars: Border Areas Show Mixed Results* [press release]. Palos Hills, IL: National Insurance Crime Bureau.

NICB. (2009c). *Hot Wheels: Vehicle Theft Continuing to Decline* [press release]. Palos Hills, IL: National Insurance Crime Bureau.

NICB. (2010). *Car Thefts Continue Downward Spiral: Western Cities Still Popular Among Car Thieves* [press release]. Palos Hills, IL: National Insurance Crime Bureau.

Pasquale, D. (2006). The Key to Auto Theft. *Police Magazine*, June 1 (http://www.policemag.com/Channel/Patrol/Articles/Print/Story/2006/06/The-Key-to-Auto-Theft.aspx).

PR Newswire. (2010). *H.E.A.T. Celebrates 25 Years of Auto Theft Awareness and Prevention in Michigan* [press release]. Livonia, MI: Help Eliminate Auto Thefts (http://www.miheat.org/new/Media/releases.htm).

SDCDA. (2010). *Undercover Auto Theft Operation Nets 51 for Selling Stolen Cars, Drugs: Task Force Partners with Military for Six-Month Crackdown* [press release]. San Diego, CA: Office of the District Attorney County of San Diego (www.sdcda.org/files/Operation%20Hotel%20California%203-5-10.pdf).

Swanson, C., Camelin, N., Territo, L., and Taylor, R. (2009). *Criminal Investigation*, 10th ed. New York: McGraw-Hill.

TXDPS. (2010). *Texas H.E.A.T. Program*. Austin: Texas Department of Public Safety (https://records.txdps.state.tx.us/DPS_WEB/Heat/index.aspx).

Wheeler, K. (2010). Vehicle Theft Investigation Ends in 51 Indictments. *City News Service*, March 5 (http://www.sdnn.com/sandiego/2010-03-05/local-county-news/vehicle-theft-investigation-ends-in-51-indictments).

CHAPTER 11

Arson Investigation

Cliff Roberson

Kaplan University

CHAPTER OBJECTIVES

After reading this chapter, you should be able to do the following:

1. Understand and describe the issues involved in arson investigations.
2. Explain why arson investigations are complex and difficult to complete.
3. Describe the duties of the first responder.
4. Explain the steps necessary to preserve the scene.
5. Determine what steps should be taken in an arson investigation.

Chapter Outline

- Introduction
- Fire Triangle
- General Issues in Arson-Suspected Fires
- Detecting Arson
- Who Investigates
- Uniform Guidelines for Fire Investigations
- Conducting a Fire Investigation
- Summary

INTRODUCTION

It is a capital mistake to theorize before one has data. Insensibly, one begins to twist facts to suit theories instead of theories to suit facts.

—Sherlock Holmes (*A Study in Scarlet*, by Sir Arthur Conan Doyle)

At common law, arson was defined as the malicious burning or exploding of the dwelling house of another, or the burning of a building within the curtilage, the immediate surrounding space, of the dwelling of another. Present-day criminal statutes have broadened the definition of arson to include the burning or exploding of commercial and public buildings (e.g., restaurants, schools) and structures (e.g., bridges). In many states, the act of burning any insured dwelling, regardless of whether it belongs to another, constitutes arson if it is done with intent to defraud the insurer. In addition, the common-law rule that the property burned must belong to another person has been completely eliminated by statute in some states. To establish the crime of arson, two elements are necessary:

1. Evidence of a burning
2. Evidence that a criminal act caused the fire

The accused must intend to burn a building or other structure. Absent a statutory description of the conduct required for arson, the conduct must be malicious and not accidental. Malice, however, does not mean ill will. Intentional or outrageously reckless conduct is sufficient to constitute malice. Motive, on the other hand, is not an essential element of arson (Wallace and Roberson, 2011).

In most states, arson is divided into degrees, depending sometimes on the value of the property but more commonly on its use and whether the crime was committed in the day or night. A typical statute might make the burning of an inhabited dwelling house at night first-degree arson; the burning of a building close enough to a dwelling so as to endanger it, second-degree arson; and the burning of any structure with intent to defraud an insurer thereof, third-degree arson. Many statutes vary the degree of the crime according to the criminal intent of the accused.

The U.S. Department of Justice published a guide entitled *Fire and Arson Scene Evidence: A Guide for Public Safety Personnel* (Technical Working Group on Fire/Arson Scene Investigation, 2000). Members of the technical working group that created the guide represented law enforcement, prosecution, defense, and fire and arson investigation communities, and their collective expert knowledge, experience, and dedication made the effort a success. The authors would encourage anyone who investigates fires or suspected arson scenes to obtain the guide and use it. As noted by then-U.S. Attorney General Janet Reno (p. iii):

> Actions taken at the outset of an investigation at a fire and arson scene can play a pivotal role in the resolution of a case. Careful, thorough investigation is key to ensuring that potential physical evidence is not tainted or destroyed or potential witnesses overlooked.

In the Introduction (p. 1), the guide observed the following:

> As Sherlock Holmes pointed out, many types of investigations are susceptible to prejudgment, but few as often as fire scene investigations. Fires, by their destructive nature, consume the evidence of their initiation and progress as they grow. Investigations are compromised, and often scenes are further destroyed by the activities of the fire service, whose primary responsibilities are to save lives and

protect property against further damage. Fire scenes often involve all manner of public entities: emergency medical, law enforcement, and fire services. Public utilities such as gas and electric companies may be involved. Passers-by, owners, tenants, customers, delivery agents all may have relevant information. The press and curious individuals attracted to large fire scenes can complicate investigations, as they make security a necessity. As has frequently been said, "A fire investigation is like a picture puzzle. Everyone involved with it has some of the pieces, but no one has the whole picture. It is up to the investigator to gather enough of these pieces together to solve the puzzle."

FIRE TRIANGLE

An arson investigation should start with the fire itself. To create and sustain a fire, three factors, known as the fire triangle, must be present:

- Oxygen
- Fuel source
- Heat

Generally, the concentration of oxygen necessary to sustain a fire must be above 16%. The fuel may be any flammable substance. The heat source needs to be at least the ignition temperature of the fuel. In a fire involving arson, one or more of the factors in the fire triangle will have been tampered with. The arsonist may have increased the fuel load by the use of flammable material or by adding accelerants such as kerosene, gasoline, or alcohol. The arsonist may increase the oxygen content of a structure by opening windows or increasing the flow of air by making holes in the ceilings or walls. Fire will generally follow the highest concentration of oxygen to its source. By ventilating a structure at the top and starting a fire at the bottom of the structure, an arsonist can cause the fire to race upward through the structure. The fire will rapidly involve the whole structure rather than be confined to one room. An arson fire involves the introduction of a heat source, which can be as simple as a match or as complex as chemicals with very low ignition temperatures. By definition a fire is considered an arson fire after all other accidental caused have been ruled out. To consider the fire an arson, the investigator should have evidence that one of the factors in the fire triangle was tampered with (Steck-Flynn, 2009).

GENERAL ISSUES IN ARSON-SUSPECTED FIRES

In only a few countries in the world do public authorities have the statutory responsibility to investigate fires and ascertain their origins and causes. The United States is one of these few. Although this appears to be an accepted responsibility of public agencies, the report of the Technical Working Group on Fire/Arson Scene Investigation (2000, pp. 3–5) identified a number of major complications in U.S. fire investigations, including:

- A fire can be a complex event whose origin and cause are not obvious.
- The training and preparation of qualified fire investigators are costly and time consuming.
- More often than not, the destructive power of the fire compromises or destroys the evidence from the outset.
- The larger the fire, the less evidence that will remain after the fire is terminated.
- Fires generally draw crowds of people, including fire, rescue, emergency medical services, utility company personnel, and health and safety personnel, which increases the chances that the fire scene security will be compromised and critical evidence will be contaminated, moved, or destroyed.
- Often, the responsibility for the investigation of a fire will be divided among different public agencies, especially where the origin of the fire is not immediately apparent.

DETECTING ARSON

The Santa Clara County, California, Fire Department is one of the few agencies in the Bay Area to staff full-time fire investigator positions, augmented by on-call personnel. Fire investigations provide information on the origins and causes of local fire problems, and this information can be shared with the local news media to promote fire safety education and arson awareness. The department also relies on Rosie, who is a Labrador Retriever trained to detect several different types of flammable liquids. Rosie and her handler were trained at the ATF Canine Training Center in Front Royal, Virginia, and have been in service together since 2004. They respond to and assist at fires within the county fire jurisdiction and in other cities in the county.

Rosie's predecessor, Dolph, could detect a substance containing a concentration of only one part per trillion (1/1,000,000,000,000,000) in the atmosphere, and his sense of smell was much more sensitive than any sophisticated equipment. Dolph could detect a half-drop of flammable liquid in the ruins of a fire. Dogs such as Rosie and Dolph, which are recertified annually throughout their working careers, claim an accuracy record of 95 to 99% in detecting an accelerant. Other breeds of dogs might become aggressive and alert to dangers, but a Lab concentrates on working to find the scent of an accelerant. According to the department, some of the benefits of using a flammable liquid detection K-9 include (SCCFD, 2011):

- Detection of small amounts of flammables
- Reduced time to find flammables at a fire scene
- Reduced time digging through the fire debris
- Reduced amount of fire debris to be analyzed by the county crime lab
- Detection of flammables on humans
- Reduction of arsons

WHO INVESTIGATES

The initial determination of who investigates a fire is difficult because most of the time it is not immediately clear whether the fire was accidental or arson. Possible agencies that may be involved in investigating a fire include:

- Law enforcement agencies
- Fire authorities
- Prosecuting attorney investigators
- Forensic laboratory experts
- Engineering specialists (fire, chemical, mechanical, or electrical)
- Private investigators on behalf of owners, insurance companies, tenants, and other interested companies.

UNIFORM GUIDELINES FOR FIRE INVESTIGATIONS

Published by the National Fire Protection Association (NFPA), *NFPA 921: Guide for Fire & Explosion Investigations* was developed as a consensus document based on the knowledge and experience of fire, engineering, legal, and investigative experts across the nation. The guide is considered the benchmark tool for fire investigations. It was originally published in 1991 and is revised every 3 to 5 years.

FIRST RESPONDERS

The first responder is usually the first public safety person to arrive on the scene, whether law enforcement, firefighter, or emergency medical services personnel. The one overriding concern of first responders is the safety of the victims, bystanders, and public safety personnel. When approaching a fire scene, the first responders should observe and note conditions and activities. Generally, the responders will need to make mental notes followed as soon as practical with permanent documentation. Information that first responders should collect includes

- Presence, location, and condition of victims and witnesses
- Any vehicles leaving the scene, bystanders, and any unusual activities near the scene
- Flame and smoke conditions, including the volume of flames and smoke; the color, height, and location of the flames; and the direction in which the flames and smoke are moving
- The type of structure and kind of occupancy (e.g., residential, business)
- Conditions of the structure, including lights, windows, doors, roof, and walls
- Conditions surrounding the scene, including blocked driveways, debris, and damage to other structures

- Weather conditions
- Any unusual circumstances at the scene
- Any fire suppression techniques used
- Status of alarms and sprinklers

PRESERVING THE FIRE SCENE

The first responders and all others involved at the scene need to take special care to preserve the evidence. One step in preserving the evidence is to observe and document the evidence at the scene. Documentation of the status of the scene should include

- Fire patterns, including multiple fire locations
- Burn injuries to victims and fire patterns on clothing
- Trailers, ignitable liquids, or other unusual fuel distribution
- Any incendiary, ignition, or explosive devices present
- Indications of any forced entry, broken locks, etc.
- Distribution of broken glass and debris
- Any shoe prints and tire impressions
- Any discarded containers, clothing, or other similar items
- Contact information for witnesses, bystanders, and victims
- Any unusual items or absence of normal contents or structural components

Threats to the evidence include the movement, removal, contamination, or destruction of evidence, such as:

- Fire suppression activities, which may wash away or dilute the evidence or destroy fire patterns
- Salvage activities, which may involve moving or removing potential evidence
- Necessary medical treatment of victims
- Witnesses and victims leaving the scene
- Personnel walking through the scene who may tamper with or remove potential evidence
- Vehicles moving across the scene, which may introduce fluids or other materials
- Power tools or equipment, which may introduce contamination from external sources
- Changing weather conditions, which may destroy potential evidence

Steps that may be taken to protect the evidence include the following:

- Limit access to the scene by preventing the presence of excessive equipment or personnel and others.
- Avoid needless destruction of property.
- Leave bodies undisturbed until their location and position have been fully documented.

- Flag items of evidence with cones or markers.
- Record observations through written notes, audio and video recordings, and photographs.
- Cover items or areas with objects or material that will not contaminate the evidence.
- Use tape or rope to isolate items or areas containing evidence.
- Collect and secure clothing from victims or suspects.
- Obtain contact information for victims and witnesses.
- Preserve transient evidence such as trace evidence or shoe prints.
- Be sure that the investigators arriving later are fully apprised of the evidence discovered and collected.

SECURITY AND CONTROL

An additional function of the first responder is to establish security and control to help fire suppression and rescue efforts. This action includes the establishment of a security perimeter, control of access into the scene, and initiation of documentation of the scene.

COORDINATION OF ACTIVITIES

Rarely will only one agency report to the fire scene. Emergency operations at the scene may involve many different agencies, and each agency will probably have a different focus. Accordingly, coordination among the agencies is essential. To assist in the coordination, first responders should establish an incident command system to allow for the systematic flow and transfer of critical scene information. The coordination planning should provide for at least:

- A command post with a point of contact and a line of communication and authority
- Staging areas to ensure that emergency and support vehicles have access into the area
- The ability to communicate critical information to responsible authorities

SUMMARY OF DUTIES OF FIRST RESPONDERS

The key person to a successful arson investigation is often the first responder. Public safety personnel tasked as first responders have critical duties at any fire scene, including

- Observe the fire and scene conditions.
- Exercise scene safety.
- Preserve the fire scene.
- Establish security and control of the scene.
- Coordinate activities.

CONDUCTING A FIRE INVESTIGATION

Individuals assigned fire investigator duties should follow the procedures outlined in NFPA 921 discussed earlier in this chapter. The established procedure is as follows:

1. Identify and contact the current incident commander and present your identification.
2. Conduct a briefing and debriefing with the commander.
3. Ascertain who has jurisdiction and authorization (legal right of entry) and identify other personnel at the scene.
4. Determine the level of assistance required and if additional personnel are needed.
5. Determine initial scene safety prior to entry; consider environmental as well as personnel safety concerns.
6. Define the extent of the scene.
7. Identify and interview witnesses at the scene.
8. Assess scene security at the time of the fire.
9. Identify resources required to process the scene.
10. Photograph or videotape the scene.
11. Describe and document the scene.
12. Process the evidence.

SUMMARY

Arson is especially difficult to investigate because often the fire destroys much of the evidence. In addition, the fire suppression efforts may also destroy evidence. It is critical for the first responder to secure the scene and document the evidence. Often the success or failure of an arson investigation will depend on the actions of the first responder. An individual assigned the duty as a fire investigator should study and follow the procedures outlined in NFPA 921.

QUESTIONS FOR DISCUSSION

1. Why is it especially difficult to investigate arson?
2. Should all fire scenes be treated as arson until it is ruled out?
3. What are the duties of a first responder at a fire scene?
4. How do arson investigations differ from other crime investigations?

BIBLIOGRAPHY

NFPA. (2011). *NFPA 921: Guide for Fire & Explosion Investigations*. Quincy, MA: National Fire Protection Association
SCCFD. (2011). *Fire/Arson Investigation*. Santa Clara, CA: Santa Clara County Fire Department. (http://www.sccfd.org/fire_investigation.html).

Steck-Flynn, K. (2009). *Crime Scene Investigation: Crime Scene Processing*. Crime & Clues, http://www.crimeandclues.com/index.php/crime-scene-investigation/40-crime-scene-processing/96-arson-investigation.

Technical Working Group on Fire/Arson Scene Investigation. (2000). *Fire and Arson Scene Evidence: A Guide for Public Safety Personnel*. Washington, D.C.: U.S. Department of Justice (www.ncjrs.gov/pdffiles1/nij/181584.pdf).

Wallace, H. and Roberson, C. (2011). *Principles of Criminal Law*, 5th ed. Upper Saddle River, NJ: Prentice-Hall.

CHAPTER 12

Financial Investigation

Michael J. Palmiotto
Wichita State University

CHAPTER OBJECTIVES

After reading this chapter, you should be able to do the following:

1. Be able to explain fraud.
2. Describe the investigative role of the federal law enforcement agencies.
3. Describe the role of Certified Fraud Examiners.
4. Know the difference in legal authority between federal law enforcement officers and Certified Fraud Examiners.

Chapter Outline

- Introduction
- What Is Fraud?
- Association of Certified Fraud Examiners
- Why Financial Investigations?
- Approach to the Investigation of Financial Crimes
- Association of Certified Fraud Examiners
- Summary

INTRODUCTION

Fraud has occurred throughout this country's history, although it seems more prevalent in our contemporary society. Today, it seems that fraud occurs daily to someone we know or in the business world. Fraud is a serious, often underrated offense that seems to be ignored by many private individuals who practice no prevention methods or are unaware that they are potential victims of fraud. The business world can be just as oblivious when they fail to put in place strategies to prevent fraud. In the last several decades, though, awareness of fraud has grown.

Fraud in America can be traced back to the colonial period when fake health cures were promoted. These medical frauds involved phony medicines, spiritual cures, and bloodletting. Also, land swindles were not unusual at the time, and either the buyer or the seller of the land could be the swindler. Immigrants or Indians were often the victims. During America's frontier period, land swindler activity increased substantially when expanding government involvement in acquisitions provided an opportunity for collusive land dealings between land swindlers and government officials. When corporations evolved in the 19th century, fraud occurred when illegal stock was issued by corporate fraudsters. Frauds involving corporations and governments have continued to persist up to the present day (Jensen, n.d.).

Before continuing, fraud itself should be defined. The variety of definitions available all seem to differ slightly. Fraud has been defined by the *American Heritage Dictionary* (2011) as "a deception deliberately practiced in order to secure unfair or unlawful gain. A piece of trickery; a swindle. One who defrauds; a cheat." Albrecht and Albrecht (2004) provided what they considered to be the most common definition:

> Fraud is a generic term, and embraces all the multifarious means which human ingenuity can devise, which are restored to by one individual, to get an advantage over another by false representations. No definite and invariable rule can be laid down as a general proposition in defining fraud, as it includes surprise, trickery, cunning, and unfair ways by which another is cheated. The only boundaries defining it are those which limit human knavery.

Fraud has several components, including deceit, intentional acts, broken trust, economical losses, secrecy, and fraudsters who may give the appearance of respectability. Joseph Wells, the founder of the Association of Certified Fraud Examiners, stated, "Fraud can encompass any crime for gain that uses deception as a principal *modus operandi*. There are but three ways to illegally relieve a victim of money: force, trickery, or larceny (Wells, 2008, p. 8).

WHAT IS FRAUD?

Fraud is a crime that can be investigated by sworn law enforcement personnel and private citizens who are trained in investigating financial crimes. Sworn law enforcement officers (federal, state, or local) have more authority and power than private fraud examiners; for example, sworn law enforcement officers have arrest powers, whereas fraud examiners do not. Both law enforcement investigators and fraud examiners must follow legal procedures in conducting an investigation dealing with fraud. It is common for former law enforcement officers to become fraud examiners and to work for corporations or operate their own business. Because financial crimes occur not only against individuals but also against corporations and nonprofit organizations, fraud examiners are often employed to determine if a financial crime has occurred. Corporations are concerned with identifying and dealing with fraud that may be causing a financial loss. They may not take legal action against fraudsters when they locate them, because they may not want the negative publicity. Generally, fraud examiners will not investigate financial crimes committed by corporations; this is generally left to law enforcement officers. A wide variety of federal statutes provide for taking criminal action against both corporations and private individuals. Individuals unfamiliar with fraud frequently rely upon auditors to locate it during reviews of a company's financial records.

Fraud examiners and financial investigators have different objectives compared to auditors. Auditing is routine and is conducted on an ongoing basis; it involves a general examination of the financial records of an organization, with opinions provided. The approach that auditors take is one of skepticism. Conversely, fraud examination occurs only with sufficient provocation, reasonable suspicion that an inappropriate act may have occurred. The object of the fraud examination is to locate the fraudster and forward the proof to the prosecutor. Fraud examinations are adversarial, thorough investigations that prove or disprove allegations of fraud (Wells, 2008).

FEDERAL INVESTIGATIONS OF FINANCIAL CRIMES

Several federal investigative agencies have been given the authority to investigate financial crimes. It would be difficult to include all of the agencies here that are involved in financial crime investigation. Instead, only two will be briefly discussed: the Secret Service and the Federal Bureau of Investigation (FBI). Listed below are the primarily financial offenses assigned to the Secret Service (2010):

- *Identity crimes* are defined as the misuse of personal or financial identifiers in order to gain something of value and/or facilitate other criminal activity. The Secret Service is the primary federal agency that investigates identity crimes, including credit card fraud, check fraud, bank fraud, false identification fraud, and passport/visa fraud.
- *Counterfeit and fraudulent identification*, as the name implies, involves possession of false identification documents or counterfeit documents.
- *Access device fraud* involves false credit cards, debit cards, computer passwords, personal identification numbers, and long distance access codes.
- *Computer fraud* involves computer crime.
- *Forgery* investigations address forged U.S. currency and bonds.
- *Money laundering* investigations focus on the laundering of monetary proceeds from criminal acts.
- *Electronic benefits transfer fraud* investigations look into food stamp fraud.
- *Advance fee fraud* investigations track Nigerian schemes, known as "4-1-9," which promise victims millions of dollars.

The FBI concentrates on corporate fraud, securities and commodities fraud, healthcare fraud, financial institution fraud, mortgage fraud, insurance fraud, and mass marketing fraud. The FBI investigates fraud under its Financial Crimes Section (FCS). The mission of the FCS is to oversee the investigation of financial fraud and to facilitate the forfeiture of assets from those engaging in federal crimes. The FCS is divided into four units: the Economic Crimes Unit, Health Care Fraud Unit, Financial Institution Fraud Unit, and the Asset Forfeiture/Money Laundering Unit:

- *Economic Crimes Unit*—Responsible for significant frauds targeted against individuals, businesses, and industries
- *Health Care Fraud Unit*—Oversees investigations targeting individuals and/or organizations who are defrauding public and private health care systems
- *Financial Institution Fraud Unit*—Identifies, targets, disrupts, and dismantles criminal organizations, and the individuals involved, who engage in fraud schemes that impact financial institutions, particularly in the areas of mortgage fraud and bank failures
- *Asset Forfeiture/Money Laundering Unit*—Identifies, targets, disrupts, and dismantles criminal organizations and individuals through strategic use of asset forfeiture, in addition to pursuing money laundering violations

ASSOCIATION OF CERTIFIED FRAUD EXAMINERS

Another form of fraud is *occupational fraud*. Occupational fraud can be defined as "the use of one's occupation for personal enrichment through the deliberate misuse or misapplication of the employing organizations resources of assets" (ACFE, 2008, p. 6). According to the Association of Certified Fraud Examiners (ACFE), occupational fraud encompasses a wide spectrum of misconduct by employees, managers, and executives. Most organizations today, regardless of their size, industry, location, or type, are confronted with occupational fraud. A primary mission of ACFE is to educate the public and anti-fraud professionals about the serious threat of occupational fraud.

Certified Fraud Examiners (CFEs) investigated 959 cases of occupational fraud between January 2006 and February 2008 (ACFE, 2008). They estimated that U.S. organizations lost 7% of their annual revenue to fraud. This loss in revenue translates to $994 billion in fraud losses. The following summary outlines the key finding of the *Report to the Nation on Occupational Fraud and Abuse* (ACFE, 2008):

- Occupational fraud schemes tend to be extremely costly.
- Occupational fraud schemes frequently continue for years before they are detected.
- The most common fraud schemes were corruption, which occurred in 27% of all cases, and fraudulent billing schemes, which occurred in 24% of frauds.
- Occupational frauds are much more likely to be detected by a tip than by audits, controls, or any other means.
- The implementation of anti-fraud controls appears to have a measurable impact on an organization's exposure to fraud.

- Among industries with at least 50 fraud cases, the largest median losses occurred in manufacturing ($441,000), banking ($250,000), and insurance ($216,000).
- Small business is especially vulnerable to occupational fraud.
- Lack of adequate internal controls was most commonly cited as the factor that allowed fraud to occur.
- After discovering that they had been defrauded, 78% of the organizations modified their anti-fraud controls.
- Occupational fraudsters are generally first-time offenders.
- The most commonly cited behavioral red flags were perpetrators living beyond their apparent means (39%) or experiencing financial difficulties at the time of the fraud (34%).

WHY FINANCIAL INVESTIGATIONS?

Fraud is a concern to both government and the private sector. Because of the seriousness of fraud, it cannot be ignored by government or the private sector. Fraud can bankrupt a government program or put a company out of business. In fact, in the past several decades companies have gone out of business because of fraud. Drexel Burnham, a financial giant in the 1980s, disappeared overnight and is considered one of the biggest failures on Wall Street. Drexel and its financial superstar Michael Milken were involved in the debt takeover of companies, which led to the culture of a get-rich mentality. Under the guidance of Milken, Drexel became deeply involved in junk bonds (debt bonds that offer a high rate of return because they are not financially solid), which were used for company takeovers. Fraud was committed both by Milken and Drexel; for example, Milken gave inside information to traders to manipulate stocks of companies that traders wanted to control. To avoid federal prosecution, Drexel paid a fine of $650 million and provided information on Milken. Milken was convicted of fraud and sent to federal prison, and Drexel went out of business when its shady financial practices were discovered (Cronin et al., 1990).

Jim Bakker was a fundamentalist evangelist who established Praise the Lord (PTL) ministries in 1975. Bakker had a PTL television channel and theme park called Heritage USA. To raise money for Heritage USA, he sold lodging space to contributors to stay once a year at Heritage. A fraud that was committed was overselling the time share space. In 1988, Bakker and several of his administrators were charged with fraud and conspiracy. They were charged with illegally taking bonuses from PTL funds, defrauding contributors to PTL, mail fraud, tax evasion, and defrauding contributors who purchased membership in Heritage USA. Bakker was sentenced to 45 years in prison and fined $500,000. PTL went into bankruptcy and was eventually sold (Groupwatch, 1990).

APPROACH TO THE INVESTIGATION OF FINANCIAL CRIMES

Financial crimes are motivated by greed, which translates to money. They differ from crimes against people and predatory crimes, such as burglary and larceny. The investigative focus concentrates on financial dealings. Financial investigators must document in detail the movement of money during fraudulent acts. They must identify the money trail and show the chain of events suggesting financial crime. If no money trail exists, the investigation may have to stop. Information valuable to a financial crime investigation can come from a wide variety of sources, such as informants, government records, business records, public records, checking and bank savings accounts, motor vehicle registrations, and real estate records, including mortgages and deeds. Additional information that may be valuable in establishing a money trail includes computer hard drives, computer disks, utility bills, credit card records, divorce records, recent purchases, and outgoing and incoming telephone records.

Financial investigators have the responsibility of obtaining evidence suggesting that financial crimes have been committed or deciding that such crimes did not occur. The investigator must decide where to look and what to look for in conducting a financial investigation, keeping in mind the resources required to do so. Financial investigators must use caution when selecting a suspect for an investigation. It may not always be easy to determine whom to target; they do not want to accuse innocent people of crimes and damage their reputations. Investigations generally begin with a suspect who might be a good source for inside information. When conducting financial investigations, investigators should seek out anyone who can provide financial information and has the authority to obtain that information.

One method of investigating fraud is to obtain what is known as *direct proof*, which proves the involvement of the suspect in the illegal financial scheme. The investigator attempts to establish an uninterrupted connection between the proof or evidence found and particular financial transactions; that is, they build a paper trail of evidence that can be documented and presented to a jury. The *indirect method* involves analyzing an individual's net worth and changes in the suspect's income and liabilities that cannot be readily accounted for.

The goal of solving a crime should be based on ethics, legal guidelines, accuracy, and a sincere search for the truth (Palmiotto, 2004). Financial investigators must follow the legal procedures required to lead to arrests and convictions. All investigations must be based on law, either federal law or state law, and all actions taken while conducting an investigation must be documented and follow proper protocol. The investigation of financial crimes is a specialized one that requires precise placement of responsibility, intensive training, and experience to develop and maintain skills (Eastman and Eastman, 1971).

ASSOCIATION OF CERTIFIED FRAUD EXAMINERS

Certified Fraud Examiners are certified by the Association of Certified Fraud Examiners (ACFE). Fraud examiners primarily study the areas of accounting, criminology, investigations, and criminal law. After a period of study, candidates must pass an examination covering their knowledge in all of these areas. In addition, to maintain their certification, fraud examiners must earn 20 continuing professional education (CPE) credits each year. Generally, Certified Fraud Examiners are accountants or former law enforcement investigators. It is a natural progression for a retired law enforcement investigator to enter the fraud investigation field (it should be noted that some private investigators who have not obtained certification also investigate financial fraud). ACFE refers to a fraud investigation as an *examination*, a term they consider to be less harsh than investigation. Fraud examiners investigate fraud for companies where workers are generally well-educated professionals. Many of the people interviewed are high-powered executives, including presidents and chief financial officers. Not everyone interviewed by fraud examiners is necessarily a suspect; the vast majority of them will not be suspects but witnesses who can provide general information about the potential offense. Fraud examiners must not be offensive, as they require the cooperation of those familiar with the business operation. Fraud examiners who are abrasive, arrogant, and rude will obtain little cooperation and information from individuals who would otherwise be willing to offer their assistance.

A fraud examination is undertaken when there exists predication or sufficient reason to initiate an examination. Fraud investigations rarely have benefit of direct evidence or eyewitnesses, and offenders do not tend to admit to fraud immediately. Like any investigation, the examination follows a number of steps, and examiners must develop a hypothesis to explain how the alleged fraud has been committed and who the suspects could be. Assumptions must be made to solve the case; initially, these assumptions are based on the known facts. Following is a summary of the steps involved (Wells, 2008):

1. Analyze the available data.
2. Create a hypothesis.
3. Test the hypothesis.
4. Refine and amend the hypothesis.

Fraud examiners must know how to review financial statements, records, and supporting documents. These documents can provide an indication of fraud upon which an examination can be conducted. Fraud examiners must conduct such reviews in a legal manner and follow the rules of chain of custody. Examiners who are weak in reading financial statements should receive extra training or work with an examiner who has familiarity with financial statements and records.

The examiner must also know how to conduct an effective interview. It should be noted that internal fraud committed by employees of a company is the most common type of fraud (Wells, 2008). Most good interviewers have excellent people skills; they are people who others want to share information with. Generally, interviews that are kept low key are the most successful. The interviewer should not be biased, and it is expected that the interviewer will be on time, dressed professionally, and fair minded in dealing with interviewees.

Fraud examiners must be able to use the powers of observation to observe behavior, displays of money, or even offenses being committed (video surveillance is useful in this regard). Surveillance involves the planned observation of people, places, and things; usually, places and things are observed to obtain information about people. Surveillance can be either mobile (following someone) or fixed (stationary). Surveillance can be valuable in obtaining information about suspects (ACFE, 2011).

Experienced fraud examiners do not initiate examinations to arouse suspicion or incriminate innocent people. They also avoid using words with negative connotations, such as *investigation* or *audit*. They conduct their inquiries in a manner that is not confrontational. The following examination methods are recommended (Albrecht and Albrecht, 2004):

- Check personnel records and company records (such as purchasing records).
- Interview former employers or unsuccessful vendors.
- Check public records, invigilation, or surveillance.
- Interview other buyers, coworkers, etc.
- Interview suspects.

Albrecht and Albrecht (2004) also outlined specific steps that a fraud examiner should take:

1. Check an employee's personnel records for evidence of liens or other financial difficulties.
2. Perform a special audit of the purchasing functions to examine trends and changes in prices and purchasing volumes from various vendors.
3. Search public records and other sources to gather evidence about the suspect's lifestyle.
4. Perform surveillance or other covert operations.
5. Interview former buyers and unsuccessful vendors.
6. Interview current buyers, including the suspect's manager (only if collusion with management is not suspected).
7. Simultaneously interview the suspected buyer and the suspected vendor.

The financial investigations of fraud examiners are similar to those of law enforcement investigators but they do not have the legal authorities given to government officials. Fraud examiners may have to be more careful than law enforcement investigators who have the power to charge someone with a crime or to conduct an interview longer than the interviewer would like. Fraud examiners cannot use the term *arrest* or testify that a suspect committed a crime. They can only present their information and let the prosecutor and jury make the decision.

SUMMARY

Fraud occurs on a daily basis. No one is free from being a victim, including individuals, married couples, small businesses, and large corporations. No organization, no matter how small or large, is immune from fraud. Any business that an individual can think of has been, currently is, or potentially will be a victim of fraud. Federal investigative agencies have been given legal authorization to investigate financial crimes. Although many federal agencies have authority to investigate fraud, this chapter concentrated on the two best known agencies with authority to investigate financial crimes, the FBI and the Secret

Service. In addition to law enforcement investigators, civilians trained in financial investigations are often employed by businesses to investigate fraud against their company. Most private financial investigators are certified by the Association of Certified Fraud Examiners. To obtain this designation, examiners must pass an intensive examination, and they must earn continuing professional education credits every year to maintain their certification.

QUESTIONS FOR DISCUSSION

1. What is fraud?
2. Provide several examples of fraud.
3. Describe the legal authority of the FBI in fraud investigations.
4. Describe the legal authority of Certified Fraud Examiners in fraud investigations.

BIBLIOGRAPHY

ACFE. (2008). *Report to the Nation on Occupational Fraud and Abuse.* Austin, TX: Association of Certified Fraud Examiners.

ACFE. (2011). *Fraud Examiners Manual.* Austin, TX: Association of Certified Fraud Examiners.

Albrecht, W.S. and Albrecht, C. (2004). *Fraud Examination and Prevention.* Mason, OH: South-Western.

Anon. (2011). *American Heritage Dictionary of the English Language,* 5th ed. New York: Houghton Mifflin Harcourt.

Cronin, M., McCarroll, T., and McWhirter, W. (1990). Predator's Fall: Drexel Burnham Lambert, *Time,* February 26, pp. 46–52 (http://www.time.com/time/magazine/article/0,9171,96948-6-6,00.html).

Eastman G. and Eastman E. (1971). *Municipal Policing.* Washington, D.C.: International Association of Chiefs of Police.

FBI. (2009). *Financial Crimes Report to the Public Fiscal Year 2008.* Washington, D.C.: Federal Bureau of Investigation (http://www.fbi.gov/stats-services/publications/fcs_report2008).

Groupwatch. (1990). *Hidden Mysteries—Religion's Frauds, Lies, Control: Praise the Lord,* Frankston, TX: HiddenMysteries.com/TGS Services (http://www.hiddenmysteries.org/religion/evange-lists/PTL.shtml).

Jensen, B. (n.d). *History of Fraud in America.* San Antonio, TX: Trinity University (http://www.trinity.edu/rjensen/FraudAmericanHistory.htm).

Palmiotto, M.J. (2004). *Criminal Investigation,* 3rd ed. New York: University Press of America.

Secret Service. (2010). *Criminal Investigations.* Washington, D.C.: U.S. Secret Service (http://www.secretservice.gov/criminal.shtml).

U.S. Department of the Treasury. (1993). *Financial Investigations,* Publ. No. 1714 (Rev. 6-93), Catalog 15271F. Washington, D.C.: U.S. Government Printing Office.

Wells, J.T. (2008). *Principles of Fraud Examination,* 2nd ed. Hoboken, NJ: John Wiley & Sons.

4

Crimes against Persons

CHAPTER 13

Homicide and Assault

Gregg W. Etter and Roger L. Pennel
University of Central Missouri

CHAPTER OBJECTIVES

After reading this chapter, you should be able to do the following:

1. Define an assault.
2. Define the crime of felonious homicide.
3. Explain the classifications of death.
4. Explain the aims of a death investigation.
5. Define wounding patterns and explain why they are important.

Chapter Outline

- Assault and Homicide Defined
- Aims of a Death or Assault Investigation
- Manner of Death
- Autopsy and the Role of the Coroner or Medical Examiner
- Motive, Method, and Opportunity: Putting the Investigation All Together
- Interviewing Witnesses
- Physical Evidence
- Summary

ASSAULT AND HOMICIDE DEFINED

The ways in which we attempt to or actually harm each other are almost infinite. Each individual state within the United States has its own statutory definition of what constitutes the crimes of assault and homicide, and the federal government has its own definition, as well. Most definitions of the crime of assault, however, center around the common law explanation as stated by Black (1968), who defined the crime of assault as "an intentional, unlawful offer of corporal injury to another by force, or force unlawfully directed toward person of another, under such circumstances as create well-founded fear of imminent peril, coupled with apparent present ability to execute attempt, if not prevented" (Black, 1968; *Naler v. State*, 1933; *State v. Staw*, 1922). In some states (e.g., Missouri and Louisiana), the crime of assault covers both the attempt and the actual resulting harm, but in others (e.g., Kansas) the crime of assault is the attempt to do harm, and the actual harm or injury is known as the crime of battery. In some states (e.g., Missouri and Louisiana), the actual amount of harm or actual potential for harm determines the degree of the crime; for example, first-degree and second-degree assault can be a felony, and third-degree assault a misdemeanor. Also, in Kansas, for example, the presence or use of a weapon as well as the degree of harm or potential for harm can distinguish aggravated assault/battery (a felony) from simple assault (a misdemeanor).

If the injury inflicted in the assault is severe enough, it can turn into a homicide. Black defined homicide as "the act of a human being in taking away the life of another human being" (Black, 1968; *Hogan v. State*, 1934; *Sanders v. State*, 1901). Black suggested that not all homicides are crimes and further subdivided his definition to explain justifiable, excusable, and felonious homicides (Black, 1968; *People v. Connors*, 1895). Felonious homicide occurs when a human being is wrongfully killed without justification or excuse in law. A justifiable homicide occurs when a human being is lawfully killed either by legal court order (i.e., death warrant for a lawful execution) or in protection of life as provided by law, such as a law enforcement officer killing a robber who is shooting at the officer. An excusable homicide is a killing that occurs either by misadventure (*homicide per infortunium*) or in self-defense (*homicide se defendendo*) (Black, 1968). Both assaults and homicides are investigated in a similar manner. The primary difference is that, in an assault, we usually have the victim available to provide evidence against their attacker. In a homicide, certain evidence can still be provided by the corpse of the victim, but unless it is a deathbed statement it is usually not verbal testimony.

AIMS OF A DEATH OR ASSAULT INVESTIGATION

Death or assault investigations aim to answer the following questions:

- *Who died or was injured?* (identification of the victim)
- *Where did the incident occur?* (actual location of the assault or killing)
- *When did the person die or get assaulted?* (time of death or injury)
- *Why did the person get hurt or die?* (cause of death or injury)
- *How did the person get hurt or die?* (manner and mechanism of death or injury)

MANNER OF DEATH

Everybody dies eventually, some sooner than others. People die every day. If you don't believe it, look in the obituary section of your local paper to see who just died. According to the Centers for Disease Control (CDC), about 803.6 people per 100,000 in the United States will die each year (CDC, 2011a). Not all deaths are criminal, but some are. The manner of death can be classified as *natural causes*, *accidental*, *suicide*, and *homicide* (Gilbert, 2004; James and Nordby, 2003).

NATURAL CAUSES

In the case of a death by natural causes, the most common type, the death is usually the result of a disease or other known infirmity. It is often expected, even by the victim. The attending physician can sign the death certificate and no further law enforcement action is required; however, if the attending physician will not sign the death certificate, it becomes the responsibility of the coroner, in which case law enforcement involvement is highly probable, if only to gather facts for the coroner. Law enforcement officers should be sure that the death is not a murder or suicide being made to look like death from a natural cause.

ACCIDENTAL DEATHS

Death in an accident or other misadventure is the second leading cause of death in the United States. An accidental death is a death caused by unintentional injuries (CDC, 2011a). Accidental deaths include automobile accidents, industrial accidents, home accidents, and most drug-induced deaths (overdoses). These deaths are investigated, as is any other death investigation, for possible civil or criminal action. Special care must be undertaken by the investigator to ensure that the death was actually accidental and not a homicide or suicide being made to look like an accident.

SUICIDE

A suicide is self-inflicted death. According to the CDC (2011a), suicide ranks as number 11 among the top 15 causes of death in the United States. The predominant ways in which people commit suicide in the United States are firearms, suffocation, and poisoning. Investigators should note that a suicide note is not always present. Suicide is sometimes faked by suspects to hide the murder of a victim, and sometimes suicide is made to look like murder by family or friends to cover suicide (usually for religious or insurance reasons). In most states, assisting a person to commit suicide is a criminal offense.

HOMICIDE

Homicide is the unlawful killing of a human being by another. According to the CDC (2011a), it ranks as number 15 of the top 15 causes of death in the United States. Common elements of the crime of homicide may include intent, malice, and aforethought.

AUTOPSY AND THE ROLE OF THE CORONER OR MEDICAL EXAMINER

In most jurisdictions, not only are law enforcement officers involved in a death investigation but so, too, is the coroner or medical examiner. Coroners, who may or may not be medical doctors, and medical examiners, who generally are medical doctors and fully qualified pathologists, may be elected or appointed, depending on the laws of the state involved. In some jurisdictions, they maintain a fully staffed investigative office, including medicolegal death investigators, who attend crime scenes with law enforcement officials. In other jurisdictions, law enforcement officials bring the evidence and the body of the victim to the coroner for examination. An autopsy is a postmortem examination of the deceased conducted by a coroner or medical examiner to determine the cause of death of the deceased. The procedure gathers evidence on the mechanism of death. The coroner determines the identity of the victim and cause of death of the individual. In homicides and suicides, coroners or medical examiners rule out accidental or natural causes (Cataldie, 2006; Fisher, 2000; Ramsland, 2008).

PRELIMINARY CONSIDERATIONS

Upon arrival at an incident, the absolute first thing that a law enforcement officer must do is to make sure that the scene of the incident is secure. This is an essential priority in any first response. Securing the scene begins with clearing the scene and making sure that there is no imminent danger to the officer or the public. This might be as simple as glancing around to see who is there and if it is safe. However, *if* the bomb is still ticking or *if* the bad guy is still there and poses a threat, it is important to keep in mind that *the first responder could get killed*. As a first responder, remember that the pool of blood that you should examine is supposed to be someone else's, *not your own*. Officers have arrived at homicide scenes where the murderer was still standing there with the smoking gun in his hand. It is rare, but it does happen. Safety first!

Contact the reporting party. Identify the reporting party and determine what occurred. What is the reporting party's role in this—victim, witness, suspect? Who else is involved? Witnesses and suspects need to be identified to conduct a proper investigation (Geberth, 2006; Weston and Lushbaugh, 2003). If applicable, secure the scene of the crime. A saying among the investigations community is that, "Evidence has legs!" This means that your evidence will walk off or be contaminated if the scene is not secured and protected. Even the simple act of too many people walking through the scene can destroy or remove hair, fiber, footprints, tire tracks, etc. Protect the scene to preserve any evidence (Fisher, 2000; Geberth, 2006; Girard, 2011; James and Nordby, 2003; Ogle, 2004; Saferstein, 2004).

The first responder needs to look for anything that could be considered as evidence. Identification of evidence by the initial responder ensures that the evidence will be properly collected, processed, and analyzed. This is a most important function. Detectives cannot examine evidence that was never identified and collected by investigators. The investigators must make sure that the evidence is legally collected; at times, investigators may need to get a search warrant or advise suspects of their Miranda rights. There is no "homicide exception" to the need to obtain a search warrant if one is needed (*Mincey v. Arizona*, 1978). The investigator also must make sure that the evidence is properly packaged, marked, turned in, and stored in such a way as to maintain the chain of custody. Evidence can be spoiled by contamination, which reduces its evidentiary value, or it can be excluded because it was collected illegally (Fisher, 2000; Geberth, 2006; Girard, 2011; James and Nordby, 2003; Ogle, 2004; Saferstein, 2004).

CRIME SCENE

Upon arriving at the crime scene, investigators should first secure the crime scene if it has not already been accomplished by the first responder. They should make sure that they have the right to legally seize any evidence present and get a search warrant when necessary (*Mincey v. Arizona*, 1978). Using procedures described in Chapter 2, the investigator should make an initial walk-through of the crime scene. The crime scene should be thoroughly diagrammed and photographed. Possible evidence includes the victim's body, biological evidence, fingerprints, trace evidence, impression evidence, and weapons. As previously mentioned, all evidence needs to be properly collected, packaged, and turned in for further analysis.

Investigators need to locate and examine the body of the victim. The body may be readily apparent, but it may have been moved by the suspect from the initial crime scene and concealed. Investigators looking for a victim's body sometime use cadaver dogs to assist in the search; these dogs are often able to detect a body that has been buried in a clandestine grave (Geberth, 2006; Hallcox and Welch, 2006). Ground-penetrating radar is also used to detect buried bodies (GSSI, 2011). Other indications of a concealed grave are changes in the color and depth of vegetation and soil at the site (Davenport et al., 1992).

When the victim's body has been located, investigators should carefully observe the position of the body (Lyman, 1999). Are any wounds visible on the body? Are any of these wounds defensive wounds? Is *rigor mortis* or *livor mortis* apparent? Is there visible decomposition of the body? Don't move the body until the coroner or medical examiner says it is all right to do so. If the intended roles are played out properly, the scene belongs to the police investigator, and the body belongs to the coroner or medical examiner. A thoroughly processed crime scene can assist in successfully solving a case.

IDENTIFYING THE VICTIM

Accurate identification of the victim is essential. The body of the victim may be whole and readily identifiable, or it may be dismembered, decomposed, or skeletonized, which makes identification more difficult. Identification papers found on the body of the victim may or may not be the victim's actual papers. Identification of the deceased is most often accomplished by family members identifying the victim. Fingerprints can be used for identification of the deceased providing that fingerprints are obtainable from the corpse (damage or decomposition may prevent this) and the victim's fingerprints are on file so they can be compared. DNA from the body or skeleton may also be used for comparison with the victim's relatives, if they are known. If the teeth of the victim are intact, identification may be possible by comparing dental records of missing subjects of the same race, gender, and age. This identification can be made by a forensic odontologist, who also makes dental comparisons for rape or child abuse cases involving teeth marks (Harvey, 1976).

Scars, marks, and tattoos on the victim's body have also been used as a means of identification, in addition to evidence of prior surgical procedures. Forensic radiologists can compare x-rays taken while the person was alive against x-rays of the remains; they are also called in for cases involving small children or babies who have been abused and suffered broken bones. A child's death may prompt taking postmortem x-rays to determine any evidence of abuse while the child was alive (Weston and Lushbaugh, 2003).

In the case of skeletonized remains, the first thing that a forensic anthropologist does is to determine if the bones are human. If so, a forensic anthropologist may be able to determine the race, sex, and approximate age, height, and weight of the deceased. Facial reconstruction of the victim is sometimes possible; such models of a victim's face can aid in identification of the victim and has been used successfully in many cases in the United States.

POSTMORTEN CHANGES AND DETERMINING THE TIME OF DEATH

Most murders are witnessed or discovered shortly after the fact; the bodies are readily found, and they bear proper identification. In a minority of homicides, though, a body is found well after the death, when a number of changes to the body have occurred. Often these bodies bear no identification. The changes that occur after death can reveal much about the individual and his or her death, including how long it has been since the death (which can be useful when determining possible motives), the time frame of the death (which can be used as a starting point in the investigation), and what types of evidence to consider collecting. As a rule, in determining the time of death, an investigator should not rely on a single factor. A great deal of variation as to the time of death may be found within a single factor.

The three major sources of evidence useful in determining the approximate time of death are corporal evidence, which is present in and on the body; environmental and associated evidence, which is present in the vicinity of the body; and anamnestic evidence, which reveals the habits and daily routine of the deceased. Corporal evidence can include the presence or absence of clothing and number of layers, the body temperature at death, and the size, physical condition, state of nutrition, location, and position of the body. The investigator would expect the body temperature to be approximately 98.6°F, although an infection, seizure, or heat injury, such as a heat stroke, may raise the temperature several degrees above 100°F. The temperature at the time of death can also be well below 98.6°F, such as in the case of shock, impaired metabolism, or hypothermia. The rate of postmortem changes will be considerably different for a muscular, young person in good physical condition suffering from no malnutrition compared to an elderly person in poor physical shape. The rate of changes also differs for a nude body in a fully extended position as opposed to a clothed individual in a fetal position.

Environmental evidence might include whether the body was indoors or outdoors, whether it was lying on the ground or buried, in water or in the desert. Other factors include the relative humidity, air currents, or precipitation. Anamnestic evidence includes the personal habits or routines of the individual; some may figure into solving the case, but others are totally irrelevant. It may be necessary to determine, for example, what type work the victim did, whether the victim's work would normally bring him or her to the location where the body was found, what type of foods the victim ate (or didn't eat), and whether the victim smoked, drank, or used drugs. What was the victim's daily routine? Was there anything different about it that day? Were there things the victim was in the habit of doing around the house that are not done? Did the victim normally drive down this road? The list of questions is endless.

The body begins the change process at the time of death. The longer the period of time between death and when the body is discovered, the less precise will be the estimation of the time of death. Changes to the body progress in a relative orderly process, and the question to be answered typically is at what point in this process was the body found?

The factor used most often to determine the time of death is *algor mortis*, or the process of the body cooling off. Geberth (2006) used the following information as a rule of thumb: If the body is warm, death occurred a few hours ago; if the body is cold and clammy, death occurred anywhere between 18 and 24 hours ago. As a general rule, the normal temperature of the healthy person is 98.6°F. The generally accepted rate of cooling is about 1.5°F per hour. So, to determine the number of hours since death, the following formula can be used: (98.6 − current body temperature) ÷ 1.5. Even assuming that this is an accurate indicator, it is still necessary for the body to have been at 98.6°F at the time of death. In the case of pneumonia or cocaine death, the temperature could be around 105°F or, in the case of heat stroke, even 110°F. In contrast, in cases of impaired metabolism, the body temperature at death could have been 93°F; it could be even lower in cases of exposure to cold (i.e., hypothermia). At some point, the body temperature loses relevance, as the body will tend to approximate the temperature of the environment. This makes it necessary to determine the rectal temperature of the body and the temperature of the environment.

Rigor mortis is a common form of determining time since death, although it is the least accurate method (Geberth, 2006). *Rigor mortis* is the stiffening of the muscles related to chemical changes occurring after death. It fixes the body in the position assumed at death. If a person dies in a seated position and *rigor mortis* sets in, the body will retain that position when moved. *Rigor mortis* is not a permanent condition. It begins at the same time throughout the body, although it first becomes evident in the shorter muscles, such as the face, becoming evident in the larger muscles later. This process generally begins in 2 to 4 hours, is completed 8 to 12 hours, and begins leaving the body at 18 to 36 hours. The beginning of the process can be accelerated or delayed, thus affecting the entire time line. If the body or the environmental temperatures are high, the onset of the process will be speeded up, while a cold environmental temperature will delay the onset.

A concept often confused with *rigor mortis* is cadaveric spasm. Cadaveric spasm is the stiffening of a single group of muscles occurring immediately after death, such as a hand still gripping the gun used to commit suicide. In contrast, *rigor mortis* is a process involving all muscles of the body, and the stiffening of cadaveric spasm does not leave the body, as in the case of *rigor mortis*.

Postmortem lividity (*livor mortis*) is the purple discoloration at the lowest parts of the body after death. When the heart no longer beats, the blood ceases to flow; gravity takes over, and the blood settles to the lowest part of the body. Without oxygen, the blood changes to a purple color. In the body of a victim lying on his back, the blood will settle to the shoulders, back buttocks, and backs of the thighs and calves. An exception to this is when the body is in direct contact with the floor (also called *blanching*). These same areas (shoulder blades, buttocks, and backs of the thighs and calves) will be a white color rather than purple, as the pressure of the floor does not permit blood flow into these areas. When the cause of death is chemical death by means of carbon monoxide poisoning, the color of these areas will be cherry red.

Livor mortis may be helpful in determining how long the victim has been dead and whether the body has been moved after death. If two parts of the body, such as the back and one side, have similar colors, then it is possible the body was moved after death. *Livor mortis* begins in approximately 30 minutes, becomes perceptible in about 1 to 4 hours, is well developed after 3 to 4 hours, and becomes fixed at 8 to 10 hours. The term "fixed" means that the *livor* patterns have settled in one position and cannot be shifted, even by moving the body to a different position. The point of fixing does not necessarily mean that the blood has lost its fluid nature, but that the blood is being obstructed from flowing out of the capillaries by the gelled blood.

The contents of the gastrointestinal tract can provide clues as to the last time the victim ate, what the victim ate, or where the victim ate. There is a general lack of agreement as to how long it takes for the stomach to empty, although Geberth (2006) suggested that the stomach empties its contents within 4 to 6 hours after a meal. If there is no evidence of food in the stomach, it may be necessary for the forensic pathologist to examine the small intestines, where food may remain for up to 12 hours. The process of the stomach emptying its contents may be affected by the type of food, the amount of food, at what rate the body metabolizes the food, and the presence of any type of medication. If there is any possibility that food may figure into the death, particularly at a residence, samples should be collected.

Postmortem decomposition is a process where the body basically turns on itself. This process has two components: autolysis and putrefaction (the major component of decomposition). Autolysis occurs when digestive juices break down the tissues of the gastrointestinal tract, which may result in perforation of the stomach within a few hours of death. During life, digestive juices act on food; during death, they act on the body.

Putrefaction occurs when bacteria within the body acts on the cells of the body, initiating a decaying process. During this process, gases are produced that distort and discolor the tissues of the body. The body begins to swell and produce a foul odor. The process is initially indicated in the area of the abdomen by a greenish color; it then spreads to the remainder of the body. A general timeline may be loosely derived from Casper's dictum regarding the rate of putrefaction: One week of putrefaction in air = two weeks in water = eight weeks buried in soil. A similar decay process occurs in the blood vessels. The blood breaks down and stains the vessels, producing a greenish-black discoloration along the blood vessels. The marbling, due to the dark color and being close to the skin, will be evident.

Some of the changes discussed above will naturally occur in most environments if the body is not found is sufficient time. Other changes only occur when a body has been placed in a particular type of environment. Adipocere is produced when a body is left in water or in a very moist environment. Adipocere is a grayish-white, cheesy, or soap-like substance consisting of fatty acids; it develops on the surface of a body that has been lying in a moist area. It usually appears first in areas with large deposits of fatty tissue, such as the face or buttocks. If a body is left in a hot, dry environment with good air circulation, the bacterial process will be retarded by the dehydration process that occurs; the result can be mummification, where the body becomes withered and shriveled up. As a rule, regardless of the environment, the body will usually proceed through putrefaction.

The body changes discussed above reflect the body's reaction to the environment, although things can happen to a body that are the result of the environment reacting to the body. These external sources may include the presence of insects, animals feeding on the body, or the depositing of plant life. The change agent most likely to appear on the body will be maggots after flies deposit their eggs on the body. The eggs planted on the body go through a precise development process. Major factors determining the rate of development are the temperature and the environmental conditions. Based on the stage of the life cycle at which the maggots are found, it is possible to determine an approximate time since death. Maturing from an egg to an adult requires about 16 to 35 days. A critical factor impacting the entire timeline is whether the flies were deposited on the body at the time it was placed in the environment. Insects may further become involved in the destruction process when roaches and other types of insects bite the skin. This is a very slow process, and such insects probably will not consume the entire body, although the small bite marks may lead investigators to believe that the source of the marks was human, as in the case of torture. If animals are suspected, the forensic pathologist will probably look for V-shaped bite marks in the bones or scratch marks surrounding the wound.

The presence of animals in either an external or internal environment will bring about other physical changes. Portions of a body found in a home may be eaten away, usually those areas not covered by clothing. If no food was available after the time of death, pets may begin feeding on their owner's body. Domesticated animals may eat only a small portion of the exposed skin, or they may eat it down to the bone. Mice and rats may also feed on the body. Occasionally plant life may grow on a body, usually outdoors but occasionally indoors. The body may have fallen on seasonal plant life that can assist in the timeline. White or yellow fungus is among the more common types of plant life found on a body.

Each of these changes may help in determining the time of death. A time of death based on only one of these factors is likely to be less accurate than one that considers each of these factors.

IDENTIFYING SUSPECTS

Suspects may be identified by the victim, by witnesses to the crime, or by informants. Suspects can be identified by physical evidence such as fingerprints or DNA, or they may confess to the crime out of remorse. The investigator often begins looking for suspects by examining all those persons who last had contact with the victim: friends, associates, enemies, family, etc. The identification of a suspect is another essential part of the investigation.

MOTIVE, METHOD, AND OPPORTUNITY: PUTTING THE INVESTIGATION ALL TOGETHER

The investigator is charged with finding out not only what happened but also who was involved and whether a crime has been committed. The development of motive, method, and opportunity is essential to any criminal homicide investigation. A suspect may have hated a victim (motive) who was beaten to death (method) and publicly stated so on many occasions, but the suspect was in prison at the time of the victim's death (lack of opportunity). All three factors are crucial in developing probable cause in the investigation using the "totality of the circumstances" doctrine as advocated in *Illinois v. Gates*, 462 U.S. 213 (1983). These factors may be proved by testimonial or physical evidence.

MOTIVE

The motive is the cause or reason why the perpetrator attacked or killed the victim (Black, 1968). There can be a single motive or a combination of motives in an assault or killing. Motives can include (Osterburg and Ward, 2010; Weston and Lushbaugh, 2003):

- Rage or other emotional factors
- Relationships (wife/husband, lover, boyfriend/girlfriend, parents, siblings)
- Revenge or jealousy
- Financial gain
- Sex (either sexual gratification or sex connected)
- Killing in the act of committing another crime
- Random or "thrill" killing

METHOD

The method is how the attack was actually accomplished or attempted against the victim. Did the suspect point a gun at the victim? Stab the victim? Strike the victim with his hands or feet? Each type of attack produces a different type of injury or, in the case of a swing and a miss, no injury at all, but it is still an assault. The investigator must be able to determine how the attack occurred in order to prove the crime.

OPPORTUNITY

In order to prove that the suspect committed the crime, the investigator must show that the suspect had the opportunity to commit the crime. Was the suspect physically present at the time of the crime? Could the suspect physically do what was necessary to accomplish the alleged assault?

INTERVIEWING WITNESSES

Witnesses are a crucial part of any assault or homicide investigation; therefore, identifying witnesses and conducting timely interviews are essential. Investigators have to get a witness' story down before it changes or the witness disappears. Don't expect witnesses to wait around for hours to voluntarily talk to an inspector. Witnesses may not even want to be involved in the case (Bennett and Hess, 1991; Gerber and Schroeder, 1974).

Many prosecutors and police prefer to have eyewitness testimony about a crime; however, eyewitness testimony can have its drawbacks and is not necessarily reliable or accurate. As an example, picture the face of a clock, and suppose that Witness 1 is standing at the 12. Witness 2 is at 2, Witness 3 is at 11, Witness 4 is at 8, and the victim is in the center of the clock. The suspect is at 6. Obviously, each witness saw what happened a little differently. It is necessary to document where every witness was in relation to the victim and suspect, as well as what they actually saw, heard, tasted, or smelled. If you don't find these witnesses and document exactly what they experienced, you can be sure that the defense attorney will! Be careful not to put words in anybody's mouth. Some investigators, for example, would not even mention finding a knife to avoid planting the idea of a knife in a witness' mind; instead, they would simply ask the witness exactly what the witness saw or heard (Pena, 1997). Accurately document what they saw or didn't see. Can the witness place the victim at the scene? Can the witness place the suspect at the scene? Did the witness hear any threats or argument? All of these questions are relevant, even those with negative answers.

Statements taken by investigators from witnesses have to be credible; therefore, witnesses must be kept separate to prevent creating a "collective memory" of what happened. We want to know what each person witnessed, not hear a compromised account obtained by group discussion. People usually mean well but they do talk to each other and memories become corrupted.

PHYSICAL EVIDENCE

Just as important and in some cases even more important is the physical evidence in the case. Ogle (2004) noted that physical evidence gives investigators valuable clues as to what happened, can prove or disprove statements by the defendant, provides the jury with a tangible object to see to strengthen the case, and is not subject to memory loss as is witness testimony. Physical evidence in homicides and assaults can consist of weapons, trace evidence, biological evidence, impression evidence, photographs, etc. Be aware, though, that, "Physical evidence has value in court proceedings only when the forensic scientist who testifies about it understands—and can explain to a jury—how the results of this analysis may be interpreted in the context of the crime scene" (Girard, 2011). Some examples of physical evidence are discussed in the following sections.

WEAPONS

Weapons are the means used by assailants to assault or murder their victims. The use of a weapon may or may not cause injury to the victim; for example, a victim who has been shot at but the bullet missed has still been assaulted. Various types of weapons may cause different wounding patterns. Walker (1983) stated that, "In an armed assault, the recovery of the weapon that was used is of primary concern, particularly if it was a firearm."

Personal Weapons

Personal weapons are the most readily available, as they consist of the assailant's various body parts (e.g., hands, head, teeth, feet). The use of body parts as a weapon can cause injury or even death. The actions taken by the suspect might be as simple as a push or a shove to cause the victim to fall off of a cliff or building. Investigators should examine possible contact surfaces such as the knuckles of the hand for abrasions, contusions, or other signs of contact with the victim. Bite marks can be matched to their owner by a forensic dentist using forensic odontology. Bite marks may be offensive or defensive wounds (*State v. Peoples*, 1980).

Blunt Instruments

A blunt instrument can be anything used as a club, a rock, a brick, an automobile bumper, etc. Blunt instruments bludgeon the victim and often leave a crushing injury, such as broken bones or contusions. Injury or death can occur. Examine the weapon for fingerprints or biological or trace evidence. This type of weapon can leave impression evidence.

Edged or Pointed Weapons

An edged or pointed weapon can be a knife, sword, axe, meat cleaver, straight razor, spear, ice pick, letter opener, or other similar object. Edged or pointed weapons can create a stabbing wound or a slashing wound. Examine the weapon for fingerprints or biological or trace evidence. The shape of the cut or puncture on the victim's body can indicate the direction of the thrust of the weapon.

Firearms

Firearms are weapons that use the explosion of a gunpowder charge to propel a projectile or bullet. Firearms are generally considered to be handguns, rifles, muskets, and shotguns. If the bullet strikes the victim, it usually causes a penetrating (puncture) or grazing (abrasion) wound. Investigators should examine the weapons, cartridge cases, and expended bullets for fingerprints, ballistic evidence, and biological evidence.

Arson (Fire and Explosives)

The definition of arson is destroying property by fire or explosives, but sometimes people are killed. Fire victims often die from the toxic gases and fumes created by the fire and do not show signs of actual burning. Bodies that are burned can display a degree of burning ranging from first degree to sixth degree. The body may be partially or almost entirely consumed by the flames, leaving only trace evidence (usually pieces of bone or teeth). A victim's body may show signs of charring and other extensive body damage. Investigators should look at fire burn patterns to determine the probable point of origin. Investigators should also look for the presence of an accelerant that would indicate that the fire had been set on purpose. Fires are sometime set to cover murders or other crimes. Explosives have different blast patterns and different chemical signatures; they often dismember victims with tremendous force. Sometimes victims are killed by the concussion of the blast, which can leave the victim with no external signs of injury but blunt injury trauma to internal organs (Walker, 1983).

Poisons

Poisons are toxic substances that can induce injury or death in the victim. While often used as a method of suicide, poison is fairly rare as a method of homicide (Geberth, 2006). Poisons may be biological or chemical, which can be solid, liquid, or gaseous. They may be administered orally, intravenously, by inhalation, or through osmosis. Poisons leave trace evidence that can be identified through chemical analysis and forensic toxicology (James and Nordby, 2003; Saferstein, 2004). Corrosion or the appearance of burning at the mouth may be present in victims who ingested a caustic substance. Dilation of the eyes may be present in poisoning from atropine or belladonna, but opiate alkaloids or nicotine cause contraction of the pupils in victims. The color of lividity on the victim's body may be affected (e.g., red vs. purplish in cyanide victims). The contents of the victim's stomach often give clues as to the poison involved (Fisher, 2000).

Other Weapons

Perpetrators have been very imaginative in the use of everyday objects as weapons. A simple pillow can be used to smother someone to death. A length of rope or an electrical cord becomes a ligature or garrote used to strangle someone. An electric curling iron is usually harmless, but when plugged in to electricity and pitched into the bathtub with one's estranged wife it becomes deadly. The possibilities are endless. Injuries will vary according to the objects used. The crime scenes often are made by the suspect to look as though a natural or accidental death occurred.

WOUNDING PATTERNS

The wound is the actual damage done by the assailant to the victim's body. Different wounding patterns are caused by the usage of different weapons. It is important for the investigator to have knowledge of and be able to recognize different wounding patterns.

Abrasion

There are three types of blunt force trauma: abrasion, contusion, and laceration. Abrasion occurs when a body scrapes against a surface and the outer layer of skin is damaged. The seriousness of the external wound depends on such factors as the force of the contact, the roughness of the surface, and the location of the wound. An injury caused by a person falling out of a moving vehicle onto an asphalt or concrete surface will result in a serious abrasion; an injury that occurs when a person slips on a grassy surface and scrapes the calf of his leg will be less serious. Abrasions are also more serious where the bone is close to the surface. Abrasions, as far as general appearance, may be considered to be the least serious type of injury, although they can be deceptive because the force of the impact may be severe enough to result in internal injuries. Abrasions form a reddish-brown scab when the skin oozes fluids and blood. An object used with prolonged force can also leave an abrasion mark on the victim; this type of injury is known as pattern abrasion. An example is the pattern left on the victim's neck when a rope or a curtain cord was used to kill the victim by means of ligature strangulation. The same result may be observed on the wrists when handcuffs or ropes are used to confine the person's hands.

Contusion

A contusion (or bruise) is an injury to a person caused by the impact of blunt force but the skin is not broken. When this blunt force contacts the skin but does not break it, blood vessels rupture, which is evident in the changing color of the skin as the blood spreads out. Often overlooked are the body organs below the surface where the blow was delivered. The location of the bruising will be immediately below or in the general vicinity of where the blow was administered. In some cases, though, this may not be true. An example of this would be a very severe blow to the forehead. At the point of contact, a pronounced swelling will be visible due to the loss of blood into the tissue, and the bruising will spread out from that location. If this is severe enough, there may be significant migration of the blood to various areas of the face. In several days, the eye may become discolored, with the blood then traveling to the cheek area, the side of the face, and ultimately to the chin and neck area. It is likely that the total healing process in this case may take several months.

The severity of contusions differs among individuals, depending on the type of tissue in the area of injury and the extent of the blood supply. Factors that may be present can affect the severity of a bruise (Knight, 1996):

- Lax tissue, such as eyelids (older people, genetic connective-tissue syndromes)
- Delicate tissues (in children and older people)
- Scanty muscle mass or obesity
- Bleeding tendency (due to alcoholism, hemophilia, taking aspirin or other anticoagulants)

Due to these variables, the intensity of the blow may not always be indicated by the appearance of the contusion. It is important for the investigator not to confuse the presence of contusions with postmortem lividity. If contusions are interpreted to be lividity, their presence may give the investigator the false impression that the victim may have been moved, when in fact the victim had not.

Evidence of a cutting injury will continue to be apparent due to the presence of a scar. In the case of a contusion, however, once the location has healed there often will be no evidence of the injury. For this reason, it is necessary to photograph the injury. The contusion will go through a series of color changes, so photographs should continue to be taken for the next several days, even up to a week, to document the changes in color and size. In the case of an abdominal injury caused by a seat belt, the extent of the initial injury may be a slightly reddened area, 2 inches wide from one hip to the other hip. Within several days, though, the injury site may well be from 4 to 6 inches wide with major discoloration, more accurately reflecting the actual severity of the contusion.

Although contusions routinely change in color after the initial impact and during the healing process, there is a lack of precision in gauging the age of contusions by their color (Geberth, 2006). It is best to simply determine whether a contusion is relatively old or new. Consider an angry female who wants her significant other arrested. She may display a contusion and report that she was assaulted several hours ago, but the color of the contusion is yellow or brownish. This would indicate that the assault, at the least, took place several days ago; therefore, it would classified as "old."

According the Bernard Knight (1996), a British forensic pathologist, medical textbooks in the past had attempted to determine a timeline of assaults based on the color of contusions. He suggested that, "It is not practicable to construct an accurate calendar of these color changes … as there are too many variables for this to be reliable." Listed below is a very general guideline to the progression of color change:

1. Red with swelling
2. Red, purple, blue
3. Greenish margins
4. Yellow cast
5. Brownish
6. Final healing, depending on size

A victim with a contusion that is yellowish or brown in color who indicates that she was assaulted the previous day is probably lying, because the contusion would be considered to be more than one day old.

When photographing contusions, a color scale should be used for accuracy and proper color when the photographs are printed. Depending on a number of variables of the camera, including the *f*/stop, the time of exposure, and the lighting of the area, the color on the photograph will often be different for the actual color of the injury.

Lacerations

A laceration is an injury due to blunt force creating a tear in the skin. This is the most serious of the three types of blunt force injuries. Although many instruments can create this injury, it will usually be an instrument that is not too sharp, in which case it would be more comparable to an incision, and not too round, in which case there may be no breaking of the skin. The tearing of the tissue is brought about by a shearing or a crushing blow. Lacerations that come to the attention of the investigator will usually be external, although it may additionally include an internal injury involving the tearing of an organ. In some cases, the force may be of such a nature that there is no external injury, only an internal injury. Lacerations normally have ragged edges, with each side possibly possessing both an abraded and a contused area. A laceration will not completely separate the two sides, as there will be a "bridging" effect due to the nerves and blood vessels. It is occasionally possible to confuse a laceration with an incision, but incisions have no bridging of the nerves or blood vessels; the two sides are completely separated.

An avulsion is a form of laceration where the force of the instrument hits at such an angle as to rip the skin and soft tissue from the bone. Another way to describe the injury would be a scooping effect.

The instrument used in the assault may be capable of transferring evidence to the body and picking up evidence from the body. Paint or any type of evidence adhering to the weapon may be left in the injury site, while fibers, hair, or blood may be transferred to the weapon. It may occasionally be possible to determine the relative size and shape of the weapon.

A laceration to the head, depending on the weapon and the force used, can be very serious. If a single blow is administered to the head, it may be difficult to determine whether the cause was a blow or a fall. It is possible that a victim's head can exhibit abrasions, contusions, and lacerations. Two things that will usually be present in this type of head injury is a fracture of the skull and bruising of the brain. A coup injury is a brain contusion located directly under the site of blunt force impact. It is caused by the bending of the skull at the fracture site, causing compression of the brain. Coup injuries are often associated with a blow to the head (moving object hitting the stationary head). A contrecoup injury is a contusion located on the opposite side of the brain from the site of blunt force impact; it is commonly the result of a fall (moving head hitting a stationary object). Either type of injury results when the brain hits the skull. It is possible to have bruises both under the fracture site and on the opposite side. In a fall, the contrecoup injury will usually be more severe than the coup injury, but the coup injury from a blow will be more severe than the contrecoup injury.

Two types of bleeding in the brain are caused by blunt force. A epidural hematoma is a blood clot that forms between the skull and the top lining of the brain (dura). This blood clot can cause pressure on the brain. A subdural hematoma is a blood clot that forms between the dura and the brain tissue. The sudden onset of such a clot is referred to as acute subdural hematoma.

Asphyxia

Asphyxia is a type of death where the body cannot take in oxygen and cannot eliminate carbon dioxide. If no oxygen can reach the lungs, the blood in the body cannot absorb the oxygen necessary for survival. This is most critical for the brain, as brain damage can occur within 4 to 6 minutes of being deprived of oxygen (Geberth, 2006). There are several ways in which a person may die of asphyxia, with some of them being almost exclusively a result of homicide and others more likely to be self-inflicted or even accidental. One indication of inadequate oxygen within the blood is the presence of cyanosis, where the skin exhibits a bluish color. Another indicator of asphyxia is the presence of petechiae, small, pinpoint hemorrhages in the whites of the eyes, although the absence of these does not mean that asphyxia was not the cause of death. Three ways of dying from suffocation are smothering, where the nose and mouth are blocked, preventing the air from reaching the lungs; choking, where the upper airway is blocked by food or some other object; and mechanical asphyxia, where pressure is applied to the outside of the body to prevent the physical act of breathing.

Items used for smothering people include the hands, a gag, a pillow, a blanket, or a plastic bag. Each of these items is readily available to an attacker. In most cases, when a plastic bag has been used, it is a case of suicide, and the person likely has consumed drugs. This is a method of suicide suggested by Humphry (1991) in his book on assisted suicide. Accidental smothering of an adult is seldom found; this is more likely to be found among babies and small children, often due to a drycleaning bag.

It is difficult to smother an unwilling adult, but where it is suspected a major source of evidence can be found in the mouth and on the face. Sufficient force used in smothering will usually produce signs of bruising or lacerations, particularly on the lips and cheeks. There may also be scratch marks on the face, in which case fingernail scrapings should be taken from the victim as well as any suspect apprehended soon after the crime. As with any crime involving an assault, there will probably be evidence of a struggle. An examination should be made of the mouth and nose for the presence of foreign material from the object used, such as fibers, feathers, or related material.

A method seldom used for homicide is choking, and it is usually classified as a natural death. It is very difficult to force an object into the upper airways of an adult. The obstruction usually responsible for this type of death is caused by attempting to swallow a too large amount of food. The Heimlich maneuver is used to dislodge the object. Choking may be more likely to occur when an individual has used an excessive amount of alcohol.

Mechanical asphyxia is usually accidental. A person who dies of a crushed chest while working on a vehicle is the victim of mechanical asphyxia caused by the jack failing to keep the vehicle elevated. Another example is when a trench collapses on trapped workers. In either of these cases, the victim's head may not be buried or crushed, but death occurs if the chest is. This is also a cause of death when a fire breaks out and large number of people stampede to the limited number of exits, crushing each other. A person on drugs or intoxicated can fall into a compressed area that restricts movement of the chest. An example of this would be rolling out of bed and becoming lodged between the bed and a wall. It is even possible for an intoxicated person to stumble or fall into such a position that his body becomes restricted and he is unable to move. Occasionally, mechanical asphyxia may be used for murder, particularly of elderly people who have little strength to fight back. In this case, a person might sit on the victim's chest and cut off oxygen to the victim's mouth and nose. The term "burked" is used to describe this method of murder, named after an individual who used this method in Scotland in 1828 to obtain cadavers to sell to medical schools.

Strangulation is caused by constriction or compression of the neck, resulting in the obstruction of blood vessels and air passages. Pressure on the carotid arteries can lead to unconsciousness in 10 seconds. The three methods of strangulation are hanging, ligature strangulation, and manual strangulation. Hanging is strangulation by means of a rope, cord, or similar ligature that is tightened by the weight of the body dropping. This method is usually suicidal, although homicide should not be ruled out until after the crime scene investigation and the autopsy. There generally must be sufficient pressure on the neck to either cut off the flow of air or interrupt the flow of oxygenated blood. The body can be fully suspended or partially suspended.

Two major factors in determining whether the hanging was a result of suicide are the position of the rope and the location of the lividity. Due to the weight of the body, the rope will leave an impression in the skin of the neck. This impression will be above the upper part of the neck, due to the weight of the body. The noose leaves a very deep impression at the point opposite the suspension point, where the knot is located. The impression at that point exhibits an inverted V shape and indicates the application of less pressure.

Once death occurs, the rope impression will remain. The pattern of the rope (pattern abrasion) will often be imparted to the neck. If it is necessary to remove the ligature at the scene, do not touch the knot; instead, cut the area opposite from the knot and then reattach the cut ends with a smaller piece of cord. It is best to let the ligature remain on the victim, letting the forensic pathologist remove it during autopsy.

Postmortem lividity patterns would be expected in several locations. If the body is in an upright position, the majority of the blood would be found in the feet and lower legs, in the hands, and in the area immediately above the rope, where it was not possible for the blood to travel any further. If the blood has not collected at the lowest portion of the body or if there are inconsistent patterns, then homicide should be considered, although homicidal hangings are rare.

Ligature strangulation is a type of death where the pressure on the neck is caused by a constricting band that is tightened by a force other than body weight. Strangulation or garroting is usually homicide, since suicide by this method is not possible. An individual attempting to do so would release the pressure when passing out. A garrote is a weapon where each end of the cord or wire is attached to a handle. As in the case of hanging, ligature strangulation also leaves a permanent groove in the neck; however, there are enough differences that we can distinguish between the two. With ligature strangulation, the mark will completely surround the neck, usually at the mid-point of the neck below the larynx. Internal injuries may be found in the neck. A tender U-shaped bone attached to the end of the tongue may be fractured. In the case of a hanging, this would not be expected because the ligature would have slid above the larynx to a higher part of the neck. The presence of petechial hemorrhages may be apparent in the whites of the eyes and skin of the face. The victim may bite his own tongue (Geberth, 2006).

The third type of strangulation is manual strangulation, also known as throttling. The pressure is caused by pressure of the hand, arm, or other limb, causing neck compression sufficient to kill the victim. This approach is homicidal, never suicidal. The hands are the most likely weapon of choice. Scratches, abrasions, contusions, and fingernail marks may be found on the victim's neck, since most likely the victim struggled. Fingernail scrapings may be found under the victim's nails. Petechial hemorrhages and cyanosis will usually be present (Geberth, 2006). As noted, both manual and ligature strangulation will often fracture the hyoid bone, a small U-shaped bone attached to the tongue. This is seldom found with hanging.

The third type of asphyxia is chemical asphyxia, which occurs when the victim inhales a gas that prevents the body from using oxygen at the cellular level. The cause of this type of death is usually due to acute exposure, where the person received a single, brief dose of the substance. The most common gas used for chemical asphyxia is carbon monoxide. Carbon monoxide is an odorless, colorless gas, usually produced by internal combustion engines. When it is inhaled, it enters the blood and attaches to the hemoglobin, resulting in death and postmortem lividity that is cherry red rather than the typical purple color. This type of death is usually suicidal; investigators should look for such things as a tube attached to the tail pipe and placed in a window or a vehicle that has no gas but the ignition is in the on position. In order to rule out homicide, an examination of the crime scene and the history of the victim are in order.

Autoerotic Deaths

Autoeroticism is a type of incident involving "sexual feeling or sexual gratification that is self-induced without having sexual relations with another" (Hazelwood et al., 1983). Such an act performed in a private setting ordinarily would be of little concern to the police, as normally no violation of the law is involved. Investigators become involved, however, when this activity results in death or a possible near-death experience. This type of activity is observed in many societies. In the United States, it involves all races and both genders, but most of the victims are white males from a middle-class background. The average age is 26.5 years old. Most knowledge of this activity comes from cases where a death has occurred, as living participants are not likely to discuss it, and the police become involved only when a death or near-death has been reported. Those unfamiliar with this activity might assume that such deaths are suicides; however, in most cases, autoerotic fatalities are accidental, although they may be homicidal, suicidal, or natural. Autoerotic fatalities are most commonly caused by asphyxia used to achieve a state of euphoria during the sexual activity. This can be accomplished by hanging (neck compression), suffocation (airway obstruction), chest compression, or oxygen exclusion. Hazelwood et al. (1983) developed a list of twelve key death scene characteristics often found at an autoerotic death scene. Not every characteristic will be present at every scene, but the scene should be examined for each of these:

- *Location*—This is usually an area where the victim was not likely to be disturbed.
- *Position of victim*—If a rope is used, the victim will usually be found in a supported position, usually on the floor.
- *High-risk agents/elements*—To enhance the level of sexual and physical pleasure, the victim likely used a rope, restrictive containers, handcuffs, gag, or some other type of restrictive mechanism.
- *Self-rescue mechanism*—This mechanism is employed to enable the victim to reduce or remove the effects of the high-risk elements. This might be the ability to stand up or having a handcuff key available.
- *Bondage*—The victim might have also used some type of a binding device, such as a rope, chain, handcuffs, or any other device that restricts movement. It is important to determine whether the victim could have put him- or herself in this position.

- *Masochism*—The scene of the death may include various means to inflict pain, especially to sexual areas. Examples include genital restraints, nipple clips, electrical wires inserted into the penis or anus, cigarettes, and ball gags.
- *Clothing/attire*—Male victims often are found wearing some type of female garment.
- *Protective measures*—The surface of the restriction, particularly a rope applied to the neck, will in most cases result in an abrasion. Some type of padding is often inserted under the rope to prevent potentially visible marks.
- *Sexual paraphernalia*—Sexual objects found in the area may include pornography, diaries, mirrors, video cameras, dildos, vibrators, or female attire.
- *Masturbatory activity*—Often there is evidence of the victim having masturbated.
- *Evidence of prior experience*—There will usually be evidence that this person has done this many times before, such as a worn spot on the wood from which the rope was suspended or semen stains from previous sessions.
- *No apparent suicidal intent*—An indication of whether there were suicidal intentions is critical. If they were planning future events, had no depression, or had not indicated such intentions, suicide in all likelihood was not the intent.

The following characteristics, at the very least, must be present for an autoerotic death determination. At a minimum, to assume an accidental death, investigators must determine that this was a solo activity, that prior evidence of such dangerous activity exists, that the victim possessed no suicidal intent, and that the victim had an expectation of privacy. When major questions arise as to how the death came about, the investigation of these deaths often hinges on a detailed examination of the crime scene and the victim's history

The pass-out game (self-asphyxiation) is a popular activity among young people to create a natural high by cutting off oxygen to the brain, but it sometimes results in death. Most literature covering this area primarily focuses on the natural high with no sexual focus. This activity may start in the preteen years. Despite distinct differences between scenes involving self-asphyxiation and those involving autoerotica, there is little indication at what point in time the activity transitions from being a game to autoerotica.

Gunshot Wounds

The condition of a victim's gunshot wound is a direct reflection of the components of the cartridge casing, among other variables. The cartridge case, bullet, bullet coating, and metal jacket contain specific elements that can be detected. Examination of a gunshot wound will reveal the presence of gunpowder (burned and unburned), soot, bullet and jacket fragments, primer compounds (lead, antimony, barium), and copper, brass, and nickel from the cartridge case (DiMaio, 1999). Wounds are categorized according to the distance from which the shot was fired—contact wounds, intermediate wounds, and distant wounds.

Contact wounds exhibit a number of recognizable characteristics. There will always be scorching at the edges of the wound, with soot deposited on the wound edges. There may be a muzzle impression, particularly if the gun had been held firmly against the victim. If a contact wound occurs to the head, soot may be deposited on both the outer and inner table of the skull. Depending on the firmness of the contact, there may be a stellate (star-shaped) wound due to gases building between the skull and the skin. The skin reaches its expansion point and then tears. With a light contact wound, the soot expands beyond just the wound edges. A contact wound over clothing will usually result in the soot and powder being deposited on the clothing but not the skin, although they will still enter the wound.

An intermediate wound is close enough for "tattooing." This tattooing is caused by grains of powder, both burned and unburned, being deposited in the skin. The density and diameter of these deposits can be measured by firing the same type of cartridge casing at various distances. The tattooing may appear from a distance of 24 to 48 inches, depending on the type of powder. Soot will be found on the body from a distance of 6 to 10 inches. This can be wiped off of the body, but the tattooing cannot. There is very little to say about the distance shot other than it is farther than the intermediate wound and will not leave any soot or tattooing. Without this, the precise range cannot be determined.

Both entrance and exit wounds can divulge additional information. At the entrance, an abrasion ring is caused by the friction of the bullet against the skin. This ring will be present regardless of the distance of the shot. There will also be a bullet wipe at the entrance where the skin wipes off debris from the bullet. As a rule an entrance wound tends to be smaller than the caliber of the bullet, circular and smooth. The smaller size is a result of the skin stretching and then rebounding after the bullet has moved through. The exit wound is usually larger in size than the entrance wound and more irregular, due to bones and other body debris becoming secondary missiles. This is especially the case when the bullet is designed to expand while in the body; thus, the size of the projectile is, in fact, larger when it exits. A situation where an exit wound may resemble an entrance wound is when the area of the exit is shored up or supported by some external item, such as a belt or some type of hard surface.

The path made by the bullet as it travels through the body is known as the bullet track. This will usually be straight, giving an accurate estimation of the angle from which the bullet was fired. An exception to this is when the bullet is deflected by a bone. Other factors that may affect the bullet track are the velocity of the bullet, the type of bullet, and whether the bullet ricocheted (Geberth, 2006).

As the bullet enters the body it causes a rearrangement of the interior of the body. A permanent cavity is created along the path of the bullet. Much larger than this cavity is a temporary cavity caused by kinetic energy transferred by the projectile's passage. This explains, for example, why sometimes with an abdominal shot organs in the vicinity suffer severe injury, but not near the bullet track.

Water Death

Drowning is not usually a means of murder. According to the FBI (2011), drowning was used as the means of death in 0.0011% (15 times out of 13,230) of the murders from 2000 to 2004. In the vast majority of drowning cases, the cause will be accidental, but it can be suicidal or homicidal. As a rule, healthy adults rarely drown unless there is an intervening reason, such as heart disease or severe cramping that happened to occur while they were in the water. There is no specific finding at an autopsy that proves the person died from drowning; it is usually a diagnosis of exclusion. When every other cause of death has been ruled out, this fact alone with evidence at the scene leads the forensic pathologist to the drowning conclusion.

The ability to swim is not an important correlate of drowning, as most victims of drowning are able to swim (Pollanen, 1998). A swimmer may attempt to perform some daring feat and too late realize that he is in trouble. Drowning in the United States is the second most common cause of death for children between the ages of 1 and 14 (CDC, 2011b). Of all non-pool drownings from 2002 to 2004 among children younger than 5 years of age, more than 80% involved children under 2 years of age (CPSC, 2007).

Not all drownings are accidental; some may be homicide or suicide. The police get called in light of the fact that a death has occurred, and the investigator may well be the only one to bring up the initial suspicion of a non-accident. What are some characteristics of a drowning death? The hands and feet of a drowning victim are wrinkled or prune like. Drowning victims may exhibit a white froth or foamy type of substance coming from the nose and mouth due to pulmonary edema. This substance may appear pink when mixed with blood. The blood results from the lungs tearing due to increased pressure during the drowning. It is possible that the lungs may contain sand or some other type of water-related debris.

The victim should always be examined for any signs of trauma, such as strangulation marks, contusions, and other wounds that are not products of an accidental drowning. Contusions, abrasions, or lacerations may be present, but the likelihood is that they are a result of underwater injuries. Injuries discovered on the top or front of the head, the top of the feet, or on the fingers and back of the hands are probably natural, based on how a body floats in death. The body should be examined for marine life bite marks. The decomposition process will cause bodies to bloat and float to the surface, but the temperature of the water may be cold enough to retard the decomposition, and the body will not float. If the water temperature rises, the decomposition process will begin and the body will float to the surface.

Diatoms can be used to determine the location where a drowning occurred, particularly when the body has been moved to another location. Diatoms are found in both freshwater and saltwater, and they differ from one body of water to another. Diatom populations also can vary seasonally within the same body of water. When diatoms are extracted from marrow (especially from the long bones), investigators can infer that these organisms became lodged in the marrow cavity while the person was drowning. The diatoms in the bone marrow can then be compared with diatoms in the body of water where the drowning was believed to have occurred.

A water death may require some additional precautions compared to other crime scenes. A body may change drastically from the time it is removed from the water until the beginning of the autopsy, so it is necessary to take photographs at both locations. Injuries to the body may be readily apparent initially but difficult to see later on. A variety of trace evidence can be obtained in drowning cases, including evidence accumulated prior to entering the water and evidence accumulated in the water. To secure as much evidence as possible, bring two clean bed sheets to the scene. Spread one sheet out and then the second one on top of that one. Place the body on top of both sheets. Fold the top sheet over the body, and then the bottom sheet. At this point, place the body in a body bag. More evidence will be collected with such a process (Castro et al., 1993).

Electrical Injury

One mode of death seldom associated with murder is an electrical injury. Many investigators will not do a crime scene search in such cases because they assume that these are natural deaths. Electrical accidents that occur to adults often occur in a work setting and involve high voltage. In many cases, knowledgeable witnesses are available who can verify that it was an accident. A suspected electrical death at a residence, however, generally receives little investigation.

Three variables are used in determining the possibility of an electrical death: the amount of current (measured in amperes), the amount of electrical resistance (measured in ohms), and the electromotive force (measured in volts). The most critical of these is amperes; 0.1 amp is sufficient current to cause ventricular fibrillation and death. Resistance is reduced in the presence of water—100,000 ohms for dry skin vs. 1000 ohms for wet skin. The number of volts in a residence is normally 110 volts. Using the formula volt/ohms = amperes, we can determine the number of amperes. Dividing 110 volts by 1000 ohms (as in wet skin or in a bathtub) gives us 0.110 amperes, which is sufficient to produce death.

A problem at such scenes is that this type of injury often leaves no external injuries, such as might be expected with lightning or high-voltage incidents. Because an electrical injury scene does not appear to be a potential crime scene, investigators may not learn of the electrocution until an autopsy is completed, if one is done at all (James and Nordby, 2003).

Central Nervous System

It is not unusual for a person to move around for a period of time, occasionally for an extended period, after receiving a serious injury. The wound may be so serious that it is surprising that the person is still alive; however, as long as the central nervous system has not been destroyed, movement is possible. An excellent example of the immediate destruction of the central nervous system is a victim being shot in the head with a powerful handgun or a rifle. Continued movement is not possible.

BALLISTICS AND FIREARMS EVIDENCE

Ballistics is the science that examines firearms-related evidence. A firearm is a mechanical device that causes a projectile to be propelled by means of gases and energy created by an explosion of a chemical compound (generally gunpowder). Each step in the process leaves telltale marks and evidence for the investigator. When the firearm is discovered, the process of examination by the investigator begins. The firearm should be photographed and where it was found documented. The firearm should be examined for fingerprints. Fingerprints may be found on the outer surfaces of the firearm, as well as on the interior of the firearm, such as on magazines or cartridges. It is difficult for someone to say he did not handle a gun when his prints are found on a cartridge inside the weapon. The firearm should be examined for make, model, serial number, finish, caliber, and barrel length. Evidence of attempts to remove or deface the serial number of the firearm should be thoroughly examined. Firearms can often be traced through their serial numbers.

As the bullet travels down the rifled barrel of a weapon, the lands and grooves of the rifling give the bullet spin. They also leave identifiable marks. Great care should be taken to recover bullets; often they can be traced to a specific firearm through ballistic examination. The exception to this rule is smooth-bore weapons such as most shotguns and some muskets. Ballistics examination can also determine the path of the bullet from the weapon to the victim.

Expended cartridges can also provide evidence such as fingerprints. When the weapon is fired the firing pin strikes the cartridge primer, causing primer marks that are specific to each weapon. In weapons that eject the expended cartridge, an ejector mark will probably be present. This mark can also be identified through ballistic comparisons to a specific weapon. The exception to this rule is a revolver, which generally does not leave an identifiable ejector mark when the cylinder is opened and the cartridges are removed. Some revolvers that use a side-gate type of cartridge ejection may leave no mark at all (DiMaio, 1999; Fisher, 2000; Warlow, 2005).

BIOLOGICAL EVIDENCE

Biological evidence is a broad category that includes body parts (flesh), bodily fluids (blood, saliva, semen, sweat, urine, feces), DNA, and other things that are or once were living, such as insects or plant evidence. Forensic toxicology involves examining biological specimens to determine the presence of alcohol, drugs, poisons, or other toxic substances that may have been used to kill the victim. Forensic serologists perform tests on blood samples to determine the type and characteristics of the blood, examine blood stains, and give testimony or presentations at trials; they also analyze semen, saliva, and other body fluids and may or may not be involved with DNA typing. Deoxyribonucleic acid (DNA) is the building block for a person's genetic makeup. Except for identical twins, everyone's DNA is different. DNA may be obtained from biological evidence, even evidence that is decades old (Rudin and Inman, 2002). Because of the danger of bloodborne pathogens or other diseases, investigators should always use universal precautions when collecting or handling this type of evidence. The analysis of bloodstain patterns by a trained investigator can reveal (Bevel and Gardner, 1997):

- The direction a given droplet was traveling at the time of impact
- The angle of impact
- The probable distance from the target from which the droplet originated
- The nature of the force involved in the bloodshed and the direction from which the force was applied
- The nature of any object used in applying the force
- The approximate number of blows struck during an incident

- The relative position in the scene of the suspect, victim, or other related objects during the incident
- Sequencing of multiple events associated with an incident
- In some cases, which hand delivered the blows from a beating

Forensic entomologists are specialists in the study of insects. Of relevance to death investigations is the fact that certain insects may use the body to serve as a host for their eggs. Over a period of time, the eggs become maggots and ultimately adults. Each insect has identifiable life cycles, which can be determined with some degree of precision, particularly taking into consideration environmental factors, such as the temperature. Forensic botanists examine leaves, seeds, and pollen found at the scene of a body or on a body.

FINGERPRINTS

Fingerprints are collected at the crime scene and off of evidence. Fingerprints may be collected from almost any surface that was touched by the suspect or victim. Sometimes fingerprints can be collected from the body of the victim (Fisher, 2000). Fingerprints are compared with those in various databases by qualified fingerprint examiners. Fingerprints are unique to the individual, so they are useful evidence in any investigation.

TRACE EVIDENCE

Trace evidence includes glass, hair and fur, fibers, paint, soils, and gunshot residue. Forensic chemists analyze various types of evidence, including trace evidence, which is often so minute that the crime scene technician may not even be aware that it has been collected. Chips of paint, for example, reveal information about the paint color, number of layers of paint and primer, source of the paint, and even the manufacturer. Forensic chemists may be able to identity small amounts of drugs, dyes, fibers, or hair. Forensic geologists can determine such things as where the suspect or victim walked by examining soil samples taken from their shoes or feet. They are capable of determining the various characteristics of soils within a sample, as well as the percentage distribution of each, and the presence of organic or inorganic substances which may ultimately narrow down its location of origin (Fisher, 2000).

IMPRESSION EVIDENCE

Impression evidence includes footprints, tire tracks, and toolmarks. Impression evidence from footprints can indicate the physical presence of the suspect or victim, direction of travel, or the scene of a struggle. Footprints can also reveal the type and brand of footwear. Several different sizes of shoes may use the same size of sole, so any indications of shoe size may be a general one. Specific imperfections or marks on the footwear may make the footwear identifiable to a specific shoe (Bodziak, 1990).

Impression evidence from tire tracks can indicate the physical presence of a vehicle, the direction of travel, and the brand and size of the tire. Many different tires can fit on a wheel, but knowing the size of the tire reduces the number of vehicles that must be considered. As with footwear, individual imperfections in the tire can make the tire more identifiable (McDonald, 1993). The three categories of toolmarks are compression (or indented) toolmarks, sliding toolmarks, and cutting toolmarks (James and Nordby, 2003). Toolmark evidence could possibly confirm the physical presence of a suspect, identify the point of entry, and reveal what type of tool was used. Toolmarks can often be matched to the individual tool or type of tool used in the crime.

SUMMARY

A successful homicide or assault investigation requires careful examination of the scene, witnesses, and evidence. Investigators must be able to identify victims, witnesses, and suspects. The successful investigator must be able to identify the suspect's motive, method, and opportunity for committing the crime. All evidence seized and interviews conducted must be done in a legal manner. The evidence must be analyzed and the investigator must be able to show how the evidence relates to the crime. These types of investigations require impeccable paperwork. An investigator's case file is the most important tool in making sure a suspect gets charged with the crime and more importantly convicted. Investigators must make sure the file is organized and accurate. It is not enough to know who committed the crime; an investigator must be able to prove it in court. Successful assault and homicide investigations require detailed, accurate, and timely police work to solve the case and get a conviction.

QUESTIONS FOR DISCUSSION

1. Explain the concept of homicide.
2. Why is identification of the deceased of primary importance to the death investigation?
3. Why is the physical location of a witness in relation to the suspect or victim important?
4. List the four common classifications of death used in the United States.
5. What is the very first thing a law enforcement officer should do upon arriving at a crime scene?
6. Define *motive*, *method*, and *opportunity*.
7. List and discuss the duties of the first responder at an assault or homicide scene.
8. Explain why wounding patterns are important to an investigation.
9. Explain *rigor mortis*.
10. What is an autoerotic death?

BIBLIOGRAPHY

Bennett, W. and Hess, K. (1991). *Criminal Investigation*, 3rd ed. St. Paul, MN: West Publishing.

Bevel, T. and Gardner, R. (1997). *Bloodstain Pattern Analysis: With an Introduction to Crime Scene Reconstruction.* Boca Raton, FL: CRC Press.

Black, H. (1968). *Black's Law Dictionary*, 4th ed. St. Paul, MN: West Publishing.

Bodziak, W. (1990). *Footwear Impression Evidence.* New York: Elsevier.

Castro, S., Galbreath, N., Pecko, J., and Zeliff, D. (1993). *Autopsy: A Forensic Manual for Criminal Investigators.* Wright Patterson AFB, OH: U.S. Air Force Institute of Technology.

Cataldie, L. (2006). *Coroner's Journal: Stalking Death in Louisiana.* New York: Putnam.

CDC. (2011a). *Mortality Data.* Atlanta, GA: Centers for Disease Control (http://www.cdc.gov/nchs/deaths.htm).

CDC. (2011b). *National Vital Statistics Report.* Atlanta, GA: Centers for Disease Control (http://www.cdc.gov/nchs/products/nvsr.htm).

CPSC. (2007). *U.S. Consumer Product Safety Commission Report.* Washington, D.C.: U.S. Consumer Product Safety Commission (http://www.cpsc.gov/).

Davenport, G.C., France, D.L., Griffin, T.J., Swanburg, J.G., Lindemann, J.W., Tranunell, V., Armbrust, C.T., Kondrateiff, B., Nelson, A., Castellano, K., and Hopkins, D. (1992). A Multidisciplinary Approach to the Detection of Clandestine Graves, *Journal of Forensic Sciences*, 37(6):1445–1458.

DiMaio, V. (1999). *Gunshot Wounds: Practical Aspects of Firearms, Ballistics, and Forensic Techniques*, 2nd ed. Boca Raton, FL: CRC Press.

FBI. (2011). *Uniform Crime Reports.* Washington, D.C.: Federal Bureau of Investigation (http://www.fbi.gov/about-us/cjis/ucr/ucr).

Fisher, B. (2000). *Techniques of Crime Scene Investigation*, 6th ed. Boca Raton, FL: CRC Press.

Geberth, V. (2006). *Practical Homicide Investigation: Tactics, Procedures, and Forensic Techniques*, 4th ed. Boca Raton, FL: CRC Press.

Gerber, S. and Schroeder, O. (1974). *Criminal Investigation and Interrogation.* Cincinnati, OH: W.H. Anderson Co.

Gilbert, J. (2004). *Criminal Investigation*, 6th ed. Upper Saddle River, NJ: Prentice Hall.

Girard, J. (2011). *Criminalistics: Forensic Science, Crime, and Terrorism*, 2nd ed. Sudbury, MA: Jones & Bartlett.

GSSI. (2011). *Ground Penetrating Radar for Forensic Investigations.* Salem, NH: Geophysical Survey Systems, Inc. (http://www.geophysical.com/forensics.htm).

Hallcox, J. and Welch, A. (2006). *Bodies We've Buried: Inside the National Forensic Academy, the World's Top CSI Training School.* New York: Berkley Publishing Group.

Harvey, W. (1976). *Dental Identification and Forensic Odontology.* London: Henry Kimpton Publishers.

Hazelwood, R., Dietz, P., and Burgess, A. (1983). *Autoerotic Fatalities.* Lexington, MA: Lexington Books.

Hogan v. State, 127 Tex. Cr. 182 (1934).

Humphry, D. (1991). *Final Exit: The Practicalities of Self-Deliverance and Assisted Suicide for the Dying.* New York: Dell.

Illinois v. Gates, 462 U.S. 213 (1983).

James, S. and Nordby, J. (2003). *Forensic Science: An Introduction to Scientific and Investigative Techniques.* Boca Raton, FL: CRC Press.

Knight, B. (1996). *Forensic Pathology*, 2nd ed. New York: Arnold.

Lyman, M. (1999). *Criminal Investigation: The Art and Science*, 2nd ed. Upper Saddle River, NJ: Prentice Hall.

McDonald, P. (1993). *Tire Imprint Evidence*. Boca Raton, FL: CRC Press.

Mincey v. Arizona, 437 U.S. 385 (1978).

Naler v. State, 25 Ala. App. 486 (1933).

Ogle, R. (2004). *Crime Scene Investigation and Reconstruction*. Upper Saddle River, NJ: Prentice Hall

Osterburg, J. and Ward, R. (2010). *Criminal Investigation: A Method for Reconstructing the Past*, 6th ed. New Providence, NJ: Lexis Nexis.

Pena, M. (1997). *Practical Criminal Investigation*, 4th ed. Incline Village, NV: Copperhouse Publishing.

People v. Connors, 35 N.Y. Supp. 472 (1895).

Pollanen, M. (1998). *Forensic Diatomology and Drowning*. New York: Elsevier.

Ramsland, K. (2008). *Beating the Devil's Game: A History of Forensic Science and Criminal Investigation*. New York: Berkley Publishing Group.

Rudin, N. and Inman, I. (2002). *An Introduction to Forensic DNA Analysis*, 2nd ed. Boca Raton, FL: CRC Press.

Saferstein, R. (2004). *Criminalistics: An Introduction to Forensic Science*, 8th ed. Upper Saddle River, NJ: Prentice Hall.

Sanders v. State, 113 Ga. 267 (1901).

State v. Peoples, 227 Kan. 127, 60S P.2d 135 (1980).

State v. Staw, 97 N.J.L. 349 (1922).

Walker, J. (1983). *Department of the Treasury: Crime Scene and Evidence Collection Handbook*. Washington, D.C.: Government Printing Office.

Warlow, T. (2005). *Firearms, the Law, and Forensic Ballistics*. Boca Raton, FL: CRC Press.

Weston, P. and Lushbaugh, C. (2003). *Criminal Investigation: Basic Perspectives*, 9th ed. Upper Saddle River, NJ: Prentice Hall.

CHAPTER 14

Sex Crimes

John Padgett

Capella University

CHAPTER OBJECTIVES

After reading this chapter, you should be able to do the following:

1. Describe the nature of sex crime investigations.
2. Explain the role of the first responder at the scene of a sex crime.
3. Comprehend the various methods used to search the scene of a sex crime.
4. List and describe the steps in a sex crime investigation.
5. Identify the various classifications of evidence related to sex crimes.

Chapter Outline

- Introduction to Sex Crimes
- Nature of Sex Crimes
- Date/Acquaintance Rape and Drugs
- Children as Victims of Sex Crimes
- Continuing Education for Investigators of Sex Crimes
- First Responder's Responsibility at the Crime Scene
- Crime Scene Investigations
- Crime Scene Search
- Nature of Sex Crime Evidence
- Photographic and Video Evidence
- Types of Evidence Encountered at Sex Crime Scenes
- Protocol of a Sex Crime Scene Search
- Glossary

INTRODUCTION TO SEX CRIMES

This chapter is designed to introduce the reader to sex crimes, sexually based offenders, and the proper scientific methods used to successfully investigate and prosecute these crimes and offenders. It is important to note that crime, criminology, and investigatory techniques and methods, as well as offenders, offender methodology, and crime evasion techniques are constantly evolving. As a scholar–practitioner, it is the reader's duty and responsibility to use the knowledge and experience gained through education, training, and field experience to move the field of criminal investigations forward with new techniques, methods, and technologies. We commit ourselves to this endeavor not for ourselves but for the innocent who cannot protect themselves from those who would victimize them.

NATURE OF SEX CRIMES

Sex crimes have long held a position among the most prominent, difficult, and controversial of criminal activities to investigate and bring to successful prosecution. Although many reasons exist for these challenges no other criminal activity has such a profound impact upon victims, families, our communities, and our country. Sexual-based offenses are not about sex; they are about power and control over the victim. The offender's desires to control and dominate the victim far exceed the actual sexual act committed. Each element of a sexually based crime is a vital component of the offender's sexual fantasy and is required in order for the fantasy to be realized. Unfortunately, as sexual offenders evolve so do their fantasies and their need for control and domination over every element of their victim's life or death. This evolution often is illustrated in unimaginable, unspeakable emotional, physical, and psychological sadistic torture of the victim and can lead to sexual homicide.

In the not too recent past, rape was deemed to be solely a male-on-female criminal offense. Today, rape also includes male-on-male and female-on-female assaults, and a husband can be charged with rape against his wife if the act is committed against her will or with the threat of or actual use of force or violence. Although most states still define rape as forced penetration of the vagina by a penis, rape laws and their wording are changing. In fact, the terms "rape" and "sodomy" have been replaced in some state penal codes with terms detailing various degrees of sexual assault or criminal sexual conduct depending on the offense and the type of force used in commission of the criminal act. Historically, criminal codes have not recognized or included males as potential victims of rape; however, as reported assaults of male victims increase, especially gang attacks against male victims, some states have begun the process of redefining their criminal codes to remove gender-specific identification in the role of victim and offender. A recent study by the National Center for Victims of Crime (NCVC) provided the following data on male victims of rape (NCVC, 2008):

- About 3% of American men—a total of 2.78 million men—have experienced a rape at some point in their lifetime.
- In 2003, 1 in every 10 rape victims was male. Although there are no reliable annual surveys of sexual assaults on children, the Justice Department has estimated that 1 of every 6 victims is under age 12.

- Approximately 71% of male victims were first raped before their 18th birthday; 17% were 18 to 24 years old, and 12% were 25 or older.
- Males are the least likely to report a sexual assault, although it is estimated that they make up 10% of all victims.
- An estimated 22% of male inmates have been raped at least once during their incarceration, roughly 420,000 prisoners each year.

This NCVC report also concluded that males are more likely to be the victims of non-homosexual gang rape than females. In these incidents, the victim is more likely to have multiple sexual acts forced upon him, and offenders are more likely to display or use weapons against him. Male victims are also more likely to experience more severe physical injuries than female gang rape victims.

The Federal Bureau of Investigation (FBI) reported that the number of reported forcible rapes dropped from 94,504 in 1989 to 89,000 in 2008 (FBI, 2009a). (Note that the figure of 89,000 was later adjusted to 90,479.) This downward trend continued, with 88,097 forcible rapes being reported to law enforcement in 2009 (FBI, 2010).

WHY DOES RAPE GO UNREPORTED?

The Rape, Abuse, and Incest National Network (RAINN, 2011) states that of all rapes nationwide, reported and unreported, only 6% of all offenders are found guilty and sentenced to prison. This equates to 15 out of every 16 sex offenders walking free. If an offender is found guilty, there is a 69% chance that he will not serve time for the crime. Reasons that factor into a lack of reporting include:

- Embarrassment
- Fear of family members' reactions
- Fear of retaliation
- Lack of faith in law enforcement and the justice system
- Revictimization
- Self-blame
- Social stigma and ostracism
- Threats and intimidation
- Trauma associated with the trial process

Sexual assault has devastating life-long consequences for survivors, families, and communities. Recognizing and understanding the chronic, long-term impacts of sexual trauma will enhance sex crime investigators' skills, allowing them to hear and see red flags that others may discount or overlook. Adult females with sexual trauma histories have been shown to have poor health and physical functioning, including higher rates of documented chronic physical illnesses, such as migraine headaches, pelvic disorders, arthritis, fibromyalgia, asthma, and gastrointestinal disorders, which cannot be attributed to psychosomatic origins or depressed mood (Golding, 1999). Research is needed to determine if the same impact is found among males with a history of sexual assault. Regardless of their gender, victims may develop sexually transmitted diseases as a result of the sexual assault and may unknowingly pass these on to their family members. Long-term emotional and psychological consequences of trauma may exacerbate survivors' physical impairments and illnesses.

Each year, an estimated 3000 sexual assaults result in conception and pregnancy (RAINN, 2011). One victim becomes two, as both the victim and unborn child face the long-term consequences of sexual assault. The victim must cope with the physical changes of being pregnant, as well as the emotional trauma of having part of the perpetrator growing inside her. She must deal with the fear of the unknown, including the impact of the perpetrator's genetic makeup on the development of the child. She must struggle with the reality of her situation, her religious and moral upbringing, and the views of her family and friends regarding such issues as pregnancy resulting from sexual assault, pregnancy out of wedlock, use of the morning-after pill, abortion, and adoption as she copes with the assault and its aftermath. She and others may question her ability to love and care for her attacker's offspring, and she fears that her attacker will resurface, claiming parental rights and subjecting her and the child to a lifetime of abuse. She may be hesitant to report the assault due to potential repercussions for her child.

The long-term emotional and psychological consequences for victims of sexual assault focus on recurring memories of the attack, issues of self-blame and responsibility, issues surrounding self-identity and self-concept, continued fears, depression, grief, anger, self-harm, escape and addictive behaviors, trust and relationship issues, role boundary and family script confusions, maladaptive social skills, power and control issues, and sexual intimacy issues. The victim may experience sleep disruptions and even insomnia due to recurring nightmares and night terrors related to the assault. Flashbacks of the assault and the surfacing of suppressed memories may occur during sexual intimacy or as a result of other triggers. The victim may experience body memories related to her attack during intimacy or as the result of other triggers. Body memories are frightening for the victim and those unaware of what is taking place. Her body will replay the physiological responses from the attack. She may tremble or shake violently, become short of breath, or even lose consciousness. She may cry uncontrollably, have difficulty hearing or seeing, smell or taste her attacker, and even vomit as she relives the attack in intense reality. Body memories are commonly associated with posttraumatic stress disorder and require professional attention.

The victim often struggles with self-blame and personal responsibility for a variety of reasons, including messages provided by the perpetrator, unsupportive family members, or disbelieving family members. Victims may view themselves as bad, unworthy, damaged, or dirty; they may feel culpable due to any biological responses of sexual arousal and pleasure during the attacks or seeking out any form of attention from the abuser to validate being loved. Victims' perceptions of self-identity and self-concept are also impacted as they internalize these messages and self-judgments. Victims may define themselves as objects of victimization rather than recognizing the strength and courage required to overcome such trauma.

Most victims have been conditioned by their attackers using fear and intimidation, which keep many victims silent and in many cases allows long-term abuse to continue for years. The fear does not end after the last physical attack, but continues for extended periods of time. Sometimes victims believe they have conquered their fears, only to later feel its grips on their lives once again. Many victims fear further sexual assaults and retaliation by the offender or the offender's family members or friends. Victims may fear undiscovered physical harm, such as infertility. Others fear that they will become perpetrators themselves and continue patterns of abuse or that their own children or other family members will be victimized, as well. Left untreated, fears stemming from sexual assault can cause paranoia or panic attacks that paralyze victims. Depression, grief, and anger result from the victim's loss of the person they were before the attack and might have become had the attack not taken place. The victim mourns for the innocence, trust, and security they had before the attack and the loss of power and personal control. Changes in relationships and unexpected lack of support from friends and family members add to the sense of loss experienced by the victim and fuel their anger. Healthy expressions of grief and anger are essential for healing; otherwise, the victim may act out these emotions in self-destructive ways, including numbing and escape through substance abuse, self-mutilation, or eating disorders, or they may even commit suicide to end the pain.

Developing and maintaining intimate relationships can be problematic for survivors of sexual trauma due to difficulties trusting their own emotions, perceptions, and assessments of other people and the settings in which they find themselves, not to mention difficulties trusting others. Role confusion exacerbates this problem, due to a lack of physical and intimate boundaries. Victims do not trust themselves to establish healthy reasonable boundaries between themselves and others due to the abnormal examples they have experienced. Judging appropriateness of parental touch may be difficult due to abuse by a caretaker. Unhealthy patterns of communication and interaction have been learned and interfere with the formation of functional relationships. Many victims find that they are uncomfortable in social settings due to the development of maladaptive or nonexistent social skills, particularly if the perpetrator kept the victim isolated from peers physically and emotionally. Society may further this isolation due to insensitivity, ignorance, and blaming of the victim. The loss of power and control can also interfere with appropriate social skill development. The victim may need to exert extreme power and rigidity to remain in control and prevent ever being victimized again. At the other end of the pendulum, the victim may relinquish all power and control, becoming passive and weak in social exchanges.

Sexual intimacy is an area of obvious anxiety for victims of sexual assault. Developing and maintaining a healthy sexual identity and intimate relationship with a mate can be a lifelong struggle for victims of sexual trauma. Victims may try to hide their sexuality under layers of baggy clothing. They may maintain extremes in body weight or practice poor personal hygiene in order to appear unattractive to potential attackers. Victims must regain ownership of their own body and develop a healthy respect for their own sexuality. Confusion related to interruptions in childhood sexual development and the differences between normal sexual impulses and urges and dysfunctional sexuality must be addressed.

Victims must learn to associate sexual intimacy and touch with pleasure rather than pain and discomfort. Sexual intimacy and relationships may be physically and emotionally threatening, uncomfortable, or even painful for the victim. Victims may emotionally or physically withdraw during intimacy, going through the motions as if not really present. Victims may even dissociate, or detach themselves from their body, during physical closeness. They may or may not be aware of this taking place and may be frightened when they realize what has happened, fearing that they are going crazy or are permanently damaged in some way. Dissociation is a common form of self-protection for many victims of sexual trauma. It is not a sign of insanity or damage, but instead a means of self-preservation that is no longer needed and now requires treatment to control and extinguish. Extreme cases of dissociation are referred to as dissociative identity disorder or multiple identity disorder.

To heal and develop a healthy intimate relationship, victims must give themselves permission to say "no" to sexual advances and to remain in conscious control during intimate relations. This requires patience from the intimate partner and open communication. Intimate partners must understand that these victims are not rejecting them, but are instead learning to identify, accept, and communicate their own sexual needs. This is a gradual process, and victims will need to feel safe, unpressured, and in control during intimate relations. They may intentionally sabotage intimate relationships due to feelings of unworthiness, discomfort, pain, or confusion related to sex. Victims may be unable to verbalize their fears and anxieties during the coupling. They may need to step away and examine their own responses before sharing these with their partner. Relinquishing control, letting go, and achieving climax may be especially difficult, uncomfortable, and even emotionally painful for the victim. Intimate satisfaction, especially for victims of sexual assault, is not dependent on achieving climax with every coupling, but instead achieving emotional closeness and a loving bond.

Ironically, many victims are unable to discern between love and the act of sex and may be unable to express genuine nurturing or concern for her intimate partner. The young victim of sexual abuse may be perceived as being highly promiscuous and sexualizing all relationships and interactions, even nonsexual exchanges. Victims may repeatedly misinterpret interactions with others (e.g., religious leaders, bosses, friends' mates, relatives), frequently reporting that they are hitting on them. They may feel that the only way to know that they are loved and cared for is through sex.

Adults with a history of sexual trauma may give their children erroneous or conflicting messages regarding relationships and intimacy. A young girl may be encouraged to openly discuss sexuality with her father only to be accused of being promiscuous when holding her boyfriend's hand. Mothers may tell their daughters that all men are evil and warn them from an early age to fear the pain of sexual intercourse. Pubescent boys may be shunned when their victimized mothers finds evidence of masturbation. Young children may be exposed to sexual content as a means to teach them about sex at an early age. When parents send children such messages regarding sexuality, a red flag is raised, suggesting a prior or ongoing history of sexual abuse of the parent and the potential for harm to the children.

DATE/ACQUAINTANCE RAPE AND DRUGS

Date/acquaintance rape is nothing new to investigators of sexual-based crimes, but the nature of the crime is changing. The recreational and criminal use of club drugs such as Ecstasy, gamma-hydroxybutyric acid (GHB), ketamine, and flunitrazepam (Rohypnol®) can have debilitating effects on those who ingest them (e.g., impaired judgment, inability to make rational decisions or give consent, memory loss, amnesia, unconsciousness, loss of coordination). As a result, law enforcement finds itself investigating more and more cases of rape where the victim has little or no memory of the incident, making successful prosecution extremely difficult. In many cases, victims may not know or understand what has happened to them, or they do not recognize the physical signs until days after the assault. When encountering a victim who claims to have been drugged or appears to have been drugged or to be under the influence, it is vital to take immediate action to seek medical testing.

The fact that a victim appears to be under the influence of drugs or alcohol must not be allowed to impact the decision to fully investigate the crime; many times investigators will fail to carefully and completely investigate an allegation of sexual assault if the victim appears to have used or is under the influence. This is a critical error on the part of the investigator and may result in the loss of critical evidence and cause irreversible damage to a future criminal prosecution of the offender. As a result of the use of the above listed drugs being used against unwitting victims, law enforcement agencies must amend their standard operating procedures (SOPs) to ensure that any sexual assault reported within the first 72 hours of the alleged victimization is provided a full and complete criminal investigation and medical examination to facilitate proper collection, preservation, and submission of evidence for investigative purposes.

CHILDREN AS VICTIMS OF SEX CRIMES

Few criminal investigations are as emotionally taxing and haunting as an investigation into the victimization of a child. This emotionality intensifies when the victimization involves an attack of a sexual nature. According to the Office of Juvenile Justice and Delinquency Prevention (Finkelhor et al., 2009), juveniles make up more than 25.8% of all sex offenders; adults, 74.2%. Of offenders committing the act of sexual violence against juvenile victims, juveniles account for 35.6%; adults, 64.4%. Among juvenile offenders, more than 59% of their victims are below the age of 12. Nine percent of these youthful offenders are 0 to 5 years of age, 16% are 6 to 12 years of age, 38% are 12 to 14 years of age, and 46% are between 15 and 17 years of age. Of these offenders, 93% are male. This report also indicated that juveniles are 24% more likely to commit sexual offenses in groups as opposed to 14% of adult offenders. Clinicians commonly refer to these juvenile offenders as "children with sexual behavior problems," but adult offenders are typically deemed to be referred to as "pedophiles."

Sexual offenses against children are often difficult to prove because, as with their adult counterparts, delays in reporting often result in the only evidence being the child's allegation and testimony. It is therefore imperative that initial interviews with child victims be conducted by a trained and experienced forensic interviewer who can elicit as accurate, informative, and detailed information as possible regarding the assault. It is advised that the child protective services investigator conduct a joint investigation with the law enforcement entity having jurisdiction over the case. The child protective services investigator will typically have training and experience working with traumatized children. Some may be trained forensic child interviewers. Inexperienced investigators and interviewers without access to skilled forensic child interviewers must be cautious not to lead or direct victims in their statements; they must also be cautious not to imply or suggest that victims "pretend," "make believe," or "play a game" as it relates to the content and context of their questions and the child's subsequent responses. Forensic child interviewers are trained to establish the child's understanding of time, place, relationship, anatomy, and sexual acts which differs extensively from adult views depending on the child's developmental stage. This can lead to defense assertions that the child's testimony was dramatized, fictional, or simply not based in reality.

Child victims of sexual crimes often experience the same fears, emotional challenges, and memory repressions as their adult counterparts, with the added component that they may feel that their very existence is based on the offender. Children often have a loyalty or love for their abusers that has been nurtured from their dependencies on their abusive caretakers.

CONTINUING EDUCATION FOR INVESTIGATORS OF SEX CRIMES

The field of sex crime investigation is a specialized one that requires extensive education and training beyond that received at the basic academy level or during in-service training sessions. Just as the FBI has recognized the individuality of sex crimes as evidenced by their categorization in their Uniform Crime Report (UCR), so, too, must state and local law enforcement agencies that investigate and prosecute these crimes. The requisite training of a sex crimes investigator should include the following courses:

- Advanced Criminal Investigations
- Advanced Crime Scene Processing
- Advance Crime Scene Photography and Videography
- Advanced Interview and Interrogation Strategies and Techniques
- Cultural, Racial, and Sexual Sensitivity Training
- Forensic Interviewing of Children and Adolescents
- Medical/Legal Terminology
- Psychology of the Sexual Offender
- Professional Ethics
- Victimology

It is imperative that this training and education be continuous in order to stay abreast of current professional developments, practices, and technologies in the field.

FIRST RESPONDER'S RESPONSIBILITY AT THE CRIME SCENE

Sexual assault has long been recognized as one of the most traumatic forms of criminal victimization in our society, as evidenced earlier in this chapter. The mental, emotional, and physical traumas, anguish, and humiliation felt by these victims can last a lifetime and affect every aspect of their future lives. The actions taken by the first responder to the scene of a sex crime will have profound effects on the final outcome of the investigation and prosecution of the case. First responders need to understand and acknowledge that the victim has already taken a monumental step in their healing process simply by exhibiting the courage to report their attack to law enforcement. Your role as first responder in a sex crime can be more important than in any other crime you investigate because the victim is most often the only witness and has reached out to you for protection, understanding, empathy, and care. Your initial response, professionalism, demeanor, and treatment of victims can determine their ability to establish the crucial components of trust and cooperation that will be vital in bringing their cases to a successful conclusion. This is true not only of adult victims but also child victims, especially considering that their offenders may have told them that the police would not believe them or would take them or their family members away if they tell anyone what happened to them.

A presentation by the Lincoln Police Department Forensic Identification Laboratory (1998) used the acronym RESPOND to describe the initial role of the first responder—R, respond; E, evaluate; S, secure; P, protect; O, observe; N, notify; D, document.

RESPOND

Upon your initial receipt of the call from the dispatcher, you should focus on officer safety, not only as it pertains to your response to the scene but also what you might be faced with once you arrive on the scene and what equipment may be necessary for you to effectively carry out your mission. You should begin focusing your professional investigative observation skills while en route, taking mental and written notes about all details you feel might be pertinent to the case. Remember to employ due regard and caution when responding to your call for assistance; if you do not make it to the scene, you help no one.

EVALUATE

Upon arrival, whether to an assault in progress or an assault completed, you should begin your evaluation of everyone and everything you come into contact with, including:

- *Victim, offender, and witnesses*—Are they in need of immediate emergency medical assistance? Do they have any visible injuries? What affect are they displaying? What is the condition of their clothing? Are they able to effectively and coherently respond to questions? Do they appear visibly under the influence? If so, how? Do you smell anything that might indicate the presence or use of alcoholic beverages or drugs? If so, what? Is the individual able to identify the offender/victim? If so, what details were they able to provide (e.g., name, physical description, clothing description, race, scars, marks, tattoos, foreign accent, unusual odor)?

- *Scene safety*—Look for anything obvious at the scene that may put you or anyone else in immediate physical danger and must be addressed before you proceed, such as live uncovered electrical wires, natural or propane gas leaks, fire accelerant, biological or chemical hazards, weapons, vicious animals, or structural damage. Do you require protective clothing, eyewear, gloves, etc.?
- *Scene assistance*—After your initial survey of the scene, determine whether you need additional emergency back-up assistance; additional non-emergency personnel support; a supervisor, investigator, or crime scene unit to respond, etc.
- *On-scene notations*—Immediately begin written documentation of everything you observe and hear, whether it be from the victim, witnesses, or offender. What were their physical, mental, and emotional states while in your presence? Did they change? Did they make any statements referring to accusations, admissions of guilt, admissions of negligence, admissions of intent, admissions of pre- or post-incident knowledge, etc.?
- *Information gathering*—Conduct cursory information-gathering interviews with possible witnesses, including neighbors, family members, bystanders, and other non-law enforcement emergency personnel who may have arrived at the scene before you.
- *Visible evidence*—Take written notes about any possible evidence that you observe that the scene and its location, being careful not to disturb the evidence. If evidence is disturbed for any reason, note why it was disturbed and by whom and where it is now. Do not attempt to replace or reposition an evidentiary item in the crime scene once it has been disturbed or moved. If dangerous or fragile evidence must be collected due to safety concerns or exigent circumstances, collect it in appropriate evidence collection containers; mark, bag, and tag all evidence collected; and log it into the evidence log.

SECURE

After initial evaluation of the scene and tending to any emergency needs, crime scene security must be implemented by establishing marked (crime scene tape or rope) perimeters (both outer and inner) accessible to authorized personnel only and manned by officers assigned to protect against unwarranted entry. The outer perimeter establishes a bright line not to be crossed by unauthorized or non-emergency personnel. The inner perimeter provides access to those directly involved in the ongoing investigation of the incident. A crime scene attendance log must be initiated to establish scene control. This log should provide the name of every person who has entered the crime scene since your arrival, beginning with you; it should include the time of their entry to the scene, time of their exit, and purpose for their being at the scene. Unauthorized personnel, including family members, witnesses, nonessential emergency personnel, officers, or supervisors, should not be allowed to enter the scene. All unassigned persons entering the inner perimeter must be logged in and escorted through the scene.

PROTECT

Now that you have taken measures to secure your scene, you must protect it from being destroyed or disturbed by nature (e.g., inhospitable weather) or by human, animal, or mechanical traffic. Locard's theory of transference must be remembered and protected against. Smoking, eating, or drinking should be strictly prohibited within the crime scene perimeter.

OBSERVE

Observation truly begins during your initial evaluation stage and continues with notations of the time you were originally dispatched and your time of arrival, basic narrative of the incident, description of the scene upon arrival, basic sketch of the scene, condition of the scene if indoors (e.g., points of forced entry, doors or windows left unsecure, internal temperature, lights on or off, condition of the interior), and condition of the scene if outdoors, including weather conditions, temperature, and possible tracks, markings, or other evidence. Take photographs or video of crowds gathered at the crime scene, etc.

NOTIFY

Once at the scene, it now falls to you to make necessary requests of support personnel, including supervisors, coroner or medical examiner, investigators, emergency medical personnel, emergency utilities personnel (gas, water, electric), and possibly relatives. Depending on your local sexual assault and child abuse protocols, you may also be responsible for notifying these team stakeholders.

DOCUMENT

From the initial receipt of the call you should have begun your documentation, which should now include the following: basic narrative with a description of the scene, crime scene attendance log, basic crime scene sketch, identification of victim, offender, witnesses, visible evidence sheet, evidence log, etc.

First responders must also be cognizant of other dangers that may arise in the moments immediately following an incident. Such dangers could arise when suspects or offenders reappear at the scene prior to additional assistance arriving. If the incident location is near a roadway where it can be observed by passing motorists, the first responder must be aware of interested observers (a.k.a., rubberneckers) who slow traffic because they are curious about what is happening at your scene and could cause a traffic accident. Many first responders have been struck and killed by preoccupied passersby while performing

SEXUAL ASSAULT SCENARIO

"I met him tonight at the bar and we had a few drinks. He asked if he could give me a ride home, I said yes. While we were driving he cut through the park. He drove to a wooded area of the park near the lake, stopped, and turned off the car. We talked for a little while and started to kiss. After a few minutes he touched my breasts and tried to unbutton my jeans. I told him to stop several times, but he started grabbing me. I opened the car door and got out. He got out of the car, told me that he was sorry, and said if I got back in the car he would drive me straight home. As I turned to walk back toward the car he grabbed me and threw me to the ground. I screamed at him to stop, but he began punching me in the face with his fist. He covered my mouth with his hand, ripped open my blouse, pulled my bra off of my breasts, and then reached down and unbuttoned my jeans. I began screaming and begging for him to stop, but he just laughed and punched me on the side of my head. I tried to curl up into a ball so he couldn't pull my jeans off or punch me, but he stood up, grabbed me by my feet, pulled my shoes off, grabbed the bottom hems on both legs of my jeans, and pulled at them until he got them off. I kept screaming for him to stop, but he jumped back on top of me and tore my underwear off. I don't know when he pulled his pants down but he forced my legs apart and forced himself inside of me. I was screaming and crying, so he put his hand over my mouth. I bit his hand as hard as I could. He pulled his hand away and screamed "Bitch!" He punched me in the face and nose and began raping me harder. When he finished he stood up, grabbed my underwear, and wrapped them around his hand where I bit him. He was bleeding. He told me to get dressed and threw my pants and shoes at me. I got dressed and he pulled me up from the ground and pushed me back into his car. He got in and drove to the park exit where the public restrooms are. He stopped, turned off the car, and told me to get out. I opened the car door and started to get out but he came around and grabbed me by my hair and walked me into the restroom, where he told me to strip and clean myself up. When I took my clothes off he picked them up, stuffed them into an orange trash bag that was in the restroom trash can, and ran from the restroom. When I heard his car start, I looked out of the restroom door and saw him beginning to drive off. When he got down the road at the curve, I saw him stop the car, get out, run toward the guardrail, and throw something over. Then he got back into his car and drove off. After awhile, the park attendant showed up and called the ambulance that brought me here."

You Are the Investigator

1. How many potential crime scenes can you identify in this scenario? Identify each and the type of crime scene it is.
2. What kinds of evidence might you find on or in the offender's possession once he has been located?
3. Might you need the services of any special forensic expert? If so, what type?

their duties at the incident location. Other threats may result from the incident you are responding to being gang related; while you are attempting to sort things out, you could discover yourself in the midst of a retaliatory drive-by shooting. First responders must be able to control their emotions, handle sudden rushes of adrenaline, work calmly and proficiently through extreme stress, and multitask, all while fulfilling their RESPOND responsibilities.

CRIME SCENE INVESTIGATIONS

When investigating a sex crime, think like the offender. Ask yourself questions like these:

- When and what route would I take and how would I identify, wait for, and approach a victim?
- Where, how, and following what path would I take the victim to make sure we were not interrupted?
- How would I deal with potential physical evidence?
- When, where, and in what state would I leave the victim, and how would I prevent her from reporting the crime and identifying me?
- When, how, and following what path would I take to make sure I got away without being noticed or identified?
- What would I do with damaged or soiled clothing, and how would I secure a change of clothing?
- What would I do about any injuries that I might have, and how could I explain these?
- Where would I go following the attack to establish an alibi, and how and when would I get there?
- Who would I likely encounter after leaving the scene?

Physical evidence must be properly identified, collected, processed, and analyzed to be accepted in court. All officers, not just crime scene technicians, should be able to properly identify, collect, and process basic crime scene evidence. To make sure that proper analysis is conducted, all officers must be aware of the capabilities of the crime laboratory serving their agency.

In cases of sexual assault, the investigator is responsible for evidence contained at the physical location where the crime took place and the evidence present on the bodies and clothing of the victim and offender. Most sexual assaults involve a relationship between the victim and attacker, which the attacker will use as a basis to claim that the attack was consensual. In these cases, it is imperative that the investigator document any evidence that supports the victim's statement to the contrary. For this reason, any signs of a struggle at the physical location should be photographed, videotaped, and documented. Signs of a struggle include broken or overturned furniture, broken dishes or glasses, items scattered around the room (especially if other areas in the home are neat and organized), and items from adjacent areas appearing to be thrown into the scene. Signs of a struggle evident on the victim's body, typically, injuries or torn or bloodied clothing, and on the attacker's body or clothing should be photographed and documented. Physical signs of the struggle will typically be photographed by medical personnel at the hospital or jail. Clothing will be collected and processed as evidence.

CRIME SCENE SEARCH

What is a crime scene? A crime scene is any location that is being investigated by law enforcement as a result of a criminal act and comprises that area where evidence may be located. The primary crime scene is where the initial crime or primary event takes place and where evidence of the criminal act may be located. If the offender or victim leaves the primary scene and travels to another location, that location would be referred to as the secondary crime scene. Secondary crime scenes are related to the primary crime scene by way of evidence from the initial crime but are not the original location of the primary event. Many times while investigating sex crimes you will discover that the primary incident occurred in one location and the offender then dropped off the victim at a secondary location, drove to another location where he threw some of the victim's personal items away, and drove home, where he parked his vehicle in the garage and then changed the clothes he was wearing at the time of the assault. The locations following the secondary crime scene are known as tertiary crime scenes. Tertiary crime scenes are other (sometimes multiple) locations that have become affixed to the primary event as a result of multiple moves on the part of the offender or victim where evidence of the primary event may be located.

How are primary, secondary, and tertiary crime scenes handled? All crime scenes are handled as though they are a primary crime scene. All evidentiary, legal, and scientific concepts and procedures that directly impact the value or usefulness of evidence in a court of law are applied equally to each of these scenes.

No two crime scenes are the same whether large or small; however, the procedures for processing crime scenes is standardized and must be followed. Investigators or crime scene investigators, through education, training, and experience, will develop individually strategic methods for applying the procedures that best fit the crime scene location and their needs at the crime scene. In doing so, these professionals exercise great caution to ensure that all evidence is located and identified without being altered or destroyed. The security and integrity of the scene are never to be compromised to make the procedures for processing the crime scene easier for investigators.

Once at the crime scene, investigators must determine the best method for processing the crime scene and what search pattern is best suited to assist them in accomplishing their goal. Many search patterns are used in the law enforcement profession, including grid searches, spiral searches, strip searches, wheel searches, and zone searches. Following standardized procedures for processing crime scenes fulfills the main goal of investigators, which is to successfully complete a thorough crime scene investigation with all evidence collected, documented, identified, marked, and submitted for processing so they will be able to accurately reconstruct the crime scene at a later date.

NATURE OF SEX CRIME EVIDENCE

Historically, investigating sexual assault cases has provided law enforcement with challenges inherently unique to sexual crimes. These crimes are often not immediately reported following their occurrence, which results in delays in evidence location and collection, initial and tertiary crime scene identification, witness location, and offender location. Each of these issues individually can raise some perplexing issues for investigators, but as a whole they have the ability to jeopardize the successful prosecution of the case and the offender.

Other pertinent challenges involve first responders. Often, the initial response to a report of sexual assault is not to the location where the offense took place. The first responder may be dispatched to the home of a relative or friend where the sexual assault was reported. As a result of their training, the first responder immediately seeks medical attention for the victim and calls for an investigator, leaving them with the responsibility of asking the victim basic fundamental questions. This scene is played out in much the same fashion when first responders are dispatched to a hospital, urgent-care, or emergency clinic where the victim is receiving medical care for an alleged sexual assault. In this case, the first responder calls for an investigator and ceases all questioning of the victim regarding the offense. This occurs most often as the result of training where they are told that due to the nature of the offense and the delicate state of the victim they are to gather only pertinent information and leave all other questioning for the investigator. It would, however, seem elementary to collect basic pertinent information from the victim:

- At what time did the incident occur?
- Where did the initial incident occur? (Inquire as to whether there were tertiary incident locations.)
- Did you know the offender?
- Did anyone see or hear what happened? Did you see or hear anyone during or immediately following the assault?
- Can you provide a description of the offender, the offender's vehicle, etc?
- Have you taken a bath, shower, or douched since the offense?
- Are you pregnant or could you have been pregnant prior to your assault?
- Are these the same clothes you were wearing at the time of the sexual assault? If not, where are they?

These basic questions can provide the investigator with crucial information that may result in the preservation of evidence, crime scenes, and even the accidental abortion of an already developing fetus unrelated to the assault.

Keep in mind that sexual assault victims and their offenders are also crime scenes and must be properly processed. The processing of victims begins at the hospital with administration of a Sexual Assault Evidence Kit (SAEK), more popularly known as a "rape kit." The collection of evidence via these kits is an extremely invasive procedure, even though it is performed by medical professionals. Investigators must be cognizant of the emotional trauma the victim has sustained prior to collecting rape evidence. The victim has already been violated by the offender and is now suffering the discomfort, humiliation, and indignation associated with the evidence collection procedure. Following collection, the evidence is properly bagged, tagged, and sealed, and a chain-of-custody transfer is made to forward the evidence to the crime lab for processing.

Once the victim has been identified and a search warrant obtained, the suspect will be processed at the hospital with a medically collected Suspect Evidence Collection Kit and possibly a Buccal Swab Kit for DNA comparison. Again, this is an invasive procedure that may result in some discomfort for the offender. Following collection, the evidence is properly bagged, tagged, and sealed, and the chain-of-custody transfer is made to forward the evidence to the crime lab for processing.

The types of physical evidence found at the scene of a sex crime are not that dissimilar to what you might find at any other crime scene, but it is associative evidence that connects the offender to the victim to the crime scene. Such associative evidence might include (Savino and Turvey, 2005):

- A used condom containing the offender's seminal fluid on the interior and the vaginal cells of the victim on the exterior
- The offender's seminal fluid in the victim's rectum
- Pubic hair of the victim intertwined in the pubic hairs of the offender
- Paint residue from the offender's workplace on the victim's clothing
- The offender's fingerprints on a glass in the sink of the victim's home
- The offender's saliva on a cigarette butt put out on the victim's abdomen

According to a study by the Georgia Supreme Court Commission on Equality (2003), in order to detect GHB in the blood, tests must be conducted within 2 to 6 hours using a urine sample; because of its slow metabolism rate, Rohypnol can be detected in the urine for up to 72 hours. Urine testing should still be performed for up to 4 days and blood tests up to 24 hours following assaults because trace amounts of these date rape drugs may still be detected (LeBeau et al., 1999). This problem again emphasizes the vital role played by first responders as it relates to response and recovery of evidence in the successful prosecution of sexual assaults, as a significant amount of time might have already passed by the time the victim realizes that an assault has taken place and reports the incident to law enforcement.

PHOTOGRAPHIC AND VIDEO EVIDENCE

Documenting evidence at crime scenes is a core component of an investigator's job. Unlike pleasure photography or videography, investigators cannot just snap photographs or video indiscriminately. Investigators must take their time, choose the best angle and the best lens, decide whether to use existing light or employ external light sources, or whether macro-photography, 1-to-1 photography, or standard photography is required. Each shot is taken with the goal of capturing every detail of the object being photographed; simply walking around snapping pictures is not an option. Investigators are required to keep a detailed log of each photograph and each video shot. This log notes various aspects of each photograph taken, such as a description of the photograph, whether polarization filters were used, whether a tripod or stand was used, which lens was used, whether a flash was used, the direction the photographer was facing at the time of the photograph, the *f*/stop and shutter speed used, and the distance to the object photographed. This photographic evidence log becomes a component of the chain of custody and is turned over to the crime lab with the investigator's photographs or video.

The use of photography in sex crime investigations is not limited to documenting the crime scene or visible injuries. Normal photography uses visible light to illuminate the subject and capture the subject on the film. Using visible light to photograph facial bruising around a victim's eye will produce an image resembling what could be viewed with the normal eye; however, employing the use of ultraviolet photography with specialized filtering will allow the camera to capture the full extent of the bruising, even that not visible to the normal eye or captured by the use of visible light photography. If the victim's injuries have completely healed and are no longer visible, reflected ultraviolet light photography has the ability to penetrate the skin and reveal bruising, scarring, impact marks, and bite marks not visible for up to 6 months or longer afterward (Robinson, 2010; Weiss, 2008).

TYPES OF EVIDENCE ENCOUNTERED AT SEX CRIME SCENES

Because sex crimes can occur virtually anywhere—indoors or outdoors, on land or in the water or in the air—crime scenes, too, can be anywhere—residence, storage shed, tent, workplace, school, restaurant, movie theater, library, park, alley, pool, junkyard, beach, restroom, classroom, crack house, church, or even in a theater of war during active military duty. They can occur in conveyances such as automobiles, trains, aircraft, watercraft, or military vehicles. Sex crimes can be committed by anyone, male or female. They can be from any walk of life, a member of any socioeconomic level. The crimes are committed by husbands, wives, brothers, sisters, mothers, fathers, uncles, aunts, grandmothers, grandfathers, babysitters, coaches, employers, coworkers, religious leaders, public service workers, school teachers, lawmakers. When investigating sex crimes, an investigator will quickly discover that there is no limit to the locations, types of offenders, or sources of evidence encountered.

Common evidence indicative of sex crimes includes blood, seminal fluid, saliva, vaginal secretions, urine, fecal matter, hair, condoms, vomit, bruising, bite marks, syringes, needles, razor blades, alcohol, and drugs. Care, caution, and preventative protection must be used whenever dealing with bodily fluids and bloodborne pathogens, as these may be infected with acquired immunodeficiency syndrome (AIDS); hepatitis types A, B, or C; human immunodeficiency virus (HIV); or tuberculosis. Be aware that there are no known cures for AIDS, HIV, or hepatitis C, and treatments for hepatitis A and B and tuberculosis are long term, lasting up to a year and a half. When encountering blood or bodily fluids, always consider it to be infected and employ all necessary precautions, as infectious organisms can live for several days outside of the body. It is also important for those involved in crime scene searches to wear disposable protective gloves, eye protection, shoe protectors, and hazmat coveralls to protect themselves from sharp objects penetrating the skin and to prevent blood and bloodborne pathogens from being transferred to their shoes or clothing. There have been many instances of emergency responders becoming infected away from the crime scene when they took off their shoes and had their hand penetrated by an infected needle, razor, or piece of glass trapped in the tread of the shoe at the crime scene.

Investigators must keep in mind that we live in the technology-rich 21st century, where low-cost, everyday technologies (e.g., flash memory cards, CDs, DVDs) capable of holding vast amounts of digital evidence are available in almost any retail store. Technology has also witnessed the creation of affordable cellular telephones, digital cameras, and digital video recorders that are pocket size with the ability to record, play, and transfer data in vast amounts in milliseconds. Computers, laptops, and netbooks come complete with editing software and webcams to produce and share information literally across the globe. When charged with conducting searches for evidence at locations controlled by suspects or offenders, investigators must be aware of these technologies, as well as internal and external hard drives, peripheral devices, and computer networks, and their capabilities when applying for search warrants. Sex offenders often take photographs or videotaped recordings of their victims during the crime to keep on hand so they can relive the event at a later date (Dutelle, 2011).

PROTOCOL OF A SEX CRIME SCENE SEARCH

The investigator's first responsibility at the crime scene is to verify that the scene was properly secured and that any evidence identified has been properly collected and processed with the chain of custody maintained. Do not shortchange or limit your crime scene search. Remember, the scene is not just the location where the penetration or other sexual act took place, but also includes all locations to which the offender and victim traveled, including the entry and exit paths of each party. When determining the boundaries of the crime scene, consider the information provided by the victim and witnesses, as well as your own perceptions of what the perpetrator was thinking when planning the attack, conducting the assault, and fleeing the area. The following procedures should be followed when conducting a crime scene search in a case of sexual assault or violent crime:

- Respond to the scene using due care.
- Provide medical emergency medical assistance to those in need.
- Evaluate your needs and possible problems.
- Secure the crime scene by establishing an outer and inner perimeter of the crime scene and begin a crime scene log for all persons entering or exiting the scene.
- Assign nonessential personal to perimeter security of the crime scene.
- Observe the crime scene and the surroundings, making notes of what and who you see.
- Make necessary notifications (e.g., supervisors, investigators, members of sexual assault or child abuse teams).

- Identify, photograph or videotape, document, and collect evidence of the crime and actions taking place before and after the crime. Collection of evidence is crucial and should include all evidence collected at the primary, secondary, and tertiary crime scenes; evidence collected from the victim; evidence collected from the offender; and statements or evidence collected from witnesses.
- Identify and locate all potential witnesses.
- Reconstruct the actions of all parties before, during, and after the crime was committed.
- Link the victim, perpetrator, and any known witnesses to the scene.
- Identify and take into custody the offender.
- Complete the district attorney's case file and prepare to reconstruct the crime scene for the court if required.
- Remember to Respond, Evaluate, Secure, Protect, Observe, Notify, and Document.

GLOSSARY

Chain of custody—The movement and location of real evidence, and the history of those persons who had it in their custody, from the time it is obtained to the time it is presented in court (Garner, 2009).

Child molestation—Any indecent or sexual activity on, involving, or surrounding a child; usually under the age of 14 (Garner, 2009).

Child pornography—Material depicting a person under the age of 18 engaged in sexual activity. Child pornography is not protected by the First Amendment, even if it falls short of the legal standard for obscenity (Garner, 2009).

Crime scene—Any location that is being investigated by law enforcement as a result of a criminal act; it is comprised of that area where evidence may be located.

Forensic odontology—A branch of forensic medicine that, in the interests of justice, deals with the proper examination, handling, and presentation of dental evidence in a court of law; it includes the identification of human remains, bite mark evaluations, postmortem identification, and dental profiling.

Habitual sex offender—A person who has been convicted of, or has pleaded guilty to, committing multiple sexually oriented offenses (Garner, 2009).

Incest—Sexual relations between family members or close relatives, including children related by adoption (Garner, 2009).

Indecent exposure—An offensive display of one's body in public, especially of the genitals (West, 2009).

Necrophilia—Sexual intercourse with dead bodies. The three types are pseudo necrophiles, regular necrophiles, and homicidal necrophiles (Hickey, 2005; Holmes, 2009; Terry, 2006).

Opportunistic sexual offender—Offenders described as exhibiting adventure-seeking, impulsive, or delinquent lifestyles; also referred to as "recreational" or "situational" offenders, as they tend to commit offenses while involved in carrying out another crime (e.g., burglary, kidnapping, robbery) (Terry, 2006).

Pedophile—An individual who is sexually attracted to prepubescent children, generally age 13 or younger. Pedophilia is defined by mental health professionals as a mental disorder, but the American legal system defines acting on a pedophilic urge as a criminal act. The focus of pedophilia is sexual activity with a child (APA, 1994, 2004).

Peeping Tom—A person who spies on another without consent, such as through a window usually for sexual pleasure; also termed *peeper* (Garner, 2009).

Primary crime scene—Location where the initial crime or primary event took place and where evidence of the criminal act may be located.

Rape—Forced sexual intercourse, including both psychological coercion as well as physical force. Forced sexual intercourse means vaginal, anal, or oral penetration by the offender. This category also includes incidents where the penetration is from a foreign object such as a bottle. Includes attempted rape, with male or female victims, and both heterosexual and homosexual rape. Attempted rape includes verbal threats of rape (BJS, 2010).

Secondary crime scene—Location related to the primary crime scene by way of evidence from the initial crime scene but is not the original location of the primary event.

Sexual predator—A person who has committed many violent sexual acts or who has a propensity for committing violent sexual acts; also termed *predator, sexually dangerous person, sexually violent predator* (Garner, 2009).

Sexual sadist—One who performs sadistic acts (real, not simulated) to derive sexual excitement from the psychological or physical suffering of the victim. Sadistic fantasies or acts may involve activities that indicate the dominance of the person over the victim. They may also involve restraint, fear, pain, humiliation, beating, burning, electrical shocks, rape, cutting, stabbing, strangulation, torture, mutilation, or killing. Sadistic sexual fantasies are likely to be present in childhood. Sexual sadism is usually chronic and is usually repeated until the offender is apprehended. The sexual sadist exhibits antisocial and violent behaviors that make outside therapy and treatment outside of institutional confinement unsuccessful (APA, 1994, 2004).

Sodomy—Oral or anal copulation between humans, especially those of the same sex (Garner, 2009).

Stalking—The act or an instance of following another by stealth. The offense of following or loitering near another, often surreptitiously, to annoy or harass that person or to commit a further crime such as assault or battery. Some statutory definitions include an element that the person being stalked must reasonably feel harassed, alarmed, or distressed about personal safety or the safety of one or more persons for whom that person is responsible. Some definitions include acts such as telephoning another and remaining silent during the call (Garner, 2009).

Statutory rape—When a person, male or female, engages in sexual intercourse with any person under the age of consent (usually 16) and not his or her spouse. Statutory rape differs from forcible rape in that overt force or threat need not be present for the violation to occur (Georgia General Assembly, 2009).

Tertiary crime scene—A location not deemed the primary or secondary crime scene; instead, it is another location (or multiple locations) that has become affixed to the primary event as a result of multiple moves on the part of the offender or victim and where evidence of the primary event may be located.

QUESTIONS FOR DISCUSSION

1. What impacts of sexual assault may interfere with your investigation and how will you handle this?
2. Using the scenario provided in the chapter, how well was the case handled? What would you do differently and why?
3. What constitutes a properly protected crime scene?
4. An ambulance took the victim to the hospital before law enforcement arrived. Her clothing and person contained vital evidence. Has the chain of custody been broken?
5. What can blood stains, a blood-splatter pattern and trail, palm prints and marks on the hood of a victim's car, scuff marks on a garage floor and stoop, partial sneaker prints, a blood trail leading inside, or a discarded soda cup tell us? Can any of this link a rapist to the victim or to a crime scene?
6. How important is crime scene photography? Video recording? Crime scene sketches?
7. What can analysis of rape-kit evidence taken by the doctor from the victim tell us? Can sperm or blood be used for DNA analysis to identify the age, sex, or race of the rapist?
8. What differences exist in the investigation of sexual assault with a child victim and an adult victim?
9. Where do you draw the line between achieving a conviction and secondary victimization?
10. What types of continuing education do law enforcement officers need to become specialized in investigations of sexual assault?

BIBLIOGRAPHY

APA. (1994). *Diagnostic and Statistical Manual of Mental Disorders*, 4th ed. Washington, D.C.: American Psychiatric Association.

APA. (2004). *Diagnostic and Statistical Manual of Mental Disorders*, 4th ed., rev. Washington, D.C.: American Psychiatric Association.

BJS. (2010). *Rape and Sexual Assault*. Washington, D.C.: Bureau of Justice Statistics, Office of Justice Programs, (http://bjs.ojp.usdoj.gov/index.cfm?ty=tp&tid=317).

Dutelle, A.W. (2011). *An Introduction to Crime Scene Investigation*. Mississauga, Ontario, Canada: Jones & Bartlett.

FBI. (2009a). Table 1: Crime in the United States by Volume and Rate per 100,000 Inhabitants, 1989–2008. In *2008 Crime in the United States*. Washington, D.C.: Federal Bureau of Investigation (http://www2.fbi.gov/ucr/cius2008/data/table_01.html).

FBI. (2009b). *Uniform Crime Reports*. Washington, D.C.: Federal Bureau of Investigation (http://www.fbi.gov/ucr/ucr.htm#cius).

FBI. (2010). Table 1: Crime in the United States by Volume and Rate per 100,000 Inhabitants, 1990–2009. In *2009 Crime in the United States*. Washington, D.C.: Federal Bureau of Investigation (http://www2.fbi.gov/ucr/cius2009/data/table_01.html).

Finkelhor, D., Ormrod, R., and Chaffin, M. (2009). Juveniles Who Commit Sex Offenses Against Minors. *Juvenile Justice Bulletin*, December (http://www.ncjrs.gov/pdffiles1/ojjdp/227763.pdf).

Garner, B.A., Ed. (2009). *Black's Law Dictionary*, 9th ed. New York: West.

Georgia General Assembly. (2009). *Official Code of Georgia*, http://www.lexis-nexis.com/hottopics/gacode/Default.asp.

Georgia Supreme Court Commission on Equality. (2003). *The Georgia Justice System's Treatment of Adult Victims of Sexual Violence: Some Problems and Some Proposed Solutions*. Atlanta: Georgia State University College of Law.

Golding, J.M. (1999). Sexual Assault History and Long-Term Physical Health Problems: Evidence from Clinical and Population Epidemiology. *Current Directions in Psychological Science,* 8(6):191–194.

Hickey, E.W. (2005). *Sex Crimes and Paraphilia*. Upper Saddle River, NJ: Prentice Hall.

Hill, G.N. and Hill, K.T. (2002). *The People's Law Dictionary: Taking the Mystery Out of Legal Language*. New York: MJF Books.

Holmes, R.M. (2009). *Sex Crimes: Patterns and Behavior*, 3rd ed. Thousand Oaks, CA: Sage.

LeBeau, M.A., Andollo, W., Hearn, W.L. et al. (1999). Recommendations for toxicological investigations of drug-facilitated sexual assaults. *Journal of Forensic Sciences*, 44:227–230.

LPD Forensic Identification Laboratory. (1998). *First Responder Crime Scene Training* [PowerPoint presentation]. Lincoln, NE: Lincoln Police Department.

NCVC. (2008). *Male Rape*. Washington, D.C.: National Center for Victims of Crime (http://www.ncvc.org/ncvc/main.aspx?dbName=DocumentViewer&DocumentID=32361).

RAINN. (2011). Rape, Abuse, and Incest National Network, Washington, D.C. (http:www.rainn.org/).

Robinson, E.M. (2010). *Crime Scene Photography*, 2nd ed. Burlington, MA: Elsevier.

Savion, J.O. and Turvey, B.E., Eds. (2005). *Rape Investigation Handbook*. Burlington, MA: Elsevier.

Terry, K.J. (2006). *Sexual Offenses and Offenders: Theory, Practice, and Policy*. Belmont, CA: Wadsworth.

Twain, M. (1909). *Letters from Earth*. New York: Harper & Row.

Weiss, S.L. (2008). *Forensic Photography: The Importance of Accuracy*. Upper Saddle River, NJ: Prentice Hall.

CHAPTER 15

Robbery

J. Harrison Watts

Washburn University

CHAPTER OBJECTIVES

After reading this chapter, you should be able to do the following:

1. Identify the criminal elements of robbery.
2. Differentiate the different categories of robbery.
3. Identify the actors and accomplices in a robbery.
4. Comprehend the various methods used to investigate robberies.

Chapter Outline

- Robbery Defined
- Categories of Robbery
- Robbery Target Selection
- Parties to the Crime
- Investigating Robberies
- Prosecuting Robberies
- Summary

ROBBERY DEFINED

Robbery is oftentimes confused with burglary. A typical scenario in Anytown, USA, is upon returning home from vacation a family finds that their residence has been broken into. They call the police department and report that they have been robbed. In actuality they have not been robbed; rather, they have been burglarized. There is a distinct difference between burglary and robbery. So what is robbery? *Robbery* is defined as using force or the threat of force to commit theft from an individual. More specifically, according to the Texas Penal Code (§29.02), a person commits a robbery if, in the course of committing theft and with intent to obtain or maintain control of the property, he intentionally, knowingly, or recklessly causes bodily injury to another or intentionally or knowingly threatens or places another in fear of imminent bodily injury or death. The family that returned home from vacation to find that their home was broken into was not robbed because the theft was not committed against their person but rather by stealth while they were away.

Each of the 50 states has a variation of the definition of robbery; however, the main elements remain the same: theft from a person and the use or threat of force. Many states have enhancements for robbery. This generally occurs when a victim is injured during the robbery or the offender brandishes a lethal weapon in the course of the robbery. An example of an enhanced robbery is reflected in the Texas statute for aggravated robbery: A person commits an aggravated robbery if he causes serious bodily injury to another; uses or exhibits a deadly weapon; or causes bodily injury to another person or threatens or places another person in fear of imminent bodily injury or death, if the other person is 65 years of age or older or a disabled person (Texas Penal Code §29.03). Some states differentiate robbery in the *first degree* from robbery in the *second degree*, depending on the circumstances surrounding the robbery. In California, every robbery of a person who is performing his or her duties as an operator of public transportation (e.g., taxi cab driver), robbery of any passenger that is perpetrated on public transportation, and every robbery that is perpetrated in a home, boat, trailer coach, or the inhabited portion of any other building is robbery of the first degree (California Penal Code §212(a)).

A second-degree robbery involves a robbery where no weapons were exhibited and where only the threat of force was used to commit the theft from an individual. When a weapon is used in a robbery, 43.5% of the time it is a firearm. Strong-armed robberies account for 40% of robberies, and a higher percentage of strong-armed robberies occur in the northeast United States as compared to the rest of the nation. The south reports more armed robberies with weapons than the rest of the nation (FBI, 2008f).

In all states, robbery is defined as a *felony crime*. Felony crimes are punishable by confinement in a state penitentiary for more than one year. Enhanced or aggravated charges of robbery result in a harsher punishment. The typical punishment for a robbery in Texas is any time in a state penitentiary from 2 to 20 years. For aggravated or first-degree robbery, the punishment is from 5 to 99 years, or life in prison.

Robbery is considered an *index crime* within the Uniform Crime Reporting (UCR) Program, which was operationalized in 1930 by the International Association of Chiefs of Police to meet the need for accurate, uniform crime statistics for the nation. The Federal Bureau of Investigation (FBI) is the federal agency that collects crime data from over 17,000 law enforcement agencies across the United States. Robbery is considered a violent crime by the UCR. Violent crimes are defined in the UCR Program as those offenses that involve force or threat of force. Surprisingly, the 2008 estimated robbery rate (145.3 per 100,000 inhabitants) showed a decrease of 1.5% compared to the 2007 rate (FBI, 2008a,b); however, over a 5-year period (2004 data compared with 2008 data), robbery showed an increase of 10.1%. The average dollar loss per robbery offense was $1315. The highest average dollar loss was for banks, which lost $4854 per offense (FBI, 2008a,g).

ATTEMPTED ROBBERY

Criminal attempt statutes generally designate that the punishment for an attempted crime would be one degree lower than if the crime was completed. In other words, in California, if an individual plans a robbery, puts on a mask, walks into a convenience store, and demands money, but the clerk brandishes a weapon from behind the counter and scares off the robber, then an attempted robbery has occurred. The California statute for criminal attempt specifies that, if the crime attempted is punishable by imprisonment in the state prison (which in this case it is), then the person guilty of the attempt shall be punished by imprisonment in the state prison for one-half the term of imprisonment prescribed upon a conviction of the offense attempted. The punishment for this type of robbery in California is a second-degree felony with a possibility to serve up to 5 years in prison, but in a criminal attempt half of that sentence would be mitigated by the fact that the robbery was an attempt.

CATEGORIES OF ROBBERY

BANK ROBBERIES

Bank robberies are unique in that a person who commits a bank robbery actually violates both state and federal statutes as they relate to robbery. Title 18, Section 2113, of the United States Code (18 USC §2113) is the federal criminal bank robbery statute. Subsection (a) of this code prohibits the taking or attempted taking by force, intimidation, or extortion of any property, money, or any other thing of value belonging to, or in the care, custody, control, management, or possession of, any bank, credit union, or savings and loan association, which are defined in federal statutes. Generally, the FBI is the lead agency in the investigation of bank robberies; however, local police departments respond to emergency calls or silent alarms in the initial response to a bank robbery. Typically, the local law enforcement agency will be the initial responding agency but will call the local office of the FBI to respond, and both agencies will work together in the investigation of the crime. If a suspect is identified, the FBI will pursue the case through the federal court system rather than the state system. There are exceptions to the rules, and one can find cases where a bank robber has been prosecuted through state courts rather than federal courts, but this would be an exception rather than the rule.

Local law enforcement agencies are considered the first responders to bank robberies, and they have special procedures that they generally follow. Police departments put into place policies that deal with the handling of the initial reporting of bank robberies in progress. Generally, the police want the robbers to get out of the bank believing that they have not been detected by the police. Most banks have silent alarms that notify the police dispatch. Officers are then dispatched to the location of the bank. Contrary to police television shows, the police may not be running with lights and sirens to the scene of a bank robbery; rather, the police prefer to use stealth to catch the robbers once they are away from the bank and innocent civilians. Local police may have predetermined hidden areas away from the bank but within eyesight of the bank entrance. When the police respond to a silent alarm in one of these areas, they wait for the robbers to come out of the bank, at which time they are taken down.

CONVENIENCE STORE ROBBERIES

Common targets of robberies are convenience stores. These stores are generally open 24 hours, which provides opportunities for robbers. The *modus operandi* or method of operation for the robber is to scope out the store and then strike quickly when the store does not have any customers in it. Most store clerks go through robbery training prior to taking a position as a clerk. The 7-Eleven Corporation implemented specific loss-prevention training, and, according to research conducted by Lins and Ericson (1998), the training implementation contributed to a 70% reduction in robberies over 20 years.

HOME INVASIONS

Home invasions are incidents where robbers make entry into a habitation while the residents are at home. The robbers generally display weapons and threaten the homeowners with violence unless they tell the robbers where their valuables and cash are located. Home invasions have been prevalent in the Asian community, as many Asian immigrants tend to keep cash in their homes rather than depositing it in banks. Kidnapping or false imprisonment charges may accompany a robbery charge in the case of a home invasion. The 2002 movie *Panic Room* is centered around a secure room built in a residence in case of a home invasion.

MUGGING

Muggings are also called *street robberies*. These types of robberies are likely to occur in parking lots, outside of shopping malls, on city sidewalks, in alleyways, and in places where people might be carrying a purse or wallet. A mugging is usually a very quick action; the victim is caught by surprise and usually offers a minimal amount of resistance. In a mugging, victims may be injured when they are pushed to the ground by their assailants. The elderly are targeted for muggings due to their perceived slow reaction time, and they typically offer little resistance. Automated teller machines (ATMs) also provide robbers with targets who have cash in hand. In fact, robberies at ATMs are such a concern that the Credit Card Accountability, Responsibility, and Disclosure Act of 2009 includes a provision for the Federal Trade Commission to study and report to Congress on the cost effectiveness of making available ATM emergency PIN technology that would enable bank customers under duress to electronically alert a local law enforcement agency. The Federal Trade Commission is researching emergency PINs or reverse PINs and alarm button technologies as a potential response to ATM robbery.

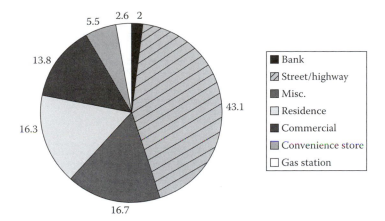

FIGURE 15.1 Robbery by location. (Adapted from FBI, *2008 Crime in the United States*, Federal Bureau of Investigation, Washington, D.C., 2008; http://www2.fbi.gov/ucr/cius2008/data/table_23.html.)

CARJACKING

California Penal Code §215(a) defines carjacking as the felonious taking of a motor vehicle in the possession of another, from his or her person or immediate presence, or from the person or immediate presence of a passenger of the motor vehicle, against his or her will and with the intent to either permanently or temporarily deprive the person in possession of the motor vehicle of his or her possession, accomplished by means of force or fear. California Penal Code §215(b) further stipulates that carjacking is punishable by imprisonment in the state prison for a term of 3, 5, or 9 years. Carjackers look for opportunities to gain control of a vehicle. This could be at a stop light or in a parking lot when the victim is just getting into the vehicle. Carjackers tend to forcibly remove the victim and take the vehicle, or they will push the victim into the passenger seat while forcing their way into control of the vehicle. The typical carjacker seeks to gain control of the vehicle rather than kidnap the victim. Victims may also be robbed of valuables, such as their jewelry, wallet, or purse, and anything that the robber can secure quickly that may be valuable.

ROBBERY TARGET SELECTION

Highway or street robberies make up the majority of all robberies. The UCR data revealed that highway robberies in 2008 accounted for 43.1% of all robberies, followed by miscellaneous robberies at 16.7% and residential robberies at 16.3% (FBI, 2008c) (Figure 15.1). Highway or street robberies are generally crimes of opportunity rather than planned robberies. The victims in this type of robbery are in the wrong place at the wrong time. They look weak, old, young, or less likely to put up resistance. Street robbers may cruise certain areas of a city looking for weak targets. Planned robberies include detailed preparations to commit robbery without being caught by the authorities. Some robberies require complex planning, but others do not. Bank robberies provide a good example of a planned robbery. Generally speaking, bank robbers watch the bank for weeks and sometimes even months in advance. They go into the bank prior to the robbery to get a feel for the layout and security. After casing the bank, a decision is made as to the suitability of the bank for a robbery.

PARTIES TO THE CRIME

Robbery is often committed by a group of individuals working together. As the complexity of the robbery increases, so does the need for accomplices. An *accomplice* is someone who knowingly, voluntarily, and with common interest participates in the commission of a crime and can be charged with the same crime(s) for which the accused will be tried (O'Connor, 2006). *Complicity* is association with a wrongful act; individuals who share in the guilt even though they do not engage in the criminal act are accomplices to the crime. A *principal* is anyone involved in committing a crime. A principal in the first degree is one who perpetrates a crime either through his or her own act or by the use of inanimate objects or innocent people. A principal in the second degree incites or abets the commission of a crime and is present actually or constructively. A person is present *constructively* when, without being present, he or she assists the principal of the first degree at the moment the crime is being committed. An *accessory before the fact* gives support to, rouses, or assists but is not actually there; an accessory after the fact receives, relieves, harbors, or assists a felon to evade arrest and conviction (O'Connor, 2006). *Complicity, principal, accessory before the fact*, and *accessory after the fact* are all different terms, each with its own distinct meaning. In accomplice law or complicity, the statutory law has evolved beyond the common law, and the case law is broad and perplexing about precisely where the lines are drawn. Complicity is a theory that can be misused by prosecutors. Only a few basic restrictions exist: First, the law does not recognize accomplices to any misdemeanor or the crime of treason. Second, an accomplice must normally be physically present during commission of the crime, but advice or words of encouragement beforehand as well as providing material assistance afterwards will create a liability. Third, no one can be convicted on the uncorroborated testimony of an accomplice alone. Finally, persons giving post-crime aid are punished less severely than those furnishing pre-crime aid. Getaway drivers are considered principal actors in the crime. Many robbers utilize getaway drivers who specialize in high-speed driving. The driver waits and acts as a lookout while the robbery is occurring. When the crime is completed, the getaway driver takes all the participants away from the crime scene. There may be witnesses outside of a location that is robbed who can describe the getaway driver and provide vehicle information.

INVESTIGATING ROBBERIES

IDENTIFYING SUSPECTS

In 2010, according to FBI statistics, 6753 persons were known to be involved in bank robbery, bank burglary, or bank larceny; Table 15.1 breaks them down by race and sex. FBI investigations had resulted in the identification of 3325 (49%) of these 6753 persons. Of

TABLE 15.1   Number, Race, and Sex of Perpetrators

	White	Black	Hispanic	Other	Unknown	Total
Male	2681	2738	479	67	232	6197
Female	255	182	15	10	10	472
Total	2936	2920	494	77	242	6669

Note: The number of persons known to be involved in the 5628 robberies, burglaries, and larcenies in 2010 was 6753. In a small number of cases (84), the use of a full disguise made determination of race and sex impossible.

Source: FBI, *Bank Crime Statistics 2010*, Federal Bureau of Investigation, Washington, D.C., 2010 (http://www.fbi.gov/stats-services/publications/bank-crime-statistics-2010/bank-crime-statistics-2010).

these 3325 identified persons, 1173 (35%) were determined to be users of narcotics and 557 (17%) were found to have been previously convicted in either federal or state court for bank robbery, bank burglary, or bank larceny.

INTERVIEWING WITNESSES AND VICTIMS

At the scene of the robbery one of the key elements to identifying suspects is to interview witnesses who may have observed essential details of the robbers. The interviews may take a considerable amount of time depending on the number of witnesses to the crime. Typically in a robbery investigation, the interviews are conducted at the scene of the crime. Many police departments have standardized witnesses statements to expedite the process. This is not the rule, however, and depending on the number of witnesses and the exact details of the crime it is not uncommon to have the witnesses accompany the investigators to the police department for interviewing.

Prior to interviewing it is important to separate the witnesses so they do not influence each other. Many times what one witness may have observed is not what a separate witness may have observed. The investigator will want to ascertain all the information and receive that information independent of any other witnesses. Details such as physical descriptions, weapon characteristics, the method in which the robber conducted the robbery, and words that the robber used are all important. When a suspect description is obtained and within a short period of time after the robbery a suspect matching that description is located in close proximity to the crime scene, that suspect can be directly transported back to the crime scene for identification by the witnesses. This process is called a *show-up*. Show-ups have been debated as they do not provide suspects with the protection of legal counsel (*Kirby v. Illinois*, 1972). In addition, the reliability of a show-up has been questioned by researchers (Steblay et al., 2003). In some cases, a suspect could be falsely identified because the clothing he or she is wearing matches the description given by witnesses. It is important to corroborate the suspect's recent path prior to the report of the robbery.

The collection of physical evidence should proceed as soon as possible. A note the robber used during the hold up would be a critical piece of evidence. Many bank robberies are executed by the robber casually entering the bank and handing a note to the teller demanding money. Generally, robbery suspects do not leave much physical evidence at the scene of the crime; however, robbers may leave fingerprints or footprints, or they may discard something that could be valuable in the investigation. It is the responsibility of the responding police officers to secure the crime scene, making sure that any physical evidence that was left at the scene is not disturbed until the investigators arrive.

CLOSED-CIRCUIT TELEVISION

In an attempt to deter robberies, many businesses utilize closed-circuit television (CCTV). The video from CCTV has improved remarkably over the past several years. Banking institutions utilize heavy video surveillance. Much of this video surveillance is now in digital form, which provides a high-quality images for police. Robbers attempt to defeat video surveillance by wearing disguises. These disguises can be quite elaborate or may be very simple. In 2005, in Tucson, AZ, three women and one man were arrested in connection with a string of robberies dubbed the "clown robbers" due to the clown disguises they wore. The break in the case came when reviews of outside surveillance videos from the robbery locations led police to the vehicle the group was using.

PROSECUTING ROBBERIES

LEVEL OF PROOF

Since larceny is an element of robbery, all the issues that exist in defining larceny are also issues in defining robbery. The common law rules that prevent the taking of real property or services from being larceny, for instance, may also prevent the forcible taking of these things from being robbery. Likewise, since the taking that results from a mistaken but honest claim of ownership is not a theft because there is no intent to deprive the rightful owner, such taking with force is not a robbery in most states because there is no theft. Hall of Fame football star Orenthal James Simpson, known commonly as O.J. Simpson, was convicted of armed robbery and ten other charges for gathering together five other men and raiding a hotel room, where they seized several game balls, photographs, and plaques. Mr. Simpson and his lawyers argued, unsuccessfully, that the incident was not a robbery but an attempt to reclaim mementos that had been stolen from him (Associated Press, 2008).

After meeting all the elements of larceny the prosecutor must then meet the requirement of force or intimidation. This element is what distinguishes robbery from larceny or theft. Purse snatchings or muggings happen so quickly that sometimes victims do not know that they have lost their property. If this is the case, the crime may be a larceny rather than a robbery. When victims do recognize the act of someone attempting to take property from them and struggle, and the perpetrator uses force to remove the property, these cases are classified as robbery. The threat of violence qualifies as force in the sense of the definition of robbery. The threat must be of an immediate nature and be specific.

SUMMARY

Robbery is defined as using force or the threat of force to commit theft from an individual. Burglary is often mistakenly referred to as robbery. Robbery is more closely aligned with theft or larceny as larceny is an element of robbery. In all states, robbery is a felony crime and punishable by incarceration in a penitentiary. Robbery is classified as being in the first degree or second degree. Some states refer to first-degree robbery as aggravated robbery. Robberies occur most often as street crimes or muggings. Robberies can be planned, such as robberies of a bank or jewelry store, or they can be opportunistic, such as convenience store robberies. Robbery is not limited to businesses and people walking on the street, as some robberies occur when perpetrators forcibly enter homes while the occupants are inside and hold the occupants hostage while taking their valuables. These robberies are classified as home invasions. Robbery is a crime that may have more than one offender per offense. An accomplice is someone who knowingly, voluntarily, and with common interest, participates in the commission of a crime and can be charged with the same crime for which the accused will be tried. In addition, an individual who assists in the planning of the robbery or aids in the concealment of the robbery after the fact could be considered complicit in the wrongful act.

Investigating robberies involves identifying suspects, collecting physical evidence, and interviewing witnesses and victims. One technology that has assisted investigators in the investigation of robberies is closed-circuit television. Proving the elements of robbery is accomplished through the testimony of witnesses and victims, as well as examining physical evidence. All of the elements of larceny plus the use or threat of the use of force to accomplish the larceny must be proven beyond a reasonable doubt.

QUESTIONS FOR DISCUSSION

1. What differentiates robbery from theft and burglary?
2. Explain the concept of complicity.
3. What are the different levels of accomplices?
4. What are the steps that a police officer should take when arriving at a robbery crime scene?
5. Explain the breakdown of robbery by location.

BIBLIOGRAPHY

Anon. (2010). Robbery—Particular Requirements. *Law Library–American Law and Legal Information*, http://law.jrank.org/pages/1982/Robbery-Particular-requirements.html.

Associated Press. (2008). O.J. Simpson Found Guilty on All Charges in Robbery–Kidnapping Trial. *FoxNews.com*, http://www.foxnews.com/story/0,2933,432663,00.html.

FBI. (2008a). Table 1, Crime in the United States by Volume and Rate per 100,000 Inhabitants, 1989–2008. In *2008 Crime in the United States*. Washington, D.C.: Federal Bureau of Investigation (http://www2.fbi.gov/ucr/cius2008/data/table_01.html).

FBI. (2008b). Table 1a, Crime in the United States: Percent Change in Volume and Rate per 100,000 Inhabitants for 2 years, 5 years, and 10 years. In *2008 Crime in the United States*. Washington, D.C.: Federal Bureau of Investigation (http://www2.fbi.gov/ucr/cius2008/data/table_01a. html).

FBI. (2008c). Table 2, Crime in the United States by Community Type, 2008. In *2008 Crime in the United States*. Washington, D.C.: Federal Bureau of Investigation (http://www2.fbi.gov/ucr/ cius2008/data/table_02.html).

FBI. (2008d). Table 3, Crime in the United States: Offense and Population Percent Distribution by Region, 2008. In *2008 Crime in the United States*. Washington, D.C.: Federal Bureau of Investigation (http://www2.fbi.gov/ucr/cius2008/data/table_03.html).

FBI. (2008e). Table 12, Crime Trends by Population Group, 2007–2008. In *2008 Crime in the United States*. Washington, D.C.: Federal Bureau of Investigation (http://www2.fbi.gov/ucr/cius2008/ data/table_12.html).

FBI. (2008f). Table 21, Robbery, by State, Types of Weapons, 2008. In *2008 Crime in the United States*. Washington, D.C.: Federal Bureau of Investigation (http://www2.fbi.gov/ucr/cius2008/ data/table_21.html).

FBI. (2008g). Table 23, Offense Analysis: Number and Percent Change, 2007–2008. In *2008 Crime in the United States*. Washington, D.C.: Federal Bureau of Investigation (http://www2.fbi.gov/ucr/ cius2008/data/table_23.html).

Kirby v. Illinois, 406 U.S. 682 (1972).

Lins, S. and Erickson, R.J. (1998). Stores Learn to Inconvenience Robbers. *Security Management*, 42(11):49–53.

O'Connor, T. (2006). *Accomplice Law*, http://www.drtomoconnor.com/3010/3010lect03.htm.

Steblay, N., Dysart, J., Fulero, S., and Lindsay, R.C.L. (2003). Eyewitness Accuracy Rates in Police Show Up and Line Up Presentations: A Meta-Analytic Comparison. *Law and Human Behavior*, 27(5):523.

5

Specialized Investigations

CHAPTER 16

Narcotics Investigation

Donald F. Vespa

U.S. Drug Enforcement Administration (Retired)

CHAPTER OBJECTIVES

After reading this chapter you should be able to do the following:

1. Describe the nature of narcotics investigations.
2. List and describe the steps in a narcotics investigation.
3. Explain the role of the case agent in a narcotics investigation.
4. Identify the various types of street narcotics.
5. Explain the role of the undercover agent.
6. Explain the role and importance of confidential informants.

Chapter Outline

- Introduction
- Case Initiation and Preparation
- Drugs of Abuse
- Surveillance
- Informants
- Undercover
- Undercover Purchase
- Operational Safety Plan

INTRODUCTION

Drug trafficking, illegal drug use, drug abuse, and violent drug-related crimes are just a few of the enormous challenges a narcotics investigator faces. In order for the narcotics investigator to be efficient and successful at fighting drug traffickers, the investigator must be creative, innovative, and dedicated to developing a basic investigative strategy to combat drug traffickers and drug organizations. The investigator must utilize all of the available resources at hand to identify, target, and eventually arrest drug traffickers. Today's drug traffickers and drug trafficking organizations are equally creative, innovative, and dedicated in their determination to distribute illegal drugs throughout our country and the world. Experience has repeatedly demonstrated that, when inadequate planning, tactics, and resources are used, deaths and injuries may result needlessly among innocent civilians, drug violators, and law enforcement personnel; therefore, it is very important that every narcotics enforcement activity be thoroughly planned by a supervisor, case agent, and participating personnel.

In the planning and execution of all narcotics enforcement operations (e.g., arrests, search warrants, undercover activity), the first priority should be given to the safety of participating personnel and the public, the second priority to the security of the money, and the third priority to the achievement of investigative objectives. It is essential that an operational safety plan be prepared for all enforcement activities. In any narcotics enforcement operation, safety should be paramount. When narcotics operations are properly planned and executed with safety in mind, the probability of injury and death are minimized.

The success of a narcotics investigation or narcotics enforcement operation is dependent in part upon reliable intelligence information. Today, drug trafficking organizations have become highly sophisticated in guarding their illegal operations from law enforcement authorities. These organizations are extremely violent, adaptable, and resourceful, so mutual law enforcement cooperation is essential in combating these sophisticated violent drug traffickers. It should be noted that, because of a single initial tip or lead, many successful large-scale drug dealers and trafficking organizations have been dismantled and put out of business. For this reason, it is very important for investigators to methodically follow all leads and tips, regardless of how trivial they seem.

One of the main goals of a drug enforcement operation is to arrest the highest level of drug violators and seize the largest quantity of illicit drugs before they reach the street. This at times can be a very daunting task due to a lack of complaining witnesses; there are only drug sellers and drug buyers. The drug investigator must develop a narcotics case based on fundamental principles of drug investigation that involve intelligence, surveillance, informants, and undercover operations. These fundamental resources are the key components in any successful narcotics investigation. The successful end result of these investigations is a reflection of the hard work and dedication to the law enforcement personnel assigned to the cases.

It is important to realize that many drug trafficking cases overlap jurisdictional boundaries; thus, it is important to develop a good cooperative relationship with other law enforcement agencies. In addition, it is equally important to work closely with the prosecutor in a narcotics investigation. The success or failure of your investigation often is determined by small procedural and legal details, all of which should be discussed with the prosecutor during the initial stages of case development. In other words, if it is at all possible, have the prosecutor on board from the beginning of your investigation to minimize potential legal problems. In this chapter, we discuss and describe some of the basic fundamental methods, principals, and techniques involved in a narcotics investigation.

CASE INITIATION AND PREPARATION

The first step in initiating a narcotics case by the narcotics investigator involves the verification of intelligence information concerning a violation of the controlled substance laws or related laws. This information may be received from a multitude of *sources of information* (SOIs), who are individuals or organizations providing occasional information without compensation. These SOIs may include law enforcement elements, both within and outside the narcotics investigator's parent agency; criminals and criminal associates; and concerned citizens. The information may also be provided by an *informant*, often referred to as a *cooperating source* or *cooperating individual*, who is an individual operating under the specific direction of law enforcement, with or without the expectation of payment or valuable consideration. This category also includes *defendant informants*, who are individuals subject to arrest and prosecution for a narcotics offense. These individuals can provide valuable information to the narcotics investigator when they have direct knowledge of the criminal activity and personal contact with the investigators.

In general, the investigator must maintain an open mind toward all information received from any source. In particular, informant assistance can be extremely valuable in narcotics cases because the informant in many cases has inside information on the criminal activities. During the initial debriefing, the investigator should establish whether or not the source has direct knowledge of the information or activities that the source is describing. If the source has no direct knowledge, the source should explain how he or she obtained the information. Every time the source names an individual, the investigator should obtain as much identifying information as possible about the individual. This should include a complete physical description and any other identifying characteristics. If the source indicates a location of criminal activity, the investigator should get as much information as possible, including addresses, geographical landmarks, and maps. The source should be asked specific questions about the drug trafficking methods, including type and quantity of drugs, smuggling routes, transportation methods, storage locations, payment amounts, clandestine drug laboratories, money movement, communications, financial assets, and narco-terrorism.

The investigator should never ask a question that compromises a law enforcement source, ongoing operation, or technical capabilities. Drug dealers are frequently aware of other criminal activities in a given area, such as robberies, burglaries, auto thefts, drive-by shootings, or homicides; therefore, the investigator should always ask the source about any other types of criminal activity for later referral to the appropriate departments or agencies. Many times a narcotics investigator has much narcotics-related information available, but it takes training and many years of experience to determine its relevancy and importance in the case. The astute investigator should evaluate the information received relative to the type of source and the circumstances of its receipt. In this process, the motivation of the cooperating individual must be scrutinized carefully.

Regardless of the source of the information, the investigator must make every effort to independently verify and corroborate the information received. This can be accomplished in several ways, one of which is surveillance of the suspected individual in question. The investigator can learn a lot of valuable information about a suspected individual by closely observing his daily activities. In addition, criminal history checks, police offense reports, traffic records, court records, public utilities, telephone records, public records, motor vehicle registration records, subsequent interviews, and informant development can all help to corroborate the information received. After the preliminary information indicating possible drug law violations or other law violations has been verified by independent sources, it is time to develop a case strategy on how best to further the investigation. It is important to remember that the overall objective of a drug case is to arrest, prosecute, and incarcerate drug traffickers to reduce drug availability in the community. In addition, the narcotics investigator should be aware of the asset forfeiture laws concerning drug traffickers and of the financial component in any drug investigation.

Regardless of whether you are investigating a low-level street dealer or a large-scale drug trafficking organization, a drug dealer's primary objective is to make a profit. Drug traffickers need cash to operate, buy silence from witnesses, pay bribes, pay legal expenses, establish stash houses, and obtain new drug sources of supply. For this reason, the assets, the financial component, are a major factor in any criminal drug organization that must be addressed by the investigator. Today's drug investigators should focus not only on the traditional objectives of arresting the drug dealer and seizing large amounts of drugs but also on identifying and locating all of the illegally obtained assets of a drug dealer or drug organization for possible seizure and forfeiture.

Proper planning of a drug investigation is crucial to whether or not the investigation will be successful. The target of the investigation and available law enforcement resources will determine the investigative response. For example, the level at which the dealer is distributing drugs is important in the planning stages of the investigation. Whether the dealer is a low-level street dealer or a large-scale multijurisdictional source of supply will determine the type of investigation initiated. All of these factors will affect the length of the investigation, type of arrests, and the amount of resources dedicated to the case. If the dealer is a low-level dealer, it might be more prudent to conduct a "buy–bust" instead of a "buy–walk," which has the potential to turn the suspect into a valuable informant or CS early on in the investigation. Remember, in many cases it takes investigative acumen to determine the credibility and value of a good CS. A narcotics investigator should not take everything a CS says at face value.

In many cases, a CS will try to embellish the information provided to the investigator. Whether the narcotics investigator chooses to conduct an undercover (U/C) agent buy or an informant (CS) buy or simply to pursue a drug possession case will depend on all of the aforementioned factors. The overall success of an investigation in part is determined by how the investigator obtains information and prepares the criminal case. To ensure successful prosecution of a case, it is wise to establish a close working relationship with the prosecutor. It would be futile to conduct an extensive complex narcotics investigation if the prosecutor refuses to present the case in court. It is always advisable to seek legal assistance early in any investigation to prevent legal problems that could negate weeks' or months' worth of investigative effort. If there is ever any question about the legality of any action, the prosecutor should be contacted before any action is taken.

In every narcotics investigation, documentation and corroboration are paramount; therefore, it is advisable to have a second investigator present as a witness during all debriefings of sources of information and confidential sources. In every narcotics investigation, a case initiation report should be submitted by the case agent or officer; this report should include details of the initial basis of the case, the major targets, and the overall objectives of the investigation. The scope of the investigation will be determined by the available intelligence information gathered on the targets of the investigation and the law enforcement resources available to conduct the investigation. Remember, technically, a narcotics case begins with the case initiation; however, in many cases, much of the investigative work begins after the arrest is made. The mere arrest of a subject is but a small part of the entire investigative process of exposing the defendant to the criminal justice system. This is especially true if the subjects arrested agree to cooperate with the authorities and additional relevant information is uncovered, which must be verified and corroborated.

Preparing a case for court requires documenting everything of importance that occurs during an investigation that leads to an arrest, as well as all subsequent post-arrest investigative efforts and procedures. All of this documentation is contained in the case file, which the case agent or officer is responsible for maintaining, updating, and periodically reviewing for completeness and accuracy. In essence, the case file is a complete chronological record of the entire investigation from case initiation to the case closing. The prosecutor may have the responsibility for the interpretation and presentation of all of the relevant evidence in court, but the investigator is tasked with the initial collection of evidentiary material to help prove the defendant's guilt. The evidence as well as the method or means by which it was obtained must not violate the laws of admissibility. The admissibility of evidence in a court of law is dependent on the manner in which the evidence was collected, processed, identified, and secured. In addition, the chain of custody of the evidence submitted must be documented. In conclusion, a drug investigator is only limited by experience, resources, ability, and hard work.

DRUGS OF ABUSE

Cocaine is a drug listed under Schedule II of the Controlled Substance Act. It is described as a white crystalline substance, chemically known as benzoylmethylecgonine, which originates from the coca plant (*Erythroxylon coca*), grown chiefly in Bolivia and Peru in the Andes Region of South America. It is considered a powerful central nervous system stimulant or "upper" and has both physical and psychological addictive properties. Known on the street as coke, flake, or snow, cocaine can be inhaled or injected into the body. It has a high melting point, so before it can be smoked it must be converted to base or crack, which has a much lower melting point. Crack, the street name for the smokable form of cocaine, resembles tiny chunks or rocks. Users smoke crack cocaine in small pipes or in tobacco and marijuana cigarettes.

When users smoke crack, they get high very quickly. Both physical and psychological dependence develops very quickly with continued crack use. Illicit cocaine is distributed as a white crystalline powder, frequently diluted by a wide variety of ingredients, including sugars such as lactose, mannitol, and inositol, as well as lidocaine, a local anesthetic. As a result of the high cost of cocaine, there is a proclivity to adulterate the substance at each level of drug distribution. The most common method of administering cocaine is by snorting the product through the nose. Large-scale cocaine dealers usually sell cocaine in kilogram quantities, whereas low-level street dealers deal in ounces or lesser gram amounts. The price of cocaine varies depending on the demand, availability, and quantity purchased.

Ecstasy (3,4-methylenedioxymethamphetamine, or MDMA) is what is commonly referred to as a synthetic or designer drug. Manufactured in clandestine laboratories, Ecstasy is a stimulant with mild hallucinogenic properties, similar in chemical composition to both 3,4-methylenedioxyamphetamine (MDA) and methamphetamine. Most MDMA seized in the United States originates in Europe. Even though the natural substance starts out in powder form, the normal dosage unit for Ecstasy or MDMA is a tablet. The tablets usually have unique designs imprinted on them. Most MDMA tablets are white to off-white in color, although some tablets are green, blue, or yellow. Ecstasy is referred to as the "love drug" or "hug drug"; on the street, Ecstasy is known simply as E or X. MDMA is frequently sold retail for $10 to $60 per tablet at all-night dance clubs known as "rave clubs." It is a Schedule I drug under the Controlled Substances Act. (Schedule I drugs have no legitimate medical purpose.)

There is a tremendous mark-up between the wholesale and retail price on MDMA. Producers of MDMA usually sell it to wholesale distributors in 10,000-tablet lots, typically charging between $1.50 and $5.00 per tablet. Subsequently, the wholesale dealers smuggle the drug into the United States via couriers. Wholesale MDMA dealers then sell the MDMA in lots of 1000 tablets to mid-level distributors, who in turn sell the drug to retail distributors. Ecstasy is popular with young adults and adolescents at rave parties because it increases the sensitivity to touch. Some of the physical effects are muscle tension, hyperthermia, blurred vision, rapid eye movements, faintness, involuntary teeth clenching, sweating, and tremors. As a result of the increase in energy, young people at rave parties dance and party continuously, resulting in dehydration, exhaustion, and high blood pressure.

Another Schedule 1 drug under the Controlled Substance Act is gamma-hydroxybutyrate (GHB), a powerful central nervous system depressant that is frequently used illicitly for its sedative and euphoric effects. Adolescents and young adults appear to be the predominant users of GHB. GHB is one of the drugs most commonly used in drug-facilitated sexual assaults due to its powerful sedative characteristics. Prior to such a sexual assault, the drug is usually covertly mixed into the intended victim's drink to mask its salty taste. It is quickly absorbed and metabolized by the body. The onset of the drug's effects normally occurs within 15 to 30 minutes of ingestion, and the effects generally last for 3 to 6 hours depending on the potency and amount of GHB administered. Vomiting is a common result of GHB consumption. An overdose of GHB can lead to respiratory depression and death.

Heroin is produced by a chemical process from raw opium obtained from the opium poppy. It is known on the street as horse or smack. It is listed under Schedule I of the Controlled Substance Act and varies in color from white to dark brown because of impurities left from the manufacturing process or the presence of additives such as cocoa, food coloring, or brown sugar. Pure heroin is a white powdery substance that is bitter in taste;

it is rarely sold on the streets. Street heroin is often sold to street addicts in a single dosage unit called a "bag," which is heavily diluted and mixed with powdered milk, sugar, starch, and quinine. Historically, heroin use in the United States has varied over periods of rising and falling demand. The demand for heroin ranges from traditional inner cities to wealthier affluent suburbs. The combination of higher purity, greater availability, and lower cost has made heroin use more appealing to young people. The new higher purity heroin can be snorted or smoked instead of being injected. Heroin comes from Mexico, Asia, and South America. The financial incentive for heroin trafficking is high. Heroin can be purchased relatively inexpensively outside the United States, but the price increases greatly after reaching this country. Mexican drug trafficking organizations using established marijuana networks have expanded their product line to include black tar and brown heroin.

Ketamine hydrochloride is a Schedule III drug under the Controlled Substance Act. Common street names for ketamine are special K, K, vitamin K, cat valium, lady K, and super K. It is a dissociative anesthetic that has a combination of stimulant, hallucinogenic, depressant, and analgesic properties. Ketamine is legally used as a preoperative veterinary anesthetic and is abused for the aforementioned properties. It is illegally used to facilitate sexual assault and often is distributed at raves, nightclubs, and private parties. Most of the ketamine illegally distributed in the United States is diverted or stolen from legitimate sources or smuggled into the United States. It can be taken orally in tablet or capsule form or snorted as a powder.

Lysergic acid diethylamide (LSD) is listed under Schedule I of the Controlled Substance Act. LSD is a hallucinogenic drug that became popular during the drug culture of the 1960s. LSD can cause delusions and hallucinations and a poor perception of time and distance. It is usually sold in the form of tablets, as thin squares of gelatin, or as impregnated paper (referred to as "blotter acid"). It is often referred to on the street as microdot or acid. All forms of LSD are sold by the dose and are normally taken orally.

Marijuana is a term that refers to the *Cannabis* plant and to any part or extract of it that produces somatic or psychic changes in an individual. Marijuana is a tobacco-like substance produced by drying the leaves and flowering tops of the plant. It varies in its potency, depending on the source and selectivity of the plant, and is commonly smoked in a variety of ways. The potency of the marijuana plant depends on its concentration of the psychoactive agent THC. The higher the concentration of THC in the marijuana plant, the higher the potency level. Sinsemilla is prepared from unpollinated female *Cannabis* plants and has an extremely high THC concentration. Marijuana price ranges vary considerable, depending on the quality and geographic location of the country. Marijuana is often referred to as pot, grass, sinsemilla, reefer, or weed. Marijuana prices fluctuate greatly depending on the geographic location and quantity purchased. It is usually sold in ounce and pound quantities.

Methamphetamine is listed under Schedule II of the Controlled Substance Act and is commonly referred to on the street as speed, crank, glass, meth, ice, or crystal. It is a synthetically produced central nervous system stimulant that induces effects similar to those of cocaine; however, it metabolizes much more slowly in the body than cocaine and thus has longer lasting effects. Ice, named for its appearance, is a smokable form of methamphetamine. Illicit methamphetamine is sold in tablets, ice, and powder forms. Powder methamphetamine can be injected, orally ingested, snorted, or smoked. It is bitter tasting and water soluble, and it ranges in color from white to reddish brown. The variations of color can be attributed to differences in the manufacturing process. Powder methamphetamine is usually snorted or injected depending on the geographic area; however, it can also be smoked or orally administered. Users experience increased alertness and a sense of euphoria along with increases in respiration, heart rate, blood pressure, and body temperature. Chronic use and abuse result in hypertension, hallucinations, memory loss, paranoid delusions, and violent behavior. The adverse consequences of methamphetamine abuse include the risk of heart failure, stroke, and prolonged psychosis. Withdrawal from the drug can result in severe depression. Historically, powder methamphetamine was chiefly made and sold by outlaw motorcycle gangs; however, large-scale Mexican drug trafficking organizations now dominate the market. These Mexico-based criminal organizations manufacture methamphetamine in large clandestine laboratories in Mexico and then distribute the methamphetamine throughout the United States via drug couriers. In addition to the Mexican methamphetamine drug laboratories, domestic "cooks" within the United States produce powder methamphetamine in small makeshift, independent mom-and-pop clandestine laboratories. Due to aggressive domestic enforcement measures and restrictions on the chemical precursors required to manufacture methamphetamine, there has been a reduction in the number of clandestine methamphetamine labs in some Midwestern states. Methamphetamine is sold by the gram, ounce, pound, or kilogram, depending on the geographic area. The price varies considerably, depending on the purity of the product.

SURVEILLANCE

Surveillance in modern-day law enforcement is a valuable and effective procedure that produces viable intelligence when all else fails. It is used for a variety of reasons and has multiple applications in the field, although the primary purpose of surveillance is to obtain information. In addition, it is frequently used to verify and corroborate information previously obtained. This also includes updating existing intelligence information to prevent it from becoming stale and ineffective. It can also be used to provide security for ongoing undercover operations, to obtain probable cause for a search warrant, to identify drug violator associates, and to provide an avenue for apprehending drug dealers in the act of committing crimes. The methods used to conduct surveillance are only limited by one's imagination and creativity. Surveillance can be by foot, motor vehicle, boat, or aircraft, or it can take place in a fixed location. A multitude of equipment is available to aid the investigator in these activities, including radios, cell phones, cameras, special surveillance vehicles, aircraft, video equipment, binoculars, high-powered telescopes, and sophisticated electronic tracking and listening equipment.

Many sophisticated large-scale drug trafficking organizations have been disrupted, dismantled, and put out of business as a result of information obtained during basic surveillance operations; therefore, it would be wise for any drug investigator to work hard at becoming proficient in the various methods, adaptations, and techniques of surveillance.

A successful surveillance is no easy task and can be a very difficult process for the inexperienced investigator. This task is compounded if the subject under surveillance is suspicious, which is often the case with paranoid drug dealers. This is the reason why basic surveillance practices and principles must be followed and implemented. Good judgment and common sense go a long way in the field of surveillance. Generally speaking, the more practice and experience an investigator has in surveillance operations, the more efficient and successful those operations will be.

Surveillance is an investigative technique that requires patience and perseverance from the investigator. Patience can be developed through practice and determination. Surveillance is a proven established investigative technique that an investigator utilizes to develop additional pertinent information to proceed with an investigation. It is one of the most valuable investigative measures that a criminal investigator can develop and use, if done correctly.

The *American Heritage Dictionary of the English Language* defines "surveillance" as the close observation of a person or group, especially of one under suspicion. In a concise law enforcement context, it simply refers to watching the bad guy without the bad guy knowing you are doing so. In a sense, the surveillance team must appear as if they are invisible to the suspect or target being observed. Maintaining this cloak of invisibility in a surveillance operation can be very difficult. Many drug violators are extremely street smart and conscious of surveillance; as a result, they are constantly looking around for indicators of police surveillance.

There are a number of terms used by surveillance members that should be defined here. The *suspect* or *target* is the person being observed. The *surveillant* is the person doing the observing. *Burned* is a term used to indicate that the surveillance has been recognized by the suspect or target. *Eye-ball* or simply *eye* refers to the law enforcement agent or officer who is the closest observer to the suspect or target. *Tail* refers to a surveillance agent or officer. *Trip* means to travel from one location to another. *Loose* refers to maintaining a discreet distance between the target and the closest surveillant. *Tight* refers to maintaining a close distance between the target and the closest law enforcement tail. A *neutral vehicle* is a non-law enforcement vehicle. A *take-away* refers to the intended direction in which a surveillance unit will follow the target.

Obviously, it is important that members of the surveillance team be in good physical condition in order to be effective. Surveillance assignments can often be very stressful and prolonged, extending over a long period of time. In addition, these assignments often occur under difficult conditions and in dangerous environments.

Surveillance team members need to be alert and have quick reflexes, keen perception, good judgment, and a good memory. Good driving skills are a must, along with keeping detailed chronological surveillance notes. All of these attributes come into play in a surveillance operation. It is very important for the team members to understand the significance of the target's actions and the relevancy of those actions in the context of the overall investigation. In many cases, though, this is not discerned until later on in the investigation. This is why it is important to keep complete and accurate notes of all details and facts during an ongoing surveillance operation.

The details and facts recorded by the surveillance officer become the basis for the content of the subsequent surveillance report, which is submitted as part of the overall investigative case file. A simple factual observance by a surveillance team member might not seem to be significant at the time, but it can be a vital bit of key information later in the investigation. It is futile to conduct a lengthy intense surveillance operation and not be able to remember important details because you forgot to take notes.

The proper attitude toward surveillance is critical. All members of the surveillance team should understand the reasons for and objectives of the surveillance assignment. This in itself is often all that is required to establish the proper attitude or mindset within the surveillance team. A surveillance operation can often be mentally and physically demanding on all members of the team as a result of long hours and little sleep. A surveillance assignment can last hours, days, weeks, or even months depending on the level and complexity of the investigation. As a result, it is crucial that all members of the team be thoroughly briefed by the supervisor and surveillance leader prior to conducting the surveillance. All members of the team should be provided with relevant target information, including physical descriptions, vehicle descriptions, aliases, criminal history, telephone numbers, license numbers, girlfriend addresses, criminal associate addresses, and photographs of the intended targets and associates. Intelligence information on a target's daily routine, individual habits, and interests should be addressed in the briefing. This information can be invaluable during a surveillance operation, especially if the team loses the target during the surveillance and needs to reestablish contact with the target. Generally speaking, the more information the team has about the target, the better the chances of success. It is important to remember that a moving surveillance can at times be compared to a fast and furious roller coaster ride. Once the operation begins, you never know when and where it will end. Members of the surveillance team are frequently confronted with unexpected conditions in the field, and the situation can change instantly. The surveillance team should always anticipate the unexpected and be prepared for the worst.

All members of the surveillance team should be equipped with the basic equipment necessary to conduct the surveillance. Some of the items and basic equipment include binoculars, maps, notepads, portable radio, extra batteries, cellular phone, GPS if available, extra clothing, and an overnight bag. In addition, the surveillance team members should all have their vehicle fuel tanks topped off. All of the vehicles should be in good working order, and the surveillance team members should always try to plan for the unexpected in any surveillance operation. Many times, the target has unexpectedly ended up driving a long distance and the surveillance team was caught off guard, assuming the subject was only running a short errand in the neighborhood. As a result, the surveillance team needs to plan ahead to be prepared for any contingency. It should be noted that prior planning can prevent or minimize many of the possible problems.

A reconnaissance of the intended area where the surveillance will begin is a vital first step in initiating a successful surveillance. This could be the target's residence, a stash house, a girlfriend's apartment, or the target's place of business. The surveillance team leader or designee should note the type of area, safety and security concerns, traffic patterns, dead-end streets, road construction, location of street lights, street names and directions, access highways, and, most importantly, good observation locations or vantage points in the immediate area. Important vantage points could be parking lots, roofs of parking garages, vacant apartments, offices, and houses. In addition, the surveillance team leader should obtain photographs of the location and the subject's vehicle, along with a sketch of the location. After this information is obtained, surveillance personnel will be better informed on how best to initiate the surveillance.

All enforcement personnel involved in the upcoming surveillance operation should be briefed and provided with all of the relevant intelligence information on the target. All equipment should be checked for proper functioning prior to departure of the team. A primary and secondary communication channel should be established in the event that a second target is developed during the surveillance, requiring dividing the surveillance team into two groups. Designated surveillance team leaders should be established prior to the surveillance operation. Some neighborhoods or locations are extremely difficult to establish surveillance in without being burned by the bad guys; therefore, to establish a covert eyeball on the target subject, it may be necessary to position a surveillance van or undercover surveillance officer on foot some distance from the target. Other ways to avoid detection would be to use various ruses; for example, a surveillance officer could feign engine trouble or could pretend to be a service repairman or maintenance worker on a job in the area. Ruse techniques are limited only by one's imagination and ability, but they may require some props to be convincing.

During night-time surveillance activities, it is important to wear dark clothing and stay out of brightly lit areas. The surveillance member, who has the eyeball, is responsible for notifying the other surveillance units when the target moves and the target's direction of travel. The surveillance member who establishes the initial eyeball in this case would not immediately be involved in the moving surveillance. In some cases, a surveillance unit will be assigned to maintain a fixed surveillance position on a given target area and will not be part of the mobile surveillance. This technique can be utilized in a number of target locations, depending on the manpower resources available. It is especially effective when the target travels or returns to an area that is extremely difficult to follow, such as a dead-end street or a long rural road leading to the target's residence. Once the target is on the move, the remaining surveillance units, which were originally pre-positioned in strategic take-away locations, are free to engage in the surveillance operation. They should key off of the surveillance leader's instructions, but if no instructions are forthcoming in a timely manner, the closest surveillance unit will take the point and the eyeball. The remaining units will establish positions to the rear of the point vehicle appropriately spaced at varying distances, depending on traffic conditions and the time of day or night.

Some surveillance units may also parallel the target vehicle on nearby streets. It is the responsibility of the lead or point surveillance unit to call out the location, direction of travel, lane of travel, and speed of the target vehicle. This information must be relayed to the other units in the surveillance team on a fairly frequent basis. The other members of the surveillance team should not have to ask the location of the target vehicle in a mobile surveillance if the lead surveillance unit is properly calling out the target vehicle location. Also, it is not necessary for the other surveillance team members to transmit their location during the surveillance operation. The lead surveillance unit should have radio communications priority, and surveillance team members should keep radio communications to a minimum. All members of the surveillance team should be aware of the approximate location of the target at all times. To avoid detection, the lead surveillance unit must rotate the lead or eyeball position periodically with other surveillance units, usually beginning with the number two unit in the surveillance caravan. If the number two surveillance unit is not able to immediately pick up the target vehicle and establish contact, then the lead or point vehicle should never relinquish the eyeball and risk compromising the entire surveillance operation by losing the target. For this reason, the change in the lead vehicle must be delayed until the number two vehicle or a substitute surveillance vehicle can come up and assume the point position. A good example of this would be when the target vehicle makes it through an intersection but the second vehicle is too far away to do so.

Timing is everything in this process, and when to change the eyeball is based on common sense, experience, and the immediate circumstances. The important thing to remember is that the eyeball or point position must be changed frequently in any successful surveillance operation; otherwise, the surveillance-conscious target will burn the surveillance operation. Visual contact must be maintained with the target vehicle until the number two surveillance vehicle is in a position to assume the number one position and take the point.

During a mobile surveillance, the target vehicle may turn either left or right or make a U-turn in the middle of the street. Some of these turns may be legal, others not. The illegal turns may be used for the specific reason of detecting or losing a surveillance tail. If the corresponding surveillance units follow the target and make such a turn, there is a good chance the target will realize that he or she is under surveillance. A wise rule of thumb in these types of cases is that, when the target vehicle turns, the lead vehicle continues straight ahead. This practice should be followed whenever possible. The number two vehicle or another surveillance vehicle would be responsible for establishing the eyeball. If the target makes a U-turn, the lead vehicle needs to continue straight ahead and immediately notify the other units of the target's evasive actions. The rear surveillance units could pull off the road, out of sight of the target vehicle, and be set up to intercept the target in the opposite direction. If the target vehicle stops beyond a hill or curve in the road, the point vehicle should notify the number two vehicle of the target's status and simply drive past the stationary target vehicle. If possible, the number two vehicle should stop before arriving at that location and the observer from the number two vehicle should exit the vehicle to get a visual on the target. Additionally, the point vehicle should also stop out of view of the target vehicle and have the observer exit the vehicle to determine what the target is doing.

In a moving surveillance, it is also important to have at least one neutral cover vehicle between the target vehicle and the closest surveillance vehicle. In many cases, the number of cover vehicles may vary considerably due, for example, to changing traffic conditions. The more cover vehicles, the less chance the bad guy is going to burn the surveillance. If there are too many cover vehicles between the target vehicle and the lead vehicle, the chance of losing the target increases. This is always a concern of surveillance team members. Generally speaking, one or two cover vehicles in heavy traffic would suffice, but more would be suitable on an open highway. This is where experience comes into play.

The distance between the vehicles may change frequently due to visibility, weather, and traffic conditions. The most likely times the target vehicle will attempt an evasive burn maneuver is upon leaving the initial location with contraband or upon arriving at the intended destination with an illegal substance. Surveillance activity is most crucial at these times. Be aware, though, that this does not preclude the suspect from randomly pulling off the highway onto the shoulder to determine if anyone is tailing him or her. This is not uncommon for experienced drug traffickers; it is simply a matter of habit.

One other important factor to always consider in any field surveillance operation is countersurveillance measures taken by the bad guys against law enforcement. Suspects involved in illegal drug trafficking have become more aggressive and violent over the years. As a result, these drug traffickers and drug trafficking organizations use some of the same surveillance methods and techniques against law enforcement officers that are being utilized against them. All surveillance personnel should be advised of the possibility of countersurveillance measures by the target and take the necessary precautions for their safety and the safety of the surveillance team. This is especially crucial after the surveillance is terminated and the surveillance team is returning to their offsite office or residence. Subsequent to the surveillance operation, the surveillance team leader or supervisor should conduct a surveillance team meeting to compare notes and discuss various aspects of the surveillance with fellow surveillance team participants in order to get a comprehensive overview of the target's activities for the final surveillance report. It is also important for the surveillance team to objectively critique their operation and make the appropriate and necessary changes in the future. There is always room for improvement in the surveillance process.

It is important to understand that there are many things to remember when conducting a moving vehicular surveillance. First and foremost, all of the surveillance vehicles should be in good mechanical condition and suited for the surveillance assignment. Brightly colored vehicles tend to stand out and are more likely to be noticed by the target than neutral-colored vehicles. The vehicles should fit the area and be as inconspicuous as possible. None of the contents of the vehicles, such as emergency lights, handcuffs, official papers, or police-related equipment, should be in view. If the vehicle is parked in a residential area, it is important to keep the police radio volume turned down low and the windows in the upright position. Many good surveillance operations have been burned by neglecting to do so.

A surveillance vehicle occupied by two officers has a number of advantages over a one-officer surveillance unit. In a two-officer unit, the observer checks locations on the map, takes detailed surveillance notes, and operates the radio. It is best if the driver can concentrate fully on operating the vehicle. The observer also has the option of exiting the surveillance vehicle for foot surveillance or to seek a better vantage point to observe the activities of the target. It is vital that the second officer maintain communications with the driver and surveillance units during this period and to keep a low profile. Additionally, if the surveillance is prolonged over an extended period of time or distance, the second officer can relieve the driver for some needed rest. Remember, it is very important to maintain surveillance eyes on the bad guy from start to finish; otherwise, key information may be missed.

Many unexpected problems and situations can develop during a foot and vehicle surveillance. Many of these problems and situations require a quick decision to be made by the surveillance team. Following are some common problems encountered and possible solutions: If the subject enters a restaurant for a meal or meeting, one or preferably two surveillance officers should enter the restaurant and take a seat near the subject, depending on the number of customers in the establishment. The surveillance officers should position themselves to the rear of the subject so the subject is not facing them directly and should try to overhear the target's conversation. If the subject meets with a second individual, it is very important to later identify that person and obtain a surveillance photograph. Particular attention should be given to any exchange of items such as a key, package, envelope, paper sack, cell phone, or briefcase. In addition, the surveillance team needs to try to identify the second subject's vehicle. The remaining surveillance units should be positioned to cover the exits of the restaurant and all routes of departure from the location. Depending on the developing circumstances at the time and the significance of the second subject, the surveillance team may have to divide into two teams to cover both subjects upon their departure from the location. This, of course, would only be necessary if they depart the meeting location in different directions.

In another scenario, the target subject might enter a movie theater, sporting event, casino, race track, or other public place. In this case, surveillance should be maintained on the subject's vehicle, and a number of surveillance officers should enter the public place to determine if the subject meets with anyone to make an exchange. As previously mentioned, the surveillance officers should try to identify the second subject and determine if any type of exchange occurred. It is important to have adequate surveillance units on the subject's parked vehicle in case the subject suddenly returns to his vehicle and quickly departs. Some very sophisticated criminals like to use decoys during the critical phases of their drug-dealing activities. This usually involves a criminal associate or unwitting subject driving the main target vehicle or a similar decoy vehicle prior to the drug transaction. As a result, the surveillance units mistakenly follow the wrong vehicle from the surveillance area, and the correct target drives off in another direction free of surveillance to do a drug transaction.

The surveillance team needs to be alert at all times and take nothing for granted during an active surveillance. If there is any doubt about the correct target vehicle and occupants, the surveillance team should visually verify that they are following the correct vehicle. Additionally, these drug criminals have been known to utilize surveillance detection methods or evasive tactics such as driving the wrong way down a one-way street, driving down a dead-end street or alley, suddenly stopping in the street, conducting erratic U-turns, or simply pulling over on the shoulder of the highway at night and turning their lights out. The surveillance team members should be aware of all of the detection and evasive methods used by the drug violators and plan accordingly; however, they must not automatically assume that all detection and evasive actions by the bad guys are indications that the surveillance has been compromised or burned. Some seasoned drug dealers routinely, almost out of habit, drive erratically and evasively due to their constant state of paranoia. If the covert surveillance team is certain that they have been compromised, though, then the surveillance operation must be terminated and continued at a later time.

When the surveillance team is operating in an unfamiliar geographic area, it is acceptable to use landmarks as points of reference instead of street names. Landmarks can be buildings, bridges, railroad tracks, or places of business. Landmark reference points are also frequently utilized in aerial surveillance. Aerial surveillance capability is a luxury not all departments can afford, but if your department or agency has access to an aircraft your success at physical surveillance is greatly increased. A small fixed-wing aircraft or helicopter is an excellent aerial surveillance tool. Each type of aircraft has its advantages and disadvantages; however, either will usually suffice. Normally, a helicopter generates a little more noise than a fixed-wing aircraft, which becomes more of a factor when dealing with surveillance-conscious subjects. The main limitation of either type of aircraft is the length of time the aircraft can stay airborne before it has to refuel. It is good to have at least two individuals in the aircraft, one being an experienced pilot and the other an experienced observer who is familiar with the geographic area. As a result of having aerial surveillance, the ground surveillance units are less conspicuous and can follow the target vehicle from a much greater distance without fear of detection. The aircraft maintains the eyeball on the target vehicle and calls out the location, direction of travel, and approximate speed to the ground surveillance units. Another advantage of having this capability is the fact that the ground surveillance can consist of a fewer number of officers or agents. Aerial surveillance has a greater success rate, offers less chance of detection, and is more efficient than traditional ground surveillance. In dealing with sophisticated surveillance-conscious drug traffickers, it is the way to go.

A stationary surveillance can be a valuable investigative tool in any long-term narcotics investigation. This type of surveillance is reminiscent of the traditional police stake-outs portrayed in movies and on television. In reality, most stationary or static surveillances can be very boring and time consuming due to the long hours required and the mundane activities associated with this investigative endeavor. This type of surveillance can last days, weeks, or even months, depending on the level of investigative intelligence being obtained. If there is very little suspicious activity, it is difficult to try to stay alert and enthusiastic.

A protracted static surveillance will try the patience and endurance of both the neophyte and seasoned narcotics officer, although this type of surveillance can be especially rewarding and has its advantages, despite its difficulties. The stationary surveillance location must be suitable to observe significant illegal narcotics-related activity without being compromised or burned. The observation post may be in a small town, large metropolitan city, or remote rural area. It must provide the surveillance officers with a clear view of the subjects and the area to be observed. In addition, the entrance and exit routes to the observation post must offer the necessary safety and security for the surveillance personnel. The observation post can be a vacant apartment, house, motor home, or motel room. In rural areas, it simply might be a heavily wooded area or secluded rocky area providing cover for the covert observers. An operational safety plan must be prepared prior to any stationary surveillance deployment. It should address all of the requirements required of a mobile surveillance, and it should be on a need-to-know basis to minimize any inadvertent compromise of the operation. It should include observation post personnel assignments, relief assignments, equipment requirements, and observation post contact information. If it is at all possible, depending on the type of enforcement operation, it is a good practice to have a mobile surveillance team available in case the subject goes mobile. The ability to act naturally or blend into the environment unnoticed during a surveillance operation is a prized asset for any surveillance team. This is where training and experience pay off in preventing the surveillance team from being detected or burned by the target. The type of clothing, facial features, mannerisms, vehicles, and race all are factors that reflect on the appearance of the surveillance team. In order not to be compromised, the surveillance team must be able to go in stealth mode during critical phases of the surveillance operation. In many cases, this is easier said than done. The surveillance officer must not show any abnormal reaction to the target of the surveillance if the target comes close. This can be difficult because of the stress factor and the adrenaline rush. Regardless, any abnormal reaction can draw attention to the surveillance officer and jeopardize the entire surveillance operation. In other words, the surveillance officer must be cool, calm, and collected when a target is encountered up close. This is a key factor in achieving a successful surveillance outcome. The million-dollar question is how to accomplish this feat and not blow the operation.

It is important to avoid looking the target directly in the eye. Direct eye contact between two individuals under these circumstances often results in a form of nonverbal communication that the target will notice and cause him to take evasive action. The second thing to avoid is not to be overly self-conscious about being a law enforcement officer. This problem is easily solved if the surveillance officer is aware of it and consciously makes an effort not to be preoccupied with this thought while conducting surveillance. The surveillance officer should act or appear no different than anyone else in the area, and there should be nothing about the surveillance officer's physical appearance that reveals the purpose of the officer's presence in the area. These are points that neophyte surveillance officers need to continuously be reminded of until assuming the proper demeanor becomes second nature. It is a common problem for inexperienced surveillance officers to prematurely assume that they have been burned by the target, although in most circumstances this is not usually the case. If the surveillance has, in fact, been compromised, though, it should be terminate and resumed at a later date.

INFORMANTS

There is an old adage in the world of narcotics investigation that informants can be your greatest investigative asset as well as your greatest liability nightmare. This adage should be remembered and not forgotten when working with informants. The term *informant* can be construed as a derogatory term when used in the presence of an informant. It is recommended to avoid using such derogatory terms when in the presence of an informant, as doing so could be a sign of disrespect and could hamper the ability of the controlling law enforcement personnel to maintain a professional relationship. For these reasons, an informant is often referred to as a confidential informant (CI) or a confidential source (CS). A CI or CS is an individual operating under the specific direction of law enforcement authority with or without the expectation of compensation.

The informant provides information on drug traffickers or provides a lawful service pursuant to the investigation of drug-related criminal acts. A defendant informant is a person meeting the above criteria but is also subject to arrest and prosecution for a criminal offense. In other words, a criminal informant is a criminally focused person with a questionable sense of loyalty acting under conflicting motives for judicial consideration. Great care needs to be exercised by law enforcement when dealing with this type of person. For our purposes here, the title *informant* does not have the same meaning as *source of information* (SOI), which is a person or business not specifically working for any law enforcement official who occasionally furnishes information to law enforcement officials without compensation. The general classification of informants can basically be divided into the following categories: average citizen, law enforcement officers, troubled or disturbed persons, criminals, and criminal associates.

Like all people, informants must be motivated to perform and apply themselves to the objective or mission. Motivation is the psychological carrot that stimulates a person to action. Understanding the motivation of any type of informant is always important in obtaining the desired results. The more motivated an informant, the more likely the informant is committed to the overall success of the required objective or mission; however, the motivation of any type of informant, especially the criminal or criminal associate informant, should be scrutinized carefully in the establishment process.

Some of the motivations of a prospective informant include fear, revenge, financial gain, ego, repentance, and perverse disposition. The prospective informant might fear criminal associates or going to prison and thus decides to cooperate with law enforcement authorities. The potential informant may be jealous of his criminal associates or may be seeking revenge due to a botched drug transaction, or he may be driven by greed. Some potential informants are simply egotistical police buffs or wannabe cops, seeking excitement and police approval. The perverse informant will try to learn police undercover methods, identify undercover officers, and try to eliminate rival drug dealer competition. This type of informant is extremely dangerous and problematic and should be avoided if possible. The truly repentant informant seldom emerges, but many informants initially claim that this is their motivating factor. The ability to identify the real motivation of the informant will greatly increase an officer's ability to successfully manage the informant. The true motivational factor ultimately will prove to be the strongest incentive for the informant's actions. When the controlling officer fails to determine the actual motives of an informant, serious control problems will develop. Successful drug investigators must be able to recognize and develop productive informants. Informants have been recruited from a multitude of sources, including referrals from other officers and agencies, arrested subjects, police intelligence units, walk-ins, call-ins, and disgruntled girlfriends, spouses, and business partners. All documented informants should be considered assets of the law enforcement department or agency, not the individual law enforcement agent or officer. Thus, the informants should be accountable not only to the controlling agent or officer but also to the department or agency.

Informants can provide independent surveillance; conduct controlled undercover negotiations; conduct controlled undercover buys; testify in court; and gather vital drug-related intelligence information. When debriefing prospective informants, investigators should first and foremost always try to determine the motivation, reliability, and intelligence level of an informant; the informant's source of knowledge about the criminal activity; and any personal interests. In addition, drug investigators should try to determine if the informant has direct or indirect knowledge of the illegal activity, has a personal vendetta involving the drug violator, was ever previously an informant, or previously falsified information. This is not an all-inclusive list, but it does cover some of the major points that investigators must address with potential informants. The past reliability of the informant or prospective informant is very important for the controlling investigator to determine. If the person has a poor track record with another department or agency and has provided false or misleading information, it might be advisable not to establish the person as an informant. The controlling officer or agent needs to try to verify all of the important drug-related information that the potential informant provides and carefully document the facts. In dealing with informants, the drug investigator should be truthful, fair, tactful, and confident, and most importantly he must maintain control. The documented informant needs to be aware of the fact that he may be required to testify in court, although all lawful means will be used to protect the informant's confidentiality. If the controlling investigator cannot control the actions of the informant, serious problems can arise and the entire investigation could be compromised. Control is very important, and the controlling investigator must establish control early on in the relationship. A rogue informant can be the investigator's worst nightmare. This is where experience dealing with informants becomes important in avoiding some of the problem areas.

When interviewing or dealing with a prospective informant, it is advisable to always have at least two law enforcement agents or officers present. Once the informant is established, he should always be able to contact at least two controlling officers. The controlling agent or officer should never meet an informant alone. All contact with the informant involving establishment, debriefing, and use should be conducted in strict confidentiality. All the information concerning the informant should be on a need-to-know basis, and all documents and reports concerning the informant's identity should be kept in a secured, limited-access location. Failure to provide confidentiality regarding the informant's identity and status might result in death, injury, or intimidation of the informant and the informant's family. The informant should be advised not to violate any criminal law in furtherance of gathering intelligence information or providing services to the law enforcement agency. In addition, informants should have no official status, implied or otherwise, as law enforcement officers or employees. Meetings with the informant outside the office should be in neutral or low-profile locations. The duration of relationships between controlling law enforcement officials and informants can be a matter of weeks, months, or even years. This process can create a bonding relationship that may lead to the loss of objectivity if a number of safeguards are not followed. It is a good practice to document all procedures and agreements involving informants or confidential sources with a law enforcement witness and supervisory concurrence.

Prior to establishment of a confidential source, a detailed CS debriefing report, criminal history checks, CS statement, fingerprints, photographs, and CS agreement should be completed. It is always important to verify the true identity of your prospective CS before utilization. It would be very embarrassing if the CS was wanted in another jurisdiction or provided you with a false name. All contact with the CS after establishment should be of a professional nature and documented for the record. There should not be any social, financial, or business contacts outside of the job between the CS and the controlling officers.

Law enforcement officers should never place themselves in a vulnerable position with a CS such that potential allegations of wrongdoing could be alleged; an example would be paying a CS alone without a witness. The CS will be your friend only as long as it benefits the CS. As a result, investigators should never put themselves in a position to compromise their professional reputation, ethics, and integrity when dealing with a CS. It is strongly suggested that a controlling investigator never meet a CS alone in the field without benefit of backup. Always remember that confidential sources are not to be trusted, and their knowledge of law enforcement operations, activities, and personnel should be kept to the minimum necessary for their successful completion of the assigned mission. In addition, statements should always be obtained from a CS whenever the CS has contact with the targets of the investigation outside the presence of the controlling officers. During the initial stages of informant establishment and utilization, informants should clearly understand their role and their relationship with the controlling law enforcement agents or officers. The informants must thoroughly understand their role and specifically follow instructions; otherwise, problems can quickly develop. The controlling agent or officer has to always be conscious of the fact that the informant may try to manipulate or control the controlling agent or officer. One example would be when a CS decides to set up a drug deal on a specific day without first checking with the controlling agent or officer. This type of irresponsible action on the part of the CS is totally unacceptable and dangerous. It establishes a bad precedent and should be strongly opposed. In addition, all informant financial transactions should be clearly documented and always witnessed by a second law enforcement individual. Close supervision of an informant demonstrates that the informant is a valued asset not only to the controlling agents or officers but also to the department or agency.

If an individual was recently arrested and is a defendant in the investigation, the drug investigator should try to obtain the defendant's cooperation immediately after the subject's arrest. No promises regarding charges against the defendant should be made; however, if the defendant decides to cooperate with the law enforcement authorities, the defendant's cooperation will be made known to the prosecutor in the case. If the defendant decides to cooperate, a thorough debriefing should be conducted for all narcotics- and non-narcotics-related information as soon as possible.

Regardless of the information the subject provides, all information should be corroborated and verified through other sources. Subsequent to a drug arrest, time is of the essence; if the defendant agrees to cooperate, there is a good chance additional drugs and money can be seized, along with additional arrests of drug violators. Sometimes this can result from a simple controlled telephone call from the cooperating defendant to other criminal associates in the investigation.

A good informant is an extremely valuable tool in providing critical information to law enforcement authorities, especially if the informant is directed and controlled correctly. In many cases, the most successful informants are individuals who have inside knowledge about drug violators or their close criminal associates. These subjects can provide the narcotics investigator with vital inside information on a drug organization by detailing and describing the clandestine smuggling/transportation methods, load vehicles, storage facilities, distribution locations, and command/control structure.

The element of trust with the informant is very important and must be established prior to any field operational activity. Trust is usually developed over a period of time in small incremental steps; therefore, the investigator must convince the informant of the importance of trust and the benefits of cooperation. Once the CS is convinced to cooperate, the investigator needs to establish the ground rules for the informant's cooperation. The confidentiality of informants is always a main concern for the informant as well as the controlling agent or officer. The ability to protect the identity and safety of the informant is a major determining factor in the informant's cooperation.

In summary, the investigator needs to identify the potential informant, obtain the informant's cooperation, establish the informant, develop the informant for maximum performance, maintain the confidentiality of the informant, utilize the informant to maintain credibility, and, most importantly, control the informant. The controlling agent or officer should always be honest, respectful, and ethical when dealing with informants.

UNDERCOVER

Most successful narcotics investigations rely on undercover (U/C) operations to obtain vital intelligence, conduct seizures involving drug-related assets, and arrest drug violators. The undercover process is an investigative technique that has been extremely successful over the years in narcotics law enforcement operations. Undercover work is a complicated form of drug investigation in which the investigator assumes the role of another person to obtain information on the drug-related activities of the drug traffickers. As a result, the U/C agent or officer can glean considerable intelligence information, not only about the individual drug trafficker but also about the entire drug distribution organization. Such information includes sources of supply, locations of major stash houses, distribution methods, key distributors, quantities and quality of drugs, drug-related assets, smuggling routes, load vehicles, and security measures utilized by the drug traffickers. There is no limit to the amount of vital intelligence information an experienced U/C agent or officer can develop, once accepted by the criminal element. Being accepted by the criminal element, though, is the hard part, and it requires skill and knowledge of the inner workings of the criminal element.

The extent of the U/C process in part is related to the scope and magnitude of the criminal element under investigation. Obviously, it would make no sense to conduct a massive extended U/C drug investigation on a small street dealer unless intelligence information connected the street dealer to a much larger scale drug distributor or organization. Thus, the scope of a particular U/C assignment often depends on how significant and connected the drug violator is. The U/C process is often used when all other traditional investigative avenues have failed to produce results. If done correctly, the U/C investigative process can reduce investigative manhours and expenses during a drug investigation. The U/C process should be well thought out in advance by all of the law enforcement participants. The length of time involved in the U/C operation, the potential end results, the complexity of the criminal organization, the propensity for violence of the drug violators, and the difficulty of introducing an undercover agent or officer to the criminal targets should all be considered in the initial planning phases of the investigation.

The prospective U/C agent or officer should first and foremost want to do the U/C assignment. It is not advisable to pressure anyone into an U/C role. The success rate in an U/C assignment in part depends on the desire and motivation of the individual agent or officer. Undercover personnel must have self-confidence, adaptability, patience, good temperament, fortitude, and courage. In many cases, all of these qualities will be needed to successfully accomplish the U/C assignment. The U/C agent or officer needs to be a quick study at times and should be able to think quickly in potentially dangerous situations.

The ability to remain cool, calm, and collected is essential in any U/C assignment. There is a degree of excitement and adventure in undercover work, but it can also be very stressful and dangerous; therefore, the undercover agent's supervisor should first evaluate the strengths and weaknesses of any potential U/C investigator to determine if the individual is suited for the U/C assignment. When assessing the suitability for an U/C assignment, the stability and overall maturity of the agent or officer must be considered, along with any special skills and talents. It would be dangerous and foolish for any supervisor to do otherwise. In reality, a successful U/C investigator should have a high degree of dramatic proficiency and a good working knowledge of the criminal world of drug dealers to successfully play the role of a criminal drug trafficker. In essence, the U/C investigator is an actor in a real life drama, on the dangerous and deadly stage of reality in the often violent world of drug dealers. The U/C investigator needs to carefully study the script (the assignment), determine the background story, assume an identity, obtain intelligence information on the violator, and establish a method to contact the target. All of this should be completed prior to any contact with the intended target.

Criminals involved in drug dealing are by nature extremely secretive, suspicious, and paranoid. As a result, it may be extremely difficult for the U/C investigator to make contact with the intended criminal target. Many times, law enforcement authorities utilize an informant to set up an U/C introduction. The informant does not have to know that the individual to be introduced to the target is a U/C operative. The other option is to use a documented informant. Obviously, the utilization of a previously reliable documented informant would be a better approach, because of the control and reliability factors. In most cases, if the informant has a trusting relationship with the target and vouches for the U/C investigator, the target will accept and be willing to do business with that person. If no informants are available, another possible approach would be for the U/C investigator to frequent places the target is known to visit in an attempt to contact the target under a ruse. This procedure requires considerable experience, a little luck, and a lot of careful planning. It is known as a *cold hit* and is more difficult to execute. It is usually done as a last-ditch effort when all previous attempts have failed.

The higher the level of drug violator, the more preparation and effort should be exercised. The propensity for violence should always be a critical factor in evaluating the undercover initiative, regardless of the amount of drugs being distributed. First and foremost, the safety of the U/C operative should be paramount in any U/C operation. The U/C investigator should try to learn as much about the target suspect as possible, including character, criminal history, history of violence, business assets, hobbies, likes and dislikes, girlfriends, favorite hangouts, and criminal associates. The more knowledge the U/C investigator has about the target, the better the agent will be equipped to deal with unexpected developments that may pop up. The other major concern is to establish a fictitious background and corresponding personal history for the U/C investigator that will pass scrutiny from a canny drug violator. The cover story and fictitious identity should have some element of truth to make them believable. If the cover story indicates that the U/C investigator is from Chicago, then it would be advisable for the agent to be familiar with that particular city and able to discuss various aspects of the area with the target. If the U/C investigator is going undercover as a laborer, it would be advisable for the agent to have some direct experience in that field of employment in case the target questions the agent about his skills. The role should fit the investigator's personality, physical characteristics, and background experience. Race, sex, language, dialect, mannerism, type of clothing, and drug knowledge can all be important factors contributing to whether or not the U/C investigator will be accepted and successful in the assignment.

Normally, the cover story does not need to be too lengthy or elaborate. In fact, it is better to keep the cover story short and simple. The less information the U/C investigator has to remember, the less chance of making a mistake in a stressful situation. In some shorter investigations, the background story may involve only a few simple facts. In other cases, if the assignment could potentially develop into a long-term investigation that requires close association with the criminal target, the cover story should be carefully planned and include specific detailed information, methods of verification, and documentary support evidence. In addition, if the U/C investigator utilizes a documented informant, the agent and the informant need to carefully rehearse the cover story prior to contact with the intended target (e.g., when and where they met, how long they have known each other). Often, the criminal target will subtly interrogate the informant and U/C investigator to check for any discrepancies in the cover story; therefore, it is very critical for the investigator and informant to be on the same page when meeting with the target. The informant literally holds the life of the U/C investigator in his or her hands.

A good informant can save time, money, and effort in making a solid contact with the target drug violator; yet, a simple mistake made by an informant can also endanger the entire operation. In order not to compromise the cover story, U/C investigators should remove all evidence of their law enforcement status prior to contacting criminal targets. This includes removing all traces of law enforcement equipment from the investigator's vehicle. A search of the investigator's vehicle should always be made prior to the undercover meet. This also applies to any alternative meet locations, such as motel rooms, apartments, or residences. A criminal target or associate may actually do a cursory search of a motel room, apartment, or residence before discussing business.

If the U/C investigator is planning on contacting the target through the use of a documented informant (CS), it would be advisable to understand the informant's motivation and prior reliability. The cover story is only as strong as its weakest link, and in many cases the weakest link is the informant. All bases must be covered with the informant prior to the U/C meeting. Informants must be advised on legal entrapment issues and made aware of the fact that they may be required to testify in a court of law in the case. Any U/C investigator who feels uncomfortable or uncertain about the motivation or sincerity of an informant should make those concerns known to their supervisors prior to the operation. All concerns involving the safety and security of the entire U/C operation need to be addressed prior to initiation of the field operation. Once all of the preliminary target intelligence information, cover story, and U/C background history are developed, it is time to make plans for an undercover meeting with the intended target.

UNDERCOVER PURCHASE

The undercover purchase of narcotics is one of the most complex and dangerous activities encountered by law enforcement authorities in today's violent world of drug trafficking; therefore, it is very important for law enforcement authorities to take all the necessary precautions and safety measures into consideration when planning and implementing an operational safety plan involving an undercover meeting or purchase. The U/C meeting is between the U/C investigator and the suspect for the purposes of negotiating the future sale of an illegal substance.

At the meeting, the quantity of narcotics, purchase price, and location of the narcotics transaction are usually discussed. The U/C investigator must try to establish some control over the terms of the future U/C purchase. The investigator must play the role of a criminal, and in essence think like a criminal when negotiating with the target. If the investigator is too easy and agrees to the initial sale price without a little haggling, a wise drug dealer will become suspicious. The price, amount, and location of the drug transaction are always negotiable. In the initial undercover meeting, much can be learned about the suspect from surveillance such as additional addresses, vehicles, potential stash houses, and criminal associates. In an undercover purchase, illegal narcotics are purchased from a known suspect or target by either an undercover agent or officer or a documented informant (CS). For prosecution purposes it is always better to have an undercover investigator purchasing the drugs than a CS. The credibility of the CS is always a concern in court; however, in many cases this is not possible so a CS is utilized to make the controlled undercover purchase. In essence, purchases made by a CS and those made by an undercover investigator are similar, but with a few exceptions. First and foremost, the CS must always be thoroughly searched along with his vehicle prior to the U/C purchase and subsequent to the U/C purchase. In addition, surveillance should always be maintained on the CS from the beginning to the completion of the transaction. This should all be documented in the relevant case reports. Regardless of who makes the undercover purchase, all of the necessary security and safety precautions need to be taken.

The two basic scenarios in an undercover purchase are the *buy–walk* and the *buy–bust*. In a buy–walk, the suspect or target is arrested at a later date after selling illegal drugs to the undercover. One obvious advantage of this is the fact that the identity of the undercover investigator or CS is not compromised at the time of arrest, and surveillance is maintained on the target to obtain additional information about the target. Several small undercover buy–walk purchases may be made before the target is arrested. This process usually helps build a stronger criminal case and results in a larger quantity of drugs being seized.

In a buy–bust, the target is arrested at the time of the narcotics sale. The location and manner in which the target is arrested should be carefully planned. Crossfire issues, officer safety, and public safety should all be addressed in the operational safety plan. One advantage in this scenario is the fact that the undercover investigator does not have to give up the buy money. There are several other advantages and disadvantages, depending on the particular case and the law enforcement resources available. A small police department that has a limited budget for the U/C purchases of narcotics is limited in the amount, type, and quantity of illegal drugs it can purchase. In addition, the limited resources may hamper the drug investigator's use of a *flash roll*, which is money shown to the drug dealer to convince the dealer to make the drug sale. Whenever a flash roll is to be used, extreme caution should be exercised to prevent theft of the money by the criminal element. The flash-roll should always be a surprise to the drug trafficker to reduce the risk of such rip-offs. Once the money is shown, it should be removed quickly to an undisclosed secure location.

There are some basic guidelines in narcotics work that are not set in concrete but would be wise to follow. One of these is never front the buy money to the drug dealer; in other words, do not give the drug dealer your money before you receive the drugs. This is a bad idea for many reasons; for example, you may lose the money and you may never see the drug dealer again. It is important to make a list or to photocopy the buy money and include it in the case file. This provides a way to identify the money at a later date. It is also a wise practice not to travel with the drug dealer to get the drugs. This raises major safety concerns for the surveillance cover team and should be avoided whenever possible. It is also a good practice not to do the drug deal in a location that is difficult for the surveillance cover team to observe or reach in case there is a safety problem; for example, inside a heavily fortified crack house with burglar bars and reinforced steel doors would not be a good choice.

The safety and security of the U/C investigator should always be the highest priority in an undercover operation. It is no secret that law enforcement personnel have been killed during robberies or rip-offs by violent drug dealers. This is the reason why the undercover investigator should carefully scrutinize the suspect's criminal background and potential for violence, such as robbery, assault, or murder. The drug dealer's level of drug distribution is also very important to analyze before an undercover transaction occurs to minimize the chance of the undercover investigator purchasing sham or "turkey dope." If the intelligence information and criminal history indicate that the targeted suspect only deals in ounces of cocaine and the informant indicates the suspect wants to sell several kilograms of cocaine for a great price, the warning signs should be flashing in big red letters for a potential rip-off. It is very important to do your investigative homework on the background of the suspected drug trafficker and establish whether or not the individual is a *bona fide* drug dealer or simply someone trying to pull a rip-off.

OPERATIONAL SAFETY PLAN

Prior to any U/C operation, whether it is a simple buy–bust or a buy–walk, a detailed operational safety plan should be formulated by the case agent or officer. All members involved in the U/C buy operation should be thoroughly briefed prior to the field operation and provided with a copy of the plan. The U/C operation must maintain a low profile where the deal is scheduled to take place to avoid being detected by the criminal element. This is absolutely essential for the overall success of the operation as well as for the personal safety of the U/C personnel.

The operational safety plan should be well thought out and carefully reviewed and approved by supervisory personnel prior to the undercover operation. The operational safety plan is usually the responsibility of the designated case agent or officer, but many times the entire narcotics unit will be involved in formulating plans for the operation. In essence, everyone has a dog in the hunt and, therefore, a voice in determining what the game plan will be. Many departments and agencies have a designated form that covers all of the required information, which should be provided in the operational safety plan. This is good practice, because such forms minimize the chances of forgetting to include important information. The operational safety plan is designed to be an operational guide for all participating parties and should be used as a road map for what to expect in the U/C operation or any enforcement action. The plan should address some alternative courses of action depending on the circumstances and should have some reasonable flexibility built into it. Many factors contribute to changes arising in a pending U/C narcotics buy. Some are under the control of law enforcement, others are not. Changes should only be made if they do not compromise the safety of the U/C personnel and if everyone can be advised of the changes.

The operational safety plan should provide a brief background of the investigation and note what is to take place, such as surveillance, U/C buy–walk, U/C buy–bust, arrest, search warrant, or a clan lab operation. The plan should indicate the person who has the money list, the amount of the flash roll, and the purchase price of the drugs. The operational plan should include the date, time, and location of the operation; specific details of the enforcement plan, such as meet location, locations to be searched, and subjects to be arrested; a basic sketch or map of the site; any photographs of target suspects; and a brief narrative of the mission instructions.

The radio communication channels should be designated along with an alternative channel. All contact cell phone information for undercover personnel should be listed, including vehicle descriptions and license numbers. The same information must also be included if the operation involves a CS. The agents assigned to monitor the body wire (kel) should be listed along with the radio channel. In addition, verbal and visual arrest signals and a danger or distress signal should be incorporated into the operational plan. It is extremely important for all law enforcement personnel involved in the operation to be familiar with these signals. All of the criminal subject's identifying information should be incorporated in the plan, including specific information on vehicles, primary or alternative address, and criminal history. A list of all personnel assisting with the operation with corresponding radio call signs, cell phone numbers, vehicle descriptions, and assignment should also be included in the plan. It is also a good practice to include the name, address, and phone number of the closest hospital or trauma unit in case there is a medical emergency. Also, the police jurisdictions involved should be indicated in the plan; because a drug deal can overlap various police jurisdictions, it is a good practice to coordinate your law enforcement activities.

Finally, a checklist at the end of the operational safety plan should include the following items: operational plan provided to communication center, communications check, cross-check, portable radios, body wire receiver check, surveillance assignments, entry tools, raid jackets/protective gear, and operational safety briefing. It is good practice to perform a cross-check with other law enforcement departments and agencies to determine if they are running any U/C operations in the area. It would be very embarrassing and dangerous for all parties if the U/C buy unknowingly involved two law enforcement departments or agencies.

Subsequent to the U/C purchase at a predetermined location, the U/C investigator should meet with other members of the surveillance team and the field supervisor to secure the drug evidence, perform a field test on the drug evidence, and obtain a quick briefing from the U/C investigator on pertinent details of the transaction. This is always a good idea, especially if the body-wire transmitter was malfunctioning and time-sensitive information must be acted on. It is also advisable for surveillance to be maintained on the suspect target after the U/C drug transaction in order to determine where the suspect travels. It is not unusual for the suspect to "trip" with the buy money to the drug supplier or a "stash" house where money and drugs are kept. It is always a good practice in drug-related investigations to follow the money. This will ultimately lead to the next level in the drug distribution hierarchy.

A thorough debriefing of all the participants involved in the U/C operation should be conducted after the operation has been completed. This can be a very productive time in the investigative process, because many of the pieces of the puzzle involving the prior U/C purchase can be gathered from all of the participating members. As a result, a complete picture of the transpired U/C event emerges. The documented times of individual observations and what was observed are crucial in preparing an accurate and detailed surveillance report to corroborate the U/C purchase. Descriptions of people, vehicles, and events connected to the U/C deal are also very important, along with any surveillance photographs or video evidence. Any U/C tape recording of the drug transaction is a key piece of evidence and should be properly labeled, dated, and marked as evidence with an exhibit number.

All evidence obtained should be clearly marked, labeled, and witnessed prior to submission to the evidence custodian. The evidence should always be documented in an acquisition report to indicate who acquired the evidence, where it was acquired, and who witnessed the acquisition. There should always be a paper trail or chain of custody for the evidence, and all the necessary documentation should be included in the investigative case file. The U/C report should also document the U/C purchase and provide the necessary facts surrounding the drug purchase. This should reflect the type and quantity of drug purchased, the location, and total price paid for the drug, along with the identity of the seller. It is also advisable to document the fact that a presumptive drug field test was conducted on the illicit drug and indicate the results in the relevant investigative report. Accurate and concise documentation is very important in any narcotics investigation. All of the hard work and long hours in the field can be worthless unless proper documentation is generated to memorialize the events, activities, and enforcement actions in the field.

QUESTIONS FOR DISCUSSION

1. What is the first step to initiating a narcotics investigation? Discuss some of the common problems associated with initiating a narcotics investigation.
2. Discuss some of the potential benefits of surveillance and the possible dangers associated with street surveillance operations.
3. List some drugs of abuse and their qualities.
4. Discuss the role of the informant in a narcotics investigation and some of the law enforcement concerns associated with working informants.
5. Discuss some of the motivating factors for informants.
6. What is the most important thing to remember when dealing with informants and why?
7. Discuss the importance of an operational safety plan and what is involved in its preparation and execution.
8. Discuss some of the personal and psychological qualities of a good undercover investigator.
9. Discuss the importance of good documentation and evidence handling in a narcotics case.
10. Discuss the importance of maintaining a good working relationship with the prosecutor.

CHAPTER 17

Cybercrime

Mark R. McCoy
University of Central Oklahoma

CHAPTER OBJECTIVES

After reading this chapter, you should be able to do the following:

1. Describe the nature of cybercrime and the various types of offenses committed in cyberspace.
2. Define cybercrime.
3. Explain the various roles digital devices play in cybercrimes.
4. Understand the different profiles of cybercrime offenders.
5. Comprehend the unique legal aspects of cybercrime investigations.
6. Explain how to collect evidence and preserve digital evidence.
7. Describe the key aspects of a cybercrime investigation.

Chapter Outline

- Introduction to Cybercrime
- Cybercrime Classifications
- Cybercrime Offenders
- The Digital Crime Scene

INTRODUCTION TO CYBERCRIME

Changes in technology have resulted in corresponding changes in the way crime is committed. Computer crime was rare 30 years ago, but rapid advances in technology, the advent of the personal computer, and easy access to the Internet have changed the way crimes are committed and thus the way they are investigated. People use computers and handheld digital devices every day to read e-mail, access the news, prepare reports, communicate with each other, analyze data, or prepare graphic information. Access to the Internet is becoming more accessible due to open Wi-Fi hotspots and easy access to broadband services. The U.S.

Census Bureau reported that in 2007 61.7% of households had Internet access, and of those 50.8% of the access was by means of high-speed broadband connections. The development and growing popularity of affordable personal computers, netbooks, smart phones, and tablet computers are presenting law enforcement with the growing challenge of computer crime and abuse. The use of computer systems for all types of activities, both business and personal, continues to grow, and the intricacy of these systems and our growing reliance on them are increasing the risk of organizations having their systems compromised by both intentional and unintentional acts (Haugen and Selin, 1999). Computer crime is a global law enforcement problem. Domestic attempts to address the problem are insufficient because cyberspace itself has no geographic or political boundaries. Countless computer systems can be simply and surreptitiously accessed through the global telecommunications network from anywhere in the world (Power, 2000). Today, terrorists and everyday criminals have the aptitude to detonate explosives in another country by means of computers, to bounce radio signals off satellites, and to disrupt computer systems controlling a country's infrastructure. Because the emerging information superhighway is without borders, computer malware and other destructive programs can be targeted at businesses or government organizations from anywhere in the world (Gene, 1995). No state possesses defensible borders when the threat is related to high technology, telecommunications, and cyberspace. The 21st century will bring greater technological innovation, as well as a legal and law enforcement community desperately battling to stay ahead of the cyberspace criminal (Krauss, 1997).

DEFINITION OF CYBERCRIME

It is difficult, at best, to come to an agreement about the definition of cybercrime. State and federal criminal statutes differ in how computer crime is defined. Britz (2004) provided some guidance: "Computer crime has been traditionally defined as any criminal act committed via computer. Cybercrime has traditionally encompassed abuses and misuses of computer systems which result in direct and/or concomitant losses" (p. 4). For the purposes of this chapter, we will define cybercrime as encompassing both of these definitions.

THE EXTENT OF CYBERCRIME LOSSES

Only a small portion of what we might call traditional computer crimes (e.g., network intrusions, computer viruses) come to the attention of the law enforcement authorities; however, many traditional crimes are now committed over computer networks and with digital devices, and these come to the attention of law enforcement on a daily basis. Although it is feasible to give an accurate description of the various types of computer offenses committed, the difficulty arises when we attempt to give an accurate overview of the extent of losses due to computer crime and the actual number of criminal offenses. The number of verifiable computer crimes is not as high as reliable estimates indicate it should be. In the results of their Computer Crime and Security survey, the Computer Security Institute (CSI, 2009) reported that the average loss per business responding to the survey from a security incident was $234,244 per year. The Uniform Crime Report (UCR) does not track traditional computer crimes or those involving the Internet and computer networks. Law enforcement officials indicate that, from their experience, recorded computer crime statistics do not represent the actual number of offenses. Experience shows that the use of sophisticated technology can actually be used to conceal a computer crime. The massive but compact storage potential of computers and the speed at which computers function ensure that computer crime is very difficult to detect, thus making it equally difficult to investigate. Investigators often do not have sufficient training to deal with crimes committed using computers or computer networks even if they involve a traditional offense such as fraud or threats. Many victims do not have a contingency plan for responding to incidents of computer crime, and they may even fail to acknowledge that a security problem exists, thus causing an underreporting of offenses.

CYBERCRIME CLASSIFICATIONS

COMPUTER AS TARGET OF CRIME

When the computer is the target, the intent of the offender is either to take information from the computer or to intentionally damage hardware, programs, or data files. Either way the offender must obtain unauthorized access to stored data using a network intrusion (hacking or cracking), social engineering, or unauthorized direct access to the computer. According to Carter and Katz (1997), these types of offenses may include the theft of intellectual property, the destruction of data, or the unlawful access to or tampering with personal, business, or government records. A national study of corporate security directors was conducted to discover the degree to which they were affected by computer crime and to identify some of the critical issues that will most likely be facing policymakers in the future. The survey found that theft was the fastest growing computer-related crime. Respondents reported that thieves most frequently targeted intellectual property, including such things as new product plans, new product descriptions, research, marketing plans, prospective customer lists, and similar information. When unauthorized access to computer networks and computers has been discovered, it is sometimes difficult to ascertain whether a law was broken, a company policy violated, or an ethical standard breached, or if the behavior simply stemmed from poor judgment (Carter and Katz, 1997). Techno vandalism is another form of computer crime that targets computers. It occurs when the unauthorized access of a computer results in damage to files or programs. Much of the techno vandalism is performed for the challenge and bragging rights rather than for profit. In these cases, the damage or loss may be either intentional or accidental (Parker, 1998). Another area involving computers as the target of crime is "hactivism." This is the practice of hacking into the website of a person, group, government, organization, or business to advocate some particular cause or political agenda. On February 7, 2000, the website of Yahoo!® was subjected to a hactivist attack that removed the site from the Internet for several hours. It was a wakeup call for everyone to discover that a website as prominent as Yahoo! could be breached and taken offline. Investigators are going to face many new and highly technical challenges when called upon to investigate crimes in which a computer or computer network is the target of the criminal activity.

COMPUTER AS INSTRUMENT OF CRIME

Some of the most common types of investigations involving cybercrime are those in which the computer or some other digital device is used as an instrument to commit a crime. In these cases, the digital device can be used as either an extremely sophisticated tool or as a potentially devastating weapon. Crimes in this category include the fraudulent use of automated teller machine (ATM) cards and accounts, conversion or transfer of bank accounts, credit card fraud, fraud via computer transactions, and telecommunications fraud. Computer-instrumental crimes depend on computers or digital devices. The Salami technique, one of the most well-known types of such crimes, allows computer criminals to take advantage of the small sums that are gained when thousands of transactions are rounded up or down and then diverting fractions of a cent on each transaction. Over time and many transactions, a large amount of money can be diverted to other accounts. An example of this technique appeared in the *Superman III* (1983) movie when Richard Pryor's character, Gus Gorman, diverted small amounts of money so he could purchase an expensive car.

Theft of service is another example of this type of computer crime. Violators commonly justify theft of service by asserting that they do no harm because they use only the available capacity and do not deprive legitimate users. Kevin Mitnick is a criminal hacker who was able to obtain access to computer and telephone systems, using services and stealing data at will. His history of computer fraud began when he was a high-school student and broke into his school district's computers. His actions eventually escalated to systematic software theft, attacks on Internet service providers, hacks into business and educational institution computers, and the theft of 20,000 credit card numbers over a 2-year period. Eventually, with the help of a computer expert from Stanford University, Mitnick was caught and pled guilty to computer and wire fraud. He was sentenced to 5 years in federal prison; upon his release, he was prohibited from using a computer for the final 6 months of his probation (Brenner, 2010).

The anonymity of the Internet has given rise to the need to investigate online fraud. Cases include online auction fraud, credit card fraud, and securities fraud. Professional thieves obtain credit cards via fake applications or by electronic theft and pass them around among their peers for profit. These types of investigations are commonplace due to the growing number of people conducting business on the Internet.

Stalking and the sexual exploitation of children have also been on the increase since the advent of personal computers. Possibly the most disturbing of these criminals are pedophiles who surf computer bulletin boards and chat rooms in search of children. Using chat and e-mail, they develop a cyberspace relationship and then seek to meet the child in person to pursue their sexual intentions. Already recognized as a serious problem, cyberstalking has produced a number of high-profile cases, such as the Megan Meir case in 2006. Megan, a 13-year-old from Missouri, met who she assumed to be a 16-year-old boy online. Megan and this boy became close online friends; he flattered Megan and showered her with compliments. The boy was actually the creation of the mother of one of Megan's friends and another adult. The flattery turned to taunts and insults, leading to Megan hanging herself in her bedroom closet. Megan's story is become all too common, and law enforcement is being tasked with investigating all types of harassment and threats in cyberspace.

COMPUTER AS REPOSITORY OF EVIDENCE

When the computer is not essential for the crime to occur, but it is related to the criminal act, it is considered incidental to the crime (Carter and Katz, 1997). In these cases, the digital device can become a repository of evidence of the crime. The crime could occur without the technology; however, computers help the crime to occur faster, permit the processing of large amounts of data, allow for the storage of data related to criminal activity, and make the crime difficult to identify and trace. Money laundering, child pornography, unlawful banking transactions, counterfeit driver's licenses, and identification cards are the most common examples of this type of computer crime.

Money laundering is a type of computer crime where computers are incidental to the crime. The movement of the money can be easily facilitated and be made anonymous by using computer systems. Both banks and casinos are closely regulated and seriously penalized for money laundering; however, the massive volume of monetary transactions that take place in the United States makes it difficult for regulators to address every large uncertain transaction. The number of such transactions is increasing as more businesses and consumers use electronic funds transfer services, and much of today's banking is conducted online.

The manufacturing, collection, and distribution of child pornography on the Internet are criminal activities that have precipitated a swift law enforcement response and new levels of public–private sector cooperation. The exchange of child pornography through the Internet is an unfortunate example of the actual human harm that can result from computer technology. Moreover, technology not only facilitates but also encourages this heinous crime. Computers are particularly advantageous to the distribution of child pornography because the activity thrives on secrecy and anonymity. The fact that individuals can access pornography and contact fellow users from their homes reduces their fear of detection. The Internet provides a wide variety of opportunities for those who trade and distribute child pornography to interact, including e-mail, websites, chat rooms, File Transfer Protocol (FTP) sites, electronic bulletin boards, and online services (Shelly, 1998). These venues allow pornographers to meet and exchange methods they have used to successfully sexually exploit children. Criminal investigations reveal that the Internet increases the ability to access images and reduces the social stigma and risk for the perpetrators. Engaging in this illicit activity on the Internet significantly reduces the chances of apprehension by law enforcement because many agencies may not be prepared to investigate these types of offenses. Technology offers offenders a double advantage through ease of access and lower risk of detection (Shelly, 1998).

CRIMES ASSOCIATED WITH THE PREVALENCE OF COMPUTERS

The prevalence of computers naturally creates new crime targets. Software piracy, counterfeiting, copyright violation of computer programs, black-market computer equipment and programs, and theft of technological equipment are all examples of crime associated with the prevalence of computers (Carter and Katz, 1997). Software piracy is one of the most common crimes committed against intellectual property and is typically committed by purchasing a single licensed copy of software and loading it onto several computers in violation of the licensing terms. Piracy also occurs when software is offered on a server available on the Internet that allows users to download popular software for a small fee. Original equipment manufacturer (OEM) unbundling consists of selling software as a standalone item that was intended to be sold packaged with specific accompanying hardware. It is not unusual for law enforcement to be contacted by software manufactures requesting help in the apprehension of someone selling pirated copies of their expensive and proprietary software. Programs that took years and millions of dollars to develop can be counterfeited in minutes with a touch of a button (Power, 2000). Although software manufactures have made attempts to prevent piracy, a computer user can duplicate an otherwise expensive product in bulk, sometimes for no more than the cost of a DVD. A study by the Business Software Alliance (http://portal.bsa.org/globalpiracy2009/index.html) estimated that the global software industry lost $51.4 billion due to software piracy in 2009. Losses in 1997 were estimated to be $11.4 billion. This dramatic increase in the cost of this type of criminal activity should signal to law enforcement the need to have investigators trained and experiences in the investigation of cybercrime activity.

CYBERCRIME OFFENDERS

The advent of cybercrime has created a new type of criminal offender. In the 1970s, perpetrators generally were computer specialists: programmers, computer operators, data entry personnel, system analysts, and computer managers or insiders. They were the only ones who knew how to operate and use the technology, and they were the only ones able to gain physical access to computer systems. In the 1980s, the type and frequency of high-technology crime changed due to advancements in personal computers and telecommunication and the advent of the Internet. External threats grew. Most information system security professionals placed the threats to computer systems at approximately 80% internal and 20% external. Into the 21st century, international crime and fraud developed and will continue to do so because of increased international networking. Threats to computer systems will come increasingly from the outside, committed by offenders across the country or around the world (Kovacich and Boni, 2000). Parker (1998) described two types of computer criminals: *outside hackers*, who attack others' computers for pleasure, challenge, curiosity, or educational experience; and *computer technology insiders*, who are presumably motivated by greed. Threats to information systems range from juvenile delinquents playing pranks to cruel hackers, white-collar criminals, career criminals, members of organized gangs, and terrorists. Successful computer criminals in many ways do not resemble the stereotype of criminals.

INSIDERS

Insiders still represent the most serious threat, and the highest risks are from the employees of a business or a government agency. These individuals have access to the physical and intellectual property of their employers. Furthermore, they are trusted and have the authority to gain access to many sensitive areas and sensitive information. When conducting a criminal investigation involving a computer-related crime, the investigation should look closely at those inside the organization who have access to the computer systems. The Computer Security Institute (CSI, 2009) reported that as much as 25% of the losses suffered by businesses were due to insiders. Investigators should look to those on the inside who have motive and opportunity to commit crimes against their employers. Security personnel are on the defensive frontline against high-technology crime, so they know where security may be weakest and they know the security controls in place in all areas of the business. Accountants and financial personnel have access to automated financial accounts and financial analyses of the business that could be used for financial gain. Management personnel generally have more access authority and can sometimes cover their crimes from their position of power in the organization. Some possible motives for insider crime could be financial gain, revenge, the challenge of getting away with it, or curiosity. Insiders rationalize committing these crimes because they feel underpaid, they have been denied a deserved promotion, or their work has gone unrecognized. In many cases, the victim organization provides the opportunity to commit the crime because they lack audit trails, access control systems, separation of duties, or methods of accountability.

OUTSIDERS

Following are six profiles of outsiders who commit computer-related crime (Parker, 1998):

1. *Pranksters* exploit others' computer systems to gain the use of a more powerful computer, gain respect from fellow hackers, build a reputation, or gain acceptance as an expert without a formal education.
2. *Malicious hackers*, also called *crackers*, exploit computers systems with the intent of causing loss or destruction to satisfy some antisocial motive.
3. *Personal problem solvers* often cause serious loss in their pursuit of a solution to their own personal problems. They believe that the victim is rich enough to afford the loss and would not miss what is taken or used.
4. *Career criminals* earn part or all of their income from crime; they use computers and exploit computer systems for financial gain.
5. *Extreme advocates* are known to have strong social, political, and religious views, and they intend to change a world situation by engaging in crime. Terrorist activity on the Internet fits into this category.
6. *Malcontents, addicts, and irrational and incompetent people* run the gamut from the mentally ill, to drug or alcohol addicts, to those wishing to gain the attention of others, to the criminally negligent.

External criminal hackers are one of the biggest challenges facing security personnel, computer crime investigators, and law enforcement professionals today. Initially, hackers were simply considered to be intelligent kids who experimented with computers, but eventually the term began to be used, incorrectly, to refer to those who illegally accessed computers for their personal pleasure, vandalism, or criminal purposes (Steven, 1984).

Hackers can be categorized as the *curious*, the *meddlers*, and the *criminals* (Kovacich, 1994). The curious break into computers to learn more about them and do not mean to cause harm to the computer system, although they sometimes do. They are the computer trespassers. The meddlers break into computers because they are interested in the challenge of breaking in and looking for weaknesses in the system. They will brag about their accomplishments to others in online chat rooms. These criminals break into computers to commit a crime for personal gain, to destroy or steal information, or to damage system files. Computer crackers choose their victims for different reasons, use a variety of methods of approach and attack, and exhibit different needs and intents. Former employees break into computers to damage them in retaliation for some perceived wrong. Technically proficient individuals break into opportune targets to feel more powerful. Thieves and spies break into computers to obtain valuable information. Malicious individuals break into medical databases to, for example, change prescriptions such that an intended victim will overdose. These types of criminals are becoming more prevalent and are creating a need for skilled investigators equipped with procedures and tools to help them collect, process, and interpret digital evidence (Casey et al., 1994).

THE DIGITAL CRIME SCENE

The investigation of some aspects of cybercrime will be the responsibility of all investigators, regardless of their assignment. We have seen that all types and manner of criminal activities can be committed using a digital device, and evidence may be stored on a digital device. Thus, burglary and homicide detectives are as likely to be involved in an investigation in cyberspace as computer crime investigators. Today, every crime scene may contain digital evidence. First responders and investigators must be aware of the possible uses of digital devices to hide evidence of a crime. The Federal Bureau of Investigation's *Digital Evidence Field Guide* lists five key facts a law enforcement officer should know about digital evidence (FBI, 2007):

1. *Many types of crime involve digital evidence.* Computers, cell phones, personal digital assistants, and other digital devices play a part in all types of crimes, from violent crimes against persons to the traditional cybercrimes.
2. *Every crime scene is a digital evidence crimes scene.* Crime scene investigators should always be alert to the possibility of digital evidence being present at a crime scene.
3. *Digital evidence can be fragile.* This type of evidence must be handled with great care to avoid altering or destroying evidence inadvertently. If not handled properly, heat, cold, and magnetic fields can destroy evidence, as can dropping a device.

4. *Digital evidence can be easily altered*. Alterations of digital evidence may be as simple as changing the file extension on a document to conceal its true identity to altering the time on a computer to make documents appear to be created at a different date and time. Investigators must be aware that some of the actions they take could change evidence.

5. *Never assume that digital evidence is destroyed*. Although fragile at times, damaged digital devices can sometimes yield evidence when handled properly. Digital forensics examiners have extracted digital evidence from burned-out computers and devices found submerged in water.

IDENTIFYING DIGITAL EVIDENCE

Investigators performing a search for digital evidence should be aware of the variety and forms of digital devices that could hold evidence. Investigators may find the following categories of digital evidence at a crime scene (FBI, 2007):

- *Commonplace*—These are the traditional types of digital media that an investigator may find. This category includes USB thumb drives, DVD/CDs, MP3 players, flash memory cards, digital cameras, and cell phones.
- *Obscure*—These are nontraditional items of digital media that are easily overlooked by investigators as a possible source of evidence. This category includes answering machines, GPS receivers, digital voice recorders, printers, copy machines, and game consoles.
- *Protected*—These nontraditional items of digital media are designed to conceal data or prevent unauthorized access. This category includes biometric devices, such as fingerprint readers, and mechanically protected devices, such as those requiring an access card or USB dongle to gain access.
- *Concealed*—These are digital media designed to hide their true purpose. This category includes USB drives disguised as pens, watches, or other everyday objects. These concealed devices can be very small and easily missed by investigators during a search.

LEGAL CONSIDERATIONS

Like other traditional crime scenes, the investigator must have the legal authority to conduct a search and seize evidence at a cybercrime scene; however, there are other legal considerations when planning a cybercrime scene search. The Electronic Communications Privacy Act (ECPA) of 1986 provides statutory procedures for intercepting wire, oral, and electronic communications. It provides protection to stored communications, such as e-mail stored on Internet service provider servers. Law enforcement conducting investigations in which there may be a need to intercept electronic communications or read e-mail that has not been delivered to its intended recipient must obtain additional legal authority. Also, the earlier Privacy Protection Act of 1980 (PPA) made it unlawful for local, state, or federal law enforcement to search or seize materials that may be publishable. The Act protects the work product of individual author's manuscripts, written conclusions, opinions, and theories of the creating author. Law enforcement should carefully consider if the PPA applies in cases where they may be searching and seizing documents of authors, publishers, newspapers, or other individuals who may be involved in the publication of these types of materials. The PPA does not apply to items considered to be contraband, such as child pornography (Britz, 2004).

COLLECTION AND PRESERVATION OF DIGITAL EVIDENCE

The collection and preservation of digital evidence must be performed in a manner that does not alter or destroy evidence and allows the proper forensic examination by trained personnel. As with all other crime scenes, the cybercrime scene must be carefully photographed, sketched, and documented; however, the digital crime scene has a few special requirements. First, crime scene investigators should never turn on a computer that is off and should never browse the files on a computer at the scene. The mere act of opening a file will alter date and time stamps that could be important to the investigation. If a computer is still running, it is important to make sure it is properly shutdown or, if that is not possible, that the power is disconnected from the system. Isolating the computer from the Internet and a power source will prevent destructive programs from being run on the machine without the investigators' knowledge. When seizing a laptop, the battery should be removed and then disconnected from any power source. Personal digital assistants and cell phones should be left off if already off and should be isolated from radiofrequency signals when possible. All digital devices should be packaged to prevent damage and should be kept away from all electromagnetic fields. Whenever possible, it is best to have a digital forensic expert on scene when collecting digital evidence.

FORENSIC EXAMINATION OF DIGITAL EVIDENCE

Proper forensic examination of digital evidence can produce useful evidence in a criminal investigation. Digital forensics has been described as an autopsy of sorts for digital media. It requires a specially trained examiner using the proper hardware and software tools to make a duplicate of the media and then analyzing data stored on the device. Forensic examinations of digital media can involve the recovery of deleted files, user names, passwords, and images and the examination of unallocated space on the device. Examiners may search for hidden files or recover encrypted documents, and they can sometimes provide an analysis of date and time stamps to establish evidentiary timelines. The proper handling and examination of digital evidence provides a forensically sound process that can be used to introduce evidence into court, along with expert testimony of the results of the examination. These exams must be performed by a trained examiner and not be attempted by crime scene investigators.

QUESTIONS FOR DISCUSSION

1. Why do you think cybercrime is so difficult to define?
2. What are the classifications of cybercrime? Provide examples of each.
3. What are the various motives of cybercrime offenders?
4. Explain the two unique legal aspects of cybercrime investigations.
5. Discuss the possible evidence that can be found in digital forensics analysis.

BIBLIOGRAPHY

Brenner, S.W. (2010). *Cybercrime: Criminal Threats from Cyberspace*. Santa Barbara, CA: Praeger.

Britz, M.T. (2004). *Computer Forensics and Cyber Crime: An Introduction*. Piscataway, NJ: Pearson Education.

Carter, L. and Katz, J. (1997). Computer Crime: An Emerging Challenge for Law Enforcement. *FBI Law Enforcement Bulletin*, 65(12):1–8.

Casey, E., Brandl, S.G., and Frank, J. (1994). The Relationship Between Evidence, Detective Effort, and the Disposition of Burglary and Robbery Investigations. *American Journal of Police*, 8(3):149–168.

CSI. (2009). *CSI Computer Crime and Security Survey 2009*. New York: Computer Security Institute (http://gocsi.com/survey_2009).

FBI. (2007). *Digital Evidence Field Guide: What Every Peace Officer Must Know*, Continuing Education Series 1.1. Washington, D.C.: Federal Bureau of Investigation (http://www.rcfl.gov/downloads/documents/FieldGuide_sc.pdf).

Gene, S. (1995). Crime in Cyberspace: The Digital Underworld. *The Futurist*, 29(5):24–28.

Haugen S. and Selin J.R. (1999). Identifying and Controlling Computer Crime and Employee Fraud. *Industrial Management & Data Systems*, 8:340–344.

Kovacich, G.L. (1994). *Hackers: From Curiosity to Criminal*. Austin, TX: Association of Certified Fraud Examiners.

Kovacich, G.L. and Boni, W.C. (2000). *High-Technology Crime Investigator's Handbook: Working in the Global Information Environment*. Boston: Butterworth-Heineman.

Krauss, C. (1997). 8 Countries Join in an Effort to Catch Computer Criminals. *The New York Times*, December, 11, p. A12.

Lange, L. (1996). Trust a Hacker Under 30? You'd Better. *Electronic Engineering Times*, August 19.

Parker, D.B. (1998). *Fighting Computer Crime*. New York: Wiley.

Power, R. (2000). *Tangled Web: Tales of Digital Crime from the Shadows of Cyberspace*. Indianapolis, IN: Que.

Shelley, L.I. (1998). Crime and Corruption in the Digital Age. *Journal of International Affairs*, 51(2):607–620.

Steven, L. (1984). *Hackers: Heroes of the Computer Revolution*. New York: Anchor Press.

CHAPTER **18**

Gang Investigation

Gregg W. Etter
University of Central Missouri

CHAPTER OBJECTIVES

After reading this chapter, you should be able to do the following:

1. Identify cultural characteristics of gangs.
2. Identify the primary and secondary crimes that gangs commit.
3. Explain motivations for gang crimes.
4. List and describe effective gang investigation techniques.
5. Identify some effective anti-gang programs and explain how they work.

Chapter Outline

- Nature of the Gang Problem
- Common Cultural Characteristics of Gangs
- Los Angeles-Based Street Gangs
- Chicago-Based Street Gangs
- Changing Nature of Hispanic Street Gangs
- Skinheads and Other White Gangs
- Asian Gangs
- Outlaw Motorcycle Gangs
- Female Gangs
- Gang Investigation Techniques
- Anti-Gang Tactics
- Anti-Gang Legislation

NATURE OF THE GANG PROBLEM

The gang problem in the United States is not new. Urban street gangs have existed in the United States since the 1820s. Gangs such as the Forty Thieves, Bowery Boys, Dead Rabbits, Roach Guards, and Pug Uglies battled in the early 1800s to gain control of their territories in the Five Points district of New York City. The Forty Thieves gang even had a pee-wee gang of youngsters called the Little Forty Thieves (Asbury, 1927). Gangs are a function of urban criminality. The street and motorcycle gangs of today have developed many of their customs and traditions from the street gangs of yesteryear. Many of the gangs still in operation today have existed for several decades, including outlaw motorcycle clubs, which date back to 1946; the Folk Nation and People Nation alliances; and the Crips and Bloods. These gangs have evolved into an almost tribal type of society. The director of the National Gang Crime Research Center in Chicago defined a gang as (Knox, 2006):

> A group is a gang when it exists for or benefits substantially from the continuing criminal activity of its members. Some element of crime must exist as a definitive feature of the organization for it to be classified as a gang. That need not be income-producing crime because it could also be crime of violence.

Anderson et al. (2009) reported the following:

> The National Youth Gang Center estimates that there were approximately 778,000 gang members and 27,000 gangs active in more than 3,500 jurisdictions served by city and county law enforcement agencies in 2007.

Modern street gangs can be described as the new urban tribes. Holmes (1971) observed that a tribe consists of a group of people who possess a common language, culture, or territory. He also noted that bonds that hold the group together revolve around the attitudes that the members of the tribe hold toward each other and the behavior patterns of cooperation and mutual assistance that act as a tangible demonstration of those attitudes. Thus, tribes work toward a common self-interest.

Criminals combine themselves into self-affiliated tribal structures to help them conduct their criminal enterprises and to avoid the police (Etter, 1998). These groups exhibit all of the characteristics of tribalism when reacting to their environment and governmental control of the territory that they occupy (Fried, 1975). Thus, in their effort to further their criminal enterprises and to avoid capture by the police, some criminals have banded together into gangs. These gangs have developed over the years into the sociological phenomenon that Fried (1975) described as secondary tribes.

Gangs have adopted a pseudo-warrior culture to facilitate their criminal society. In this pseudo-warrior culture, gang members view themselves as street warriors, race warriors, or road warriors. Violence is seen as a legitimate tactic to achieve ends, and gang members will use violence to achieve their desired ends or goals (Elder, 1997). Objectives of violence include: warnings, intimidation, control of turf, control of trade, control of personnel, revenge, etc. In addition, the use of violence increases the member's warrior status within the gang (Etter, 1998).

Gang members can gain status for themselves by exhibiting antisocial traits. They pick street names for themselves that enhance this violent image. Jackson and McBride (1986) observed that

… a lack of self-discipline and a violent temper are unacceptable traits in the non-gang society, but in the gang system he can turn these "liabilities" to his advantage by letting go completely and building a reputation as a *vato loco* ("crazy guy").

They further suggested that the pseudo-warrior culture practiced by gangs promotes violence and bravery by its members in support of the goals of the gang:

Similarly, the gang member knows that if he is killed by a rival gang during a fight, he will be viewed as a fallen hero by his home boys. His name will appear for years to come painted in gang graffiti throughout the barrio, and his exploits will be told again until reality is forgotten and a legend created.

COMMON CULTURAL CHARACTERISTICS OF GANGS

Gangs can be a strictly local affair with no national gang affiliation or alliances, but many gangs choose to affiliate with a nationwide brand-name gang, such as the Latin Kings from the People Nation. Although this occurs, no central gang structure exists in the United States. Each gang operates somewhat independently, often driven more by their cultural affiliation with their chosen group than a broader formal alliance. Sometimes sets of the same gang may even fight each other. Gangs in this country often operate somewhat like fast-food franchises, each bearing the corporate logo of Crips or Latin Kings but independently owned and operated. Although each gang is somewhat different, modern gangs exhibit several common cultural characteristics.

SELECTIVE MEMBERSHIP

One of the ways that gang members protect themselves from law enforcement is by selective membership. You can't just run out and join an urban street gang. The fact that the Mafia is not an equal-opportunity employer is well known (Gage, 1971). Prospective gang members are often screened by race, sex, religion, language, ethnicity, and other cultural factors (Asbury, 1927; Etter, 1998; Knox, 2006; Thrasher, 1936; Yablonsky, 1962). Racial and ethnic homogeneity has become the norm among gang members (Nadel, 1996), although this is changing somewhat in the center of the country (e.g., Omaha, NE; Davenport, IA; Little Rock, AR; Memphis, TN), where whites and females are likely to be incorporated into more traditional Los Angeles- or Chicago-based street gangs than they would be in Chicago or on the coast. One of the simplest and most effective tools in this screening process is *vouching*. This means that someone has to nominate someone for membership in a gang. That member is then responsible for that person's conduct within the gang. If that conduct is unsatisfactory, the gang may impose negative sanctions on both the offender and the person who proposed the offender. Language has been another screening tool, as it offers a means of protection and a means of communication. How many police officers speak Sicilian, Vietnamese, Chinese, Japanese, Russian, or Spanish fluently enough to conduct a legal interrogation under *Miranda v. Arizona*, much less infiltrate and be able to pass as a member of the group? Even when officers do speak the language, gang members often use a subdialect (e.g., Spanish speakers will use Calo or Spanglish) or street language to confuse the issue (Jackson and McBride, 1986). The average age of gang members is traditionally believed to be 12 to 25, but some groups have admitted members as young as 7 or 8, and some older members tend to hang on.

INITIATION RITES ARE OFTEN VIOLENT

Every tribe has a rite of passage that allows young people to transcend from childhood into full adult membership in the group. Gangs are no exception, and they often have elaborate initiation rites for anyone who becomes a member of the gang. In the inner city, the gang has replaced society in the lives of its members. In these rites of passage, a prospective member of the group is required to prove their worth to the group and their skills as a warrior who is willing to fight and die for the tribe or gang. In the most common of these initiation rites, gangs may "beat in" a new member. This involves the prospective member being physically attacked and beaten by several gang members for a period of time. This proves the new member's worth in combat to the gang and affirms that person's warrior status in the group. It also adds to the oft-repeated gang custom of "blood in, blood out." The initiate is often required to commit a crime in front of witnesses. This virtually eliminates most police informants or undercover police officers, as their agencies will not allow them to undertake such conduct. The crimes might be as simple as stealing something in front of witnesses to participating in a robbery or drive-by shooting. The object of this type of initiation is to impress upon prospective gang members that they are now criminals and there is no turning back. Most gangs are not a co-ed operation. As a general rule, females are not allowed to join the gang or have any say in its operations; however, as previously noted, some gangs are beginning to allow female members to become full members of the gang. In areas where this is occurring, female members often have the option of being "sexed in." This involves having sex with either every member of the gang or a set number of gang members (often determined by a roll of the dice). Female members who choose this option are not as highly thought of as those who choose to be beat in. Because of the longevity of many of these street gangs (some have lasted over 50 years), another option, being "blessed in," is sometimes available to prospective members who are relatives of existing members (e.g., son, daughter, grandchild); however, many still choose to be beat in out of tradition. This is especially true for Hispanic gangs.

GANG FUNERAL RITES ARE OFTEN OBSERVED

Just as a group member is given a formal rite of passage into the group, that member is also given a formal rite of passage into the next world. Members of the group gather as a show of unity to mourn their deceased member. The deceased is usually buried in the full colors or uniform of the group. Mourners from the group also attend in full colors or uniform. Group affiliation is often listed on the funeral program. Retaliatory drive-by shootings or other acts of violence often occur in close proximity to the funeral rites.

GANGS HAVE A CODE OF CONDUCT FOR THEIR MEMBERS

Just as in any tribal structure, gangs have rules. These rules are made by the elders of the tribe, or gang. Rules among criminal groups are not new. The Mafia's code of behavior, called *Omertà* ("manliness"), has been around since 1282 (Arlacchi, 1987; Gage, 1971). Thrasher (1936) noted that youth street gangs adopt codes of conduct that reflect their environment. Typically these rules represent a type of situational morality that exists only within the gang; for example, if you are a Disciple, it is okay to shoot at a Latin King, but leave the Folk alone. Sometimes these rules are very formal and contained in written constitutions; sometimes the rules are passed on as oral history to new members. The rules are rigidly enforced, and rule breakers are punished. Most of the punishments are physical in nature and sometimes include the death of the violator or the violator's family. Typical of the rules and oaths taken by gang members is the following example from Kansas Department of Corrections Sergeant Terry Dunn, who seized this handwritten example from a gang member at the Hutchinson Correctional Facility in 1997:

Westside 2 Lincoln Block Gangsta Disciples

1. I solemnly swear myself into the Lincoln Block Gangsta Disciples.
2. I will represent part of this organization in life & death.
3. I swear never to disrespect myself or a member of the Gangsta Disciple Nation.
4. I swear to accept all orders from the King of Kings & appointed chiefs & chosen ones.
5. I will not affiliate myself with no other organization, set, or abide by any of their laws or ways, except Gangsta Disciples.
6. I swear to assist all members mentally & physically as well as I can!
7. I will never disrespect my organization by any means.
8. I swear to never disrespect, scandalize, or conspire against the organization.
9. I will always greet each member of the Gangsta Disciples with the closing of the fists and the uprising of the pitchforks.
10. It will be death before dishonor of my organization Gangsta Disciples (Westside L.B.G.D.)
11. I swear to keep all doings of the organization under a code of silence.
12. I solemnly swear myself into the Gangsta Disciples–Westside Lincoln Block Gangsta Disciples—til death do us part!

In a gang, absolute and unquestioned loyalty to the group is demanded above all else. This loyalty supersedes any family ties, religious beliefs, friendship ties, or other loyalties. The gang becomes the gang member's family and tribe. The gang members, as a group, often have no respect for the law or fear of going to jail. Going to jail is often considered as just the cost of doing business. Sometimes incarceration can build a member's status in a gang, making them a loyal veteran of the group. Jail is a good place to train gang members in how to commit new criminal acts. Jail is also a good place to recruit new members into the gang.

GANGS OFTEN CLAIM TERRITORY

Gangs, like tribes, claim and defend their territories, often to the death. Gangs mark their turf with graffiti to show ownership and to warn rival gangs against trespassing. Hispanic gangs are the most territorial, although this is changing as some of these gangs (e.g., MS-13 and La-18) have gone transnational. Asian gangs are the most mobile and therefore the least territorial. White gangs often make political proclamations about "white homelands," and their territorial claims are largely symbolic. Outlaw motorcycle gangs are known to enforce the "100-mile" rule and demand payment of a street tax or permission to operate in their area.

GANGS MAINTAIN AN INTERNAL ORGANIZATION AND STRUCTURE

Many modern urban street gangs pattern their customs, habits, and internal organizations after the Mafia, in light of the organizational success of the Mafia in its progression from a neighborhood street gang in New Orleans and New York in the late 1800s to the present-day Mafia operations that extend over Europe and the United States (Gage, 1971). By operating as a series of families and as a commission, the Mafia has an organization and chain of command capable of supporting global-scale operations. In short, the Mafia has gone from retail to wholesale. Mafia members do not sell individual dosage units of drugs on the street corners. Street gang members still do. Gangs in the United States have adopted either a formal or informal structure for their operations.

A more formal gang organizational structure has been adopted by Chicago-based street gangs, outlaw motorcycle gangs, Mara Salvatrucha 13 (MS-13), and most Asian street gangs. In a formal organizational structure, each gang member has a designated position within the gang with specific duties and responsibilities. Although a formal organizational chart may not be hanging on the wall of the gang's clubhouse, gang members know their place within the gang's organizational structure and what is expected of them as gang members of that particular group. As in any other group, there may be infighting to see who will be the boss or leader. The organizational structure may be based along business or military lines. Many gangs follow the Mafia's organizational structure, but Asian gangs are more likely to model themselves after the Chinese Triads or the Tongs from California. The larger a gang becomes, the more likely that they will adopt a more formal organizational structure.

An informal organizational structure has been adopted by Los Angles-based street gangs, skinheads, and various Hispanic street gangs. Gangs organized with an informal structure believe in the concept of a "leaderless resistance." It is their belief that any leader would be targeted and probably killed or captured by enemies of the gang (police or other gangs); therefore, they attempt to decide things by group consensus. In this type of group, they might, and often do, acknowledge senior members of the group as OGs, or "original gang-sters" (a type of senior advisor), but the OGs do not always have command capability.

GANGS MAINTAIN AN INTERNAL AND EXTERNAL MEANS OF COMMUNICATION

Gangs rely on oral histories to pass on the history, traditions, rules, and folklore of the gang. This is a secure way to pass information as documents can be seized and used as evidence of gang membership in court. Thus, the exploits of Folk Nation Disciple leader "King Larry Hoover" are passed on mostly by word of mouth to new members of the Black Gangster Disciples, and knowing the meaning of each point of the Folk Nation's six-pointed star (love, life, loyalty, wisdom, knowledge, understanding) is required of new members. The culture of the gang is passed in this way from generation to generation.

In gangs, the use of graffiti or tagging is a time-honored tradition. Often called the newspaper of the streets, graffiti marks turf, declares war, mourns the dead, shows disrespect for rival gangs, sings the praises of gang members, and is used to issue challenges. Crossing out or putting upside down another gang's symbols or graffiti shows disrespect. Hispanic gangs call their gang graffiti *plaqueso* ("places"). The slang term *plaquesos* is derived from the Spanish *placa*, meaning a "sign" or "plaque." When Hispanic gang members talk of writing graffiti on a wall they refer to it as throwing a *placa* on the wall. It is not just graffiti. It proclaims to the world the status of the gang and offers a challenge to rivals. Moreover, graffiti writing is a skill, an acquired skill, that requires a great deal of time and practice to perfect (Jackson and McBride, 1986).

Hand signs are used by gang members for identification, intimidation, challenges, and general communication. Whenever a gang member flashes a hand sign at a person, he in effect is saying, "Here's who I am. Who are you?" Los Angeles-based gang members talk of throwing a sign, while Chicago-based gang members speak of representing. Hand signs provide a definite statement as to the identity and often intentions of gang members; for example, when a witness is testifying in court during the trial of a gang member, a gang member flashing a hand sign could be considered an act of intimidation toward that witness.

Language is used to exclude non-members of the group. Most police do not speak Spanish, Sicilian, or Vietnamese, for example, fluently enough to understand what is going on. Slang or street language is liberally inserted into conversations to exclude those who would not understand. The use of street names or aliases is common, as is the use of code in communications, drug tallies, and other communications.

Gang members are Internet savvy, and many of the gangs now have websites. These websites are used as a means of communication and require password access to some areas of the website. They are also used as a means of recruitment, and interested parties can inquire about gang activities. They are graffiti in an electronic format. Gang members also make extensive usage of cellular communications. Texting is prevalent. Prepaid cell phones are popular because they are almost untraceable and are thrown away after a particular time period.

GANG MEMBERS ARE FOND OF TOTEMS OR PARAPHERNALIA TO SHOW MEMBERSHIP

Symbols contained on or within tattoos, clothing, or jewelry often are used by gang members as totems to identify themselves as members of the group and to show loyalty to the group. Identification with the group is a primary reason for tattoos. Not everyone who has a tattoo is a gang member, certainly, but gang members, supremacists, and biker group members often have tattoos showing affiliation with their group. A tattoo is a permanent mark on the body and therefore symbolizes a lasting commitment to the group. It is not something done lightly or without thought. The group member who places a tattoo on his body makes a visible public statement about his acceptance of the group into his life forever.

Criminals have long used tattoos to identify themselves to each other and to show their contempt for the rules of society. Tattoos fall into three basic categories: (1) alphanumeric (numbers and letters that spell out the intended message, often in code); (2) symbolic/pictorial (symbols and pictures that identify the gang or religious affiliation); or (3) a combination of both alphanumeric and symbolic/pictorial. Knowledge of these symbols can be useful to law enforcement officers investigating gang activity and in identifying gang members.

Similar to tattoos among gang members is the practice of branding or applying burn marks with, for example, a lit cigarette. A gang member will either place such marks on his own body or allow another gang member to do so. Many investigators believe that burn marks reflect a willingness to engage in criminal activity or an individual's toughness. Three burn marks generally refer to "my crazy life," or the gang life. They are normally arranged in a triangle (also seen as a tattoo).

Clothing is more than a fashion statement with gang members. Outlaw motorcycle gang members wear sleeveless jackets bearing the logo or colors of their groups. Patches denote various rankings, crimes, or sexual exploits of the biker. In street gangs, expensive athletic clothing in the gang colors is favored by many gang members. The fancy clothing not only exhibits economic success to observers but also provides a means of instant identification. The University of North Carolina (UNC), for example, has the colors of light blue and white. The Neighborhood Crips have adopted this team as their own because their color is light blue, and they feel that the NC in the university's logo could stand for "Neighborhood Crips"! Also, the ram that is used as a mascot by the university is considered by the gang to be a symbol of strength and power. Thus, a 14-year-old gang member will be viewed with respect and envy by his peers if he wears a starter jacket with the gang totem that cost $150, a $30 baseball cap with a logo, and a pair of athletic shoes with laces in the gang colors that cost another $150.

Local tee-shirt companies print up special runs of shirts with gang logos upon request. Gang-related jewelry showing logos, drug symbols, or weapons is also popular among street gang members. African American street gang members began a custom referred to as *sagging*, where they wear their pants down low. Sagging has been adopted by most other street gangs, as well.

GANGS ENGAGE IN CRIMES TO MAKE MONEY

Although gangs receive some financial support from their members in the form of dues, their primary means of financial support is through the commission of crimes. The *differential opportunity theory*, proposed by Cloward and Olin (1960), suggests that a criminal subculture develops when youths see no legitimate means of achieving economic success, and the members of the group use criminal acts as a means of achieving economic success. In his research of the gang as an American enterprise, Padilla (1993) confirmed this view and observed that

> Similar to other business organizations, the gang's survival is heavily dependent on its capacity to develop and maintain a sound financial base. Funds are needed for meeting a wide range of organizational needs, such as the purchase of weapons, making rent payments, bailing members out of jail, and paying attorney's fees.

Thus, the crimes of drug trafficking, prostitution, weapons dealing, gambling, theft/fencing, extortion/loan sharking, and arson are committed by gang members to make money. Related crimes, such as pornography, homicide/assaults, rape, robbery, burglary, and political corruption, often are committed to support the primary crimes.

The sale of illegal drugs is a primary source of income for most gangs. Most gangs only deal in one or two drugs. They view this as a business and often refer to drugs as the "product." Drugs are also used as an alternative currency. Gang employees such as prostitutes and street-level drug dealers are often paid in drugs. A few gangs do not sell drugs at all, but most do because it is the quickest and most efficient way to raise money for the gang.

Not only is prostitution the world's oldest profession but it has also been a very reliable money maker for gangs. Prostitutes may be either male or female; both female and male prostitutes service male clients. Generally, gang members are not prostitutes themselves. The prostitutes are often drug addicts and become *de facto* employees of the gang due to their addiction. The gang members act as their pimps and pay them off in drugs.

Gangs by their very nature have weapons because of the violent nature of the business that they are in. They also often deal in weapons illegally. Weapons are acquired through legal purchases, smuggling, theft, or fencing operations. They are sometimes sold to raise cash. In the gang pseudo-warrior culture, the possession of a weapon raises the gang member's warrior status in the gang.

Gambling operations such as running the numbers and off-track betting have been traditional mainstays of gangs. Floating crap games are also common. Asian gangs favor high-stakes card games such as Pai Gow. Legalization of gambling, lotto, parimutuel betting, etc., has shifted revenues from the gangs to the state in many areas.

Gang members are not above stealing something; in fact, it may be required as a part of initiation rites. But, where you have dope, you have junkies, so why take the risk? Have the junkies steal for their daily fix, then act as the fence and pay the junkie off in drugs. "Steal-to-order" burglary rings are formed when gangs use junkies to steal merchandise that will be sold to raise money for the gang. Weapons are often acquired in this way.

One of the most traditional ways for a gang to exercise control over a region is to collect "tributes" from the residents or businessmen in the neighborhood. The protection racket is one of the oldest scams used by the gangs that is still in operation. Tributes are paid to gangs for permission to do business in their territories. Businessmen are approached by gang members who offer to help them keep their businesses "safe" in this high-crime area. Businesses that pay come under the protection of the gang that controls that turf. Any other criminal who attacks that business or patrons of that business has to answer to the local gang. If a business owner refuses, gang members will break windows, knees, etc., until the owner relents. This is sometimes called a *street tax*. Also, other drug dealers have to pay a fee to the gang to sell dope on their corner.

Extortion is common when a gang discovers a secret (e.g., embezzlement, adultery, pedophilia) and uses that knowledge to blackmail the victim into payment or cooperation; for example, a high school principal who visits a gang-controlled prostitute for an evening of pleasure may get more than he bargained for. He might be blackmailed into allowing that gang to either deal or recruit in his school.

One way that gangs acquire merchandise, cars, and businesses is through the practice of loan sharking. Loan sharking is popular among gangs dealing with a population of poor people who do not use banks; desperate and poor people have little access to the formal banking system. Gangs loan them money at outrageous interest rates that sometimes are compounded hourly. Failure to repay such loans can be fatal. Gangs often acquire an interest in a legitimate business in this way.

Arson to collect insurance is another time-honored way to make money. In fact, many Asian gangs and outlaw motorcycle gangs specialize in arson; however, arsonists don't stay bought (see discussion on extortion). Arson is sometimes used by a gang for retaliation or intimidation.

GANGS WILL BUY OR INVEST IN LEGITIMATE BUSINESSES

Gangs often acquire an interest in or outright possession of businesses inside of their territory. This type of hostile takeover is often facilitated by a businessman's default on a debt to a loan shark or drug dealer. Sometimes a gang buys a business to invest their profits from other enterprises. Business ownership has many advantages for a gang. It provides employment for gang members (thus keeping their parole officers happy); it acts as a front to commit other crimes; it gives the gang a base from which to recruit; and it allows the gang to launder illicitly earned money back into the legitimate business community.

Businesses are often used by gangs and other criminals as a convenient means of laundering proceeds from other criminal activities. Gangs tend to acquire businesses that are cash heavy, such as restaurants, game rooms, catering services, escort services, vending machines, or automobile repair shops. Al Capone went to jail not for his gang-related murders or crimes but for income tax evasion. This point has not been lost on the current crop of gangsters. Strandberg (1997) observed that

Any retail business that accepts cash can be used as a money laundering operation. According to John R. Kingston, special supervisory agent with the FBI's Economic Crimes Unit, a crook can buy the business and take it over, and all he has to do is increase his profits by ten or twenty percent by adding cash to it.

LOS ANGELES-BASED STREET GANGS

A discussion about Los Angeles-based street gangs is primarily one about two major groups: Crips or Bloods. They are sworn enemies, but they have several things in common. Both groups were started by high school students in the Compton/Los Angeles area in the late 1960s. Both groups combined some existing youth gangs into the new groups. The subunits of both groups are called *sets*. Sets run from about 10 to about 40 members each. The sets are usually named after streets in Los Angeles, but sometimes local street names are also used. Both groups have now expanded from coast to coast. They use violence for the sake of violence, as a show of toughness, and they view themselves as street warriors. Initially, both groups were composed largely of African Americans and Hispanics. This has changed somewhat as the gangs have expand across the United States.

CRIPS

The Crips were formed around 1968 in the Compton/Los Angeles area by combining several smaller local street gangs. One of the original gangsters was Raymond Lee Washington (1953–1979). He was one of the founders of the Baby Avenues gang, which morphed into the Crips, and was killed by a rival gang member. Another of the early founders of the Crips was Stanley "Tookie" Williams (1953–2005). Williams helped to expand the Crips in Los Angeles during the early 1970s. He was arrested for a quadruple murder in 1979 and convicted. He attempted to reform in prison and was the author of a children's book, but he was executed for his crimes.

The Crips membership originally consisted largely of blacks and Hispanic males. The Crips began expanding across the United States in the 1980s as a result of drug wars. As this expansion occurred, in some areas (e.g., Omaha, Davenport, Little Rock, Memphis) whites, Native Americans, and Asians began to be admitted, as well as females. Crips have a loose organization that does not openly acknowledge a single leader. They do recognize OGs in some sets. An individual Crips set usually ranges in membership from 10 to 40. Sometimes the Crips sets are allies, but sometimes they fight among themselves. The Crips are loosely allied with the Folk Nation in Chicago. In some areas of the country, they compete for drug trade turf.

The Crips' primary color is blue, which can be traced to the Washington High School colors in South Los Angeles; however, the Grape Street Crips favor purple, the Spooktown Crips use brown, and the Asian Boy Crips wear yellow. Crips often wear blue bandannas and do-rags or other articles of blue clothing. They use the letter "C" in place of "B" in writing to disrespect the Bloods. Crips are fond of calling each other "Cuzz" and calling themselves "Blood Killas" (BKs). A sign of disrespect toward Crips is use of the word "Crabs."

BLOODS

The Bloods were formed around 1968 in the Compton/Los Angeles area. It is believed that the Bloods arose as a reaction to formation of the Crips. Drug trafficking led to their quick expansion across the United States in the 1980s. Originally, membership was restricted to blacks and Hispanics, but others are allowed to join today. Bloods favor the color red; they wear red bandannas or do-rags and other articles of red clothing when they "flame up." The Bloods often require that initiates receive a dog-paw mark, often burned in with a cigarette, on their right shoulder. Bloods members may also sport a tattoo of a dog (usually Mack truck logo) or a tattoo or burn scar of MOB (Member of Blood or Money over Bitches). Bloods will often refer to the Pirus, who were one of the original Blood gangs. Bloods use a crossed-out "c" in words in a show of disrespect for Crips. A term of disrespect for Blood is "Slobs." Blood sets, typically 10 to 40 members each, initially had a loose organization with no defined leader. Today, the Bloods are allied with the People Nation, and they recognize OGs. Blood sets may not like each other, but they seldom fight among each other. In 1993, the United Blood Nation was formed in the New York City jail system. It has rapidly spread down the East Coast of the United States. It has breathed new life into the Bloods across the United States as the reformation spread back to the west coast. As a result, the Bloods nationwide have begun to adopt a more formal organizational structure.

CHICAGO-BASED STREET GANGS

Chicago-based street gangs are divided into Folk and People Nations. They usually favor a structured organization and even carry business cards. War sweaters were originally popular among these groups and were worn like high-school letter sweaters. They maintain websites and other Internet communications.

FOLK NATION

The Folk Nation is a loose alliance of 28 gangs that originated in Chicago-area jails in the late 1950s and early 1960s. They now operate from east of the Rocky Mountains to the East Coast. The gangs in the Folk Nation generally have a paramilitary structure and organization. They favor formal constitutions and oaths. Early founders include the three "kings," David Barksdale, Jerome "Shorty" Freeman, and Larry Hoover.

Folk Nation gang members generally align to the right in dress and symbols. They prefer to use two or more colors to represent their gang, and the way in which the colors are worn denotes the particular set. The Gangster Disciples like to wear blue and black as their colors, and their preferred symbol is the six-pointed star representing "King David" (David Barksdale, 1947–1974), who was one of the founders of the group (Petrone, 1994).

The Folk Nation is involved in political movements as well as criminal acts. Their political organization in the Chicago area is called 21st Century VOTE. The Folk are very territorial and have been known to engage in turf wars. Membership is largely black and Hispanic in the Chicago area, but it varies elsewhere. Some Folk sets are highly mobile, while others have been on the same few blocks for 50 years. Although originating in the Chicago area, the Folk Nation has spread into over 35 states. They are even beginning to move to the West Coast in small numbers. They are loose allies with the Los Angeles-based Crips. Their criminal and political empire is also attempting to expand (Knox, 2006).

PEOPLE NATION

The People Nation is a loose alliance of 28 gangs that originated in Chicago-area jails in the late 1950s and early 1960s. The People Nation now operates from east of the Rocky Mountains to the East Coast, although smaller groups are beginning to migrate to the west coast. The gangs of the People Nation have a paramilitary structure and organization. Several of the gangs are affiliated with the Nation of Islam religious movement. The People Nation favors formal constitutions and oaths.

Founder Jeff Fort is credited with uniting the members of 50 Chicago street gangs into the Black P Stone Nation, which evolved into the People Nation (Knox, 2006). The original group was ruled by 21 person commission called the Main 21. The largest of these People Nation gangs are the Black P Stones, Cobra Stone, El Rukn, Gaylords, Latin Counts, Latin Kings, and Vice Lords. These groups have a multistate presence. Other smaller People Nation gangs may not have an area of operation that is very far outside of their neighborhood, but they have managed to exist for over 50 years.

A People Nation gang member generally aligns to the left in dress and symbols. Many of the People Nation gangs use a five-pointed star as a symbol to honor one of the original founders, Jeff Fort, who is Muslim. People Nation gangs are identified by the two or more colors they wear and their arrangement. The El Rukn usually wear black, red, and green, but sometimes blue and red. The Vice Lords favor black and gold or black and yellow (Petrone, 1994).

The People Nation is involved in political movements as well as criminal acts. Their political organization in the Chicago area is known as PUSH. They are very territorial and engage in turf wars. People Nation members represent a variety of Muslims, black, Hispanics, and whites. Although originating in the Chicago area, the People Nation has spread into over 35 states. They are loose allies with the Los Angeles-based bloods. Their criminal and political empire is also attempting to expand (Knox, 2006).

CHANGING NATURE OF HISPANIC STREET GANGS

Traditional Hispanic street gangs are largely a local affair. They may have existed for generations, with older members sliding into a less active *veterano* status. Young people join the same gangs that their parents or grandparents belonged to. These traditional Hispanic gangs are extremely territorial and have low mobility from their local barrios. They traditionally view themselves as street warriors. The changing nature of the drug wars in the 1980s and transnationalization of the modern drug trade after the 1990s have caused massive changes in the traditional local Hispanic gang cultures.

The drug wars of the 1980s brought about a change in the overall patterns of gang involvement in most communities. Chicago- and Los Angeles-based street gangs began to expand across the United States. Local gangs were swept up into national gang affiliations either by choice or by force; thus, many Hispanic gangs became Folk or People, Crips or, to a lesser extent, Bloods. These gangs became more mobile than their predecessors, leading to conflict between the Folk Nation and People Nation. It was fueled by immigration issues when newcomers joined the national affiliates because they might not have been as readily accepted into local Hispanic gangs.

Bucking this trend are the two rival transnational gangs: the 18th Street gang and the Mara Salvatrucha 13 (MS-13). Both gangs started in the Rampart District of Los Angeles. The 18th Street gang was formed in the late 1960s as an outgrowth of the Clanton 14 gang. The subunits of Diesiocho (XV3) are cliques whose membership varies from 50 to 100. The 18th Street gang is estimated to have 15,000 members in the Los Angeles area alone and 65,000 worldwide. Beginning as a traditional street gang, the 18th Street gang quickly developed a reputation for being aggressive and violent. The membership was originally people of Mexican decent; however, as the gang has expanded across the United States and into Central and South America, other Hispanics, Middle Easterners, Asians, and Caucasians have been allowed to join in some areas. The 18th Street gang has an organized hierarchy within each clique, but they have no overall recognized national or international leadership. Groups do communicate or coordinate with each other. The 18th Street gang has forged alliances with Mexican drug trafficking organizations and Colombian cartels. They are highly mobile and very adaptive to law enforcement counter-measures (Walker, 2010).

Their chief rivals are the Mara Salvatrucha 13. The MS-13 gang was started by Salvadorian refugees in the Rampart section of Los Angeles during the late 1980s as a defense against established Los Angeles street gangs. MS-13 is active in 42 states and Washington D.C., Mexico, Honduras, El Salvador, and Guatemala. The FBI estimates that there are 6000 to 10,000 members in the United States and even more overseas. The MS-13 has adopted the colors of blue and white, taken from the colors of the national flag of El Salvador. Membership in the MS-13 was originally restricted to people from El Salvador, Ecuador, Mexico, Honduras, and Guatemala, but now other Latinos are permitted to join. Spanish is the primary language used. Ethnicity rather than race is a factor. Ages range from 11 to 40. Females are permitted to join the MS-13 on the East Coast but not on the West Coast. The MS-13 has rapidly spread across the United States. When they move into a new area they are very flashy and wear their colors openly. When police respond, they tone down colors or use more subtle markings. MS-13 members are very open about the types of crimes they commit. They adapt quickly and change tactics to meet local needs.

Many of the MS-13 members have had paramilitary training or experience. Machete attacks by MS-13 members along the East Coast and in Central America have decapitated many victims. Notes are often left with the bodies of the victims, and fingers are chopped off the hands of gang rivals. Permission to kill is called a "green light." MS-13 assassinations have strict rules that call for at least one head shot to the victim. The murder weapon (usually a gun) is often sent to other cities to be used in another murder.

The MS-13 is organized into cliques that have regular business meetings with agendas, goals, and reports. Originally, these cliques operated totally independently of one another, but recent attempts have been made by MS-13 members from the West Coast to become more formally organized through *misas janeras* ("conferences"). Their goal is to be the leading Hispanic gang (Etter, 2010).

SKINHEADS AND OTHER WHITE GANGS

White gangs tend to be local affairs or sets of national gangs. The exception is skinheads. Skinheads fall into a special category, as their crimes are often more racial or political than they are economic. With regard to Cloward and Ohlin's (1960) theory of differential opportunity, skinheads would fall under retreatism and rebellion. They arrived in the United States from the United Kingdom in the 1970s and have since spread across the country. They operate in small groups of 10 to 25 with very little leadership or organization. Skinheads believe in a leaderless resistance and view themselves as race warriors. They often find themselves opposing African American gangs in some jurisdictions because of their racial beliefs. Although most other gangs ignore the skinheads as being irrelevant to the big picture of making money, they will sell weapons to them or buy weapons from them. Skinheads do, however, commit crimes to make money and support the gang. They have been involved in burglary rings, robberies, and the manufacture of methamphetamine, among other crimes. Skinheads often ally with other neo-Nazi groups (Etter, 1999).

ASIAN GANGS

Asian street gangs have existed in the United States since the first rush of Chinese immigration during the gold rush of the 1840s in California (Asbury, 1933). The Asian gangs have either operated independently (e.g., Oriental Lazy Boys in Wichita) or sought gangs with a national affiliation (e.g., Asian Boyz Crips). More often they are affiliated or controlled by more traditional Asian organization such as the Triads or Tongs. They have a formal organizational structure within their groups and are highly mobile. Asian gangs maintain extensive communications with other Asian gang members and often coordinate or cooperate in criminal ventures; however, there is no overall leadership structure in the United States for Asian gangs. Asian street gangs favor bright colors, but they tend to emulate their Hispanic or African American counterparts in the neighborhoods they occupy. One difference is that they will often display a streak of color through their hair when they are about to engage in some gang activity. This is a custom that has been borrowed from the Yakuza, a Japanese organized crime group. Specialized crimes of Asian gangs include arson, auto theft, and home invasions.

OUTLAW MOTORCYCLE GANGS

Biker gangs, or outlaw motorcycle clubs, began in 1935 in the United States with the Outlaws Motorcycle Club, but after World War II they expanded rapidly. The International Outlaw Motorcycle Gang Investigators Association estimated that there are at least 375 Outlaw motorcycle clubs in the United States and over 100 elsewhere in the world (IOMGIA, 2003), ranging from fewer than 25 members within a single chapter to several thousand members; hundreds of chapters exist worldwide. Many of the smaller outlaw motorcycle clubs are allied with larger ones for protection or drug distribution.

Biker gangs have a warrior philosophy, and gang members view themselves as road warriors. They want to ride free of governmental controls. Bikers reject society and societal norms. They are proud of their "FTW" philosophy and racist views. A weapons culture is common. Crimes among outlaw motorcycle gangs are economically motivated. Bikers are highly mobile; yet, many outlaw motorcycle clubs are highly territorial and enforce the 100-mile rule, which means that no one can operate within 100 miles of their territory without obtaining their permission and paying a street tax. At any given time, some outlaw motorcycle clubs are at war with others. Alliances between the groups often shift as needed to support the activities of the group. Outlaw motorcycle clubs usually maintain a strict formal style of organization. Individual clubs or chapters may elect or appoint officers of the club. Management directives are enforced by a sergeant at arms or an enforcer. Members pay dues and are required to attend meetings. The membership is all adult males. The member must own an American-made motorcycle. The biker clubhouse is a place to meet, train, party, and conduct club business. Admission is by invitation only. Clubhouses are often fortified and booby-trapped. Electronic security systems are not uncommon. Weapons are frequently stored there, along with stolen motorcycles.

Outlaw motorcycle clubs engage in crime for economic reasons, often at the wholesale level of trafficking. Their recent role as methamphetamine producers has been diminished by the large amounts of Mexican methamphetamine that have become available in the U.S. market. Some outlaw motorcycle groups (e.g., Banditos, Mongols) have formed alliances with Mexican drug trafficking organizations to transport drugs into and across the United States. Other clubs (e.g., Hell's Angels, Pagans, Outlaws) have formed alliances with Asian Triads and Canadian gangs to transport drugs from Canada into the United States. The largest outlaw motorcycle groups currently operating in the United States are the Hell's Angels, Outlaws, Banditos, Pagans, and the Sons of Silence (Barker, 2007). They are expanding, but not as fast as some of the Chicago- or Los Angeles-based street gangs. The biker lifestyle appeals to a small minority of the motorcycle population. They are exhibitionists and truly are the "one percenters" they seek to be.

FEMALE GANGS

Females are the minority in gang life in the United States. Most gangs traditionally only admit males to full membership; thus, most female gang members in the United States fall into one of three basic groups:

- *Ladies' auxiliary*—Girls hang with male gang members and adopt the identity of the gang without becoming actual voting members. They may wear the colors of the gang. This is the traditional role that has often been imposed on females when male gang members do not let them join the gang as full voting members. This is changing, especially in the Midwest.
- *Hardcore*—Girls actually join a specific gang as full voting members with the approval of male members of the gang. This is becoming more prevalent in some areas of the Midwest.
- *Girl gangs*—Girls form their own gangs and engage in criminal activities independent of male-dominated gangs.

The most significant difference between male and female gang members is adult gang membership. Very few of the women continue their membership in the gang when they become adults. The most common reasons are that they grow out of it, most become mothers, and many realize it is too crazy (Moore and Hagedorn, 2001).

In her research studying female gangs for the Chicago Crime Commission, Lindberg (1999), found two trends in female gangs. First, it is not as easy now for female gang members to go undercover as it used to be. In the past, females were shielded from the high-profile activities of the gang, such as drive-by shootings or other hits; therefore, rival gang members did not recognize them when they came into their neighborhood. Because they are more active in gang activities, the girls are more likely to be recognized by opposing gang members. Second, because girls are joining gangs at a younger age, many male gang members fear that the actions of young and undisciplined females may upset the stability of the street operations or put the gang in imminent danger. These females have a reputation for overreacting, often violently, to petty or delicate matters without considering the consequences.

GANG INVESTIGATION TECHNIQUES

By their very nature the investigation of gang crimes is a more complicated task than a normal criminal investigation. This is because the crimes are committed by groups rather than by individuals. The complex and interconnected relationships between rival gangs make any gang investigation or prosecution complicated. The patterns of criminality by gangs and gang members often mean that today's "victim" is tomorrow's perpetrator. Witness tampering or intimidation is rampant, making prosecutions difficult. Because of this, training in gangs and gang characteristics is essential for both investigators and prosecutors.

IDENTIFICATION OF GANGS AND GANG MEMBERS

Programs! Programs! You can't tell the players without a program! Unlike baseball players, although gang members could arguably be said to wear an identifying uniform of sorts, their names and numbers are seldom printed on the back of their shirts. Thus, figuring out who is who and where they belong in a gang investigation is of primary importance.

How do you identify a gang member? More importantly, how can you prove it in a court of law? To investigate gang-related crimes it is necessary to identify gang members and to develop the knowledge base required to understand the complex relationships in an organized crime or gang crime case in order to develop probable cause in conspiracy and Racketeer Influenced and Corrupt Organization (RICO) types of investigations. Specific criteria have been adopted by most law enforcement agencies to document individuals who are gang members. An example of these criteria is those adopted by the Wichita Police and the Sedgwick County Sheriff's Department, which must apply before a suspect can be classified as a gang member (Etter and Swymeler, 2008):

> *Note:* An individual must meet two (2) of the following criteria to be documented as a gang member. Same applies to other hate groups.
>
> 1. When an individual admits membership to a gang/hate group and displays knowledge of gang activities consistent with such membership
> 2. When reliable informant identifies an individual as a gang member
> 3. When an informant of previously untested reliability identifies an individual as a gang member and it's corroborated by independent information
> 4. When an individual resides in or frequents a particular gang's area and affects their style or dress, use of jewelry, symbols, or tattoos
> 5. When an individual who has not been previously identified as a gang member or hate group member has been arrested several times in the company of identified gang or hate group members for offenses that are consistent with gang activity
> 6. When there are strong indications that an individual has a close relationship with a gang but does not exactly fit the above criteria, in which case he or she shall be identified as "gang/hate group associate"

Identification of gang members allows investigators to make associations with groups and to identify the relationships between gangs, which are so essential to successful gang investigations. This is critical in developing suspects in multi-perpetrator crimes. Information must be obtained in a legal fashion. Most agencies have developed policies and procedures to cover how gang intelligence information can be obtained, how creditability of information is determined, how it must be stored, and who has access to this information. Gang investigators should be trained or familiar with the gang dynamics, characteristics, and traits in their city and surrounding cities.

INVESTIGATION OF A GANG CRIME

The problem with a gang crime is that it is usually a group offense. We are not looking for one suspect who beat up the victim; instead, we are looking for six guys basically wearing the same clothes, and they all beat up the victim. Multiple suspects are a fact of life in the investigation of a gang crime. Physical evidence is needed to corroborate the statements of witnesses and victims. Anderson et al. (2009) pointed out some things that a crime scene investigator must look for when investigating a gang crime:

- Were multiple weapons involved? Indications would include different caliber bullet casings or projectiles found at the crime scene, different types of weapons left at the crime scene, or multiple wounds on the victim.
- Does the physical evidence, such as fingerprints, blood, or DNA, indicate that more than one person was involved?
- Was anything left behind at the crime scene that might indicate group behavior (e.g., clothing, notes, multiple vehicles)?
- Is any security video available at or near the crime scene that might have captured the suspects?
- Did fresh graffiti appear in the area either before or after the crime?
- Was the victim a gang member? On what do you base your findings (see above sample gang criteria)?

When developing their criminal case, the investigator should look for signs of gang behavior, such as other gang members being present and either backing up the assailant or apparently witnessing the crime. These other gang members might have prevented others from interfering while the crime was being committed. Members of the gang often say or yell the gang's name during the commission of the crime or throw hand signs that represent the gang. Gang members often position a lookout to watch for the police or other rival gangs and alert the others when these dangers present themselves. Cars are an important part of gang crimes. Stealing a car and driving that car to commit a crime such as a drive-by is an important element of the crime. Identification of the driver can lead to arrests of the rest of the group. Another important piece of solving the crime puzzle is finding out who obtained or was holding the weapon. Weapons are often acquired for the purpose of committing a crime, and finding out where the gun came from or went is crucial (Anderson et al., 2009).

When interviewing witnesses, the investigator should determine the number of suspects, their descriptions, and the specific actions of each suspect. Did the suspects arrive or leave together? Were the suspects wearing the same types or colors of clothing? Were gang signs thrown or a gang name mentioned? How did the suspects interact together (e.g., were directions or orders being given, was there a lookout)? Did multiple people participate in the crime? Witnesses should be separated and witness statements should be gathered immediately before the witnesses can be contaminated by group discussion of the events or be forced to recant their statements by gang members or their associates (Anderson et al., 2009).

ANTI-GANG TACTICS

Anti-gang tactics that have proven effective in some jurisdictions include warrant round-ups, which can take large numbers of gang members off of the streets. Coordination with parole and probation authorities provides good intelligence, and association with a known gang member can be a cause of a parole violation for a parolee or probationer. Intensive patrol in open-air drug markets or high crime areas does not totally stop all gang crime, but it suppresses it and makes it difficult for the drug dealers to do business. Closing off streets by means of simple barricades has worked to restrict access to certain areas and reduce drive-bys or getaways in high crime areas.

ANTI-GANG LEGISLATION

Most states have statues defining what is a gang. A typical gang definition statute is that of the Commonwealth of Virginia:

> §18.2-46.1. Definitions.
>
> As used in this article unless the context requires otherwise or it is otherwise provided:
>
> "Act of violence" means those felony offenses described in subsection A of §19.2-297.1.
>
> "Criminal street gang" means any ongoing organization, association, or group of three or more persons, whether formal or informal, (i) which has as one of its primary objectives or activities the commission of one or more criminal activities; (ii) which has an identifiable name or identifying sign or symbol; and (iii) whose members individually or collectively have engaged in the commission of, attempt to commit, conspiracy to commit, or solicitation of two or more predicate criminal acts, at least one of which is an act of violence, provided such acts were not part of a common act or transaction.

Many states prohibit membership in a gang, but statutes such as this can face constitutional challenges (Anderson et al., 2009). Many states allow gang crime or gang membership to be used as a sentence enhancer when gang membership is a factor in the crime. Some cities have passed municipal ordinances against gangs or gang activities. These criminal laws have had mixed results. Research has shown that the statutes are not used uniformly, and many have faced legal challenges (VA DCJS, 2008)

In order to combat street gang members standing around on street corners and creating open-air drug markets, the City of Chicago passed an anti-loitering ordinance that defined loitering as "remaining in one place without any apparent purpose." It allowed Chicago police officers to order individuals to move or be arrested. From 1992 to 1995, 43,000 people were arrested based on this ordinance; however, the Supreme Court found that the ordinance was unconstitutionally vague and struck it down in 1999 (*City of Chicago v. Jesus Morales*, 1999).

The state of California has adopted the unique tactic of suing the various gangs and obtaining civil court injunctions to prohibit the gang or members of the gang to be at a certain street corner or other specific location. Gang members who show up at the prohibited site may by cited for contempt of court. This legal tactic has met with some limited success.

QUESTIONS FOR DISCUSSION

1. What are the primary crimes that gangs commit to make money?
2. Explain how gangs protect themselves from infiltration by the police and rival gangs.
3. Explain the three primary type of gang initiation rites.
4. What are the two primary groups that Chicago-based street gangs divide themselves into?
5. How has the nature of Hispanic gangs changed over the past 20 years?
6. Explain how female gang members are different from males in their gang activities.
7. Describe how gang crimes are different from other crimes.
8. Explain how a gang member is identified by law enforcement.
9. Describe an effective anti-gang tactic used by law enforcement.
10. Are anti-gang laws effective? Why or why not?

BIBLIOGRAPHY

Anderson, J., Nye, M., Freitas, R., and Wolf, J. (2009). *Gang Prosecution Manual*. Washington, D.C.: Office of Juvenile Justice and Delinquency Prevention, U.S. Department of Justice.

Arlacchi, P. (1987). *Mafia Business: The Mafia Ethnic and the Spirit of Capitalism*. London: Verso.

Asbury, H. (1927). *The Gangs of New York: An Informal History of the New York Underworld*. New York: Old Town Books.

Asbury, H. (1933). *The Barbary Coast: An Informal History of the San Francisco Underworld*. New York: Garden City Publishing.

Barker, T. (2007). *Biker Gangs and Organized Crime*. Newark, NJ: Lexis Nexis.

City of Chicago v. Jesus Morales, 527 U.S. 41 (1999).

Cloward, R. and Ohlin, L. (1960). *Delinquency and Opportunity: A Theory of Delinquent Gangs*. New York: The Free Press.

Elder, A. (1997). Inside Gang Society: How Gang Members Imitate Legitimate Social Forms. *Journal of Gang Crime Research*, 3(4):1–12.

Etter, G. (1998). Common Characteristics of Gangs: Examining the Cultures of the New Urban Tribes. *Journal of Gang Research*, 5(2):19–33.

Etter, G. (1999). Skinheads: Manifestations of the Warrior Culture of the New Urban Tribes. *Journal of Gang Research*, 6(3):9–23.

Etter, G. (2010). Mara Salvatrucha 13: A Transnational Threat. *Journal of Gang Research*. 17(2):1–17.

Etter, G. and Swymeler, W. (2008). Examining the Demographics of Street Gangs in Wichita, Kansas. *Journal of Gang Research*, 16(1):1–12.

FBI. (2008). *The MS-13 Threat: A National Assessment*. Washington, D.C.: Federal Bureau of Investigation (http://www.fbi.gov/page2/jan08/ms13_011408.html).

Fried, M. (1975). *The Notion of Tribe*. Menlo Park, CA: Cummings.

Gage, N. (1971). *The Mafia Is Not an Equal Opportunity Employer*. New York: McGraw-Hill.

Holmes, L. (1971). *Anthropology: An Introduction*, 2nd ed. New York: Ronald Press.

IOMGIA. (2003). *Proceedings of the 29th Annual International Outlaw Motorcycle Gang Investigators Association Conference*, Scottsdale, AZ, September.

Jackson, R. and McBride, W. (1986). *Understanding Street Gangs*. Placerville, CA: Custom Publishing.

Knox, G. (2006). *An Introduction to Gangs*, 6th ed. Peotone, IL: New Chicago School Press.

Lindberg, K. (1999). *Girls in Gangs: The Girls Behind the Boys*. Chicago, IL: Chicago Crime Commission.

Miranda v. Arizona, 384 U.S. 436 (1966).

Moore, J. and Hagedorn, J. (2001). Female Gangs: A Focus on Research. *Juvenile Justice Bulletin*, March, pp. 1–11.

Nadel, B. (1996). NYC DOC Slashes Gang Violence. *Corrections Forum*, 5(9).

Padilla, F. (1993). *The Gang as an American Enterprise*. New Brunswick, NJ: Rutgers University Press.

Petrone, F. (1994). *The Street Gang Identification Manual*. Elgin, IL: Gang Prevention, Inc.

Strandberg, K. (1997). Money Laundering. *Law Enforcement Technology*, 24(7):28–33.

Thrasher, F. (1936). *The Gang: A Study of 1,313 Gangs in Chicago*, 2nd ed. Chicago, IL: University of Chicago Press.

VA DCJS. (2008). *Use of Anti-Gang Statutes Contained in the Code of Virginia*. Richmond, VA: Department of Criminal Justice Services.

Walker, R. (2010). *18th Street Gang: An Aggressive and Violent Criminal Street Gang*, Robert Walker's Gangs OR Us, http://www.gangsorus.com/18th_street.htm.

Yablonsky, L. (1962). *The Violent Gang*. New York: Macmillan.

6

Putting It All Together

CHAPTER 19

Legal Issues in Criminal Investigations

Frank DiMarino
Kaplan University

CHAPTER OBJECTIVES

After reading this chapter, you should be able to understand the following:

1. Criminal laws are part of broad penal codes enacted by state legislatures or the U.S. Congress.
2. Because states enact comprehensive penal codes that define crimes and establish penalties, different behaviors may be treated as crimes in one state but not in another.
3. Public perception about criminal behavior changes over time, so what conduct is considered to be a crime may also change.
4. Criminal statutes define what constitutes a crime by defining the crime through the use of elements or components of a criminal offense.
5. Criminal statutes must be sufficiently specific so persons of ordinary intelligence have fair notice that the contemplated conduct is forbidden by the statute.
6. The punishment for felony offenses includes possible sentences of more than a year in confinement.
7. A grand jury must determine whether probable cause exists that a crime was committed and that the defendant committed the crime before a defendant can be charged with a felony.
8. Misdemeanors are lesser offenses that include a possible sentence of no more than a year or less of incarceration.
9. Police officers are entitled to arrest individuals for misdemeanors, even for seat belt violations, committed in their presence.

10. First responders to a crime scene must be aware that the initial crime scene investigation can be pivotal to discovering the identity of the perpetrator and gathering crucial evidence.

11. Processing a crime scene includes marking the location of the evidence, sketching and photographing the scene, measuring relevant distances, taking investigative notes, and collecting the evidence.

12. The collection of fungible evidence, such as drugs, money, certain weapons, and contraband, must be marked and accounted for with a chain-of-custody document to protect the integrity of the evidence.

13. An arrest warrant protects an individual from an unreasonable seizure and may only be issued upon a showing of probable cause to believe a suspect is committing or has committed an offense.

14. The exclusionary rule renders evidence that has been unlawfully obtained inadmissible at trial.

15. The judge decides whether any of the evidence that the parties want to use is illegal or improper.

16. Probable cause may be based upon information shared among law enforcement agencies, crime databases, and observations made by investigators.

17. A police officer may arrest without a warrant provided that a felony or a misdemeanor is committed in the officer's presence.

18. During an investigatory stop, police officers are permitted to frisk the person for weapons provided that the officers have an articulable, reasonable suspicion and that the officers are acting to protect their safety.

19. Criminal profiles may be used as the basis to conduct an investigatory stop.

20. Probable cause to search is a finding that there is a fair probability that evidence of a crime or fruits of a crime will be found in a particular location.

21. Facts within an affidavit that are considered "stale" cannot be used to support a probable cause determination.

22. Before entering a private residence, police officers must abide by their state's "knock and announce" statutes.

23. Exigent circumstances, such as the hot pursuit of a suspect, may justify a warrantless search.

24. A prosecutor has special ethical obligations in criminal cases.

25. If contraband or evidence of a crime is found during an inventory search, that evidence may be seized.

26. A prosecutor must disclose to the defense any exculpatory evidence and evidence that may be used to attack the credibility of a witness.

27. A prosecutor must seek justice in each case, which may include dismissing charges when the evidence is insufficient to convict.

28. A defendant who is unable to afford a lawyer to represent him at trial may have a court-appointed lawyer.

Chapter Outline

- Introduction
- Criminal Law
- Felonies
- Misdemeanors
- Legal Considerations and the Crime Scene
- Arrest
- Search and Seizure
- Criminal Procedure

INTRODUCTION

This chapter describes the substantive and procedural laws that govern criminal prosecutions from the crime scene investigation through to the verdict rendered by a jury. The formation of substantive criminal law—the standards that apply to behavior and conduct within a society and the punishments attached to violations of those standards—is controlled by statutes enacted by the U.S. Congress and state legislatures. Criminal offenses are divided into two major classifications: felonies and misdemeanors. Felonies are offenses where the punishment exceeds one year of incarceration and misdemeanors are lesser offenses where the defendant can be sentenced to a year or less in jail.

Knowledge of legal requirements and standards that apply to the collection and preservation of evidence is necessary so the integrity of the crime scene is preserved and evidence can be admissible as exhibits during a trial. The protection of a crime scene and the comprehensive documentation of investigative activity and observations are crucial to apprehending suspects and bringing them to justice. An accurate chain of custody that documents the transporting and handling of evidence ensures that evidence is properly stored and analyzed so it can be relied upon during a criminal prosecution.

The arrest of an individual represents one of the most controlling interactions between the police and society. The Fourth Amendment to the U.S. Constitution requires that all arrests be made in accordance with a warrant supported by probable cause. Probable cause to arrest can be based on numerous factors, especially in light of technological improvements in the sharing of criminal information among law enforcement agencies. Exceptions to the warrant requirement include when it is impractical to get a warrant because of potential harm to society or in cases where the defendant may flee. Less intrusive than an arrest are police encounters where persons are stopped based on the reasonable suspicion by the police that criminal activity is afoot. Such a stop is of limited duration, and police are allowed to question the suspect, frisk the suspect to avoid harm to the police, and detain the suspect until the suspicion is dispelled.

Searches for evidence often provide productive opportunities to further the criminal investigation and to gather information to support a criminal prosecution. The Fourth Amendment also mandates that a search be conducted only with a warrant that is supported by probable cause. Although there are exceptions to this warrant requirement based on exigent circumstances, such exceptions are narrowly interpreted, and they must not be the result of police conduct that has contributed to creating the exigent circumstances.

Rules of criminal procedure govern the conduct of criminal prosecutions and affect the manner of criminal investigations; for example, custodial interrogations require that specific constitutional warnings be provided to a suspect or incriminating statements could be excluded from trial. Likewise, a criminal defendant is afforded representation by counsel at all critical stages of a prosecution. The criminal investigator must diligently follow the rules of criminal procedure to ensure that evidence is gathered lawfully and that its later use and effectiveness at trial are not compromised.

CRIMINAL LAW

The body of law that sets forth offenses and penalties for violations is known as criminal law. As lawmakers, legislators consider societal customs and behaviors and enact laws that prohibit certain activities, such as theft, or mandate that certain activities take place under penalty of law, such as paying taxes. Common law principles that emanated from 18th-century English law form the foundation of many criminal laws such as addressing theft, murder, and burglary. Currently, many criminal laws are part of broad penal codes enacted by state legislatures or the U.S. Congress. Generally, criminal behavior can be divided into two categories. First, *malum in se* crimes are those offenses that are inherently bad; these crimes include, for example, murder, rape, assault, and robbery. Second, *malum prohibitum* crimes are those crimes that are not inherently wrong but instead are made a crime because of legislative action. Such crimes are against public policy and include, for example, failure to file income tax returns, false reports of crimes, drinking in a public place, and speeding.

Most states enact a comprehensive penal code that defines crimes and establishes maximum penalties for violations. The Texas Penal Code, for example, was written to establish a complete "system of prohibitions, penalties, and correctional measures to deal with conduct that unjustifiably and inexcusably causes or threatens harm to those individual or public interests for which state protection is appropriate." The Texas code defines such crimes as assault, murder, robbery, arson, money laundering, theft, sexual assault, and fraud.

Because states are able to enact their own criminal laws, different behaviors may be treated as crimes in one state but not in another; for example, the sale of alcoholic beverages is not permitted on Sundays in some states, but other states place few or no restrictions on the sale of alcohol. State legislators, as the representatives of citizens within a state, are empowered to enact laws that reflect what they believe society deems is acceptable and unacceptable conduct. Although legislatures take into account the public perception of crime, it is important to note that public perception tends to change over time and among regions, so what is considered a crime may also similarly change over time.

The Federal Criminal Code as enacted by Congress is contained in several titles or major sections. Title 18 defines many crimes that are often used by prosecutors and investigators in bringing federal charges, including the interstate transportation of stolen property, wire fraud, bank fraud, and embezzlement of funds from a federally insured bank. Title 26 defines most crimes related to tax violations, such as income tax evasion and failures to pay tax.

The criminal justice system in America relies upon the enforcement of criminal laws and following procedural rules relating to the investigation and prosecution of a criminal case. Substantive criminal laws generally define what acts constitute crimes. Statutes specify the elements of each crime. The elements of the offenses are the component parts of the criminal act that must be proven beyond a reasonable doubt by the government during a prosecution.

Wisconsin Statute 943.10 specifies that a burglary occurs when any person intentionally enters any room within or any structure used as a building or dwelling, an enclosed railroad car, an enclosed portion of any ship or vessel, a locked enclosed cargo portion of a truck or trailer, a motor home or other motorized type of home, or a trailer home, whether or not any person is living in any such home, with intent to steal or commit a felony therein and without consent of the person in lawful possession. The elements of burglary are (1) intentional entry; (2) of any building, dwelling, or other specified area; (3) with intent to steal or commit felony; and (4) without permission.

Criminal statutes must be sufficiently specific such that prosecutors and investigators will not broadly interpret them and prosecute individuals for criminal acts not contemplated by the legislatures. In 1972, the Supreme Court decided the significant case *Papachristou v. City of Jacksonville*, which concerned the interpretation of criminal statutes. The Court considered a vagrancy statute that provided criminal penalties for "common night walkers, … persons wandering or strolling around from place to place without any lawful purpose or object, habitual loafers, … persons … frequenting … places where alcoholic beverages are sold or served, persons able to work but habitually living upon the earnings of their wives or minor children." Upon the arrest of eight defendants for what was argued to be seemingly innocent conduct, the Court determined that this vagrancy statute was void for vagueness. In other words, the statute on its face, "fail[ed] to give a person of ordinary intelligence fair notice that his contemplated conduct is forbidden by the statute." The Court concluded that the statute encouraged arbitrary and erratic arrests and convictions by giving almost unfettered discretion to the police. Without specific standards governing the exercise of police discretion, the statute became a convenient tool for "harsh and discriminatory enforcement by local prosecuting officials, against particular groups deemed to merit their displeasure."

FELONIES

A felony offense is defined as a crime that carries a punishment of more than a year of incarceration. The investigation of felony offenses is treated as a priority for most investigative agencies, and more resources are devoted to the investigation of felony crimes. Felonies include such crimes as robbery, rape, murder, identity theft, bank fraud, bribery, insurance fraud, and money laundering. The investigation of felonies generally involves more investigative resources than minor offenses because of the more complex nature of the crime, the greater harm to the victim, and the deleterious impact upon society. Consequently, the punishment that a judge imposes on an offender who has committed a felony may also be more severe.

The Fifth Amendment to the U.S. Constitution requires that all felony cases be indicted by a grand jury. This means that a prosecutor must establish that it is more probable than not that a felony has been committed and that the defendant committed the felony. The standards that a grand jury employs to decide the cases before them are not as stringent as at trial; for example, the grand jury may consider hearsay evidence, but a trial jury may not unless the evidence is covered by an exception provided for in the rules of evidence. Also, the trial jury must use the standard of beyond a reasonable doubt to determine guilt, but the grand jury uses the probable cause standard to indict.

Generally speaking, in about 90% of the felony cases, the defendant pleads guilty rather than exercising his or her right to a trial before a jury. Often, a guilty plea is the result of dropping a charge or otherwise limiting the amount of incarceration or other punishment that a defendant would have to endure. Such plea bargaining has its critics, as defendants usually do not have the same bargaining influence as the government. On the other hand, plea bargaining does result in efficiently disposing of the charges through a conviction and frees up limited criminal justice resources to try other cases. The conviction of a felony carries the loss of certain civil rights, such as the right to vote, serve on juries, obtain certain professional licenses, or receive specified governmental benefits.

MISDEMEANORS

A misdemeanor is a crime less serious than a felony and carries a maximum penalty of one year or less in confinement. Misdemeanors include such crimes as shoplifting, disorderly conduct, vandalism, trespass, and public intoxication. A misdemeanor is charged by a formal accusation made in a charging document by a prosecutor. A grand jury does not consider the charging of misdemeanors. Misdemeanors committed in the presence of a police officer may justify an arrest without securing a warrant. In *Atwater v. City of Lago Vista* (2001), the Supreme Court held that a police officer could arrest the driver of a vehicle for a seat belt violation, even though the arrestee was a mother with a child in the back seat of the car, because officers may arrest for misdemeanors committed in their presence. Similarly, in *Virginia v. Moore* (2008), the Court upheld a warrantless arrest for driving with a suspended license despite a state law requiring that the defendant appear pursuant to a summons because police officers may arrest for misdemeanors committed in their presence. An offense occurs in the "presence" of an officer when the arresting officer, with the aid of all his senses, such as sight, smell, and hearing, determines that an offense is being committed.

LEGAL CONSIDERATIONS AND THE CRIME SCENE

As former U.S. Attorney General Janet Reno recognized, "Actions taken at the outset of an investigation at a crime scene can play a pivotal role in the resolution of a case. Careful, thorough investigation is key to ensure that potential physical evidence is not tainted or destroyed or potential witnesses overlooked." The first responder to a crime scene must be aware that the crime scene will have present the most productive evidence when the first responder arrives. The suspect may still be in the area. Physical evidence, such as clothing, weapons, casings or shells, fingerprints, toolmarks, residue, fluids, footprints, tire marks, and fibers may all be present when law enforcement authorities first arrive but may vanish due to inclement weather, the actions of the victim, or the conduct of bystanders. If the crime scene is not properly protected, witnesses to the crime may leave the area without being identified. The first responder must not only protect others from injury or loss of life but also control the crime scene so that the area is protected, evidence is collected and preserved, and destruction and contamination of evidence are minimized. Quick action in light of an understanding of criminal investigations may mean the difference between finding crucial evidence or losing evidence that could lead to a successful prosecution.

First aid to any victims and evacuation to a medical facility take priority over controlling a crime scene. Similarly, examinations at the scene by a medical doctor of any deceased victim also have priority.

Nonetheless, appropriate actions must be taken to preserve the integrity of the scene by isolating and controlling the scene. The boundaries of a crime scene must be identified, established, protected, and secured by diligent police officers. Proper security must be implemented so evidence is not altered, rearranged, destroyed, lost, concealed, or removed without authority. Police can secure a crime scene by roping off the area and patrolling its boundaries.

Protection and control of a crime scene continue until investigators have thoroughly processed and released the scene from police control. Processing the crime scene includes marking the location of evidence, sketching the scene and location of the evidence, photographing the crime scene, measuring relevant distances, completing investigative notes, collecting and cataloguing the evidence, and transporting the evidence.

The police officer who responds to a crime scene should take the following actions:

1. Provide needed medical attention.
2. Record the location, date, time of arrival, and weather conditions.
3. Try to identify the suspect and apprehend if in the vicinity or contact supervisor so appropriate bulletins can be issued.
4. Call for more officers so the scene can be adequately protected.
5. Protect any evidence that may be destroyed by placing boxes or other appropriate covering over the evidence.
6. Identify victims, witnesses, and suspects; take note of their names, addresses, phone numbers, and other relevant information.
7. Prepare investigative notes that include a description of the scene, including odors, openings, lighting, and other observations.

The priority of these actions depends on the nature of the crime scene and circumstances of the offense.

The collection of evidence and reporting of investigative activity must be trustworthy and complete so they can be appropriately considered at a criminal trial that may take place months or even years after the crime is committed. Photographs and sketches are usually important exhibits at trial. Likewise, the collection of fungible evidence such as drugs, money, weapons, and other items must be sufficiently marked as evidence, recorded in an evidence log, and properly controlled with a chain-of-custody document so the evidence can be readily admissible at trial. Evidence must be collected, preserved, inventoried, packaged, transported, and submitted to the lab or evidence custodian in accordance with the department's standard operating procedures to ensure the integrity of each piece of evidence to serve as a later trial exhibit if necessary.

ARREST

The Fourth Amendment of the U.S. Constitution sets forth the controlling standard for arrests made by law enforcement officers. The Fourth Amendment states: "The right of the people to be secure in their persons, houses, papers, and effects, against unreasonable searches and seizures, shall not be violated, and no Warrants shall issue, but upon probable cause, supported by Oath or affirmation, and particularly describing the place to be searched, and the persons or things to be seized." An arrest warrant protects an individual from an unreasonable seizure and may only be issued by a judicial officer with probable cause, based on an affidavit, to believe the arrestee is committing or has committed an offense. In *Johnson v. United States* (1948), the Supreme Court stated:

> The point of the Fourth Amendment … is not that it denies law enforcement the support of the usual inferences which reasonable men draw from evidence. Its protection consists in requiring that those inferences be drawn by a neutral and detached magistrate instead of being judged by the officer engaged in the often competitive enterprise of ferreting out crime.

For violations of the Fourth Amendment, a criminal procedure doctrine known as the *exclusionary rule* renders evidence gathered during an "unreasonable" search or arrest inadmissible at trial. The Fourth Amendment thus guarantees both a substantive right and procedural protection for criminal defendants.

PROBABLE CAUSE TO ARREST

The judicial officer authorizing the warrant must consider the facts and circumstances presented in the warrant application and affidavit in a practical, common-sense manner. The factual statements in the affidavit of the officer requesting the warrant must provide a "substantial basis" for the probable cause determination that a crime has been committed and who the perpetrator is. The facts stated in the affidavit must be current and recent; they must not be stale. The warrant itself must describe with particularity the person to be arrested and the crime alleged to have been committed. Generally, reviewing courts give great deference to a judicial officer's decision to issue a warrant.

The standard of probable cause may be satisfied by relying upon numerous facts and circumstances learned through a criminal investigation. First, probable cause may be based on the direct observations of the officer; for example, the officer may observe a criminal offense or suspicious activity and report the events observed in an affidavit to support a warrant. Police may also draw conclusions about criminal activity based on their experience and special training regarding suspicious behaviors that are not, at first take, apparently criminal.

Second, probable cause may be based on information or evidence obtained during an investigative detention or a "Terry stop." The Terry stop is described in more detail in the section on investigatory stops and reasonable suspicion. The purpose of this type of police encounter is to resolve a reasonable suspicion that a law enforcement officer may have about criminal activity that may be occurring or is about to occur. During a Terry stop, the officer may conduct a pat-down or a frisk to protect his safety or public safety. This limited pat-down may result in the officer discovering contraband that could be used to establish probable cause to arrest; for example, during a Terry stop, a police officer may frisk a suspect because a bulge in the suspect's pants pocket could be a concealed pistol. During such a pat-down, the officer may find illegal drugs in the suspect's pocket that could be used to establish probable cause for a drug arrest. Evidence that is in plain view or obtained from a consensual search may also establish probable cause to arrest.

Third, probable cause may be based on information provided by an informant who has a proven track record of reliability. (Of course, reliable information from an informant may also create reasonable suspicion and justify an investigatory stop.) The reliability of an informant's tip is evaluated on a sliding scale. Increased corroboration will be necessary before acting on a tip from an informant who is of uncertain or unknown trustworthiness. On the other hand, less corroboration may suffice if the information is from a known previously reliable source. To properly assess the reliability of an informant's knowledge, an investigating officer should obtain as much detailed information concerning two specific areas. First, how did the informant obtain the information about the specific criminal activity? Did the informant learn of the information through personal observation, hearsay from acquaintances, direct conversation with the suspects, or some combination of these? Second, why should the police officer believe the informant? Has the informant been reliable in the past so the informant has a proven track record or are there independent circumstances that corroborate the informant's knowledge that render the informant's statements trustworthy?

Fourth, probable cause may exist based on information provided by other law enforcement sources. Law enforcement agencies may share information that cumulatively may amount to probable cause to identify the perpetrator and the offense. Federal, state, and local agencies are sharing more information regarding criminal activities by participating in joint task forces, regional fusion centers, and special crime prevention initiatives. Additionally, crime databases such as the U.S. Department of Treasury's Financial Crimes Enforcement Network (FinCEN) stores and evaluates financial transaction information to aid law enforcement in the investigation of money laundering, bank fraud, terrorist financing, and other financial crimes. These sources, taken together with other investigative activity, may aid in establishing probable cause. Notably, probable cause cannot be established through information based on mere suspicion received from an anonymous source. The Supreme Court decided in *Florida v. J.L.* (2000) that an anonymous tip that a person carrying a gun, without more, does not give rise to probable cause that a crime was committed or even reasonable suspicion to justify an investigatory stop and frisk. For a tip to be considered sufficient to amount to a reasonable suspicion or probable cause, it must come from a source with demonstrated reliability.

ARRESTS CONDUCTED AT PRIVATE BUILDINGS

If the arrest is to occur on premises that are owned by a third party such as a parent, friend, or acquaintance of the suspect to be arrested, the arrest warrant alone does not grant authority to the arresting officer to enter the private building to make the arrest. Instead, to enter the premises legitimately, the arresting officer must have an independent legal justification. Specifically, the arresting officer must have a search warrant, the owner's consent, or exigent circumstances to lawfully enter the premises to make the arrest. Exigent circumstances include such situations that would lead a reasonable person to believe that, unless an entry into the premises and an arrest are made immediately, the suspect may flee, destroy evidence, or continue in violent criminal activity.

WARRANTLESS ARRESTS

For an arrest to occur legitimately, it must be pursuant to a warrant or based on an authorized exception to the warrant requirement of the Fourth Amendment; for example, under common law, a law enforcement officer may arrest without a warrant a person for any felony committed in the officer's presence. Some states have codified this common law principle to give statutory authority to officers (and, in some cases, other persons) to make an arrest for felonies committed in their presence. Section 2935.04 of the Ohio Revised Code on Criminal Procedure, a statute effective for over a half a century, provides that, "When a felony has been committed, or there is reasonable ground to believe that a felony has been committed, any person without a warrant may arrest another whom he has reasonable cause to believe is guilty of the offense, and detain him until a warrant can be obtained." After making a warrantless arrest, an officer must promptly secure a judicial determination of probable cause. Obviously, a considerable amount of risk to the officer and to third parties accompanies an arrest. To promote officer safety, an officer should restrain the arrestee as soon as possible so the arrestee cannot flee or inflict harm. Second, the officer should search the arrestee for weapons and any contraband. The search should include the arrestee's clothing, bags, containers, and other items within the arrestee's reach and control. Third, the officer should conduct a protective sweep of the immediate area of the arrest to ensure that weapons or other armed persons are not present; for example, if an arrest occurs in a two bedroom apartment, an officer is justified to look in each bedroom and other rooms, including the closets, to ensure that an armed person is not present in the apartment that may harm the officers.

CUSTODIAL INTERROGATION

After a person is apprehended and before any questioning occurs, the arrestee should receive his Miranda warnings. In *Miranda v. Arizona* (1966), the Supreme Court held that no confession is admissible that is obtained through custodial interrogation unless the suspect is first advised of his Fifth Amendment rights. To comply with the *Miranda* decision, a suspect needs to be informed of the following: (1) He or she has the right to remain silent, (2) anything that is said may be used against him or her in court, (3) he or she has the right to consult with an attorney and to have an attorney present during questioning, and (4) if he or she cannot afford an attorney, one will be appointed. Providing an oral and written advisement of these rights, along with a signed waiver from the suspect, significantly contributes to the admissibility of any confession that a suspect may provide and rebuts any claim of compelled self-incrimination.

INVESTIGATORY STOPS AND REASONABLE SUSPICION

It is important to realize that not all encounters between law enforcement and individuals arise to the level of an arrest; for example, in *Terry v. Ohio* (1968), the Supreme Court decided that police are authorized to stop a person for a limited time, ask for identification, ask questions about what they are doing, and, to ensure that the officer's safety is protected, conduct a pat-down and a frisk. The range of permissible police activities must be reasonably related to the original purpose for the stop. For this brief encounter to occur legitimately, a police officer must only have a reasonable suspicion that criminal activity is afoot rather than satisfying the higher standard of probable cause.

To satisfy the reasonable suspicion standard to conduct an investigatory stop, an officer must have a reasonable, objective, and articulable suspicion, based on the "totality of circumstances," that a person is engaged in criminal activity. Mere hunches or generalized suspicions are insufficient. The police officer must be able to articulate objective reasons why he believed criminal activity was occurring; an officer's subjective intentions are not relevant.

To find a reasonable suspicion, courts rely on a police officer's personal observations and the officer's knowledge that a crime has been committed. Reasonable suspicion may arise based on an officer's observation of several seemingly innocent activities, such as two men at night walking back and forth on a sidewalk and stopping and talking in front of a jewelry store, that may cumulatively create reasonable suspicion. Courts are willing to defer to the observations and conclusions of the police. It is understood that an experienced officer can infer criminal activity from conduct that seems innocuous or innocent to a lay observer. Flight from the police may trigger reasonable suspicion; for example, in a high crime area, a person's unprovoked flight upon seeing the police can justify an investigatory stop. Importantly, however, a generalized suspicion of criminal activity based solely on race does not justify an investigatory stop.

When an officer holds a person beyond the amount of time necessary to accomplish the purpose of the stop, the stop rises to the level of an arrest that must be supported by probable cause. There is no bright-line rule to define when an investigatory stop transforms into an arrest. Instead, on a case-by-case basis, courts consider the diligence of police in speedily resolving their reasonable suspicion, the nature of any physical restraints or commands placed on a suspect's liberty, and whether the police removed the individual to another location. Courts use a balancing test between the limitations placed on a person's liberty and the need to protect the safety of the police officer and the public.

As mentioned, under *Terry v. Ohio*, during an investigatory stop, if the officer reasonably believes his safety or public safety is at risk, he may pat-down or frisk a suspect's outer clothing. The frisk should be limited to a search for weapons and may not be used as a subterfuge to search for evidence of criminal activity.

CRIMINAL PROFILES

Law enforcement officers frequently use drug courier profiles as a means to halt drug trafficking and possession. These profiles are based on an accumulation of law enforcement experience regarding traits and characteristics that generally would be noticeable for someone in possession of drug contraband. Such profiles serve as a valuable means for officers to be more alert to likely criminal activity, although such profiles may vary among locations and regions and become outdated over time. Although courts have differed in rulings regarding law enforcement use of drug profiles, some general rules emanate from the cases. First, the drug courier profile itself cannot justify an arrest but it may justify an investigatory stop. In other words, the fact that a suspect meets a profile does not create probable cause to arrest; at most, it may create a reasonable suspicion on the part of the officer that criminal activity is afoot that would prompt a Terry stop. Second, to justify such a stop, the officer will need to provide a reasonable, objective, articulable suspicion based on the officer's observations and experiences. As Chief Justice Rehnquist stated in *United States v. Sokolow* (1989): "A court sitting to determine the existence of reasonable suspicion must require the [law enforcement officer] to articulate the factors leading to that conclusion, but the fact that these factors may be set forth in a 'profile' does not … detract from their evidentiary significance." The key is that the law enforcement officer must provide sufficient information to justify the stop. Third, and crucial to a successful prosecution, unless the underlying investigative stop is valid, any later search, arrest, or seizure of contraband will be invalid.

SEARCH AND SEIZURE

A search is the governmental invasion of a person's privacy. Not all privacy interests, however, are protected by the Fourth Amendment. The Supreme Court uses a two-part test to determine the legitimate existence of privacy that should be protected by the Fourth Amendment. First, the individual must have a subjective expectation of privacy, and, second, society must be prepared to recognize that expectation as objectively reasonable. So, items that are abandoned, exposed to the public, or obtained by consent from the party are not protected by the Fourth Amendment because there is no reasonable expectation of privacy in such items. Whether governmental action constitutes a search depends on how intrusive the action is. An example of a minimal intrusion that does not constitute a search is the use of a drug canine to perform a sniff test to determine the presence of drugs. The sniff test may be conducted without infringing upon the Fourth Amendment rights.

PROBABLE CAUSE TO SEARCH

A search warrant protects an individual's privacy interest in his or her home and possessions against unjustified police intrusions. Similar to arrest warrants, search warrants also require a showing of probable cause. Probable cause to search is simply a "fair probability" that contraband, evidence of a crime, instrumentalities of a crime, or fruits of a crime will be found in a particular place. If there is probable cause to believe the item sought will be in the place, but is not there at the time of issuing the warrant, the judicial officer may authorize an anticipatory search warrant. Investigating officers seeking a warrant must prepare an affidavit that provides to the judicial officer a "substantial basis" to support a finding that probable cause exists. The affidavit must contain sufficient facts so the warrant can state with particularity the place to be searched and the items to be seized. As with arrest warrants, such facts may be based on the officer's experience and special training, information from a reliable and known informant, sources that can be independently corroborated, and other investigative activity. Facts obtained from a prior illegal search, however, cannot be relied upon to support a finding of probable cause. In addition, facts within an affidavit that are considered "stale" cannot be used to support a probable cause determination.

SEARCH WARRANTS

As mentioned, the Fourth Amendment requires that a warrant describe with "particular[ity] ... the place to be searched and the persons or things to be seized." This clause has been interpreted to protect against wide-ranging exploratory searches, so an individual's privacy is safeguarded from unfettered police intrusions. Many search warrant applications will include a photograph of the place to be searched, with the house number clearly marked so the agents executing the warrant will not make a mistake. It is also good practice to incorporate by reference into the warrant the affidavit so the attachments to the warrant may cure a warrant lacking sufficient particularity or that contains such mistakes as transposed house numbers or wrong addresses. An example of a catch-all phrase included in some warrants is "evidence of crime at this date unknown." Such a phrase, when coupled with the affidavit incorporated by reference into the warrant and the warrant itself, may be deemed to sufficiently limit police discretion in executing the warrant. In *Andresen v. Maryland* (1976), the Supreme Court determined that a similar catch-all phrase did not render the warrant insufficiently particular. Thus, a warrant authorizing seizure of "fruits, instrumentalities and evidence of crime at this [time] unknown," when read in context with the rest of the warrant application, properly authorizes a search for evidence relevant to the warrant's specified offense of false pretenses.

"KNOCK AND ANNOUNCE" STATUTES

When executing a warrant on a private dwelling, officers must comply with "knock and announce" requirements. Under common law, police officers could not forcibly enter a residence to execute a search warrant unless they first knocked at the door, identified themselves as officers of the law, announced their reason for requesting admittance into the home, and were refused admittance. In *Wilson v. Arkansas* (1995), the Court held that the "knock and announce" principle is an element of the Fourth Amendment reasonableness inquiry. The Supreme Court has determined that "every householder, the good and the bad, the guilty and the innocent, is entitled to the protection designed to secure the common interest against unlawful invasion of the house." About 34 states and the federal government have enacted "knock and announce" statutes requiring that law enforcement officers knock and announce their presence prior to making a forced entry. The federal "knock and announce" statute provides: "The officer may break open any outer or inner door or window of a house, or any part of a house, or anything therein, to execute a search warrant, if, after notice of his authority and purpose, he is refused admittance." The exceptions to the "knock and announce" requirement include: (1) when the officer reasonably believes that there may be a risk to the safety of the officer or others; (2) when the occupants already are aware of the officer's presence and his purpose so the knock and the announcement would be a useless gesture; and (3) when the officer reasonably believes that knocking and announcing his presence would lead to the destruction of evidence or escape of suspects.

WARRANTLESS SEARCHES

Warrantless searches, according to the Supreme Court "are *per se* unreasonable under the Fourth Amendment—subject only to a few specifically established and well-delineated exceptions." Likewise, a search that is unsupported by probable cause is also generally unlawful. There are, however, some exceptions to the general rule that probable cause and a warrant are required to conduct a search; for example, recall the earlier discussion about Terry stops, where police are permitted to stop someone based on articulable suspicion. Once a person is stopped, the police are able to conduct a pat-down and frisk in order to protect officer safety.

PROTECTIVE SWEEPS

Similarly, if police officers enter a residence to make an arrest or conduct a search, according to *Maryland v. Buie* (1990), they are permitted to conduct a protective sweep to ensure that no one is hiding who may cause injury. Officers may conduct a limited protective sweep that consists of a cursory inspection of "closets and other spaces immediately adjoining the place of arrest from which an attack could be immediately launched." Such a protective sweep may extend to a nonadjoining area only if officers have a "reasonable belief based on specific and articulable facts that the area to be swept harbors an individual posing a danger to those on the arrest scene." If during the protective sweep officers find contraband, that contraband could be seized and used as evidence.

SEARCHES INCIDENT TO AN ARREST

When a person has been arrested, an officer may also conduct a warrantless search incident to a valid arrest. During a search incident to a lawful arrest, the officer may search for both weapons and evidence beyond the arrestee's person to the area within the immediate control of the arrestee. This includes searches of containers found on the arrestee or within his reach.

PLAIN VIEW

Police may also seize evidence that is in plain view without a warrant, provided that: (1) officers have not violated the Fourth Amendment in arriving at the place from which the evidence could be plainly viewed; (2) the incriminating character of the evidence is immediately apparent; and (3) items are not disturbed to discern the evidentiary value of an item in plain view. This means that police may lawfully seize evidence in plain view when executing either a search warrant or an arrest warrant. Notably, the plain view doctrine has been extended to include "plain touch," "plain smell," and "plain hearing."

EXIGENT CIRCUMSTANCES

Officers may also conduct a warrantless search under exigent circumstances, which include, for example, such circumstances where evidence is subject to destruction, the safety of the officers or the public is threatened, the suspect may flee before a warrant is able to be obtained, or the police are in a "hot pursuit" of a suspect. The "hot pursuit" exception includes those circumstances only when the police have made an immediate and continuous pursuit of a suspect from the original crime scene. In drug cases, police may secure a residence in such a way as to guard against the destruction or removal of evidence until a warrant is obtained; for example, securing the perimeter and all inhabitants may safeguard against the destruction of evidence. In addition, if authorities have a reasonable belief that police safety or the safety of the general public is at risk, officers may enter a dwelling and conduct a complete search without a warrant. Police may inspect any place where they have a reasonable belief that dangerous items may be found. Courts examine the totality of circumstances to determine whether exigent circumstances exist. Specifically, courts will consider the gravity of the offense that underlies the need for the search and the reasonableness attached to the manner in which the search was conducted. The prosecution may need to show that a telephone warrant from a magistrate was not available and that the conduct of the police did not improperly create the exigent circumstances such that the circumstances were contrived.

CONSENT SEARCHES

A search may also be based on the permission that has been granted by a person who is authorized to grant permission. Such consent searches, conducted without a warrant, are lawful provided that consent was given voluntarily by someone who had the authority over the location to give consent. Consent may be express (e.g., in writing) or implied through actions. To determine whether consent was voluntarily given, courts will weigh such factors as age, intelligence, education, ability to communicate in a particular language, and length of time that the person was subject to questioning or detention.

VEHICLE SEARCHES

Concerning the search of vehicles, when police arrest an occupant of a motor vehicle they can only search the passenger compartment of the vehicle incident to the arrest if: (1) the arrestee is unsecured and within reaching distance of the vehicle, or (2) it is reasonable to believe that evidence relevant to the crime of arrest will be found in the vehicle.

INVENTORY SEARCHES

After a lawful seizure of property, police may conduct a warrantless search of the property to satisfy three purposes: (1) to protect the owner's property while it is in police custody, (2) to properly account for the property and protect the police against claims of lost or stolen property, and (3) to protect the police from potential harm. Inventory searches must be conducted according to standardized operating procedures. If contraband or evidence of a crime is found during an inventory search, that evidence may be seized.

Finally, it is worth emphasizing that courts have repeatedly recognized the sanctity of a home under the Fourth Amendment and required, except in rare circumstances, a warrant to enter. As the Supreme Court has stated: "At the very core of [the Fourth Amendment] stands the right of a man to retreat into his own home and there be free from unreasonable governmental intrusion." In the case of *Kyllo v. United States* (2001), Justice Antonin Scalia described the protection afforded a home and said that any physical invasion of the structure of the home, "by even a fraction of an inch, was too much … and there is certainly no exception to the warrant requirement for the officer who barely cracks open the front door … In the home, our cases show, all details are intimate details, because the entire area is held safe from prying government eyes."

CRIMINAL PROCEDURE

Criminal procedure is governed by constitutional doctrine, statutory requirements, case law, and court rules. If criminal procedural rules are violated, a successful prosecution is at risk depending on the harm to a defendant's constitutional rights to a fair trial. Procedural rights are meant to ensure that a level playing field is afforded to a defendant so the defendant, for example, is not compelled to incriminate himself, is able to discover the evidence that the government intends to use at trial, and is allowed to challenge the credibility of witnesses through cross-examination.

INDICTMENT

At the beginning of a criminal prosecution, rules of procedure afford the defendant the opportunity to be made aware of the charges and to ensure that probable cause exists to support the charges. For felony charges, a prosecutor prepares an indictment, which is the charging document that alleges specific violations of criminal statutes by stating dates, places, the manner in which the statute was violated, and other pertinent facts regarding the commission of an offense. The indictment is presented to a grand jury, which, after hearing evidence about the charges, determines whether probable cause exists to provide a "true bill." Generally, once an indictment is issued by the grand jury, the defendant may be arrested or ordered to appear in court pursuant to a summons. In federal cases where there is significant risk of harm to the public or where the defendant may flee, the defendant may be arrested upon a criminal complaint and warrant for his arrest. In such cases, an indictment may be presented to the grand jury within 30 days of the arrest.

INITIAL APPEARANCE

The first appearance of the defendant in court is known as the initial appearance. At this hearing, the defendant is advised of his rights to remain silent and to have counsel represent him at trial. The magistrate also makes a determination as to the conditions of pretrial release or bail that should be set for the defendant by assessing the gravity of the offenses, the strength of the evidence, and the likelihood that the defendant may flee or cause harm to society while awaiting trial.

ARRAIGNMENT

The second hearing in which the defendant appears in court is the arraignment. During the arraignment, the judge may read the indictment, or the defendant may waive its reading and ask the defendant how he pleads to the charges. In federal court, the presiding judicial officer at an arraignment is usually a magistrate judge, who is not authorized to take a guilty plea to a felony offense; therefore, at all felony arraignments in federal court conducted by a magistrate judge, defendants plead not guilty. At the arraignment, the judge also establishes obligations on the part of the government to provide to the defendant discovery of the evidence and reciprocal discovery obligations on the part of the defendant pertaining to expert witnesses and alibi witnesses.

SUPPRESSION HEARING AND THE EXCLUSIONARY RULE

Dependent upon whether a confession was obtained from the defendant or evidence was seized during a search, the defense may file motions to suppress and a suppression hearing may be held to admit evidence about how a search was conducted or a confession obtained. If a motion to suppress is granted, then such evidence may be excluded from the trial pursuant to the exclusionary rule, which mandates that evidence obtained unlawfully not be considered by a jury so as to deter police conduct that violated the defendant's constitutional rights.

TRIAL

During the trial itself, the jury is admonished that the defendant is presumed to be innocent of the charges and can only be found guilty if the government is able to prove the defendant's guilt beyond a reasonable doubt. At trial, the defendant is entitled to zealous representation by a defense counsel and may confront the witnesses through cross-examination. Additionally, the defendant cannot be compelled to testify. To reach a decision, the jury must return a unanimous verdict. If convicted of the charges, the defendant is entitled to have his case heard on appeal if he complies with the time requirements of filing an appeal after his conviction.

PROSECUTORS

The prosecutor plays a significant role in the criminal trial and provides legal advice to law enforcement while the criminal investigation is proceeding. Should the prosecutor only be an advocate for the government in seeking a conviction? What ethical obligations are imposed upon a prosecutor? The Supreme Court has commented on these questions and has set forth the law regarding the role of the prosecutor in the American criminal justice system; for example, the prosecutor must disclose to the defendant all evidence that is exculpatory in nature or reflects payments or rewards to criminal informants, as well as the prior convictions of prosecution witnesses. The ethical obligations of a prosecutor were emphasized in *Berger v. United States* (1935), where the Supreme Court said:

> [The prosecutor] is the representative not of an ordinary party to a controversy, but of a sovereignty whose obligation to govern impartially is as compelling as its obligation to govern at all; and whose interest, therefore, in a criminal prosecution is not that it shall win a case, but that justice shall be done. As such, he is in a peculiar and very definite sense the servant of the law, the twofold aim of which is that guilt shall not escape or innocence suffer. He may prosecute with earnestness and vigor—indeed, he should do so. But, while he may strike hard blows, he is not at liberty to strike foul ones. It is as much his duty to refrain from improper methods calculated to produce a wrongful conviction as it is to use every legitimate means to bring about a just one.

QUESTIONS FOR DISCUSSION

1. What is the difference between *malum in se* and *malum prohibitum* crimes?
2. What are the differences between a felony and a misdemeanor?
3. What types of evidence can be found at a crime scene?

4. How should an investigator record where evidence was found at a crime scene?

5. What is a chain of custody and why is it important?

6. How can an investigator establish probable cause to justify seeking an arrest warrant?

7. What should an officer do if the person to be arrested will be found in someone's private home?

8. What are the exceptions to the general rule that an arrest must be conducted only with a warrant?

9. What are the circumstances to consider when determining the reliability of an informant's tip?

10. What can an officer do during an investigatory stop?

11. What are the considerations to determine whether a protective sweep has legitimately uncovered evidence of a crime?

12. What is the purpose of the exclusionary rule?

BIBLIOGRAPHY

CONSTITUTION AND STATUTES

Texas Penal Code, Title 1. Introductory Provisions. Chapter 1. General Provisions. Section 1.02. Objectives of Code (http://www.statutes.legis.state.tx.us/docs/pe/htm/pe.1.htm).
U.S. Constitution, Amendment IV.

CASES

Andresen v. Maryland, 427 U.S. 468 (1976).
Arizona v. Gant, 556 U.S. ___, 129 S.Ct. 1710 (2009).
Atwater v. City of Lago Vista, 532 U.S. 318 (2001).
Brady v. Maryland, 373 U.S. 83 (1963).
Coolidge v. Hampshire, 403 U.S. 443 (1971).
Gideon v. Wainwright, 372 U.S. 335 (1963).
Florida v. J.L., 529 U.S. 266 (2000)
Johnson v. United States, 333 U.S. 10 (1948).
Katz v. United States, 389 U.S. 347 (1967).
Kyllo v. United States, 533 U.S. 27 (2001).
Mapp v. Ohio, 367 U.S. 643 (1961).
Maryland v. Buie, 494 U.S. 325 (1990).
Miranda v. Arizona, 384 U.S. 436 (1966).
Papachristou v. City of Jacksonville, 405 U.S. 156 (1972).
Roviaro v. United States, 353 U.S. 53 (1957).
Silverman v. United States, 365 U.S. 505, 511 (1961).
Strickland v. Washington, 466 U.S. 668 (1984).
Terry v. Ohio, 392 U.S. 1 (1968).
Thornhill v. Alabama, 310 U.S. 88 (1940).
United States v. Sokolow, 490 U.S. 1 (1989).
Virginia v. Moore, 128 S. Ct. 1598, 1607 (2008).
Wilson v. Arkansas, 514 U.S. 927 (1995).

BOOKS, JOURNALS, AND ARTICLES

ABA. (1993). *ABA Standards for Criminal Justice: Prosecution and Defense Function*, 3d ed. Washington, D.C.: American Bar Association.

Bajaj, S. (2009). Policing the Fourth Amendment: The Constitutionality of Warrantless Investigatory Stops for Past Misdemeanors. *Columbia Law Review*, 109:309–349.

Berger v. United States, 295 U.S. 78 (1935).

Black, H.C. (1951). *Black's Law Dictionary*, 4th ed. St. Paul, MN: West.

Bulzomi, M.J. (1997). Knock and Announce: A Fourth Amendment Standard. *Law Enforcement Bulletin*, 66(5):27–32 (http://www2.fbi.gov/publications/leb/1997/may976.htm).

Conom, T.P. (1991). Bulwarks of Liberty: Presumption of Innocence and Reasonable Doubt. *The Champion*, December, pp. 18–23 (http://www.nacdl.org/public.nsf/GideonAnniversary/Index1/$FILE/PresumeInnocence.pdf).

Del Carmen, R.V. (2007). *Criminal Procedure Law and Practice*, 7th ed. Belmont, CA: Thompson Wadsworth

Dietz, L. et al. (2011). Witnesses. In *American Jurisprudence*, 2nd ed., Vol. 81. St. Paul, MN: West.

Eleventh Circuit U.S. Court of Appeals. (2010). *Pattern Jury Instructions (Criminal Cases)*. Washington, D.C.: Judicial Council of the U.S. Eleventh Judicial Circuit (http://www.ca11.uscourts.gov/documents/jury/crimjury.pdf).

Judicial Conference of the United States. (2004). *Handbook for Trial Jurors Serving in the United States District Courts*. Washington, D.C.: Administrative Office of the United States Courts (www.txwd.uscourts.gov/jury/docs/handbookfortrialjurors.pdf).

Kamisar, Y. (1991). The Fourth Amendment and Its Exclusionary Rule. *The Champion*, September/October, pp. 20–25 (http://www.nacdl.org/public.nsf/GideonAnniversary/Index1/$FILE/4ExclusionaryRule.pdf).

U.S. Courts. (2011). *Federal Courts*. Washington, D.C.: United States Courts (http://www.uscourts.gov/understand03/content_1_0.html).

USDOJ. (2000). *Crime Scene Investigation: A Guide for Law Enforcement*. Washington, D.C.: Office of Justice Programs, U.S. Department of Justice (http://www.ncjrs.gov/pdffiles1/nij/178280.pdf).

Worrall, J.L. (2007). *Criminal Procedure from First Contact to Appeal*, 2nd ed. Boston, MA: Allyn & Bacon.

CHAPTER 20

Preparing the Case for Court

Cliff Roberson
Kaplan University

Gwynne Birzer
Hite, Fanning & Honeyman, LLP

CHAPTER OBJECTIVES

After reading this chapter, you should be able to do the following:

1. Explain the necessity for accurate police reports.
2. Understand the basic rules of evidence
3. Explain the process of admitting documents into evidence
4. Know how to prepare for court testimony.
5. Understand what is expected of witnesses during direct examination and cross-examination

---

Chapter Outline

- Introduction
- Preparation
- Testimony in Court
- Accuracy of Police Reports
- Chain of Custody of Evidence
- Personal Credibility

INTRODUCTION

This chapter discusses preparing a case for court from the lead investigator's viewpoint. Although both authors are attorneys, the chapter is not directed toward counsel preparation for trial, but toward the steps that the lead investigator needs to take to prepare for trial. As former police officer Carole Moore noted (Birzer and Roberson, 2011):

Students who want to make good grades hit the books prior to taking a test. Witnesses who expect to be called to present evidence in court should take their cues from college kids and study the material that's likely to be a part of the course.

PREPARATION

Effective witnesses do not simply arrive in court the day of the trial, do battle with the defense attorney or attorney for the opposing party, and convince the jury that they are telling the truth and that the defendant or witness for the other party is not being entirely truthful. Effective witnesses prepare for court. Preparing for and testifying in court are everyday experiences for some witnesses. Even when it becomes a common occurrence, the witness must understand that, unless the information can be conveyed to the jury in the proper manner, all the work done during the arrest, questioning, and charging of the defendant may be wasted.

As is discussed later in this chapter, an average witness is *almost always* a prepared witness. A superior witness is *always* a prepared witness. Chapter 4 discussed preparing field notes and report writing. In this chapter, we look at preparing to use those notes and reports in court. Successful court testimony begins with accurate preparation of notes and reports. One of the most important steps in preparing for court is to proofread again those notes and reports. If any errors or mistakes are discovered, it is important not to make any changes but to report the problems to the counsel who is calling you as a witness. Reports should always be prepared as if they will be used in court.

On receiving the summons to appear in court, the witness should attempt to contact the prosecutor or attorney for the party that is calling him or her as a witness. In most large cities and counties, prosecutors—like the police—are overworked and understaffed and may not return telephone calls before meeting the witness in the court hallway. The witness should not depend on the prosecutor or counsel to make the job of testifying easy. The attorney may not have carefully examined the file before appearing in court and may rely on the reporting witness to carry the day. If a critical aspect of the case is not evident from reading previous reports or statements, the witness should ensure that the attorney is informed of this fact *before* the start of the trial—not just before taking the witness stand. The reason is this: The attorney may be engaged in last-minute plea bargaining or settlement discussions or may make an opening statement to the judge or jury that will later prove to be false if he or she is not made aware of all the important facts surrounding the case.

After discussing the case with the attorney, the witness will await his or her turn to testify. Depending on the nature of the case and the attorney's preference, the witness may testify first or last. Although jurors are told not to consider anything that is not admitted into evidence, they will sometimes form unofficial opinions of persons on the basis of their observations. If the witness is required to remain outside the courtroom, he or she should also remain attentive and professional. In addition, the witness should be cordial but avoid joking with other witnesses—and especially avoid laughing with the opposing counsel. Jurors who observe these antics may believe that the witness is not serious about what is occurring in the courtroom and therefore may discount his or her testimony.

Having reviewed any previous reports or statements, refreshed the memory, and talked with the attorney, the witness is ready to take the stand and testify. Dress regulations for court appearances vary according to the jurisdiction. An effective witness strives for a professional, conservative look. In reality, jurors should pay attention to the testimony and not what the witness is wearing, but flashy clothes, rings, gold chains, or other out-of-the-ordinary dress may cause a juror to concentrate on the witness's clothing at a critical part of the testimony instead of listening. The witness does not have to wear a three-piece suit with a white shirt but should dress in a manner acceptable for court. Not suitable for court are cowboy boots, jeans, or a leather miniskirt.

TESTIMONY IN COURT

Some individuals are uncomfortable standing or sitting in front of a group and talking. Being an uncomfortable witness is different than being an unprepared witness. Being uncomfortable may prove to make an effective witness, while being unprepared will never make an effective witness. Occasionally, a witness may be required to testify in a deserted courtroom with only the court personnel present, such as in a closed hearing; however, the majority of a person's testimony will occur in public. Moreover, the witness will be subjected to cross-examination by the opposing attorney, who will attempt to destroy the witness's credibility.

Even if you were not a member of the debating team in high school or college or you avoided taking public speaking classes, you may, with proper training, learn to communicate in a professional manner while testifying. This oral skill can be mastered with practice, but only if you are familiar with the purposes of both direct examination and cross-examination. In the following subsections, we briefly discuss this aspect of the judicial process.

To testify in court effectively, it is helpful for witnesses to understand the aims or goals of direct examination. Most attorneys who call witnesses attempt to satisfy two generally accepted objectives during direct examinations:

1. To present all legally sufficient evidence to support the charges or claims filed against the opposing party or defendant
2. To convince the fact finder of the integrity of the evidence and, ultimately, the truth of the charge or claim

OATH OR AFFIRMATION

Before a witness is allowed to testify, the witness is required to declare that he or she will testify truthfully, by oath or affirmation administered in a form calculated to awaken the witness's conscience and impress the witness's mind with the duty to do so. The requirement of an oath is designed to ensure that every witness gives accurate and honest testimony. The oath requirement is intended to preserve the integrity of the judicial process by awakening the witness's conscience and making the witness amenable to perjury prosecution if he or she lies (*United States v. Zizzo*, 1997). Federal Rule 603 states that a witness need not swear an oath but may merely affirm that he or she will testify truthfully. An affirmation can be given in any form calculated to awaken the conscience of the witness and impress on the witness the duty to tell the truth. Permitting the witness to testify under an affirmation as well as oath is designed to remove many of the objections that certain members of some religious groups have. As a practical matter, if a witness prefers to affirm rather than take the oath, court personnel should be notified prior to the witness taking the stand.

OPPORTUNITY FOR WITNESS TO EXPLAIN OR DENY THE STATEMENT

The basic common law foundation consists of affording the witness an opportunity of either admitting or denying that a prior inconsistent statement was made and, if he admits it, of explaining the circumstances of the statement. The traditional method of confronting a witness with his inconsistent statement prior to its introduction is the preferred method of proceeding. In fact, where the proponent of the testimony fails to do so, and the witness subsequently becomes unavailable, the proponent runs the risk that the court will properly exercise its discretion not to allow the admission of the prior statement.

REFRESHING A WITNESS'S MEMORY

Often a witness when testifying will forget vital information. When this occurs, the counsel who is conducting the questions may attempt to refresh the witness's memory. As a general rule, a counsel may use anything that will help trigger the witness's memory as long as the matter does not provide new information to the witness or is likely to create a false impression. In cases where the witness is a police officer, this often involves the use of a police report or field notes to refresh the officer's memory.

If the witness remembers after he or she has reviewed the police report or other item, then the witness may testify according to his or her refreshed memory. In this case, while the other party (defense) may examine the document or other item, the refreshing item is not evidence since it was only used to jog the witness's memory. In this case, if the item is not introduced, it is not evidence; therefore, it does not need to be authenticated or to comply with the best evidence rule.

If the memory is refreshed while the witness is testifying to overcome the fear that the witness who says that his memory is refreshed is really remembering only what he just read from the document, certain procedural safeguards apply. As previously noted, the opposing party is allowed to inspect the document, and the opposing party is allowed to cross-examine the witness regarding the refreshment of memory before the witness is allowed to continue his testimony. In addition, the opposing counsel is allowed to enter into evidence the relevant portions of the document. If the latter is true, the best evidence rule applies.

Counsel should always request that a witness review documents before trial for two reasons. First, it is more efficient in presenting the case if counsel is not required to follow the procedure necessary to refresh a witness's memory and establish that his memory has been refreshed. Second, when a witness requires that his memory be refreshed in court, this lack of memory about the incident creates a negative impression on the jury.

If the witness's memory has been refreshed before trial, this fact may be addressed by opposing counsel during cross-examination, and generally the opposing counsel will be allowed to review the document and introduce relevant parts of it into evidence.

REQUIRED STEPS TO REFRESH RECOLLECTION

State rules of evidence may vary, but generally the below steps are required for in-court refreshing of a witness's memory:

1. Counsel establishes that the witness's memory is exhausted and that the witness cannot testify fully and accurately from memory.
2. There is a document or other item that will refresh the witness's memory.
3. Counsel shows the document to the witness and allows the witness to read or examine it silently.
4. Counsel then asks the witness if he now recalls the matter independent of the document; that is, the witness's memory is refreshed.
5. If the witness states that he now recalls the matter independent of the document (i.e., his memory is refreshed), the opposing counsel is permitted to question the witness about the issue of whether the memory has been refreshed.
6. The witness is then allowed to testify.
7. If the witness testifies that he cannot recall the matter even after reviewing the document, counsel may then try to have the document entered as evidence of past recollection recorded.

EXCERPT FROM *BAKER V. STATE*

Baker was convicted of murder in the first degree in a criminal court in Baltimore, MD. On appeal, Baker challenged the conviction on the basis that the Court denied him the opportunity to refresh the recollection of a police witness by showing him a report written by a fellow officer. Following is an excerpt from *Baker v. State*, 35 Md. App. 593, 597 (Md. Ct. Spec. App. 1977):

> **Court's opinion:** In permitting a witness to refresh his recollection by consulting a memorandum, the courts are in accord with present psychological knowledge. A distinction is drawn, in the analysis of the memory process, between *recall*, which is the reproduction of what has been learned, and *recognition*, which is recall with a time factor added, or an awareness that the recall relates to past experience. It is with recognition that the law is principally concerned in permitting a witness to revive his recollection. The psychological evidence is clear that in thus allowing to be brought to mind what has been forgotten, the law is following sound psychological procedure.

It is, of course, hornbook law that when a party seeks to introduce a record of past recollection, he must establish:

1) that the record was made by or adopted by the witness at a time when the witness did have a recollection of the event, and

2) that the witness can presently vouch for the fact that when the record was made or adopted by him, he knew that it was accurate.

Court decision: Judgment convicting appellant was reversed because appellant was entitled to refresh the recollection of police officer by using the report written by a fellow police officer.

STAGES OF EXAMINATION

- *Direct examination*—This is comprised of the initial questions put to the witness by the counsel or party that called the witness.
- *Cross-examination*—After conclusion of direct examination, the opposing party may examine the witness. During cross-examination, the counsel generally may asking leading questions. On cross-examination, the witness may be questioned as to his honesty, any bias the witness may have, the witness's opportunity to observe the incident, the witness's memory, and subjects discussed during direct examination.
- *Redirect and recross-examination*—After cross-examination, the calling party may conduct a redirect examination over matters covered during cross-examination followed by recross-examination. Often during redirect and recross the court will restrict the introduction of new subjects because new subjects are generally outside of the scope of the testimony.

OBJECTIONS TO QUESTIONS

Often when a witness is testifying, the opposite party will object to the form of the question. Some of the more common objections include the following:

- The question is open ended and calls for undirected narrative. This restriction is designed to keep the witness from answering with irrelevant or otherwise inadmissible evidence.
- The question is leading. It is a question that suggests an answer. (Note: Leading questions may be asked on cross-examination.)
- The question was an argumentative question designed to make or emphasize some point or to argue to the jury rather than elicit information.
- Relevance objections arise when the question either asks a questions or calls for an answer that is not relevant to the proceedings

IMPEACHMENT OF A WITNESS

Impeachment refers to the process of attacking the credibility of a witness. The rules of evidence in most states provide that the credibility of any witness may be attacked by any party, including the party calling the witness. Under common law, a party who called a witness could not impeach that witness unless the court declared the witness a "hostile witness." This is no longer the rule. The rationale for the common law rule rested on assumptions concerning a party's presumptive support of a witness called by that party and the need to protect the witness from harassment. The federal rules of evidence recognize that a party does not necessarily vouch for a witness; in fact, a party may have no choice but to call an adverse witness in order to prove a case. Prior to the court declaring a witness to be hostile, the party calling the witness must first establish that the witness is uncooperative.

TEN COMMANDMENTS FOR WITNESSES

Following is a list of "Ten Commandments" for witnesses (County of San Diego, CA, District Attorney's Office, 1995):

1. Tell the truth. In a trial, as in all other matters, honesty comes first.
2. Do not guess. If you do not know, say so.
3. Be sure you understand the question. You cannot possibly give a truthful and accurate answer unless you understand the question.
4. Take your time and answer the question asked. Give the question as much thought as is required to understand it, formulate your answer, and then give the answer.
5. Give a loud, audible answer. Everything you say is being recorded. Do not nod your head yes or no.
6. Do not look for assistance when you are on the stand. If you think you need help, request it from the judge.
7. Beware of questions involving distance and time. If you make an estimate, make sure everyone understands that you are making an estimate.
8. Be courteous. Answer yes or no, and address the judge as Your Honor.
9. If asked if you have talked to the prosecutor, admit it freely if you have done so.
10. Avoid joking and making wisecracks. A lawsuit is a serious matter.

These commandments are as valid for a seasoned witness as they are for a first-time witness. Each rule is based on both common sense and years of court experience by attorneys. The first and most basic rule of testimony requires that the witness tell the truth. Although the idea that witnesses should always tell the truth seems obvious, reality and emotions can sometimes cause individuals to slant their testimony to assist an attorney or to ensure that the defendant is portrayed in a bad light. Failure to testify truthfully has several consequences. The most obvious issue is that the witness is sworn to tell the truth. Violation of this oath can lead to criminal charges or the destruction of the person's reputation. In addition, the witness's credibility may be destroyed in front of the court or jury, with the result that they disbelieve all of the witness's testimony and find for the other party. This result is the exact opposite of what was intended by slanting or stretching the truth to help out the attorney or place the defendant in an unfavorable light. Who can forget the problems caused in the O.J. Simpson case when everyone learned that Detective Mark Fuhrman of the Los Angeles Police Department had "forgotten" using racial slurs in the past?

Close to the first rule is the second, which requires that the witness not try to help the case by guessing. If the witness is unsure, a simple statement to this effect is sufficient. Such a statement shows the jury that the witness is human and may not have all the answers to every question.

The third rule simply requires that the witness understand the exact question that is asked. At first glance, this rule appears simple to follow; however, many times attorneys will ask several questions in one sentence. If the witness is unsure of the exact question, a request should be made to repeat or clarify the question.

The fourth rule requires the witness to think through both the question and the answer instead of blurting out a response. Taking a few seconds to form the answer in your mind before responding to the question is a good practice.

The fifth requirement mandates that the witness answer in a loud and clear voice. Remember, appellate courts have only the written transcript of what occurred when they review a case on appeal. The court reporter will not transcribe a nod of the head or estimate the distance between the witness's hands when he or she is demonstrating a gesture or an action of the witness. If the witness uses motions during the testimony, they should be accompanied by an accurate oral description.

The sixth commandment may seem harsh, but it exists for the witness's benefit. The witness must understand that no one but the judge can intervene during direct examination or cross-examination. The attorneys may raise objections, but the court must decide whether the objections are valid. When objections are made, the witness should refrain from speaking until the objection is ruled upon by the court.

The seventh rule is one that most witnesses will violate at least once. Typically, the witness states a distance during direct examination. For example, in response to the prosecutor's question about the distance between the witness and the defendant, the witness may state, "The defendant was 20 feet from me when I observed the weapon." On cross-examination, the defense attorney may ask the witness to point out an object in court that is 20 feet from the witness stand. If the witness is mistaken about this distance, the defense attorney will clearly point out this mistake and will then ask how the witness could be certain about the distance between the witness and the defendant on the night in question when the witness cannot even make an accurate estimate in the calm and secure setting of a courtroom.

The eighth commandment is also basically common sense, but it can also build an witness's credibility. The witness should be seen as a professional and not as someone who does not respect authority.

The ninth rule ties in with the first rule because it requires the witness to answer a question truthfully. Discussing the case with the attorney who called before you testify is not improper.

The last commandment also pertains to the witness's credibility. The defendant's liberty is at stake during the trial. The witness should be professional and calm when answering every question. Once called to testify, the witness should approach the witness chair or, as it is sometimes called, the witness box and turn to the court personnel to be sworn in. The witness will be asked to swear or affirm to tell the truth, the whole truth, and nothing but the truth. Once the witness is sworn in, the court personnel will tell the witness to be seated.

The witness should wait for this invitation because doing so shows respect for the court and allows the attorney to appear to be in control of the courtroom. Once the witness is seated, the attorney calling the witness will ask a series of questions about the witness's knowledge of the crime, one of the individuals involved in the case, or the incident. This questioning is *direct examination*. Following is a series of preliminary questions most attorneys use to start the questioning:

1. Would you please state your full name for the record?
2. What is your occupation?
3. How long have you been employed by [employer]?
4. Do you, on this day, feel you are properly trained to perform the duties for which you are employed?
5. On [the date and time in question], what was your assignment?
6. On that date and time, what, if anything, unusual did you observe while on this assignment?
7. At what location did you observe this unusual occurrence?
8. Is that location in the [city, county, state] of [city, county, state]?
9. Please tell the jury what you observed.

The purpose of these questions is to allow the witness to become comfortable on the stand and to give the jury some background information about the witness. Such questions also set the stage for the more critical testimony about the witness's observations and reactions. In some jurisdictions, these questions are known as *foundational questions* because they establish the witness's jurisdiction and authority to act.

When a party calls a witness, the party is allowed to ask only direct questions (with some minor exceptions that are not relevant to this text). Such questioning is accomplished through direct examination. A direct question is open ended and does not suggest the answer to the person being questioned. Once the attorney finishes with direct examination, the attorney for the other side has a right to cross-examine. *Cross-examination* allows asking either direct or leading questions. A *leading question* is phrased in a way that suggests an answer to the person being questioned.

After establishing the jurisdiction for the witness to act, the attorney will question the witness about his or her knowledge of the case. The witness should listen to each question and ensure that he understands what is being asked. If not clear what the exact question is, the witness should state this fact and ask the prosecutor to restate the question. "I'm not certain I understand your question; would you please restate it?" is one way to ask for clarification. If the question is understood, the witness should pause for a second and then answer. This pause should follow every question; as is discussed subsequently, it becomes extremely important during cross-examination. When answering a question, the witness should answer only what was asked. Following is an example of a witness answering more than was asked:

> *Question:* Did you observe anyone at that location?
> *Answer:* Yes, as I pulled up to the service station, he saw me and fled from the scene. I then lost sight of him for several minutes, but observed him one block from the scene of the crime.

Not only is the witness's response defective on several grounds, but it also creates more questions than it answers. Furthermore, without clarifying some of the issues in the witness's answer, the attorney may have opened the door for the other attorney to question whether a certain individual was the same person who fled from the service station. Following is a specific series of questions dealing with the issues the witness raised.

> *Question:* Did you observe anyone at that location?
> *Answer:* Yes, I did.
> *Question:* Whom did you observe?
> *Answer:* I saw the defendant.
> *Question:* Would you point to that person if he or she is in court and, for the record, describe what the person is wearing?
> *Answer:* Yes, it is the person sitting at the table to my right/left, wearing a blue suit.
> *Question:* How far away were you when you saw the defendant?
> *Answer:* I was about 15 feet from him.
> *Question:* What was he doing when you first saw him?
> *Answer:* He was backing out of the service station office.
> *Question:* What, if anything, did he do next?
> *Answer:* He looked toward me and fled.
> *Question:* Where did he go?
> *Answer:* He ran south on Broadway Street.
> *Question:* What did you do at that time?
> *Answer:* I entered the service station to check on the welfare of the people inside and was informed by Mr. Smith that the defendant had just robbed them at gunpoint.
> *Question:* Once you heard this, what did you do?
> *Answer:* I asked Mr. Smith if he could describe the individual who robbed him.
> *Question:* What, if anything did Mr. Smith say?
> *Answer:* He gave me a description of the individual who robbed him.
> *Question:* What, if anything did you do next?
> *Answer:* I called the police.

The difference between the two sets of questions and answers is apparent. The second set gives the jury more complete facts about the incident and establishes why the witness could recognize the defendant even though he lost sight of the defendant for several minutes.

CROSS-EXAMINATION

Once the witness has answered the questions posed by the attorney who called the witness, the attorney for the other party has the right to ask questions on cross-examination. Unlike trials in the movies, cross-examination seldom results in witnesses breaking down and recanting their previous testimony; rather, it is a series of questions designed to attack the credibility of witnesses by showing weaknesses in their original testimony or by establishing a motive or bias on their part.

Cross-examination is an art that has several purposes. It takes substantial preparation to master effective cross-examination of a witness. Most attorneys will not ask a question they don't already know the answer to. All witnesses should be aware of these objectives so they can better understand the questions being asked of them by defense attorneys. Depending on the jurisdiction, some questions or issues may not be raised on cross-examination; however, the general objectives of cross-examination include, but are not limited to, the following ten points:

1. To develop favorable matters that were left unsaid on direct examination
2. To introduce all of a conversation or document, if the witness has testified to only a part of the content
3. To demonstrate that the witness is lying
4. To establish that the witness could not have seen or heard what he or she has claimed
5. To test the witness's ability to hear, see, remember, and relate facts with accuracy
6. To establish the witness's bias or prejudice
7. To establish any interest the witness may have in the outcome of the case
8. To impair the witness's credibility
9. To impeach the witness by any means permitted by law
10. To set up unanswered questions for argument to the jury in summation

Just as with direct examination, the witness should pause before answering any question. This pause is critical because it allows the other attorney to object to the question and prevent its answer from coming before the jury. Attorneys, during cross-examination, can and will use numerous tactics or techniques to discredit the witness's testimony.

The witness should know the facts surrounding the case. An unprofessional and embarrassing response by the witness is to say, "I don't recall, but I put it in my report." Rest assured, the attorney for the other party will know the facts—and will have the opportunity to read the report again while the witness is testifying. In addition, the opposing attorney has the other party's version to draw on. Even though parties do not always tell their attorneys the complete truth, the defense is provided with another perspective on the facts that can be used to attack the witness.

Furthermore, the witness should always maintain a professional, courteous attitude. Some attorneys will argue with witnesses, others will be condescending, and some may even sneer. No matter what tactic is used, the witness should always maintain professionalism.

The witness must be prepared to be cross-examined and respond in a positive manner. Positive responses in such situations reinforce in the jury's mind that the witness is a professional simply doing a job.

If the witness makes a mistake during testimony and is caught by the opposing attorney, the witness should readily admit to the mistake. Nothing damages your credibility more than letting an opposing attorney lead you down a path of rationalizations in an attempt to justify an obvious mistake.

The witness's voice and body language should convey the attitude of a calm professional. The voice should be loud enough for all the jurors to hear, but not so loud as to distract from what is being said. The witness should also avoid squirming on the witness stand. If the testimony has proceeded for more than two hours and the witness must use the restroom, the witness should politely ask for a brief recess.

The witness should not despair if opposing counsel appears to be winning. After cross-examination, the prosecutor is allowed to conduct a *redirect examination*, which is the prosecutor's opportunity to clarify any issues raised during cross-examination.

ACCURACY OF POLICE REPORTS

As noted by veteran police officer Kimberly Clark, writing a police report is boring (Clark, 2006). In fact, it is hard work and time consuming. But, you should not forget that many people will be reading and scrutinizing every word in the report. If the bad guy gets arrested, a copy of the report goes to the prosecutor's office and the bad guy's attorney will get a copy. An inaccurate police report of the incident in question is a gift to the defense. If you have documented all the facts from the interviews and the investigation, closed all loopholes, answered all questions, and addressed all issues that could possibly be raised, then the chances of successful prosecution of a bad guy are vastly improved. Following are the five most common errors found in police reports:

1. Failure to provide sources of information
2. Failure to report significant details
3. Failure to write neatly and clearly
4. Use of poor English including misspelled words
5. Failure to maintain objectivity.

Biggs (2001, p. 11) distinguished between an average investigator and a superior one:

- The *average investigator* looks at a group of people near a crime scene and thinks, "There is a group of people standing around my crime scene."
- The *superior investigator* looks at the same situation and thinks, "There is a group of people standing around my crime scene and each of them knows something about this case. It's my job to get them to tell me what they know and then figure out how to get the ones who do not want to talk to me to do so anyway."

The morning of the trial is not the day to discover errors in the reports. When you first receive notice of a court appearance, immediately review the notes and reports associated with your investigation of that case. This will generally occur several months or even years after the crime. Review the reports and question each fact or word. Consider the following court testimony (Birzer and Roberson, 2011):

Defense counsel (DC): Now, sir, you attacked the victim after she was already injured. Isn't that correct?

Witness (investigator): No.

DC: Your name is [name], correct?

Witness: Yes.

DC: You were the investigator on this case, correct?

Witness: Yes.

DC: You reported the events as they occurred, correct?

Witness: Yes.

DC: And you reported the events as accurately as you could recall them, correct?

Witness: Yes.

DC: You reviewed and signed the report we are referring to today, correct?

Witness: Yes.

DC: Now, sir, your report reads: "I raped her in a blanket and called for an ambulance." Correct?

Witness: But, sir, I meant "wrapped."

DC: Not my question, sir. My question was whether or not your report reads, and I quote, "I raped her in a blanket and called for an ambulance." Correct?

Witness: Yes.

DC: How many other errors are in your report?

STANDARD FORM POLICE REPORTS

Another factor to examine when preparing for trial concerns whether the police report was completed on a standard form in which several portions of the form are preprinted on the form. An additional step is involved if your department or agency uses standard forms with information already filled in. You need to check to see if there are any discrepancies between the preprinted information contained in the report and the actual facts of the case. Consider the following paragraph which was taken from an ad posted on a DWI website (http://d-w-i.org/dwipolicereports.html):

> Because police reports are used as an official record in a DWI case, this is especially troubling for a DWI suspect. Using pre-written police reports creates a false account of the drunk-driving arrest. A skilled defense attorney may be able to obtain copies of the officer's other DWI reports within a certain time frame to determine whether or not the he or she is using pre-written reports. If the defense attorney can prove that the officer's reports were pre-written, it will definitely diminish the officer's testimony.

CHAIN OF CUSTODY OF EVIDENCE

In criminal cases, a question of authenticity arises when something is seized from a defendant and then introduced at trial, and the defendant disputes that it is his or argues that the thing has been altered in some way. One way for the prosecution to authenticate the evidence is to establish a chain of custody. Courts have been permissive in determining whether the government has established a sufficient chain of custody. The evidence rule in most states is that gaps in the chain of custody go to weight and not admissibility (*United States v. Miller*, 1993); for example, a one-year gap in the chain of custody for contraband goes to the weight and not the admissibility of the evidence when there was no showing of bad faith on the part of government officials, who are entitled to a presumption that they did not alter the proffered evidence.

The most important chain of custody is the one from the original seizure of the evidence to the analysis of the substance. Given the fungibility of drugs, it is essential to make a connection between the substance seized from the defendant and the substance actually tested. Any substantial gap in this chain of custody or any indication of alteration should be treated as fatal, because otherwise there is an unacceptable risk that the test does not reflect the contents of the substance seized (*United States v. Casamento*, 1989). A gap in the chain occurring after testing can be treated more permissively, given the admissibility of the testing procedure itself and the fact that the only purpose for introducing the substance in court is to illustrate the testimony of government witnesses.

Testimony of a witness who has personal knowledge as to a piece of evidence is a classic way of authenticating the evidence. Someone who is an eyewitness to the signing of a document may authenticate the document. A layperson can identify handwriting based on familiarity with the handwriting. A signature may be identified by testimony of a person familiar with the signature. It is not essential that the witness have been present when the signature was executed, but sufficient foundation must be established in order for a lay person to verify a signature or handwriting.

Handwriting, fingerprints, blood, hair, clothing fibers, and numerous other things can be authenticated by comparison with specimens that have been authenticated. Sometimes the comparison can be done by the jury; at other times, an expert witness will be required, especially when scientific knowledge is needed to make a valid examination of the samples. The trial judge has discretion to exclude specimens when questions as to their authenticity will be confusing, excessively time consuming, and not relevant to the proceedings.

Sometimes the characteristics of an item will themselves serve to authenticate the item. A letter may be authenticated, for example, by content and the circumstances indicating it was a reply to a duly authenticated letter. One who is familiar with the voice of another may authenticate a conversation or identify the speaker on a tape or other recording; however, if the tape or recording is offered for its truth, hearsay problems still will exist and must be solved following satisfaction of the authentication requirement.

PERSONAL CREDIBILITY

Consider this except from the *Los Angeles Times* (Gold and Gottlieb, 2005):

> Dr. Park Dietz, a California psychiatrist, is a legend in law enforcement circles. He is a specialist in a strange niche market that involves telling corporations how to prevent mass workplace killings and celebrities how to avoid obsessed fans. He has, said fellow forensic psychiatrist Steven Pitt, "no peer in our business."

Compare that excerpt to this one the same day (Gold, 2005):

> The capital murder convictions of Andrea Yates were thrown out by an appeals court Thursday, three and a half years after she told investigators that she had methodically drowned her five children in the bathtub to spare them from eternal damnation and to punish herself for being a bad mother. The court overturned the verdicts because an expert witness for the prosecution, Dr. Park Dietz, mistakenly told the jury that an episode of the television drama "Law & Order"—in which a woman drowned her children in a bathtub—aired shortly before the Yates killings. In the purported episode, the mother was acquitted of murder because she was judged insane, according to the witness.

Prior to this mistake, Dr. Dietz was considered by many to be a professional witness on matters involving mental issues in criminal cases. After his mistake in the Yates case, his creditability as a witness was seriously diminished, and his value as an expert witness was greatly reduced because of this mistake, even though this was probably an innocent mistake. Whenever he testifies in the future, he will be subject to be cross-examination by the opposing party because of this mistake. The Dietz situation is an excellent example as to why witnesses should be careful when testifying to make sure that their testimony is correct. Any misstatement or untruth will subject the witness to continuing harassment in the future. The golden rule is do not testify as to a certain fact unless you are certain you are correct. If you are uncertain, express those concerns in court while on the stand.

QUESTIONS FOR DISCUSSION

1. Why is it important to submit accurate police reports?
2. What are the consequences of misstating facts in a criminal trial?
3. Explain how to refresh a witness's memory.
4. Why is it important to build a reputation for honesty on the witness stand?
5. What reasons can you think of that support the need to be well prepared to testify on the witness stand?

BIBLIOGRAPHY

Biggs, M. (2001). *Just the Facts: Investigate Report Writing*. Upper Saddle River, NJ: Prentice Hall.

Birzer, M. and Roberson, C. (2011). *Introduction to Criminal Investigation*. Boca Raton, FL: CRC Press.

Clark, K. (2006). *How to Really, Really Write Those Boring Police Reports*. Flushing, NY: Looseleaf Law Publishing.

County of San Diego, CA, District Attorney's Office. (1995). *Ten Commandments for Witnesses*. San Diego, CA: District Attorney's Office.

Gold, S. (2005). Yates Case Turns on Trial Error. *Los Angeles Times*, January 7, p. A-1.

Gold, S. and Gottlieb, J. (2005). Defense Derides Psychiatrist as a Witness-for-Hire: Forensic Specialist Park Dietz Was Paid $50,000 by the Prosecution to Testify Whether Andrea Yates Could Distinguish Right from Wrong. *Los Angeles Times*, January 7, p. A-1.

Roberson, C. and Birzer, M.L. (2010). *Introduction to Private Security*. Upper Saddle River, NJ: Prentice Hall, p. 246.

United States v. Casamento, 887 F.2d 1141 (2d Cir. 1989).

United States v. Miller, 994 F.2d 441 (8th Cir. 1993).

United States v. Zizzo, 120 f.3d 1338 (7th Cir. 1997).

INDEX